pelling and Diction

ective Sentences

continued

Effective Sentences

Larger Elements

continued

Larger Elements

Hodges' Harbrace Handbook

THIRTEENTH EDITION

Hodges' Harbrace Handbook

THIRTEENTH EDITION

John C. Hodges

Winifred Bryan Horner
Texas Christian University

Suzanne Strobeck Webb
Texas Woman's University

Robert Keith Miller
University of St. Thomas

HARCOURT BRACE

HARCOURT BRACE COLLEGE PUBLISHERS
Fort Worth Philadelphia San Diego New York Orlando Austin
San Antonio Toronto Montreal London Sydney Tokyo

Publisher: **Christopher P. Klein**
Executive Editor: **Michael Rosenberg**
Acquisitions Editor: **John Meyers**
Product Manager: **Ilse Wolfe West**
Developmental Editor: **Michell Phifer**
Project Editor: **Matt Ball**
Art Director: **Brian Salisbury**
Production Manager: **Kathleen Ferguson**

Mary Stoughton and EEI Communications for copyediting and editorial services

ISBN: 0-15-508132-2
Library of Congress Catalog Card Number: 97-72177

Copyrights and Acknowledgments appear on page C-1 and constitute a continuation of the copyright page.

Address for orders:
Harcourt Brace College Publishers
6277 Sea Harbor Drive
Orlando, FL 32887-6777
1-800-782-4479

Address for editorial correspondence:
Harcourt Brace College Publishers
301 Commerce Street, Suite 3700
Fort Worth, TX 76102

Website address:
http://www.hbcollege.com

Harcourt Brace & Company will provide complimentary supplements or supplement packages to those adopters qualified under our adoption policy. Please contact your sales representative to learn how you qualify. If as an adopter or potential user you receive supplements you do not need, please return them to your sales representative or send them to: Attn: Returns Department, Troy Warehouse, 465 South Lincoln Drive, Troy, MO 63379.

Printed in the United States of America

7 8 9 0 1 2 3 4 5 6 039 9 8 7 6 5 4 3 2 1

Preface

A compact yet comprehensive guide, the *Hodges' Harbrace Handbook, Thirteenth Edition* offers practical, well-organized, and easily accessible advice for writers. Specific examples throughout the book demonstrate the principles of writing that are applicable to both course work and professional tasks, and frequent cross-references establish how these principles inform each other.

The Thirteenth Edition is a complete revision of the Twelfth. While recognizably the same book that generations of writers have come to trust, the handbook is now easier to use and understand. To revise it, we followed several principles:

1. Whenever possible, we have explained the reasons or purposes for specific elements of grammar, style, punctuation, and mechanics. Students learn faster and write better when they understand the reasons behind the rules.
2. We have updated the examples, drawing principally upon contemporary American writers and including examples of student work.
3. In sample sentences that are revised to illustrate the principles being taught, we have introduced handwritten corrections so that the revision is more readily apparent.

4. We have extensively revised the exercises by increasing the number that encourage students to write or revise in context, by making many exercises the focus of class discussion, and by providing exercises that give students writing practice.
5. We have significantly expanded our discussion of writing with computers; we have integrated this discussion throughout the book and identified the sections with an icon instead of isolating this material in a separate chapter.
6. ESL Similarly, we have expanded our discussion of writing difficulties common to dialect and ESL, doing so *in context* rather than placing these concerns in a separate chapter. This decision is in response to changing national demographics and our determination not to make international students feel as if their needs were being addressed only as an afterthought. Because many of their problems are ones that American students face as well, some concepts are not separated out as relating only to ESL students.
7. We have eliminated the "Notes" and reduced the number of "Cautions" to make the text more straightforward and to give more emphasis to the "Cautions" that remain.

Those familiar with past editions will also note some major structural changes. To emphasize our commitment to writing as a process, we have divided what used to be a single chapter, "The Whole Composition," into two: "Planning and Drafting Essays" and "Revising and Editing Essays." Three versions of a new student essay illustrate these chapters, and we have expanded our discussion of invention and revision. Similarly, we divided what had been a one-hundred-page chapter on the research paper into two: "Research Finding and Evaluating Sources" and "Research Using and Citing Sources." This division makes it easier for students to locate information. "Finding and Evaluating Sources" now contains a significantly expanded discussion of how to use electronic resources; "Using and Citing Sources" discusses the most recent MLA and APA guidelines and illustrates writing from sources with two new student essays.

In response to requests from users, we have created two other chapters new to this edition. "Writing under Pressure" builds on material previously located in "Writing for Special Purposes" to give it more emphasis and make it more useful. Chapter 36, "Writing Arguments," expands on the discussion of critical thinking introduced in Chapter 35 and helps students understand an important type of academic writing previously unaddressed in the book.

The chapter on manuscript format has been heavily revised and retitled "Document Design." Because most students compose their papers on computer, this chapter provides tips for electronic preparation and submission of documents.

Although we have considerably expanded the section covering the writing process with new chapters and more material, *Hodges' Harbrace* remains a handbook first and a rhetoric second. We have tried to change existing chapter titles and subtitles as little as possible. And while we have made the book easier to teach and easier to consult, we have not compromised its well-established integrity. On the contrary, we have worked hard to improve it. As a result, the new edition will respond to the changing needs of writers well into the next century.

The following supplements accompany the *Hodges' Harbrace Handbook, Thirteenth Edition.*

Instructor Supplements

Instructor's Manual

Harcourt Brace Guide to Teaching First-Year Composition

Harcourt Brace Sourcebook for Teachers of Writing

Harcourt Brace Guide to Teaching Writing with Computers

Harcourt Brace Guide to Writing across the Curriculum

Diagnostic Test Package to accompany the Harbrace Handbook, 13e

Transparency Acetates to accompany the Harbrace Handbook, 13e

Instructor's Correction Chart

Test Bank to accompany the Harbrace Handbook, 13e

Student Supplements

Harbrace College Workbook, 13e

Harbrace Basic Writer's Workbook

Harbrace ESL Workbook

Working Together: A Collaborative Writing Guide

Harcourt Brace Guide to Peer Tutoring

Harcourt Brace Guide to Citing Electronic Sources

Resourceful Reader, 4e

Writing in the Disciplines, 3e

Merriam Webster's Dictionary (softcover)

Merriam Webster's Collegiate Dictionary, 10e

Software

Writing Tutor V

Harbrace Online 3.1

Harbrace CD-ROM

ExaMaster Test Bank to accompany the Harbrace Handbook, 13e

For additional information on the supplemental materials available for *Hodges' Harbrace,* please visit the *Harbrace* Website at http://www.harbrace.com/english

Acknowledgments

For the material on English as a Second Language, a feature new to the Thirteenth Edition, we are indebted to **Judith B. Strother** *at the Florida Institute of Technology* and **Irene Juzkiw** *at the University of Missouri.* Their special expertise added a much needed feature to the *Hodges' Harbrace.*

The following individuals gave us their advice and experience, which shaped the Thirteenth Edition.

Focus Group Participants

Donald Andrews, *Chattanooga State Technical Community College;* Mary Jo Arn, *Bloomsburg University;* Susan Becker, *Illinois Central College;* Honora Berninger, *Hillsborough Community College;* Tim Biehl, *Tarrant County Junior College;* Tracy Bird, *Hillsborough Community College (student);* Cathy Bridges, *Hillsborough Community College (student);* Teresa Chasteen, *Hiwassee College;* Carol Cinclair, *Brookhaven College;* Sean Claflin, *Hillsborough Community College (student);* Linda Clark, *Maryville College;* Mark Dawson, *Faulkner University;* Cody Dolnick, *University of San Diego;* Josh Edmonson, *Hillsborough Community College (student);* Dave Esselstrom, *Azusa Pacific University;* Bernie Felder, *St. Joseph's University (student);* Sally Fitzgerald, *Chabot College;* Angela Forsman, *University of South Florida (student);* Jim Frank, *Cleveland State Community College;* Jean Marie Fuhrman, *University of Central Florida;* Judith Gallagher, *Tarrant County Junior College;* Danny Glover, *University of South Florida (student);* Barbara Goldstein, *Hillsbor-*

ough Community College; Adrienne Goslin, *Cleveland State University;* Michele Grantle, *St. Joseph's University (student);* Angie Green, *Lee College;* Rusty Green, *University of South Florida (student);* Mary Beth Gugler-Matthews, *Pasco-Hernando Community College;* Patsy Hammontree, *University of Tennessee-Knoxville;* George Hanson, *University of California at San Diego;* Beth Hedengren, *Brigham Young University;* Kathryn Henkins, *Mt. San Antonio College;* Susan Hines, *Middle Georgia College;* Mary Hostenner, *St. Joseph's University (student);* Maggie Jenkins, *Pellissippi State Technical Community College;* Myra Jones, *Manatee Community College;* Jim Knox, *Roane State Community College;* Robert Lamm, *Arkansas State University;* Ernest Lee, *Carson-Newman College;* Susan Lowdermilk, *Texas Wesleyan University;* John Martino, *California Polytechnic State University-Pomona;* Melissa Mazzei, *University of South Florida (student);* Jeanne McDonald, *Waubonsee Community College;* Alan Merickel, *Tallahassee Community College;* Judy Michna, *DeKalb College-Dunwoody;* Robert Miller, *Tennessee Temple University;* Jody Millward, *Santa Barbara City College;* Jason Murray, *Pasco-Hernando Community College (student);* Marlene Musinca, *Villanova University (student);* Jennifer Olsone, *St. Joseph's University (student);* Mary Padget, *Tennessee Technical University;* Karen Peterson, *Hillsborough Community College (student);* Ron Puckett, *Polk Community College;* Bob Renk, *Trinity Valley Community College;* Ashley Richmond, *Delaware County Community College (student);* Stephanie Sanchez, *University of South Florida (student);* Jack Scanlon, *Triton College;* Marie Schein, *Tarrant County Junior College;* Karen Sidwell, *St. Petersburg Junior College;* Laurel Smith, *Vincennes University;* Marcia Songer, *East Tennessee State University;* Barbara Stewart, *Long Beach City College;* Megan Striker, *St. Joseph's University (student);* Bill Summer, *Delaware County Community College (student);* Brian Talbert, *Villanova University (student);* Michelle Tarlene, *Delaware County Community College (student);* Tom Tuggle, *Gainesville College;* Donte Williams, *Pasco-Hernando Community College (student);* Michael Woodard, *St. Joseph's University (student);* and Driek Zirinsky, *Boise State University*

Phone Interviews

Paul Clee, *Tacoma Community College;* Joseph Colavito, *Northwestern State University;* Cynthia Denham, *Snead State Community College;* Gabrielle Gautreaux, *University of New Orleans;* Eloise Grathwohl, *Meredith College;* Angie Green, *Lee College;* Diana Kilpatrick, *Palm Beach Community College;* Bruce Kirle, *Trident Community College;* John Launt, *Central Piedmont Community College;* Dara Llewellyn, *Florida Atlantic University;* Mike Matthew, *Tarrant County Junior College;* and Lisa Williams, *Jacksonville State University*

Manuscript Reviewers

Dorothy Ashe, *West Hills Community College;* Myrtle B. Beavers, *Okaloosa Walton Community College;* Jon G. Bentley, *Albuquerque Technical-Vocational Institute;* Tim Biehl, *Tarrant County Junior College;* Steven Brahlek, *Palm Beach Community College;* Ann Camy, *Red Rocks Community College;* Thomas E. Fish, *Cumberland College;* Gabrielle Gautreaux, *University of New Orleans;* Lynn M. Grow, *Broward Community College;* Ruby Johnson, *Wallace State Community College;* George M. Kelly, *Hinds Community College;* Wanda Martin, *University of New Mexico;* Barbara McMichael, *Gwinnett Technical Institute;* Kathryn Raign, *University of North Texas;* Eula Thompson, *Jefferson State Community College;* Heidemarie Z. Weidner, *Tennessee Technical University;* and Lisa Williams, *Jacksonville State University*

Marketing Phone Interviews

Donald Andrews, *Chattanooga State Technical Community College;* Linda Bensel-Meyers, *University of Tennessee-Knoxville;* Lorraine Cadet, *Grambling State University;* George Cox, *Johnston Community College;* Margaret DeHart, *Trinity Valley Community College;* MaryBeth DeMeo, *Alvernia College;* Wendy Jones, *County College of Morris;* Paul Kleinpoppen, *Florida Community College at Jacksonville;* Carol Lowe, *McLennan Community College;* Judy Michna, *DeKalb College-Dunwoody;* Bill Newman, *DeKalb College;* Mary Padget, *Tennessee Technical University;* Ken Rosen, *University of Southern Maine;* Marcia Songer, *East Tennessee State University;* Bill Spencer, *Delta State University;* and Ken Wolfskill, *Chowan College*

Marketing Survey Participants

Elizabeth Addison, *Western Carolina University;* David Anderson, *Butler County Community College;* Gordon Anderson, *Delgato Community College;* Vic Aquino, *Green River Community College;* Rozel Arant, *Northeast Louisiana University;* Ellen Arl, *University of Southern California at Sumter;* Dorothy Ashe, *West Hill Community College;* Charles Avinger, *Washtenau Community College;* Jan Balakiam, *Kean College;* Juanita Barnes, *Grambling State University;* Carol Bays, *Northern Michigan University;* Sue Bennett, *New Mexico Junior College;* Dianne Bladel, *Florida Community College at Jacksonville;* Valerie Blue, *Nashville State Technical College;* William Bode, *Southern College;* Jesse Bogan, *Morris Brown College;* Odon Bologan, *Delaware State University;* Gene Booth,

Albuquerque Technical-Vocational Institute; Steven Brahlek, *Palm Beach Community College;* Floyd Brigdon, *Trinity Valley College;* Jessica Bryan, *Troy State University;* Patricia Burnes, *University of Maine-Orono;* Russell Burrows, *Weber State University;* Lorraine Cadet, *Grambling State University;* Susan Calovini, *Austin Peay State University;* Mike Campbell, *Yakima College;* Ayne Cantrell, *Middle Tennessee State University;* Linda Carmichael, *East Tennessee State University;* Allison Carpenter, *University of Delaware;* Jerry Carr, *Hinds Community College;* Julie Cary, *Georgia State University;* Harriet Castratsaro, *Indiana University at Bloomington;* Judy Cheatham, *Greensboro College;* Merlin Cheney, *Weber State University;* Elizabeth Chesla, *Polytechnic University;* Dennis Ciesielski, *Peru State College;* Dennis Clark, *Eastern Illinois University;* Sarah Cogne, *West Liberty State College;* Rocky Colavito, *North Western State University;* Anna Coles, *Baldwin-Wallace College;* Elaine Coneq, *Southwest Mississippi Community College;* Mark Connelly, *Milwaukee Area Technical College;* Judith Corbin, *Eastern Illinois University;* Moira Cordel, *University of Detroit Mercy;* Richard Cornelius, *Bryan College;* George Cox, *Johnston Community College;* Anne Crane, *St. Edwards University;* Patricia Crane, *Nazarene Bible College;* Carol Creekmore, *DeKalb College at Rockdale Center;* Leslie Cronin, *Widener University;* Marilyn Curall, *Valencia Community College;* Martha Davenport, *Olympia College;* MaryBeth DeMeo, *Alvernia College;* Cynthia Denham, *Snead State Community College;* C. J. Denne, *College of New Rochelle;* Dennis Dooley, *Wofford College;* Paul Drake, *Spartenburg Technical College;* Sean Dugan, *Mercy College;* Sallie Duhling, *Gainesville College;* Mike Eason, *Tarrant County Junior College;* Donna Edsel, *Muskingum College;* Mark Edmonds, *St. Leo College;* Jolly Faught, *Cumberland College;* Steve Feldman, *George*

Mason University; Donald Fritz, *University of Texas Pan American;* Hank Galmish, *Green River Community College;* James Gamble, *University of Arkansas at Monticello;* Maryanne Garbowsky, *County College of Morris;* Bill Gary, *Henderson Community College;* Gabrielle Gautreaux, *University of New Orleans;* Louise Gearhart, *Hogerstown Junior College;* Julia Gergits, *Youngstown State University;* Jim Gilchrist, *Iowa State University;* Karen Gillenwaters, *Brazo Sport College;* Margaret Gillio, *Northern Michigan University;* Owen Gilman, *St. Joseph University;* Lewis Graham, *Olympia College;* Eileen Gregory, *University of Dallas;* Kevin Griffith, *Capital University;* Huey Guagliardio, *Louisiana State University-Eunice;* Rachel Guppta, *Charles Mott Community College;* Janet Haddock, *Northeast Louisiana University;* Joanne Haen, *Kansas City Community College;* Carol Hall, *Victoria College;* Jeff Hammond, *St. Mary College of Maryland;* Elree Harris, *Westminster College;* Judy Hart, *Frank Phillips College;* Susan Hartman, *Reading Community College;* Jane Haywood, *University of Mary Hardin Baylor;* Betty Lou Heimbold, *University of Cincinnati-Clermont College;* Doris Helbig, *Florida Atlantic University;* Cindy Hess, *Elizabethtown College;* Alice Hines, *Hendrix College;* Michael Hood, *Belmont Abbey College;* Sue Howard, *Duquesne University;* Tom Hruska, *Northern Michigan University;* Marsha Huntineton, *Everett Community College;* John Hyman, *The American University;* Deborah Jacobs, *Prestonburg Community College;* Melanie Johnson, *Wallace State Community College;* Wendy Jones, *County College of Morris;* Nancy Kennedy, *Edmonds Community College;* Janice Kidd, *Lake Land College;* Lola King, *Trinity Valley College;* Paul Kleinpoppen, *Florida Community College at Jacksonville;* Jim Knox, *Rowan State Community College;* Dan Landau, *Santa Monica College;* Susan Lang, *Southern Illinois University at Car-*

bondale; Rosemary Lanshe, *Broward Community College;* Russ Larson, *Eastern Michigan University;* Gail Laurson, *Southeast Community College;* Ernest Lee, *Carson Newman College;* William Lenz, *Chatham College;* Diane Lestourgeon, *Widener University;* Sarah Liggett, *Louisiana State University;* Salvatore Lisanti, *Westchester Community College;* Frank Littler, *Palm Beach Community College;* Alice Loftin, *Tusculum College;* Kim Long, *Shippensburg University;* Richard Louth, *Southeast Louisiana University;* Carol Lowe, *McLennan Community College;* Laura Maas, *Olivet College;* Cheryl Martin, *Roanoke-Chowan Community College;* Linda Martin, *Florida Community College;* Linda McGinley, *West Liberty State College;* Tom McKay, *Truman College;* Victoria McLure, *South Plains College;* Barbara McMillan, *Union University;* John Moore, *East Illinois University;* Nelda Moore, *Jones County Community College;* Janet Morczek, *Daly College;* David Moreland, *Louisiana State University;* John Morris, *Cameron University;* Tina Murdock, *Clear Creek Baptist Bible College;* Christopher Nielson, *Widener University;* Connie Nunley, *Truett McConnell Junior College;* Susan Oldrive, *Baldwin-Wallace College;* Penny Olson, *Bay Mills Community College;* Peter Olson, *Hillside College;* Mary O'Reilly, *Rider University;* Joyce O'Shay, *Stark Technical College;* Sam Overstreet, *Maryville College;* Pat Palmer, *Olympia College;* Nancy Parker, *Embry Riddle Aeronautical University;* Jane Parks, *Dalton College;* Mildred Pate, *Georgia Southern University;* Mary Peddicord, *Pearl River Community College;* Rita Perkins, *Camden County College;* Donna Prescott, *Green Mountain College;* Janice Quass, *Grand View College;* Carole Raybourn, *Morehouse College;* Mary Jo Reiff, *University of Kansas;* David Rosen, *University of Maine at Machias;* Ken Rosen, *University of Southern Maine;* Kenny Rowlette, *Liberty University;* Rebecca Rowley, *Clovis Community College;* Mark Schmidt, *University of Arkansas at*

Monticello; Geoffrey Schramm, *University of Maryland at College Park;* Kathleen Sherfick, *Albion College;* George Shields, *Kentucky State University;* Erlene Smith, *Pearl River Community College;* William Smith, *Piedmont College;* Marcia Songer, *East Tennessee State University;* Jacqueline Stark, *Los Angeles Valley College;* Philip Stirling, *Ferris State University;* Jim Stuart, *Kellogg Community College;* Marilyn Styne, *Wilbur Wright College;* Joan Sweitzer, *Lake City Community College;* George Teffner, *University of Pittsburgh at Bradford;* Sandra Thompkins, *Hiwassee College;* Nancy Tuten, *Columbia College;* Linda Underhill, *Alfred University;* Louis Van Keuren, *Green Mountain College;* Ben Varner, *University of Northern Colorado;* Frank Vaughan, *Campbell University;* Donna Walker-Nixon, *University of Mary Hardin Baylor;* James Wallace, *University of Akron;* Jonathan Walters, *Norwich University;* W. G. Walton, *Meredith College;* Jay Ward, *Thiel College;* Bill Waterson, *Lees McRae College;* Michael Webster, *Grand Valley State University;* Bob Welsh, *Webster University;* Mike Westerfield, *Michigan Christian College;* Katherine Wheatcroft, *Bucknell University;* Ron Wheeler, *Johnson Bible College;* Judy Whitis, *Olivet Nazarene University;* Jeanne Williams, *Southwest Mississippi Community College;* Ken Wolfskill, *Chowan College;* Jim Wood, *Green River Community College;* Randall Woodland, *University of Michigan-Dearborn;* Laura Writer, *Ottawa University;* and Norma ZanRheenes, *Western Michigan University*

For the daunting task of copyediting and proofreading the manuscript, we thank Mary Stoughton, Senior Editor, and the staff at EEI Communications.

For help with details from research to manuscript preparation, we are indebted to Camille Langston, Susan Perry, Denise Stodola, and Paul Teske.

Finally we wish to give special thanks to the editorial and marketing staff at Harcourt Brace for their two and a half years of preparation for the Thirteenth Edition: Michael Rosenberg, Executive Editor for English; John Meyers, Acquisitions Editor; Michell Phifer, Developmental Editor; Ilse Wolfe West, Senior Product Manager; Kimberly Allison, Special Projects; and Katie Frushour and Laura Newhouse, Editorial Assistants. From the production staff, for their amazing efforts to bring all phases of this edition together, we thank Matt Ball, Project Editor; Kathy Ferguson, Senior Production Manager; and Brian Salisbury, Senior Art Director.

Contents

MECHANICS

PUNCTUATION

SPELLING AND DICTION

EFFECTIVE SENTENCES

LARGER ELEMENTS

Grammar

Chapter 1
Sentence Sense

Writing a clear, precise sentence is an art, and you can master that art by knowing the different kinds of sentences and the ways they function. You can also revise your sentences more effectively if you recognize the different parts of speech and the ways they work together. Knowing how to revise will help you become a more flexible, effective writer. (For explanations of any unfamiliar terms, see the Glossary of Terms.)

The parts of a sentence An English sentence divides into two parts.

> SUBJECT + PREDICATE
>
> **Gabriel** + **hung** the picture on the wall.
>
> The **towel** + **is wet.**

These parts, the subject and the predicate, are the two essential elements of an English sentence. The **subject** is what the sentence is about and answers the question "Who?" or "What?" The **predicate** says something about the subject (see 1a) and contains a word that expresses action or state of being. In the sentence above, *hung* expresses the action Gabriel took, and *is wet* expresses the state of the towel. The pattern is **SUBJECT + PREDICATE**, which is the basic order of English sentences.

1a Verbs form the predicate of sentences.

A verb functions as the predicate of a sentence or as an essential part of the predicate. You can recognize a verb by observing its form as well as its function.

> Marco **walks.** [verb by itself]
>
> Marco **walks** very fast. [verb plus modifier]

Verbs can be compound, that is, composed of more than one verb.

> Marco **walks** and **arrives** on time.

A verb can consist of more than one word. The **auxiliary** is often called a *helping verb* or *verb marker*. The verbs *have* and *be* are auxiliaries and follow the pattern of **AUXILIARY + VERB. Modals** such as *can/could, may/might,* and *shall/will* follow the same pattern and express such things as ability or possibility; *shall/will* expresses future tense. (See chapter 7 for a complete discussion of verbs.)

> The fight **had started** by then.
>
> He **will be studying** late.
>
> Mara **should go** now.

Other words sometimes intervene between the auxiliary and the verb.

> I **have** not **paid** my dues.
>
> Television **will** never completely **replace** radio.

Verbs with prepositions When verbs are followed by a preposition (often called a **particle**), they are called

phrasal verbs. A preposition combines with a verb to mean something different from the verb standing alone. For example, the meaning of the verb *turned* is different from the meaning of the combination *turned out.*

> Martha **turned** the car **out of the way**. [prepositional phrase modifying the verb *turned*]
>
> Nothing **turned out** the way she expected.

Some examples of verbs with prepositions are *look up, burn down, phase out, turn off, watch out, put off, try on.* If a phrasal verb has a direct object, the verb and the preposition can often be separated. The preposition can come before or after the object.

> She **looked** the word **up** in the dictionary.
>
> She **looked up** the word in the dictionary.

If the object is a pronoun, the preposition must follow the object.

> She **looked** it **up** in the dictionary.

ESL The meanings of such verbs can be found in a good ESL dictionary, together with an explanation of whether or not they are separable. (See chapter 19, page 207 for ESL dictionaries.)

1b Subjects, objects, and complements can be nouns, pronouns, or word groups serving as nouns.

(1) Subjects of verbs

Except for imperatives, which are commands, or requests, in which the subject, *you,* may be understood, all grammatically complete sentences contain stated subjects—nouns, pronouns, or word groups serving as nouns. In the following sentences, the subjects are in boldface and the verbs are in italics.

Louisiana *produces* delicious yams.

Does **North Carolina** also *grow* yams?

In commands or requests, the subject is often understood.

[**You**] *Take,* for example, Louisiana and North Carolina.

Subjects of verbs may be compound.

Louisiana and **North Carolina** grow yams. [compound subject]

To identify the grammatical subject of a sentence, first find the verb, then use it in a question beginning with *who* or *what,* as shown in the following examples:

The runner leaped the hurdle.	The book was read by Nan.
Verb: **leaped**	Verb: **was read**
WHO leaped? **The runner** (not the hurdle) **leaped.**	WHAT was read? **The book** (not Nan) **was read.**
Subject: **runner**	Subject: **book**

Subjects usually precede verbs in sentences. Common exceptions occur in questions and after the words *there* and *it,* both of which fill out a sentence without altering the meaning.

Was the *book* interesting? [verb + subject]

There *were* no *refusals.* [there + verb + subject]

It is not easy *to study* on a sunny spring day. [it + linking verb + infinitive subject]

(2) Objects of verbs

Verbs denoting action often require a **direct object** to receive or show the result of the action. Such verbs are called **transitive** verbs. (See chapter 7.) Sometimes a word that shows to whom or for whom the action occurred (**indirect object**) comes between the verb and the direct object. In the following sentence, the objects are in boldface.

> The clerk sold **her** the expensive **briefcase.** [indirect object: *her;* direct object: *briefcase*]

Like the subjects of verbs, direct and indirect objects are generally nouns or pronouns.

To identify a direct object, find the subject and the verb and then use them in a question ending with *whom* or *what,* as shown in the following example:

> Juana silently took his hand.
>
> Subject and verb: **Juana took**
>
> Juana took WHAT? **hand**
>
> Direct object: **hand**

Direct objects in sentences like the following are directly affected by the action of the verb.

> A tornado leveled a city in Nebraska. [The subject, *tornado,* acts. The object, *city,* receives the action.]

Knowing how to change from *active* to *passive voice* can also help you identify an object. When you make a verb passive, the object of the active verb becomes the subject of the passive verb. The original subject is either omitted or incorporated into a phrase beginning with *by*. (See also examples on pages 80 and 83 of chapter 7 and in 29d(1).)

Active The Eagles finally **defeated** the **Lions.** [*Lions* is the direct object of *defeated.*]

Passive The **Lions were** finally **defeated.** [*Lions* is the subject of *were defeated;* the original subject is omitted.]

The **Lions were** finally **defeated** by the Eagles. [The original subject is incorporated into a phrase.]

A form of *be* (such as *is, are, was*) is added when an active verb becomes passive.

Some verbs (such as *give, offer, bring, take, lend, send, buy,* and *sell*) can have both a direct object and an indirect object.

Linda gave Felipe a new bicycle. [subject + verb + direct object: **Linda gave bicycle.**]

Linda gave a bicycle TO WHOM? **Felipe** [indirect object: **Felipe**]

Direct and indirect objects of verbs can be compound.

She likes **peas** and **spinach.** [compound direct object]

We offered **Elena** and **Octavio** a year's membership. [compound indirect object]

(3) Subject and object complements

Nouns, pronouns, and adjectives are used as subject and object complements. (See 1c.) A **subject complement** refers to, identifies, or qualifies the subject and helps complete the meaning of the forms of *be* (*am, is, are, was, were, been*), linking verbs (such as *seem, become*), and sensory verbs (such as *feel, look, smell, sound, taste*). These verbs are often called **intransitive verbs.** (See chapter 7.)

Leilani is my **sister.** [*Sister* identifies *Leilani,* the subject.]

Violence became **inevitable.** [*Inevitable* describes or qualifies *violence,* the subject.]

The rose smelled **sweet.** [*Sweet* describes *rose.*]

An **object complement** refers to, identifies, or qualifies the direct object. Object complements help complete the meaning of verbs such as *make, name, elect, call, paint.*

We elected Jesse **president.**

The flaw made it **worthless.**

(4) Word order

Becoming thoroughly aware of English word order—usually **SUBJECT + VERB + OBJECT** or **COMPLEMENT**—will help you recognize subjects, objects, and complements. Careful study of the five most common sentence patterns will reveal the importance of word order.

Pattern 1

SUBJECT + VERB.

The **children did** not **listen.**

The **lights** on the patrol car **flashed** ominously.

Pattern 2

SUBJECT + VERB + OBJECT.

Mice frighten elephants.

Elephants frighten mice.

Kenya's **athletes** often **win** the **marathon.**

Pattern 3

SUBJECT + VERB + INDIRECT OBJECT + DIRECT OBJECT.

Jan showed Karl the **book.**

The **company will** probably **send me** a small **refund.**

In some sentences (especially questions), the direct object does not always take the position indicated by these basic patterns.

What **event do** Kenya's **athletes** often **win**? [direct object + auxiliary + subject + verb]

Pattern 4

SUBJECT + LINKING VERB + SUBJECT COMPLEMENT.

My son's **name is Aaron.**

The **fence was white.**

Pattern 5

SUBJECT + VERB + DIRECT OBJECT + OBJECT COMPLEMENT.

I named my **son Aaron.**

I painted the **fence white.**

Exercise 1

Label all subjects and verbs (including auxiliaries and prepositions) in the sentences below. Next, label all direct and indirect objects and complements. Be prepared to discuss the basic sentence patterns (and any variations) and the types of verbs used.

1. He desires no real companionship.
2. Alliances once forged become invaluable.
3. The workers must take off their normal clothing and put on protective gear.
4. The artist has created a masterpiece.
5. In the newspaper article, the journalist gives us a detailed description of the latest industrial accident and its environmental consequences.
6. Football games and popular music need players, arenas, and fans.
7. The new manager suggests that the employees revise their former work habits.
8. They have not always been hospitable to their family and friends.
9. There was one painting so expensive that it astounded the auctioneer.
10. Academic writing, particularly journal articles, can be full of valuable information but can be difficult to decipher unless the reader is willing to take the time to understand it.

1c There are eight classes of words—the parts of speech.

Words are traditionally grouped into eight classes or parts of speech: **verbs**, **nouns**, **pronouns**, **adjectives**, **adverbs**, **prepositions**, **conjunctions**, and **interjections**. Verbs, nouns, adjectives, and adverbs (called **vocabulary** or **lexical words**) make up more than 99 percent of all words listed in the dictionary. But pronouns, prepositions, and conjunctions—although small in number—are important because they are used over and over in speaking and writing. Prepositions and conjunctions (called **function** or **structure words**) connect and relate other parts of speech. Prepositions and conjunctions, as well as interjections, are also the only word classes that do not change their form. (For a summary of the form changes of the other parts of speech, see **inflection** in the Glossary of Terms.)

The function and form of each of the eight parts of speech listed in the chart below are discussed on the following pages. (See also the corresponding entries in the Glossary of Terms.) The chart shows the relationships among parts of speech, form, and function in the following sentences.

Compassionate friends generously offered her shelter from the Nazis' persecution.

	Form	Function	Part of Speech
Compassionate	*-ate* ending	modifier	adjective
friends	*-s* (plural)	subject	noun
generously	*-ly* ending	modifier	adverb
offered	*-ed* (past)	verb of predicate	verb
her	objective case	indirect object	pronoun
shelter	singular	direct object	noun
from	invariable	connector	preposition
the	invariable	modifier	adjective
Nazis'	*s'* (plural possessive)	modifier	noun
persecution	singular	object of the preposition	noun

Here, one part of speech—the noun (a naming word that forms the plural with *-s* and the possessive with *'s* or *s'*)—is used as a subject, a direct object, a modifier, and an object of a preposition.

A dictionary labels words according to their parts of speech. Some words have only one classification—for example, *notify* (verb), *sleepy* (adjective), *practically* (adverb). Others have more than one label because they can function as two or more parts of speech. The label of a word therefore depends on its use in a given sentence. The word *living,* for instance, can be a form of the verb *live* (as in *are living*), an adjective (*a living example*), or a noun (*makes a living*). Another example is the word *up:*

They dragged the sled **up** the hill. [preposition]

She follows the **ups** and downs of the market. [noun]

"They have **upped** the rent again," he complained. [verb]

Kelly ran **up** the bill. [part of a phrasal verb]

The **up** escalator is broken again. [adjective]

Hopkins says to look **up** at the skies! [adverb]

The following chart lists some words showing the common endings that mark different parts of speech.

Noun	Verb	Adjective	Adverb
correlation	correlate	correlated	
motivation motivator motive	motivate	motivational	motivationally
negotiation negotiator	negotiate	negotiated	
progress	progress	progressive	progressively
recognition	recognize	recognizable recognized	recognizably
sensation sense	sense	sensory	
validation validity	validate	valid	validly

(1) Verbs *notify, notifies, is notifying, notified*
write, writes, is writing, wrote, has written

A verb is an essential part of the predicate. (See **1a**.)

> He **is** no longer **writing** those dull stories.

Two suffixes frequently used to make verbs are *-ize* and *-ify:*

> *terror* (noun)—*terrorize, terrify* (verbs)
>
> *real* (adjective)—*realize* (verb)

Verbs often add prepositions to form **phrasal verbs.** (See **1c(6)**.)

> Joseph **turned out** the light.

CAUTION Verbals (infinitives, participles, and gerunds) cannot function as the predicate of a sentence. (See **1d**.)

(2) Nouns *nation, nations, nation's, nations'*
woman, women, kindness, kindnesses
Carthage, United States, William, NASA
breakthrough, buddy system, sister-in-law

Nouns function as subjects, objects, complements, appositives, and modifiers, as well as in direct address and in absolute constructions. (See **noun** and **absolute construction** in the **Glossary of Terms**.) Nouns name persons, places, things, ideas, animals, and so on. The articles *a, an,* and *the* signal that a noun is to follow (a *chair*, an *activity*).

> **McKinney** drives a **truck** for the **Salvation Army**.

Suffixes frequently used to make nouns are *-ance, -ation, -ence, -ism, -ity, -ment, -ness,* and *-ship*.

relax, depend (verbs)—*relaxation, dependence* (nouns)

kind, rigid (adjectives)—*kindness, rigidity* (nouns)

Words such as *father-in-law, Labor Day,* and *swimming pool* are generally classified as *compound nouns*.

ESL Nouns can also modify other nouns. These noun modifiers are almost always singular even when the noun they modify is plural: *sophomore students, office buildings*. Common exceptions: *men students, women doctors*. A noun modifier used with a number is singular and has a hyphen: a *4-door car, 10-year-old children*.

ESL ***Count/noncount nouns*** (See 22a(1) for use of articles.)

Count nouns are words that represent individual items that can be counted and cannot be viewed as a mass, such as *book, child,* or *atom*.

Count nouns can be either singular or plural and are preceded by words such as *many, few, a few, a number,* and *several* with the plural. Use either indefinite (*a, an*) or definite articles (*the*) with count nouns. (See 22a(1).)

Noncount nouns, such as *humor* or *furniture*, represent an abstract concept, a mass, or a collection and do not have an individual existence. Modifiers such as *much* or *a little* can be used with noncount nouns but never *a* or *an*. They usually have only a singular form.

(3) **Pronouns** *I, me, my, mine, myself*
you, your, yours, yourself
he, him, his; she, her, hers; it, its
we, us, our; they, them, their
this, these; who, whom, whose; which, that
one, ones; everybody, anyone

A pronoun is a word that can substitute for a noun in sentences. Pronouns change form according to their function. (See chapter 5.)

> **They** bought **it** for **her**. **Everyone** knows **that.**

(4) **Adjectives** *shy, sleepy, attractive, famous, historic*
three men, *this* class, *another* one
young, younger, youngest; good, better, best

Adjectives modify or qualify nouns and pronouns—and sometimes gerunds. (See page 21.) Generally, adjectives appear immediately before the words they modify.

> **These difficult** decisions, whether **right** or **wrong,** affect all of us.

In the following example, *strong* is a predicate adjective (subject complement), a word that modifies the subject and helps complete the meaning of the sentence. (See 4b and 7.)

> **Competitive** gymnasts look **strong.**

Suffixes such as *-al, -able, -ant, -ative, -ic, -ish, -less, -ous,* and *-y* can be added to certain verbs or nouns to form adjectives:

> *accept, repent* (verbs)—*acceptable, repentant* (adjectives)
>
> *angel, effort* (nouns)—*angelic, effortless* (adjectives)

The articles *a, an,* and *the* are often classified as adjectives. Noun modifiers are also often classified as adjectives. (See 1c(2).)

(5) Adverbs *rarely* saw, call *daily, soon* left, left *sooner*
very short, *too* angry, *never* shy, *not* fearful
practically never loses, *nearly always* cold

As the examples show, adverbs modify verbs, adjectives, and other adverbs. In addition, an adverb can modify a verbal, a phrase, or a clause.

Adverbs that do not modify any verb in the sentence are said to modify the sentence as a whole and are called *sentence modifiers*. They are separated from the rest of the sentence by a comma.

> *Honestly,* Jo wasn't speeding.
>
> *In fact,* I wasn't even there.

(6) Prepositions *on* a shelf, *between* us, *because of* rain
to the door, *by* them, *before* class

A preposition has an object (except when it is part of a phrasal verb such as *look up*), which is usually a noun or a pronoun. The preposition establishes a relationship such as space, time, accompaniment, cause, or manner between its object and another part of the sentence. The preposition with its object (and any modifiers) is called a *prepositional phrase*.

> ***With* great feeling,** Martin Luther King, Jr., expressed his dream ***of* freedom.**

The preposition may follow rather than precede its object, and it can be placed at the end of the sentence:

What was he complaining **about?** [*What* is the object of the preposition. COMPARE "He was complaining about what?"]

Some prepositions, called **phrasal prepositions,** can contain more than one word.

According to Georgeanne, it was a bad experience.

The following list contains the most commonly used phrasal prepositions.

Phrasal Prepositions (two or more words):

according to	by way of	in spite of
along with	due to	instead of
apart from	except for	on account of
as for	in addition to	out of
as regards	in case of	up to
as to	in front of	with reference to
because of	in lieu of	with regard to
by means of	in place of	with respect to
by reason of	in regard to	with the exception of

Prepositions can combine with verbs to form **phrasal verbs.** (See **1a**.) They can also combine with other words to form certain idioms.

ESL Some prepositions, such as *by/until* and *except/besides,* pose special problems. *Until* means a continuing situation that will come to an end at a definite time in the future. *By* means an action that will happen at or before a particular time in the future.

I will finish my work **by** six o'clock.

I will be away **until** next Tuesday.

Besides means *with* or *plus* and usually "includes," while *except* means *without* or *minus* and usually "excludes."

Besides a salad, we had soup and crackers.

We had everything we wanted **except** a salad.

(For other preposition problems, consult the Glossary of Usage or one of the ESL resources listed in chapter 19 on page 207.)

(7) Conjunctions cars *and* trucks, in the boat *or* on the pier
will try *but* may lose, *neither* Ana *nor* Miguel
I worked *because* Dad needed money.
The river rises *when* the snow melts.

Conjunctions are connectors. The **coordinating conjunctions** (*and, but, or, for, nor, so,* and *yet*), as well as the correlatives (*both–and, either–or, neither–nor, not only–but also, whether–or*), join sentence elements (words, phrases, or clauses) of equal grammatical rank. (See also chapter 26.) The **subordinating conjunctions** (such as *because, if, since, until, when, where, while*) join subordinate clauses to independent clauses. (See 1e, pages 24–25.)

Words like *consequently, however, nevertheless, then,* and *therefore* (see the list on page 41) serve as conjunctive adverbs (or adverbial conjunctions).

Don seemed bored in class; **however,** he did listen and learn.

(8) Interjections

Interjections are exclamations. They can be followed by an exclamation point or by a comma.

Wow! Oh, that's a surprise.

Exercise 2

Using your dictionary, classify each word in the following sentences according to its part of speech.

1. She walks with the grace of a beautiful swan.
2. Neither wisdom nor wit can be learned by silence.
3. She picked Marie for a friend and then picked on her throughout their friendship.
4. He thought of his small, weak legs, his fragile, slender hands and drew himself up into a miserable little blob in the corner of the cushy recliner.
5. Smart enough to see the potential of her current situation for being promoted in the company, Elaine took to helping her supervisor during lunch and working during evenings and weekends.

1d A phrase is a group of words that functions as a single part of speech.

A **phrase** is a word group that lacks a subject and/or a predicate and functions as a single part of speech (noun, verb, adjective, adverb). A short simple sentence can be expanded by adding word groups that function as adjectives or adverbs. (See 1c(4) and 1c(5).)

(1) Kinds of phrases

A phrase is a group of grammatically related words that function as a single part of speech (noun, verb, adjective, or adverb). Phrases are generally classified as follows:

Verb Phrases The flowers **have wilted. Have** you **watered** them? Gerald **has looked up** the word. I **might have been told.**

Noun Phrases **The heavy freeze** killed **fruit trees.** They elected Alexandra **vice president.**

Prepositional Phrases Parking **on campus** is prohibited. We were racing **against time.**

Participial Phrases **Exploring the beach,** we found many treasures. The picnic ground, **covered with trash,** looked pretty bad.

Gerund Phrases **Swimming across the lake** is fun. They loved **playing in the water.**

Infinitive Phrases He wanted **to go to the movie.** He asked **me to go with him.**

Absolute Phrases **The lunch having been packed,** we were ready to go. The star left the gym, **reporters following him eagerly.** (See **absolute phrase** in the Glossary of Terms.)

Appositive Phrases John, **my brother,** is here today. June 21, **the longest day of the year,** is my birthday.

Noun phrases serve as subjects, objects, and complements, while **verb phrases** serve as predicates. **Prepositional phrases** may modify nouns, pronouns, adjectives, adverbs, or verbs. **Appositive phrases** substitute for and expand the meaning of nouns: Millicent, *my oldest sister.*

As you learn to recognize phrases, give special attention to verb forms in word groups that are used as nouns, adjectives, or adverbs. Although such verb forms (called *verbals*) are much like verbs because they have different tenses, can take subjects and objects, and can be modified by adverbs, they cannot function as the predicate of a sentence. These verbal phrases can serve only as adjectives, adverbs, or nouns.

Verbal phrases in sentences

Shoppers **milling around** did not buy much. [participial phrase, *milling around* (see **participle** in the Glossary of Terms), modifying the noun *shoppers*]

Some people win arguments by **just remaining silent.** [gerund phrase (see **gerund** in the Glossary of Terms), object of the preposition *by*]

The group arrived in a van **loaded with heavy equipment.** [participial phrase modifying the noun *van*]

Vernon went to Boston **to visit relatives.** [infinitive phrase, *to visit relatives* (see **infinitive** in the Glossary of Terms) modifying the verb *went*]

(2) Phrases used as nouns

Verbal phrases

Verbals may be classified as participles, gerunds, and infinitives. **Verbals** and **verbal phrases** function as adjectives, nouns, or adverbs. **Gerund phrases** are always used as nouns. **Infinitive phrases** are often used as nouns (although they can also function as modifiers), and a **prepositional phrase** occasionally serves as a noun as well ("*After supper* is too late!").

Nouns	Phrases Used as Nouns
The **decision** is important.	**Choosing a major** is important. [gerund phrase—subject]
She likes the **job.**	She likes **to do the work.** [infinitive phrase—direct object]
He uses my garage for **storage.**	He uses my garage for **storing his auto parts.** [gerund phrase—object of a preposition]
He wants two things: **money** and **power.**	He wants two things: **to make money** and **to gain power.** [infinitive phrases in a compound appositive]

Appositive phrases

An **appositive phrase** identifies, explains, or supplements the meaning of the word it adjoins.

> Johnnycake, **a kind of cornbread,** is native to New England.

(3) Phrases used as modifiers

Prepositional phrases nearly always function as adjectives or adverbs, and **infinitive phrases** can also be used as adjectives or adverbs. **Participial phrases**, however, are used as adjectives, and **absolute phrases** are used as adverbs. (See also **sentence modifier** in the Glossary of Terms.)

Adjectives	Phrases Used as Adjectives
It was a **sad** day.	It was a day **for sadness.** [prepositional phrase]
A **destructive** tornado roared through the city.	**Destroying everything in its path**, a tornado roared through the city. [participial phrase containing a prepositional phrase]
My **wet** clothes felt cold.	**Soaked with water**, my clothes felt cold [participial phrase containing a prepositional phrase]

Adverbs	Phrases Used as Adverbs
Drive **carefully.**	Drive **with care on wet streets.** [prepositional phrases]
She sang **joyfully.**	She sang **to express her joy.** [infinitive phrase]
Today I could feel the warm sun on my face.	**My eyes shaded against the glare**, I felt the warm sun on my face. [absolute phrase] (See the Glossary of Terms.)

The preceding examples demonstrate that although phrases function in the same way as single-word modifiers, they are not merely substitutes for single words. Phrases can express more than can be packed into a single word.

Exercise 3

Underline each phrase in the following passage. Then note whether the phrase functions as a noun, an adjective, an adverb, or an appositive.

[1]Within the past few years, more science fiction movies, many of which deal with issues surrounding the Internet, have appeared at theaters. [2]This increase has occurred despite science fiction's previous reputation, negative but perhaps accurate, which suggested that most of its fans were incredibly nerdy and unpopular teenage boys. [3]Such a reputation, however negative it once was, is currently undergoing a change. [4]Indeed, some movies, including the films *Hackers* and *The Net,* directly contradict the implications suggested by this reputation, and they suggest that nerdiness is "cool," particularly if it involves computer expertise. [5]In fact, this trend may be changing primarily because the use of computers is more common and popular than ever before.

[6]Although computers, too, are often associated with geeky young men, sociological reality is changing this notion as well. [7]In fact, in many science fiction films today, women are the "geeky-yet-cool" heroines, one example being the female lead in *Hackers*. [8]Indeed, her character, surrounded by teen male geeks, is the one who possesses the most sophisticated computer knowledge. [9]This increase in female roles and characters may help account for the genre's ever-increasing popularity.

1e Recognizing clauses helps in analyzing sentences.

A clause is a group of related words that contains a subject and a predicate.

(1) Independent clauses

An **independent clause** has the same grammatical structure as a sentence and contains a subject and a predicate. In the example below, the independent clause is in bold.

> **The boy chased the dog,** although he couldn't catch him.

(2) Subordinate clauses

A **subordinate clause** is a group of related words that contains a subject and a predicate but cannot stand alone. Such clauses often begin with words like *because* and *since*. In the example below, the subordinate clause is in bold.

> Maria received the gold medal **because her performance was flawless.**

Subordinate clauses provide additional information about the independent clause and establish the relationship of the additional information to the independent clause. Unlike an independent clause, a subordinate clause is grammatically dependent and functions within a sentence as an adverb, an adjective, or a noun.

> The last ship carrying passengers had recently arrived in the Ross Sea, **which was closed by ice most of the year.** [adjective clause]

> I had to leave the meeting early **because I became ill.** [adverb clause]

Geologists know **why earthquakes occur.** [noun clause—direct object]

The following conjunctions are commonly used to introduce, connect, and relate subordinate clauses to other words in the sentence.

Words Commonly Used as Subordinating Conjunctions:

after	in case	supposing that
although	in that	than
as (far/soon) as	inasmuch as	though
as if	insofar as	till
as though	lest	unless
because	no matter how	until
before	now that	when, whenever
even if	once	where, wherever
even though	provided (that)	whether
how	since	while
if	so that	why

Relative pronouns also serve as markers of those subordinate clauses called **relative clauses.** (See chapter 5, page 56.)

that what which who, whoever
whom, whomever whose

Subordinate clauses used as nouns

Nouns	**Noun Clauses**
The **news** may be false.	**What the newspapers say** may be false. [subject]
I do not know his **address.**	I do not know **where he lives.** [direct object]
Give the tools to **Rita.**	Give the tools to **whoever can use them best.** [object of a preposition]

Karen's **protest** amazed me.	The fact **that Karen protested** amazed me. [appositive]

The conjunction *that* before a noun clause can often be omitted.

I know she will come.

Subordinate clauses used as modifiers

Two types of subordinate clauses—adjective clauses and adverb clauses—serve as modifiers.

Adjective clauses Any clause that modifies a noun or a pronoun is an adjective clause. Such clauses, which nearly always follow the words they modify, usually begin with relative pronouns but may sometimes begin with words such as *when, where,* or *why.*

Adjectives	Adjective Clauses
Everyone needs **loyal** friends.	Everyone needs friends **who are loyal.**
The **golden** window reflects the sun.	The window, **which shines like gold**, reflects the sun.
My sister lives in a **peaceful** town.	The town **where my sister lives** is peaceful.

If not used as a subject, the relative pronoun (*who, whom, that, which,* and so on) in an adjective clause can sometimes be omitted:

He is a man **I admire.** [COMPARE "He is a man *whom I admire.*"]

Adverb clauses An adverb clause usually modifies a verb, but it also may modify an adjective, an adverb, or even the rest of the sentence in which it appears. Adverb clauses are ordinarily introduced by subordinating conjunctions.

Adverbs	Adverb Clauses
Next, the disk controller failed.	**After I backed up my files,** the disk controller failed.
His popularity dropped **locally.**	His popularity dropped in areas **where people knew him.**

Some adverb clauses may be elliptical. (See also 25b(3).)

If I can save enough money, I'll go to Alaska next summer. **If not,** I'll take a trip to St. Louis. [Clearly implied words are omitted.]

Exercise 4

Underline the independent clauses in the following paragraph. Then find the subordinate clauses, place brackets around them, and label each as a noun clause, an adjective clause, or an adverb clause.

[1]The late 1970s are most often remembered for disco music and polyester styles, tacky as they may have been. [2]Still, an aggressive kind of music, different from the popular disco styles, was coming out of Austin, Texas, at the time. [3]This new sound—punk—had grown out of the music of other bands, earlier British punk bands. [4]A club named Raul's became very popular, spawning a surge in the local music scene, and very soon Austin was swamped with new bands, all playing their original songs to devoted fans as well as other musicians.

[5]The punk movement, ever in opposition to disco, took on a decidedly nonpolyester look. [6]In fact, the look was very different, usually consisting of a torn white T-shirt, scruffy jeans, a leather biker jacket, spiked hair, and safety pins, many of which were strategically placed.

[7]The movement thrived in Austin for about seven or eight years, but was hindered by the closing of Raul's,

which had been sold by its aging owner. [8]While this event reduced the number of places where new bands could play, fresh, original music continued to live in Austin, a town still known for being on the cutting edge of music.

1f Sentences may be analyzed by form and function.

The form of a sentence is identified by the number and kinds of clauses it contains. The function of a sentence refers to its purpose.

(1) Examining sentence forms

a. A **simple sentence** consists of a single independent clause:

I [subject] **had lost my passport.** [predicate containing a verb and a direct object]

b. A **compound sentence** consists of at least two independent clauses and no subordinate clauses:

I had lost my passport, but **I did not worry about it.** [A comma and a coordinating conjunction (*but*) link the two independent clauses.]

c. A **complex sentence** has one independent clause and at least one subordinate clause:

Although I had lost my passport, I did not worry about it. [A subordinate clause—indicated here by *although* and followed by a comma (see 12b)—precedes the independent clause.]

d. A **compound-complex sentence** consists of at least two independent clauses and at least one subordinate clause:

When I lost my passport, **I ordered** a new one, but **I did not worry** about it. [*When* signals the subordinate clause; *but* connects the two independent clauses.]

(2) Examining the purpose or function of sentences

English sentences make statements (**declarative**), ask questions (**interrogative**), give commands or make requests (**imperative**), and make exclamations (**exclamatory**).

Declarative	She refused the offer. [statement]
Imperative	Refuse the offer now. [request or command]
Interrogative	Did she refuse the offer? She refused, didn't she? She refused it? [questions]
Exclamatory	What an offer! And she refused it! [exclamations]

Be aware of the forms and functions of the sentences you read and note how writers use them to achieve particular effects. (See also chapter 30.) In your own writing, think about what you want your readers to understand from each sentence and make sure you have used the forms and functions that will most effectively express your thoughts.

Exercise 5

Analyze the passage below: (1) Identify the form (simple, compound, complex, or compound-complex) and the function (declarative, interrogative, imperative, or exclamatory) of each sentence. (2) Underline the independent clauses. (3) Bracket subordinate clauses and note whether they are noun, adjective, or adverb clauses.

[1]Certainly something had to be done. [2]Just think: Matthew and Nathan had told me four times in as many minutes just how bored they were and how much they really didn't appreciate it. [3]I have to think of something for them to do, I mused, looking at the pile of books on the table in front of me, since whether they were bored, or I was bored, or we were all bored, I was sure of one inescapable fact: I had to finish reading six chapters for an exam the following day.

[4]As I saw it, the best way to handle their boredom was to get them to go outside and play; I suggested this because I had reached my wits' end, and I was relieved when they hurried outside.

[5]In fact, they were ecstatic! [6]Had they been, perhaps, waiting until I gave them my seal of approval? [7]Were they behaving like frustrated, lazy couch potatoes merely because they were afraid they'd anger me by asking to go outside? [8]At that point, I decided it was time for a break, so I, too, went outside and joined in their fun.

Exercise 6

Write ten sentences of your own. Make sure you write at least one simple sentence, two compound, three complex, and one compound-complex. Make at least one of the sentences declarative, one interrogative, one imperative, and one exclamatory. Identify the main and subordinate clauses in your sentences, and label the subordinate clauses as noun, adjective, or adverb.

Chapter 2

Sentence Fragments

A **fragment**, an incomplete sentence starting with a capital and ending with a period, is ordinarily avoided in formal writing. Fragments can be difficult to recognize within a context.

> He enjoys flowers and shrubs. **Which help screen him from the street.**
>
> Raymond began to tap out the rhythm. **First on the table and then on the counter.**

Fragments are often phrases or subordinate clauses. In the above examples, the fragments (in bold) can be corrected by making them independent sentences or by connecting them to an adjoining sentence.

> He enjoys flowers and shrubs. **They help screen him from the street.**
>
> Raymond began to tap out the rhythm, **first on the table and then on the counter.**

Testing for fragments You can ask three questions to help identify fragments:

1. Is there a verb? If not, supply one or attach the fragment to a related sentence (2a). Remember, a verbal is not a verb.
2. Is there a subject? If not, supply one or attach the fragment to a related sentence (2a).
3. Is there a subordinating conjunction? If so, remove it or attach the subordinate clause to a related sentence (2b).

Occasionally, writers deliberately use fragments for emphasis. For example, writing that mirrors speech often contains grammatically incomplete sentences or expressions. Similarly, exclamations and answers to questions are often single words, phrases, or subordinate clauses written as sentences.

> **Understand?** [question with an implied subject (*you*), informal use]
>
> **Unbelievable! No pain, no gain.** [exclamation and phrases, informal use]
>
> Why does Camilla's radio always play classic rock? **Because that is her favorite kind of music.** [subordinate clause, answer to a question, informal use]
>
> I don't remember a world without language. From the time of my earliest childhood, there was language. **Always language, and imagination, speculation, utters of sound. Words, beginnings of words.** —SIMON J. ORTIZ [phrases, literary use. Repetition links the first fragment to the preceding sentence and telegraphs Ortiz's emphasis in the second fragment.]

! CAUTION Have a good reason for any sentence fragment you allow to stand.

2a Phrases are sometimes mistakenly punctuated as sentences.

Verbal phrases, prepositional phrases, parts of compound predicates, and appositives are sometimes written as fragments. They can be revised in one of the ways listed below.

1. *Make the phrase into a sentence by supplying the missing subject and/or verb.*

He reached the top. ^He was Panting and puffing all the way.

I'm getting an ice cream cone. ^I want One scoop of chocolate swirl and one of butter pecan.

2. *Attach the fragment to a related sentence.*

He reached the top, ~~top.~~ Panting and puffing all the way.

I'm getting an ice cream cone ^with One scoop of chocolate swirl and one of butter pecan.

2b Subordinate clauses are sometimes mistakenly punctuated as sentences.

These fragments can be revised in one of the ways listed below.

1. *Remove the subordinating conjunction and supply the missing elements.*

They tried to understand Arturo's objections. They ~~Which~~ were unfounded.

2. *Attach the fragment to a related sentence.*

They tried to understand Arturo's objections, which ~~objections. Which~~ were unfounded.

3. *Reduce the fragment to a single-word modifier and include it in the related sentence.*

They tried to understand Arturo's ^unfounded objections. ~~Which were unfounded.~~

Exercise 1

Revise each item below to eliminate the sentence fragment. In each case, explain why you chose to revise as you did. If any fragment does not require revision, explain your reason for allowing it to stand.

1. Walking to the grocery store. I bought a Sunday paper.
2. His sister tried to give him a call. Because his boss gave him the raise he recently requested.
3. His mother patiently awaited her son's late return. Which proved to be a great inconvenience.
4. She criticized the taxi driver who had driven her. Very harshly, but calmly.
5. After I finished my paper. I wanted to watch television a while.

Exercise 2

The paragraph below contains several fragments. Follow the guidelines in **2a** and **2b** to revise the paragraph so it contains no fragments. Give your reasons for revising each fragment as you did.

[1]Most of the kids in her neighborhood—Marcy, Jake, and Bernadette—owe their sense of security to the Barnwells, the older couple living at the end of the block. [2]Not just because Mrs. Barnwell takes the time to help them with their homework whenever their parents are at work. [3]The Saturdays at the park, the snacks Mr. Barnwell makes once in a while in the late afternoon, and the woodworking projects they encourage kids to begin and that sometimes are visible in their front yard. [4]These are just as valuable. [5]Their official roles as neighborhood babysitters are more complex than one might think. [6]Though it's easy to see that if you take the time to think about it. [7]You're not likely to forget it. [8]Some people report hearing that they never had children because they decided not to

have any. [9]But that's not really what happened. [10]Unfortunately, they were unable to have them. [11]Making them both rather sad and leaving them with a lot of extra love to give. [12]In fact, the kinds of disappointments we all have to face in some form. [13]They can alter, or change, the way we deal with other people, many times for the better. [14]People changing positively in the way they interact with the world. [15]People may become kinder to each other. [16]Because the most important things people have in this world are their relationships with others.

Chapter 3

Comma Splices and Fused Sentences

A **comma splice** consists of two (or more) independent clauses joined simply by a comma. It is an error that occurs only in compound or compound-complex sentences. A **fused sentence** (also called a *comma fault* or *run-on sentence*) occurs when neither a conjunction nor appropriate punctuation joins two independent clauses.

> **Comma Splice** The current was swift, he swam to shore.
>
> **Fused Sentence** The current was swift he swam to shore.

Both comma splices and fused sentences can be corrected by separating the clauses with a semicolon or period or by joining them with a conjunction.

To separate:

1. Independent clauses may be separated by placing a period after each clause.

   The current was swift. He swam to shore.

2. Independent clauses may be separated by a semicolon (see 14a).

   The current was swift; he swam to shore.

The semicolon relates but keeps separate two grammatically equal units of thought: **SUBJECT + PREDICATE; SUBJECT + PREDICATE.** Writers generally do not use the semicolon between parts of unequal grammatical rank.

A comma, a semicolon, or a period can be used between independent clauses not linked by a coordinating conjunction when the clauses are short, parallel in form, and unified in thought.

> They came, they fought, they died.

The comma emphasizes similarity in idea and grammatical structure, the semicolon emphasizes difference, and the period denotes separation.

To link and relate:

1. A comma can be inserted before the appropriate coordinating conjunction (*and, but, or, nor, for, so, yet*—see 12a).

   The wind was cold**, so** they decided not to walk.

   They decided not to walk**, for** the wind was cold.

2. One clause can be subordinated to the other (see 12b).

   The wind was so cold **that** they decided not to walk.

   Because the wind was cold**,** they decided not to walk.

3. One of the clauses can become an introductory phrase (see 12b).

   Because of the cold wind, they decided not to walk.

Ways to recognize independent clauses and distinguish them from phrases and subordinate clauses are fully explained in chapter 1, especially 1d and 1e.

ESL *For students who learn British English as a second language* British usage, contrary to American practice, commonly links independent clauses with a comma. When writing for American readers, however, follow the American practice.

3a Commas occur between independent clauses only when they are linked by a coordinating conjunction (*and, but, or, for, not, so, yet*). (See also 14a.)

Comma Splice Women's roles have changed radically in recent decades, women now make up a larger percentage of the workforce.

Revised Women's roles have changed radically in recent decades, **for** women now make up a larger percentage of the workforce. [coordinating conjunction *for* added after the comma]

OR Women's roles have changed radically in recent decades; women now make up a larger percentage of the workforce. [A semicolon separates the independent clauses.]

Comma Splice He was not an outstanding success at his first job, he was not a complete failure either.

Revised He was not an outstanding success at his first job, **nor** was he a complete failure. [Note the shift in the word order of subject and verb after the coordinating conjunction *nor*.]

OR He was **neither** an outstanding success at his first job **nor** a complete failure. [a simple sentence with a compound complement]

Comma Splice I ran over some broken glass in the parking lot, it did not puncture my tires.

Revised I ran over some broken glass in the parking lot, **but** it did not puncture my tires. [the coordinating conjunction *but* added after the comma]

OR **Although** I ran over some broken glass in the parking lot, it did not puncture my tires. [Addition of *although* makes the first clause subordinate: see 12b.]

To avoid a fused sentence, use a period or a semicolon between independent clauses not linked by a coordinating conjunction.

Fused She wrote him a love letter he answered it in person.

Revised She wrote him a love letter. **He** answered it in person. [each independent clause written as a sentence]

OR She wrote him a love letter; he answered it in person. [independent clauses separated by a semicolon: see 14a]

The comma is also used to separate a statement from a tag question.

You can come, can't you? He rides a bike, doesn't he?

They couldn't be wrong, could they—not all those millions!

—WILLIAM GOLDING

Exercise 1

Connect each pair of sentences in two of the following ways: separate them with a semicolon, join them with a coordinating conjunction, reduce one to an introductory phrase, make one subordinate with a subordinating conjunction. (See the list of subordinating conjunctions in 1e(2).)

1. My dad loves to cook. I bought him some cookware for Father's Day.
2. Esteban wants to see the latest horror movie. He has already looked up the movie schedule in the newspaper.
3. She enjoys seeing paintings at the art museum. She hates having to pay extra for special exhibits.
4. Monica may disagree strongly with the guidelines set by the student representative committee. She also has a great deal of power in that organization.
5. There used to be a coffee house down that street. I remember seeing it when I was in New York last year.

Exercise 2

Revise any sentence that needs it. Put a check mark after correctly punctuated sentences.

1. Matthew lumbered out of his bedroom and walked down the hallway to the living room, on the coffee table he found the remote control before stumbling to the couch to sit down.
2. My friend has taken her nephews to baseball games each season this may explain why they enjoy the sport so much.
3. Those children dropped the frisbee they had found we picked up the colorful disk and began to throw it back and forth.
4. The guests seem partial to the eating and dancing, which we thought would put them in a festive mood.
5. Today almost all of my aunts and uncles arrived in San Antonio to attend the family reunion this weekend, and almost all of them will be staying at our house.
6. One evening I was working on my homework, a five-page paper due the following week, even with the television turned off, I had a hard time concentrating.
7. Fruits and sorbet make light, satisfying desserts, heavier desserts include cakes and cookies.
8. Between the department store and diner near the corner of Fifth and Starr is a health-food restaurant except for three seafood dishes, all the entrées are vegetarian.
9. Through careful negotiation, an agreement was reached for the sake of the two companies, they were united into one corporation.
10. A successful party requires plenty of brightly colored decorations, the space for dancing, eating, and talking. That is what we need to celebrate Maria's birthday.

3b Semicolons occur before conjunctive adverbs or transitional phrases that are placed between independent clauses. (See also 14a.)

Comma Splice Sexual harassment is not just a women's issue, after all, men can be sexually harassed too.

Revised Sexual harassment is not just a women's issue**; after all,** men can be sexually harassed too. [independent clause**;** *transitional phrase***,** independent clause.]

Fused Sentence The nineteenth-century European imperialists left arbitrarily drawn boundaries in Africa therefore, each country is composed of a mix of languages and cultures.

Revised The nineteenth-century European imperialists left arbitrarily drawn boundaries in Africa**; therefore,** each country is composed of a mix of languages and cultures. [independent clause**;** *conjunctive adverb***,** independent clause.]

Below is a list of frequently used conjunctive adverbs and transitional phrases.

Conjunctive adverbs:

also	however	next
anyhow	incidentally	nonetheless
anyway	indeed	otherwise
besides	instead	similarly
consequently	likewise	still
finally	meanwhile	then
furthermore	moreover	therefore
hence	nevertheless	thus

Transitional phrases:

after all	even so	in the second place
as a result	for example	on the contrary
at any rate	in addition	on the other hand
at the same time	in fact	
by the way	in other words	

Unlike a coordinating conjunction, which has a fixed position between the independent clauses it links, many conjunctive adverbs and transitional phrases either begin the second independent clause or take another position in it.

She believed daily exercise has many benefits; **however**, she couldn't fit it into her schedule. [The conjunctive adverb begins the second independent clause. See also 14a, page 156.]

She believed daily exercise has many benefits; she couldn't, however, fit it into her schedule. [The conjunctive adverb (set off by commas) appears later in the clause.]

COMPARE

She believed daily exercise has many benefits, **but** she couldn't fit it into her schedule. [The coordinating conjunction has a fixed position.]

Exercise 3

Write five correctly punctuated compound sentences using various conjunctive adverbs and transitional phrases to connect and relate independent clauses.

3c Divided quotations can trick you into making a comma splice. (See also chapter 16.)

Comma Splice "Who won the lottery?" he asked, "how much money was in the pot?"

Revised "Who won the lottery?" he asked. "How much money was in the pot?"

Comma Splice "Injustice is relatively easy to bear," says Mencken, "it is justice that hurts."

Revised "Injustice is relatively easy to bear," says Mencken; "it is justice that hurts."

Exercise 4

Comma splices and fused sentences have been incorporated into the following paragraph. Indicate how the comma splices and fused sentences could be revised, and mark sentences that need no revision with a check mark.

1"I really like magazines and newspapers," he said "I read the sections discussing world news and business because they use my mind. 2I read the sections discussing entertainment and gossip," he continued, "because the stories are either informative or so unusual that I can't put them down. 3When I was in the hospital, I read the sections of the newspaper that discussed medical issues many articles in this section often focus on what can go wrong, this one, however, discussed the credentials and success rates of local hospitals."

4"I also read a lot of books, particularly in the evening it's a good way to relax and exercise my imagination. 5There's not one genre or type I read religiously. 6Someday, I'd like to read more science fiction books I always see them at the bookstore, but I haven't bought any yet."

Exercise 5

First, review chapter 2 and study chapter 3. Then identify and mark the sentence fragments (SF), comma splices (CS), and fused sentences (FS) in the following passage. Next, write down why you classified them as you did, indicating how they could be revised. Put a check mark after each sentence that needs no revision.

[1]He looks frail, thin. [2]Almost vulnerable. [3]The baggy gray sweater I gave him for his birthday is loosely pulled around him like a cape his shoulders are stooped. [4]And he holds a book. [5]There is a sound, however, in my father's voice it is a tone of tired strength.

[6]We sit alone at the kitchen table only a few hours after the funeral. [7]"From day to day, we all must wear our painful experiences as a sign to others," he says with the vigor of pride and past victories, reading from the journal he's kept for the past fifty years, his constant companion. [8]"Here then is a glimpse of the sign I send to you," he says, however he still smiles and speaks of healing, happiness, and the future. [9]He tells me stories about my mother. [10]The idea being that the stories we tell are important parts of the real lives we live. [11]After a few moments, he looks at me directly and leans in closer. [12]"In our stories, we can live with complete abandon" he says this in a respectful cadence. [13]"In life, we must proceed slowly, gradually. [14]Primarily with balance and stealth. [15]Never with insensitivity."

Chapter 4

Adjectives and Adverbs

Adjectives and adverbs are modifiers that qualify, restrict, or intensify the meaning of other words. They also describe degrees of comparison. **Adjectives** modify nouns and pronouns; **adverbs** modify verbs, adjectives, and other adverbs.

Adjectives	**Adverbs**
a **quick** lunch	eat **quickly**
armed squads	**heavily** armed squads
She looked **angry.**	She looked **angrily** at me.
the **most brilliant**	shined **more brilliantly**

The articles *a, an,* and *the* are often classified as adjectives.

ESL See 22a(1) for the use of articles.

Adverbs that modify verbs commonly describe how (manner), when (time), or where (place) the action occurred.

Manner We walked **quietly.**

Time We arrived **later.**

Place We walked **home.**

Adverbs can also modify verbals (gerunds, infinitives, participles) and whole clauses as well. (See 1d, page 20.) Whole clauses may even function as adverbs. (See 1e, pages 26–27.)

Walking rapidly is good for you. [adverb *rapidly* modifying gerund *walking,* which serves as the subject]

When my family visited my aunt's house in San Francisco, my grandmother would search for me among my many cousins.
—RICHARD RODRIGUEZ
[an adverbial clause of time modifying the verb *would search*]

The *-ly* ending is usually associated with adverbs formed from adjectives (*lightly*), but certain adjectives formed from nouns also have the *-ly* ending (*cost, costly*). A number of words can function as either adjectives or adverbs (*fast, well*), and a few adverbs have two acceptable forms (*quick, quickly; slow, slowly*). When in doubt, consult the dictionary for the labels *adj.* and *adv.* and any usage notes.

Nouns used as adjectives are almost always singular: *sophomore students, executive women.* Common exceptions are **man** and **woman,** which change to the plural when they modify a plural noun: **men doctors, women doctors.**

4a Adverbs modify verbs, adjectives, and other adverbs.

Leela played her part ~~perfect~~ perfectly. [The adverb *perfectly* modifies the verb *played.*]

The plane departs at ~~a reasonable~~ a reasonably early hour. [The adverb *reasonably* modifies the adjective *early.*]

Most dictionaries still label the following as informal usage: *sure* for *surely, real* for *really,* and *good* for *well.*

Informal The Broncos played **real good** during the first quarter.

Formal The Broncos played **very well** during the first quarter. [appropriate in both formal and informal usage—see also **19b**]

Exercise 1

In the following sentences, convert any informal or unacceptable modifier into an adverb acceptable in academic writing. Put a check mark after each sentence that needs no revision.

1. He called loud to her.
2. The local known celebrity walked into the nightclub but did not stay.
3. She was happy to finish as quick as she did.
4. He doesn't get to go out as regular as he would like since he started his new job.
5. When I have the chance to watch MTV, I surely do enjoy it.
6. He was well-trained and sang good.
7. In a cloud of smoke, the guitarist appeared very sudden on the stage.
8. I don't do well on tests when I have to write that rapid.
9. That night the house seemed abnormal quiet.
10. They dance most energetic when they go to the club.

4b There is a distinction between adverbs used to modify verbs and adjectives used as subject or object complements.

A common error is to use an adjective as an adverb or an adverb as an adjective.

The actor looked *angry*. [subject complement]

The actor looked up *angrily*. [adverb]

Object complements (usually adjectives or nouns) modify the direct object as they help complete the meaning of such verbs as *make, name, elect, call, find, consider*. (See also **1b(3)**.)

They found Collette **trustworthy**. [The adjective *trustworthy* refers to the direct object *Collette* and completes the meaning of the verb *found*.]

CAUTION Do not omit the *-d* or *-ed* of a past participle used as an adjective. (See also **7a**, pages 87, 88.)

The dog was too frighten^ed^ to go to him.

Exercise 2

Using adjectives as complements, write two sentences that illustrate each of the following patterns.

Subject + linking verb + subject complement.
Subject + verb + direct object + object complement.

4c Many adjectives and adverbs change form to indicate the degree of comparison.

Generally, shorter adjectives (and a few adverbs) form the comparative by adding *-er* and the superlative by adding *-est*.

large, larger, largest

quick, quicker, quickest

Most two-syllable adjectives with stress on the first syllable also form their comparative or superlative by adding *-er* or *-est*. For words whose base form ends in *-y*, change the *-y* to *-i* when adding the comparative or superlative ending. (See 18d(3).)

lucky, luckier, luckiest

Longer adjectives and most adverbs form the comparative by using *more* (or *less*) and the superlative by using *most* (or *least*).

fortunate, more/less fortunate, most/least fortunate

rapidly, more/less rapidly, most/least rapidly

A few common modifiers have irregular forms.

little, less, least

good/well, better, best

bad/badly, worse, worst

far, further/farther, furthest/farthest [See the Glossary of Usage.]

When in doubt, consult your dictionary.

(1) The comparative denotes a greater degree or refers to two in a comparison.

Make sure to complete the comparison, and always make clear what the subject is being compared with. In the examples, the conjunction *than* signals the second element being compared.

The metropolitan area is much **bigger** now **than** it was five years ago.

Dried apples are **more** nutritious per pound **than** fresh apples. [a comparison of two groups]

More embittered **than** ever, the chief demanded that Joseph halt the march in Rocky Canyon and hold a council.

—DEE BROWN

Note that the comparison may be implied by the context.

> She wrote **two** papers, and the instructor gave her a **better** grade on the second.

The comparative form when used with *other* sometimes refers to more than two.

> Bert can run **faster** than the *other* players.

(2) The superlative denotes the greatest degree or refers to three or more in a comparison.

> The interests of the family are **best** served by open communication.
>
> Bert is the **fastest** of the three runners.
>
> **OR**
>
> Bert is the **fastest** runner of all.

The superlative occasionally refers to two, as in "Put your *best* foot forward!"

Usage accepts comparisons of many adjectives or adverbs with absolute meanings, such as "a *more perfect* society," "the *deadest* campus," and "*less completely* exhausted." But many writers make an exception of *unique*—using "*more nearly* unique" rather than "more unique." They consider *unique* an absolute adjective—one without degrees of comparison.

(3) A double comparative or superlative is incorrect.

> Our swimming hole is much ~~more~~ shallower than Crystal Lake.
>
> That was the ~~most~~ funniest movie.

Exercise 3

Provide the appropriate comparative or superlative form of the modifier given in parentheses.

[1]"This fish weighs (little) than the one I caught yesterday," Uncle Verne said as he reeled in his line. [2]But this isn't the (bad) day for fishing. [3]Uncle Verne, a veteran fisherman, finds the silver shad the (useful) lure available for catching bass. [4]A (lively) bait has never before been produced. [5]Its movement attracts even the (tiny) of bass. [6]Of course, Uncle Verne hopes to haul in the (big) fish of all; however, at times one must be prepared to deal with the (small) fish. [7]When a big bass strikes at the bait, only the (strong) fisherman will be able to fight the battle. [8]Although, physically, Uncle Verne appears to be the (weak) fisherman in the boat, when the catch is weighed at the end of the day, there is no doubt he is good.

4d Use of a word group or a noun as an adjective can be awkward or ambiguous.

Many word groups or nouns effectively modify other nouns (as in *reference* manual, *windfall profits* tax, *House Ways and Means* Committee), especially when appropriate adjectives are not available. Avoid such forms, however, when they are awkward or confusing.

Awkward	Many candidates entered the president race.
Better	Many candidates entered the presidential race.
Confusing	The Representative Landor recess maneuvers led to victory.
Better	Representative Landor's maneuvers during the recess led to victory.

4e A single rather than a double negative is correct.

The term **double negative** refers to the use of two negatives within a sentence or clause to express a single negation. Like the double comparison, the double negative is considered incorrect.

> He did **not** keep ~~**no**~~ records.
>
> I can~~**not**~~ do **no**thing about it.

Because **hardly, barely,** and **scarcely** already denote severely limited or negative conditions, use of **not, nothing,** or **without** with these modifiers creates a double negative.

> I could~~**n't**~~ **hardly** quit in the middle of the job.
>
> The motion passed with ~~**not**~~ **scarcely** a protest.

ESL Cumulative adjectives follow a specific order. Writers often use up to three adjectives to modify a noun. English requires that the adjectives occur in the following order: determiners, subjective opinion (beautiful, happy, angry), physical description (size, shape, age, and color), origin, material, purpose.

> that ugly brick building their large English watercolor
>
> Dad's old threshing machine a round Italian pizza dish

Using more than three adjectives before a noun is awkward and is usually avoided.

Exercise 4

After you have reread rules **4a** through **4e** and have studied the examples, correct all errors in the use of adjectives or adverbs in the sentences below. Also eliminate any awkward use of nouns as adjectives, and correct double negatives. Put a check mark after any sentence that needs no revision.

1. I have more work to do now than I used to.
2. The job advertisement asked for young willing intelligent native Spanish speakers to apply.
3. The restaurant was so packed I couldn't hardly move.
4. Although I didn't change the recipe much, the soup seemed much more tastier than usual.
5. He said it was easy the biggest turnout they had ever seen.
6. They never went nowhere new.
7. The professor says that it is very difficult to judge the poetry writing contest.
8. The coffee tastes real well when he adds some raw sugar to it.
9. The young man believed he led a much fuller life than his friends.
10. The bookstore information person told me they had run out of that novel.

Chapter 5 Case

Case refers to the form of a noun or pronoun that shows its relation to other words in a sentence. For example, the different case forms of the boldfaced pronouns below, all referring to the same person, show their different uses.

> **I** [the subject] want **my** [modifier showing possession] cousin to help **me** [direct object].

I, the subject, is in the *subjective* (or nominative) case; *my,* showing possession, is in the *possessive* (or genitive) case; and *me,* the object, is in the *objective* case.

ESL Although many languages include the subject pronoun in the verb, in English it must be stated except in certain imperatives. (See 1b(1).)

Pronouns also have singular and plural forms.

> **We** [plural subject] want **our** [plural modifier] cousins to help **us** [plural direct object].

The personal pronouns Personal pronouns identify the speaker (first person: *I, we*), the person spoken to (second person: *you*), and the person or thing spoken about (third person: *he, she, it, they*). The pronouns *I, we, he, she,* and *they* have distinctive forms for all three cases and for both singular and plural. *You* is the same in both singular and plural, and *you* and *it* change case form only in the possessive.

Modifiers that indicate ownership or a comparable relationship are in the **possessive case.** A few possessive pronouns (such as *mine* and *theirs*) sometimes function as nouns.

That book is **mine.**

	Singular	Plural
Subjective	I	we
	you	you
	he, she, it	they
Possessive	my, mine	our, ours
	your, yours	your, yours
	his, her, its	their, theirs
Objective	me	us
	you	you
	him, her, it	them

CAUTION Although *their* and *they* can be confused in spoken English, *their* is the possessive pronoun; while *they* is subjective. These must be distinguished in written English.

~~they~~ *their* book ~~they~~ *their* house

See Glossary of Usage for confusion of *their, there, they're,* and *there're.*

The pronouns *my, our, your, him, her, it,* and *them* combine with *self* or *selves* to become **intensive/reflexive pronouns,** which are used primarily for emphasis.

Jake, **himself,** brought it here.

Intensive/reflexive pronouns also often refer to a noun or pronoun already mentioned in the sentence. They always follow the person or thing to which they refer.

Jake saw a picture of **himself.**

CAUTION Do not use *myself* or *me* in place of *I* in a compound subject.

> Jake and ~~**myself**~~ *I* brought it here.
>
> ~~**Me and Jake**~~ *Jake and I* brought it here.

Hisself and *theirselves,* although the logical forms for the reflexive pronouns (possessive plus *-self* as in *myself, yourself, herself*), are not accepted in formal English; instead, use *himself, themselves.*

> James and Jerry painted the house by ~~theirselves.~~ *themselves*

Relative pronouns Relative pronouns (*who, whom, which, whose,* and *that*) introduce clauses that refer to a noun in the main clause.

> **Julieta, who** is my sister, lives in Atlanta.

Who, whose, and *whom* ordinarily refer to people; *which* to things; and *that* to either. The possessive pronoun *whose* (in place of an awkward *of which*) sometimes refers to things:

> The poem, **whose** author is unknown, has recently been set to music.

	Singular or Plural
Subjective	who, which, that
Possessive	whose
Objective	whom, which, that

(See also 1e.)

CAUTION Do not confuse *who's* and *whose.* (See Glossary of Usage to distinguish between them.)

5a Pronoun form in compound constructions varies.

Multiple *subjects or subject complements* are in the subjective case.

> **She and her father** buy groceries on Saturday morning.
>
> I thought **he or Dad** would come to my rescue.
>
> It was **Maria and I** who solved the problem. [See 5f.]

The first person pronoun *I* occurs last in a compound construction.

> ~~Me and~~ Ricardo *and I* are good friends.

Multiple objects of prepositions are in the objective case.

> between Merrill and ~~I~~ *me*   with Amanda and ~~I~~ *me*

You can test the case of a pronoun after a preposition by eliminating the accompanying noun or pronoun.

> Gabriel gave it to (Edwyn and) me.

Multiple objects of verbs or verbals and *subjects of infinitives* are in the objective case.

> Clara may appoint **you or me.** [direct object]
>
> They lent **Tom and her** ten dollars. [indirect object]
>
> He gets nowhere by scolding **Bea or him.** [object of gerund]
>
> Dad wanted **Sheila and me** to keep the old car. [subject of the infinitive]

If an appositive follows a pronoun, normal case rules still apply.

> *We* ~~Us~~ students need this.
>
> Dylan told ~~we~~ *us* girls to go home.

Exercise 1

Choose the correct pronoun in the parentheses in each of the following sentences. Explain your choice.

1. Two of my friends, Cherise and (she, her), went hiking last weekend.
2. After dropping Sandy and (he, him) off at work, I went to see Leann and (she, her).
3. There is a great deal of competition between Mark and (he, him).
4. It was Marlene and (she, her) who left the milk out on the counter.
5. Students like Lori and (I, me) have many things to do before the semester starts.
6. After the dinner party the hosts spoke privately with two of the guests, Gabriela and (he, him).
7. My family and (I, me, myself) wanted Mark and (she, her) to phone soon.
8. Ms. Brown will hire a new employee, either Cody or (she, her).
9. Are Lorna and (they, them) still planning to meet at the movies this afternoon?
10. (He, Him) and (I, me) were in the same peer group in composition class last semester.

5b The use of a pronoun in its own clause determines its case.

(1) *Who* or *whoever* as the subject of a clause

The subject of a verb in a subordinate clause takes the subjective case, even when the whole clause is used as an object:

> I forgot **who** won the game. [*Who* is the subject of the clause *who won the game*. The clause is the object of the verb *forgot*.]

He has consideration for **whoever** needs his help. [*Whoever* is the subject of the clause *whoever needs his help*. The clause is the object of the preposition *for*.]

(2) Confusing constructions with *who* or *whom*

Such expressions as *I think, he says, she believes,* and *we know* can follow either *who* or *whom*. The choice depends on the position of *who* or *whom* in its own clause.

Walter picked Jan **who** he knows speaks well. [*Who* is the subject of the verb *speaks*.]

Walter picked Jan **whom** he knows we all respect. [*Whom* is the object of the verb *respect*.]

(3) Pronouns after *than* or *as*

In sentences with implied (rather than stated) elements, the choice of the pronoun form is important to meaning:

She likes Clarice more than **I**. [subjective case, meaning "more than I like Clarice"]

She likes Dana more than **me**. [objective case, meaning "more than she likes me"]

He talks with Jerry as much as **her**. [objective case, meaning "as much as he talks with her"]

5c *Whom* for all pronouns used as objects in formal written English

Pronouns take their form according to their use in a subordinate clause. *Whom*, the form used for the object of a verb or a preposition in a subordinate clause, is often misused.

They helped the people ~~**who**~~ whom they liked.

Gabriel liked all the people ~~who~~ *whom* he met that day.

This is a friend ~~who~~ *whom* I write to once a year.

I don't know ~~who~~ *whom* he voted for.

In spoken English, the pronoun *who* is commonly used when it occurs as the first word in the sentence, even when it is the object of a verb or preposition. Dictionaries increasingly accept this usage, although in formal writing it is better to use the traditional *whom* as the object even when it is the first word in a sentence.

Informal **Who** do you want to speak to?

Formal **Whom** will they elect president?

Whom is omitted (or *that* substituted) in sentences where no misunderstanding would result.

The friend he relied on moved away.

The friend that he relied on moved away.

Exercise 2

Using the case form in parentheses, convert each pair of sentences in the following paragraph into a single sentence.

[1a]Lee Harvey Oswald was the prime suspect in the president's assassination. [1b]Jack Ruby killed him in front of millions as live television cameras recorded the event. (who) [2a]In fact, we got news of the president's assassination from Walter Cronkite. [2b]Walter Cronkite was the CBS news anchor. (who) [3a]After the president was shot, stunned bystanders stood around crying and rubbing their eyes. [3b]The bystanders had been cheering and calling to Kennedy as he rode by in the motorcade. (who) [4a]Today, people still wonder if Oswald was really guilty. [4b]At the time, the Warren Commission labeled Oswald the lone as-

sassin. (whom) [5a]Since Kennedy's assassination, numerous authors have written on the subject of the president's murder. [5b]These authors have been labeled "assassination buffs" by the press. (who)

Exercise 3

In the sentences below, insert *I think* after each *who.*

1. It was the Reverend Martin Luther King, Jr., who won the 1964 Nobel Peace Prize.
2. Mary Wollstonecraft Shelley, who is the author of *Frankenstein,* was married to poet Percy Bysshe Shelley.
3. Joan Didion, who is a journalist, has written about cultural and political conflicts in such works as *Miami* and *Salvador.*

In the following sentences, complete each comparison by using first *I* and then *me.* Explain the difference in meaning.

4. My sisters enjoyed her more than ________.
5. David likes you as much as ________.

5d A pronoun before a gerund uses the possessive form.

A pronoun follows the convention of using a possessive noun before a gerund.

I appreciated Tom's helping Denise.

The possessive form of the pronoun is used before a gerund (a verb form ending in *-ing* and used as a noun).

I appreciated ~~him~~ *his* helping Denise.

The *'s* to show possession is often not heard in rapid speech, but it must be included in writing.

~~Susan~~ *Susan's* stopwatch

CAUTION The *-ing* ending marks both gerunds and participles. A participle is a verbal used as an adjective; a gerund is a verbal used as a noun. The possessive case precedes gerunds, but not participles. The sentences below have different meanings. In the first sentence *sitting* is a participle modifying *the man* who annoys us; in the second sentence his *sitting* is what annoys us.

> The man sitting (participle modifying *man*) at the desk annoyed us.
>
> The man's sitting (gerund acting as subject) at the desk annoyed us.

5e Pronouns use the objective form for the subject or the object of an infinitive.

> They wanted Dave and **me** to help **him**.

5f Pronouns use the subjective form for a subject complement.

> That certainly could be **she** sitting near the front. [COMPARE "She could be sitting. . . ."]
>
> It was **I** who first noticed the difference. [COMPARE "I first noticed. . . ."]

Informal English accepts *It's me* (*him, her, us,* and *them*).

Exercise 4

Following the guidelines for formal written English, choose the appropriate form of the pronouns in parentheses. Remember: choose *whom* when the pronoun functions as an object and *who* when it functions as the subject of a verb or as a subject complement.

1. Margaret believes she knows (who/whom) will win the election.
2. When problems arise, Winifred knows (who/whom) to call on and when.
3. I'm not sure (who/whom) left that coat here.
4. I contacted the person (who/whom) you suggested.
5. She must know (who/whom) they are and where they came from.
6. Do you know (who/whom) I ran into at Sharon's party?
7. That's a person (who/whom) I hardly know.
8. Is that the professor (who/whom) you were talking about?
9. At registration, (whoever/whomever) I asked for directions was very helpful.
10. To find out (who/whom) murdered (who/whom), you'll have to read the whole book.

Exercise 5

Find and revise all pronoun forms in the following paragraph that would be inappropriate in formal English. Put a check mark after each sentence that needs no revision.

1Marcie and Chris wanted Elizabeth and I to go to the movies with them. 2In fact, they wanted us—Elizabeth and I—to choose the movie we would all see. 3As for Elizabeth and I, we both like movies, but Chris and Marcie like them more than we. 4Marcie didn't know this, however, and she strongly urged us to come with them. 5Moreover, Elizabeth and I, stammering a response, did not suggest to Chris and her that we really didn't want to go with them. 6Eventually, I whispered to Elizabeth, "It looks like those two are going to force you and me to go to the movies even though they could go by themselves." 7She replied, "Although we really don't have to go, they would probably be mad if we didn't." [8]Obviously, we two had wanted to do something other than go to the movies, but neither of us actually spoke up. [9]Unfortunately, the movie was really awful, and Chris and Marcie enjoyed the movie no more than we did, although they generally enjoy movies more than us. [10]When all was said and done, though, it was Elizabeth and I who I blamed for us having a bad time.

Chapter 6 Agreement

A verb and its subject or a pronoun and its antecedent agree when their forms indicate the same number and person. Notice below that the singular subject takes a singular verb and that the plural subject takes a plural verb. (If you cannot easily recognize verbs and their subjects, study 1a and 1b.)

Singular	The **car** in the lot **looks** shabby. [*car looks*]
Plural	The **cars** in the lot **look** shabby. [*cars look*]

Lack of subject-verb agreement occus chiefly in the use of the present tense. Except for forms of *be* and *have* (*you were, he has eaten*), verbs in other tenses do not change form to indicate the number and person of their subjects. For a list of various forms of *be* and the subjects they take, see page 79.

A pronoun must agree with its antecedent (the noun that the pronoun refers to) in number. (See also chapter 28.)

Singular	A **wolf** has **its** own language. [*wolf–its*]
Plural	**Wolves** have **their** own language. [*wolves–their*]

A pronoun also must agree with its antecedent in gender. See 6b.

the **boy** and **his** mother [masculine antecedent]

the **girl** and **her** father [feminine antecedent]

the **garden** and **its** weeds [neuter antecedent]

6a Verbs must agree with their subjects.

Agree means that the subject and verb must match. That is, if a subject is plural, the verb must have a plural form, and if the subject is singular, the verb must have a singular form. (If you cannot easily recognize verbs and their subjects, study **1a** and **1b**.)

Singular The **rose** in the vase **is** wilted. [*rose is*]

Plural The **roses** in the vase **are** wilted. [*roses are*]

Because only present-tense verbs change form to indicate the number and person of their subjects, most problems with subject-verb agreement occur when present tense is used. It is easy to confuse the endings of *verbs* (where *-s* indicates **singular**) with those of *nouns* (where it indicates **plural**).

subject + *s*	**verb + *s***
The students need attention.	The student needs attention.
Zinnias bloom best in the sun.	A zinnia blooms best in the sun.

If the subject of your sentence is singular but is not *I* or *you,* the verb needs the *-s* ending:

That talk show host asks silly questions. [The sound of the *-s* may be masked in speech if the word that follows begins with an *s*.]

ESL Although some languages do not permit clusters of more than one consonant at the end of a word (such as the *sks* in *asks*), English requires the addition of an *-s* to make most nouns plural and to form third-person singular verbs.

Since grammar checkers cannot catch agreement errors, it pays to be alert for situations that cause them.

(1) Other words between the subject and the verb

The **rhythm** of the pounding waves **is** calming. [*Waves* is the object of a prepositional phrase, not the subject.]

All of the dogs in the neighborhood **were barking.** [*Dogs* and *neighborhood* are both objects of prepositional phrases. *All* is the subject.]

Phrases such as *accompanied by, along with, as well as, in addition to, including, no less than, not to mention, together with* generally introduce a prepositional phrase and do not affect the number of the subject.

Her **salary** in addition to tips **is** just enough to live on.

Tips in addition to her salary **are** just enough to live on.

(2) Endings of subjects and verbs not clearly sounded in rapid speech

Economists seem concerned [might sound like **Economist seem** concerned, but the former is correct].

She **ask** Sybil first.

(3) Subjects joined by *and*

My two best **friends** and my **fiancé hate** each other.

The **coach** and the **umpire were** at home plate.

Writing on a legal pad and **writing with a computer are** not the same at all. [gerund phrases—COMPARE "Two actions are not the same."]

A compound subject that refers to a single person or unit takes a singular verb.

> The **founder and president** of the art association **was** elected to the board of the museum.
>
> The **creator and director** of *Schindler's List* **is** Stephen Spielberg.

(4) Subjects joined by *either . . . or*

> John or Doris **writes** to us regularly.
>
> Neither Carol nor Ted **is** excluded from the meeting.
>
> Either Patty or Tom **was** asked to preside.

If one subject is singular and one is plural, the verb agrees with the subject nearer to the verb.

> Neither the basket nor the **apples were** expensive.
>
> Neither the apples nor the **basket was** expensive.

The verb also agrees in person with the nearer subject.

> Either Frank or **you were** going to hire her anyway.
>
> Either you or **Frank was** going to hire her anyway.

(5) Inverted word order or *there + verb* constructions

> VERB + SUBJECT
>
> Hardest hit by the snows and subzero temperatures **were** the large **cities** of the Northeast.
>
> *There* + VERB + SUBJECT
>
> There **are** several **ways** to protect yourself from a tornado.

(6) Relative pronouns (*who, which, that*) used as subjects

Stoddard Hall, which is the computer science building, is always open.

It is the **doctor who** often **suggests** a diet.

It is among the **books that are** out of print.

This is the only **store that gives** triple coupons. [COMPARE "Only one store gives triple coupons."]

It is not bigger discounts but **better service that makes** the store successful. [COMPARE "Better service (not bigger discounts) makes the store successful."]

He is one of **those who agree** with my decision. [*Who* refers to *those,* a plural pronoun. The plural form of the verb is necessary for agreement.]

(7) *Either, one, everybody, all, any, some, none,* and other such indefinite pronouns

Each, either, one, everybody, and *anyone* are considered singular and so require singular verbs.

Either of them **is willing** to shovel the driveway.

Each has bought a first-class ticket.

Everybody in our apartment building **has** a parking place.

Depending on the sentence, *all, any, some, none, half,* and *most* can be either singular or plural.

Wendy collects comic books; **some are** very valuable. [COMPARE "Some comic books are very valuable."]

The bank would not take the money because **some was** foreign. [COMPARE "Some money was foreign."]

Use a singular verb with singular subjects preceded by *every* or *each* and joined by *and:*

Every cat and dog in the county **has** to be vaccinated.

Each fork and spoon **has** to be dried carefully.

Placing *each* after a plural subject does not affect the verb form:

The cat and the dog **each have** their good points.

(8) Collective nouns and phrases

Collective nouns and phrases refer to a group of individual things as a unit. (See **1c**.) Whether they require a singular or a plural verb depends on whether the sentence refers to the group as a whole or to the individual items in the collection.

ESL *For students who learn British English as a second language* British usage treats collective nouns as plural.

British	The committee **are** meeting tonight.
American	The committee **is** meeting tonight.

Treat collective nouns as singular when writing for American readers.

Singular (regarded as a unit):

The **committee is** meeting today.

Ten million gallons is a lot of oil.

The **jury convenes** today.

The **number is** very small.

Plural (regarded as individuals or parts):

The **majority** of us **are** in favor.

Ten million gallons of oil **were spilled.**

A **number were** absent.

Although the use of *data* and *media* as singular nouns (instead of *datum* and *medium*) has gained currency in informal English, most writers still use *data* and *media* as plural nouns in formal written English.

Formal	The media **have** shaped public opinion.
Informal	The media **has** shaped public opinion.
Formal	The data **are** in the appendix.
Informal	The data **is** in the appendix.

(9) Linking verbs

Linking verbs include the forms of *be* (*am, is, are, was, were, being, been*), the verbs referring to the senses (*look, feel, smell, sound, taste*), and some others such as *appear, become, grow, make, prove, remain,* and *seem.*

His favorite **snack is** graham crackers.

Those **speakers sound** odd.

Mom's vegetable **soup makes** my tastebuds rejoice.

Because the pronoun *what* is singular or plural depending on whether the word (or word group) it refers to is singular or plural, the verb agrees with its complement in sentences like this:

What I think **is** my own **business.**

What our parents gave us **were memories** to be cherished.

(10) Titles of single works, words spoken of as words, nouns plural in form but singular in meaning

Ren and Stimpy **sticks** in the memory. [The TV show itself, not the characters in it, sticks in the memory.]

Kids **is** informal for *children.*

Nouns that look like they are plural but are treated as singular include *economics, electronics, measles, mumps, news,* and *physics.*

Measles **is** a serious disease.

Economics **is** important for a business major.

Some nouns (such as *athletics, politics, series, deer,* and *sheep*) can be either singular or plural, depending on the meaning:

Statistics is an interesting subject. **Statistics are** often misleading.

A **series** of natural disasters **has** occurred recently. Two **series** of natural disasters **have** occurred recently.

The **sheep strays** when the gate is left open. **Sheep stray** when the gate is left open.

Exercise 1

Use each of the following to make a complete sentence. Be sure that subjects and verbs agree.

1. My books and my pen . . .
2. It is my mother who . . .
3. Everyone . . .
4. Neither the (singular subject) nor the (plural subject) . . .
5. The list of volunteers . . .

6b Pronouns agree with their antecedents.

The subject of a verb and the subject complement are in the **subjective case.**

Subjective He left early. **Who** noticed? [subjects of verbs]

It was **I** on the phone. [subject complement—COMPARE "*I* was on the phone."]

The object of a verb, verbal, or preposition is in the **objective case.**

Objective Marcella blamed **me.** [direct object]

Telephoning **them** is a nuisance. [object of verbal]

I gave **him** the book. [indirect object]

To **whom** was it addressed? [object of preposition]

Pronouns should agree in number and gender with the noun or phrase (antecedent) to which they refer.

The cousins gave us **their** [plural modifier referring to cousins] help.

George gave us **his** [masculine pronoun referring to George] help willingly. Lucinda, on the other hand, gave us **her** [feminine pronoun referring to Lucinda] help grudgingly.

When referring to a noun that can include both men and women, you can avoid the pronoun *he* by dropping the pronoun.

A student should hand ~~his~~ papers in promptly.

You can also avoid the problem by recasting in the plural, in the passive, or in the imperative.

> Students should hand their papers in promptly. [plural]
>
> Papers are to be handed in promptly. [passive]
>
> Hand your papers in promptly. [imperative]

Chapter 7 Verbs

Verbs express the action in a sentence. They show what someone (or something) does (see 1a), whether the subject is singular or plural and what its relationship to the audience (first, second, or third person) is (see 1b, 6a), when an action occurred, who did it, and whether it is hypothetical or conditional. They are the heart of a sentence.

Tense Verbs change form to show whether an action happened in the present, the past, or the future. This change of form is called **tense**, and through tense a verb can show, for example, that one action began yesterday and is still going on, but that another action began yesterday and ended yesterday. English traditionally recognizes six tenses: three simple tenses and three perfect tenses.

Simple Tenses

Present: We often write letters.
Past: After graduation, we wrote letters.
Future: We will write letters after graduation.

Perfect Tenses

Present: We have written letters since graduation.
Past: We had written letters after graduation.
Future: We will have written letters before graduation.

A **perfect tense** refers not only to the time in which the action began but also to the time in which the action is completed.

Tenses are based on primary forms called principal parts (*ask, asked, asked, asking*). (See 7a.)

ESL Those whose first language is not English often find the English tense system confusing. The tenses described above actually refer to time relationships rather than to tense forms (of which English actually has only two—present and past). To express the idea that an action happened at some unspecified time, English uses the simple tenses, either present or past. To specify how the complex time relationships of completed actions are to be understood, English speakers combine the auxiliary verb *have* with one of the principal forms of the verb to form the perfect tense: have asked. *Will* combines with a different principal form to show future time: *will ask*.

Regular and irregular verbs The way a verb forms its past tense determines its classification as regular or irregular. A **regular verb** takes the *-d* or *-ed* ending to denote the past tense.

Regular *laugh* (*laughs*), *laughed*
believe (*believes*), *believed*

Irregular verbs do not take the *-d* or *-ed* ending. They form their past tense in other ways (see pages 83–86).

Irregular *eat* (*eats*), *ate*
run (*runs*), *ran*
cut (*cuts*), *cut*

Auxiliary verbs **Auxiliary verbs** (or helping verbs) combine with other verbs to indicate tense, voice, or mood. **Modal auxiliary verbs** join the present form of the verb to make requests, give instructions, and express doubt, certainty, necessity, obligation, possibility, or probability.

Checklist of Auxiliary Verbs

Auxiliary Verbs		Modal Auxiliary Verbs	
be	have	shall	may
am	has	should	might
is	had		must
are		will	
was	do	would	can
were	does		could
been	did		
being			

The present form of a verb combines with *shall* or *will* to show the future tense. (See the Glossary of Usage for the limited use of *shall*.) *Have* combines with the past participle of a verb to show the perfect tense, and forms of *be* combine with the past participle of a verb to form the passive voice (see page 80). *Be* also combines with the present participle (the *-ing* form of a verb) to show the progressive (an action in progress). *Do* joins the present form of the verb to express emphasis or form questions.

ESL In English, the present progressive expresses action that is occurring now, whereas the simple present expresses activities that occur at an unspecified time (timeless or habitual present):

I am boiling eggs.	The act of boiling eggs is occurring now.
I boil eggs.	The act of boiling eggs is habitual.

She **will** go. [future tense]

She **has** gone. [perfect tense]

She **is** laughing. [present progressive]

She **was** laughing. [past progressive]

She **will be** laughing. [future progressive]

The book **is** read often. [passive voice—present tense]

The book **has been** read often. [passive voice—present perfect tense]

I **do** like that chocolate pie. [emphasis—present tense]

Did she like chocolate pie? [question—past tense]

I **should** study tonight. [obligation]

I **might** study tonight. [possibility]

In formal writing, *can* refers to ability; *may* refers to permission. (See the **Glossary of Usage**.)

I **can** skate fast. [ability]

May I borrow the car? [permission]

Although the auxiliary always precedes the basic verb, other words may intervene.

Have the members **paid** their dues?

Television **will** never completely **replace** newspapers.

ESL In English, when more than one auxiliary precedes a basic verb, the modal comes first, followed by the auxiliary showing perfect tense (*have*), then the progressive form (*been* + *-ing*) or passive voice (*been* + *-ed*).

We should have been basting the turkey more often. [The modal *should* is followed by the perfect tense marker *have* and the progressive *been basting*.]

The turkey should have been basted more often. [The modal *should* is followed by the perfect tense marker *have* and the passive *been basted*.]

***Forms of* be** The most irregular verb in the English language is *be*. It has eight forms: *am, are, is, was, were, be, been, being.*

That may **be** true. He **was being** difficult.

Following is a list of forms of *be* used with various subjects in the present and past tenses.

	First	Second	Third	
Present	I am	you are	he/she/it is	[singular]
	we are	you are	they are	[plural]
Past	I was	you were	he/she/it was	[singular]
	we were	you were	they were	[plural]

Some dialects use *be* in place of *am, is,* or *are,* the present forms of *be*. Some dialects also use *be* with the present participle to indicate habitual action. In formal written English, use the conventional forms of *be,* as shown in the list above.

She ~~be~~ is a fine hockey player.

He ~~be~~ is walking to class.

Be can serve as a linking verb between a subject and its complement. (See **1b**.)

Gabriel **is** a very good student.

ESL English recognizes two kinds of verbs, those that express states of being (sometimes called **stative** verbs) and those that express action (**dynamic** verbs). Some verbs have two meanings, one stative, the other dynamic: I have [possess] time to waste. [stative] I was having [experiencing] trouble understanding him. [dynamic]

Voice **Voice** indicates the relationship between the action of the verb and the subject. Two kinds of relationships are possible: active and passive. **Active voice** emphasizes the subject as the **doer** of the action. **Passive voice** deemphasizes the doer of the action and makes the subject the *receiver*. (See also 29d(1), and the Glossary of Terms.) To make an active verb passive, use the appropriate tense form of *be* with the base verb.

Active	The dog **chases** the cat. [The subject *dog* acts on the object *cat*.]
Passive	The cat **is chased** by the dog. [The subject *cat* is acted upon. The prepositional phrase identifying the doer of the action could be omitted.]

Most writers choose the active voice because it is clearer, more precise, more concise, and more vigorous than the passive. Use passive voice only when you have good reason. (See 29d(1).)

Transitive and intransitive verbs In the examples above, the subject and the object of an active verb (the actor and the receiver of the action) switch places when a verb becomes passive. The subject of a passive verb receives the action. This transformation to passive voice is possible only with verbs that accept a direct object—**transitive verbs**. Although an **intransitive verb** can take a subject complement, it does not accept a direct object and cannot be made passive. (See the Glossary of Terms.)

Transitive	The hammer **bent** the nail. [*Nail*, the direct object, receives the action of *hammer*.]
Intransitive	The bell **looks** fragile. [The subject complement, *fragile*, identifies *bell*.] The bell **feels** smooth. [The adverb *smooth* modifies the verb.]

Some verbs can be transitive or intransitive, depending on the sentence.

Transitive	Claudia **studies** the book.
Intransitive	Claudia **studies** all night.

A dictionary will indicate if a verb is transitive, intransitive, or both.

Mood **Mood** indicates speakers' or writers' attitudes about what they are saying. The **indicative mood** makes statements—a definite attitude; the **imperative mood** issues commands or requests—an insistent attitude; and the **subjunctive mood** expresses situations that are hypothetical or conditional—a tentative attitude. (See also 7d.)

The following conjugation of the verb *see* shows the relationships among tense, person, voice, and mood. It also shows how auxiliary verbs help make a verb passive and also form the perfect tenses.

THE CONJUGATION OF A VERB

Indicative Mood

Active Voice		*Passive Voice*	
Present Tense			
Singular	*Plural*	*Singular*	*Plural*
1. I see	we see	I am seen	we are seen
2. you see	you see	you are seen	you are seen
3. one (he/she/it) sees	they see	one (he/she/it) is seen	they are seen
Past Tense			
1. I saw	we saw	I was seen	we were seen
2. you saw	you saw	you were seen	you were seen
3. one saw	they saw	one was seen	they were seen

Future Tense

1. I shall (will) see	we shall (will) see	I shall (will) be seen	we shall (will) be seen
2. you will see	you will see	you will be seen	you will be seen
3. one will see	they will see	one will be seen	they will be seen

Present Perfect Tense

1. I have seen	we have seen	I have been seen	we have been seen
2. you have seen	you have seen	you have been seen	you have been seen
3. one has seen	they have seen	one has been seen	they have been seen

Past Perfect Tense

1. I had seen	we had seen	I had been seen	we had been seen
2. you had seen	you had seen	you had been seen	you had been seen
3. one had seen	they had seen	one had been seen	they had been seen

Future Perfect Tense (seldom used)

1. I shall (will) have seen	we shall (will) have seen	I shall (will) have been seen	we shall (will) have been seen
2. you will have seen	you will have seen	you will have been seen	you will have been seen
3. one will have seen	they will have seen	one will have been seen	they will have been seen

Imperative Mood

Present Tense

See.	Be seen.

Subjunctive Mood

	Active Voice	*Passive Voice*
	Present Tense	
Singular	if I, you, one see	if I, you, one be seen
Plural	if we, you, they see	if we, you, they are seen
	Past Tense	
Singular	if I, you, one saw	if I, you, one were seen
Plural	if we, you, they saw	if we, you, they were seen
	Present Perfect Tense	
Singular	if I, you, one have seen	if I, you, one have been seen
Plural	if we, you, they have seen	if we, you, they have been seen

Past Perfect Tense (same as the Indicative)

7a Verbs have at least three principal parts.

The three principal parts of verbs are the simple present form (*see*), which is also part of the infinitive (*to see*); the past form (*saw*); and the past participle (*seen*). (See **principal parts** in the Glossary of Terms.) The present participle (*seeing*) is often considered a fourth principal part.

The **present form** can be a single-word verb (*demand*) or a combination of a single-word verb and a helping verb (*is demanding, can demand*). Unless the verb is irregular, the **past form** can also be a single-word verb with *-d* or

-ed (*demanded*). (See page 76.) It can be combined with helping verbs (*might have demanded*).

This checklist of principal parts includes regular and irregular verbs that are sometimes misused.

Checklist of Principal Parts of Verbs ✓

Present	Past	Past Participle
arise	arose	arisen
ask	asked	asked
attack	attacked	attacked
awaken	awakened OR awoke	awakened
bear	bore	borne/born
begin	began	begun
blow	blew	blown
break	broke	broken
bring	brought	brought
burst	burst	burst
choose	chose	chosen
cling	clung	clung
come	came	come
dive	dived OR dove	dived
do	did	done
drag	dragged	dragged
draw	drew	drawn
drink	drank	drunk
drive	drove	driven
drown	drowned	drowned
eat	ate	eaten
fall	fell	fallen
fly	flew	flown
forgive	forgave	forgiven
freeze	froze	frozen
get	got	got OR gotten

continued

continued from previous page

give	gave	given
go	went	gone
grow	grew	grown
hang (things)	hung	hung
hang (people)	hanged	hanged
happen	happened	happened
know	knew	known
ride	rode	ridden
ring	rang	rung
rise	rose	risen
run	ran	run
see	saw	seen
shake	shook	shaken
shrink	shrank OR shrunk	shrunk OR shrunken
sing	sang OR sung	sung
sink	sank OR sunk	sunk
speak	spoke	spoken
spin	spun	spun
spit	spat	spat
spring	sprang OR sprung	sprung
steal	stole	stolen
sting	stung	stung
stink	stank OR stunk	stunk
strive	strove OR strived	striven OR strived
swear	swore	sworn
swim	swam	swum
swing	swung	swung
take	took	taken
tear	tore	torn
throw	threw	thrown
wake	woke OR waked	woken OR waked
wear	wore	worn
weave	wove	woven
wring	wrung	wrung
write	wrote	written

Some troublesome verbs, especially the following, are easy to confuse and tricky to spell:

PRINCIPAL PARTS OF TROUBLESOME VERBS

Present	Past	Past Participle	Present Participle
lay	laid	laid	laying
lead	led	led	leading
lie	lay	lain	lying
loosen	loosened	loosened	loosening
lose	lost	lost	losing
pay	paid	paid	paying
set	set	set	setting
sit	sat	sat	sitting
study	studied	studied	studying

Exercise 1

Respond to the questions written in the past tense with a past tense verb; respond to the questions in the future tense with a present perfect verb (*have* or *has* + past participle). Follow the pattern of the examples.

EXAMPLES
Did it really happen? Yes, it really happened.
Will the bubble burst? The bubble has burst.

1. Will they run a mile?
2. Did she give it to you?
3. Did the daffodil bloom?
4. Will the pond freeze?
5. Did her cat have kittens?
6. Will they bring lasagna?
7. Did anyone pitch a no-hitter?
8. Will they arrive early?
9. Did you go to the movie?
10. Has the battery died?

Participles in predicates

Participles are never used alone as the predicate of a sentence. When an *-ing* form is part of the predicate, it always has at least one helping verb. Both the past and present participles can work as modifiers and they can also form part of the predicate:

pastries *baked* last week [past participle]	We *baked* pastries last week. [sentence]
heat waves *rising* from the road [present participle]	Heat waves *rise* from the road. [sentence]

Be especially careful not to confuse nouns modified by participles with actual sentences. (See 2a.)

When the subject causes the action, combine the helping verb with the *-ing* form (**present participle**); when the subject is affected by the action, use the *-ed* form (**past participle**). These forms are sometimes referred to as *present progressive* and *past progressive* tenses.

She **was filing** the briefs. [subject acts]

The briefs **were being filed.** [subject acted upon]

He **has asked** them. I **was asked.** I **will be asking** questions.

They **have begun. Had** he **begun**? It **is beginning** to snow.

CAUTION Although it is easy to remember a clearly pronounced *-d* or *-ed* (*added, repeated*), it is sometimes harder to remember a needed *-d* or *-ed* in such expressions as *supposed to* or *used to* when the sound is not emphasized in speech. (See 4b.)

Yesterday, I ~~ask~~ asked myself is the judge prejudiced?

He ~~use~~ used to smoke.

I am not ~~suppose~~ supposed to be the boss.

She ~~talk~~ talked to Ellen yesterday.

7b Confusion of *sit/set* and *lie/lay* and *rise/raise*

You will pick the correct form most of the time if you remember that you can *set, lay,* or *raise* something, but you yourself *sit, lie,* or *rise*. Thinking of these verbs in pairs and learning their principal parts can help you remember which form to use.

Present	Past	Past Participle	Present Participle
sit	sat	sat	sitting
lie	lay	lain	lying
rise	rose	risen	rising
set	set	set	setting
lay	laid	laid	laying
raise	raised	raised	raising

Set, lay, and *raise* mean "to place or put something somewhere." For example, to *set* the table means to *lay* the silverware next to the plates. *Sit, lie,* and *rise,* the intransitive verbs of the pairs, mean "be seated" or "get into a horizontal position" or "get up." For example, *you sit down* or *lie down* or *rise up*.

Sit **Sit** down. **Sitting** down, I thought it over. He **sat** up.

Set I **set** the clock. It **had been set** there.

Lie **Lie** down. **Lying** down, I fell asleep. He **lay** there for hours.

Lay We **laid** these aside. These **had been laid** aside.

Rise I **rise** before daylight. I **rose** even earlier yesterday. I am **rising** earlier each day.

Raise I **raise** the window each night. I **raised** the window last night. I am **raising** the window to clear the smoke.

Exercise 2

Without changing the tense, substitute the appropriate form of *sit/set, lie/lay,* or *rise/raise* for the italicized verbs in the following sentences.

1. Last week they *established* their plans for the trip.
2. I often *rest* on the old stone wall and watch the sunset.
3. I *lifted* the window shade.
4. I try to *get up* in time to work out each morning.
5. After he weeded the garden, Chen decided to *nap* on the front porch.
6. I *am putting* your book on the front porch.
7. I have *slept* here for at least three hours.
8. Hugh was *sprawling* on the couch when I arrived.
9. Marcella *got up* in time to see me off.
10. Kalynda was *adjusting* her watch.

7c Tense forms express differences in time.

(1) The meaning of tense forms

Tense is not the same as time. Although tenses refer to time (see page 75), the actual tense forms often do not reflect divisions of actual time. For instance, as the following examples show, the present tense form is certainly not restricted to present time. It can refer to past and future occurrences as well. Furthermore, auxiliaries and other words in the sentence can also indicate time.

Present tense (timeless or habitual present, now)

I **see** what you meant by that remark.

Dana **uses** common sense. [habitual action]

Mistakes **are** often **made.** [passive verb, habitual action]

Blind innocence **sees** no evil. [universal or timeless truth]

In 1939 Hitler **attacks** Poland. [historic present]

Joseph Conrad **writes** about what he **sees** in the human heart. [literary present]

The store **opens** next week. [present form, used with the adverbial *next week* to denote future time]

I **am trying** to form an opinion. [present progressive form indicating action occurring now]

Past tense (past time, not extending to the present)

I **ate** the cake.

They **played** a good game.

We **were continuing** our work. [continuing action in the past]

The paper **was reviewed** by two people. [passive]

Adolpho **used to be** happy. [COMPARE "Adolpho was happy then."]

Future tense (at a future time, sometime after now)

We **will see** the movie.

Shall we **try** a different road?

He **will be having** his dinner. [progressive]

A different color **will be used.** [passive]

Present perfect tense (sometime before now, up to now)

I **have taken** the prize.

She **has** consistently **broken** her previous records.

Has Michelle **been using** her talents? [progressive]

Deer **have been seen** in those woods. [passive]

Past perfect tense (before a specific time in the past)

Terese **had planned** to meet with me before school.

After Shawn **had left** for work, he realized it was a holiday.

Had they **been sailing** along the coast? [progressive]

My computer **had been crashing** for weeks. [passive]

When they married, they **had known** each other for ten years.

Sometimes the simple past can replace the past perfect.

Tawanda **had talked** [*or* **talked**] to me before class started.

Future perfect tense (before a specific time in the future)

Our bumpers **will have rusted** by the time he changes his mind.

The future perfect is almost always replaced by the simple future.

After graduation, I **will have seen** [*or* **will see**] my dreams come true.

Exercise 3

For each sentence, explain the differences in the meaning of the tense forms separated by slashes.

1. It has rained/had rained for days.
2. Jean cut/did cut/was cutting her hair.
3. My mother-in-law had bought/will have bought the car by then.
4. Time flies/does fly/has flown/had been flying by rapidly.
5. Zora Neale Hurston writes/wrote of a woman's search for her true identity in *Their Eyes Were Watching God*.

(2) Logical sequence of tense forms

Combinations of tense forms can make very fine distinctions in relation to actual time.

When the speaker **finished**, everyone **applauded.** [Both actions took place at the same definite time in the past.]

Collette **has stopped walking** at night because she **had heard** that several women were mugged. [Both forms indicate action at some time before now, but *had heard* indicates a time before the action indicated by *has stopped.*]

When I **had been** here for two weeks, I **learned** that my application for financial aid **had been denied.** [The *had* before *been* indicates a time before the action described by *learned* and *denied.*]

Infinitives The present infinitive expresses action occurring at the same time as, or later than, that of the main verb; the present perfect infinitive shows action that occurred before the time shown by the main verb:

I want **to show** you my new trick. [present infinitive—for the same time as the main verb, *want*]

He preferred **to go** home. [present infinitive—for time later than *preferred*]

I would like **to have won** first place. [present perfect infinitive—for time before the main verb *would like.* COMPARE "I wish I *had won.*"]

ESL ***Infinitive and gerund phrases after verbs*** Although there is no set rule for the correct usage, certain verbs are followed by infinitives, and others by gerunds.

I offered **to help** her.

I avoided **calling** her.

Some of the most common verbs followed by a gerund are *appreciate, avoid, consider, delay, discuss, enjoy, finish, keep (on), mention, mind, postpone, suggest.*

I **mind missing** the party.

Some of the most common verbs followed by an infinitive are *agree, appear, ask, decide, expect, intend, need, plan, pretend, promise, refuse, want.*

I **decided to go** home.

Some verbs that are followed by a noun or a pronoun + an infinitive are *advise, allow, ask, encourage, expect, force, invite, remind, require, want.*

I **encouraged** Mac **to study** with her.

The verb *go* is followed by the gerund in certain expressions that for the most part concern recreational activities.

Let's **go swimming.**

Participles The present form of participles expresses action occurring at the same time as that of the main verb; the present perfect form indicates action that took place before that of the main verb:

Planning for the election, he decided what he should advocate. [The planning and deciding were simultaneous.]

Having built the house themselves, they felt a real sense of pride. [The building took place first; then came their sense of pride.]

Exercise 4

In the following paragraph, insert the appropriate form of the word in parentheses so that the events in the paragraph form a logical sequence.

[1]Last night I (going) (seeing) the college's spring revue. [2]When I (arriving) at the auditorium, everyone (standing) in line (waiting) (getting) in. [3]As soon as the doors (opening) everyone (rushing) (finding) their seats. [4]I (finding) mine right away and (sitting) down, but I (standing) up often for all the other people who (sitting) in my row. [5]After the lights (dimming), the music (beginning), and the curtains (opening), the cast (beginning) (singing) and (dancing) and I (losing) all track of time until the curtain (coming) down for the intermission. [6]After the intermission, an entirely different cast (performing) from the one that (beginning). [7]I (being) (startling) until I (remembering) the article in the campus paper that (reporting) how a dispute between the producer and the director (is settling).

7d Although rare, the subjunctive mood is still used for specific purposes.

The subjunctive mood, though rare, still occurs in fixed expressions such as *so be it, be that as it may, as it were,* and *God bless you* and is also used to express certain other meanings.

Forms for the subjunctive

For the verb *be:*

PRESENT, singular or plural: **be**

PAST, singular or plural: **were**

For all other verbs with third-person singular subjects, the subjunctive omits the characteristic *-s* ending:

PRESENT, singular only: **see** [The *-s* ending is dropped.]

Examples
It is important that Nancy **see** me first.
Suppose we **were** to leave before she does.
The prosecutor insisted that the witness not **avoid** the question.

Alternatives
Nancy **has to see** me first.
Suppose we **leave** before she does.
The prosecutor urged the witness not **to avoid** the question.

Should and *would* (past forms of *shall* and *will*) are also used for the subjunctive.

Subjunctives are used under the following conditions:

1. **After *that* with such verbs as *demand, recommend, urge, insist, request, suggest, move***

I demand that the parking ticket **be** voided.

I suggested that she **move** to a new apartment.

The committee requested that we **adjourn.** [COMPARE "The committee wanted to adjourn."]

2. **To express wishes or (in *if* or *as if* clauses) a hypothetical, highly improbable, or contrary-to-fact condition**

I wish I **were** in Ashville.

If I **were** you, I'd accept the offer.

Eat as if every meal **were** your last.

Although formal English still calls for *should* in conditional clauses, informal English accepts *would,* just as it accepts *will* instead of *shall*—except in questions such as "Shall we go?"

I wish she would leave.

3. **As *had* rather than *would have* in *if* clauses expressing an imagined condition**

   If he had ~~**would have**~~ arrived earlier, he wouldn't have lost the sale.

   OR

   Had ~~If~~ he ~~**would have**~~ arrived earlier, he wouldn't have lost the sale.

Exercise 5

Explain the use of the subjunctive in the following sentences in each of these situations: (a) a formal letter of application and (b) an informal letter to a friend.

1. Had Linda been here, she would have explained everything.
2. She insisted that Victor be heard.
3. I wish that Inez were here.
4. If there should be a change in policy, we would have to make major adjustments.

Exercise 6

Compose five sentences illustrating various uses of the subjunctive.

7e Unnecessary shifts in tense or mood can confuse readers. (See also 27a.)

He *came* to the meeting and tried ~~*tries*~~ to take over. [shift in tense from past to present]

It is necessary to restrain an occasional foolhardy park visitor. If a female bear *were* to mistake his friendly intentions and *supposes* him a menace to her cubs, he would be in trouble. [shift in mood from subjunctive to indicative] But females with cubs ~~were~~ are only one of the dangers. [a correct sentence if standing alone, but inconsistent here with the present tense in the preceding sentence and therefore misleading] All bears are wild animals and not domesticated pets. It is therefore an important part of the park ranger's duty to watch the tourists and above all ~~don't~~ not to let anyone try to feed the bears. [shift in mood from indicative to imperative]

Exercise 7

Look carefully at the following passage to note any errors or inconsistencies in tense and mood or other problems with verb usage and revise as needed.

[1]It is hard for me to realize that it were only three years ago that I first begin to send e-mail to my friends. [2]Today I got most of my mail (except for bills) online, and I also did much of my other business online, too. [3]For instance, I can paying my bills electronically since I had an account at an electronic bank, and I can also ordering almost any thing I wanted from a catalog that I could have looked at on the World Wide Web. [4]I even buys my last car online. [5]Of course, I go to a dealer and drove a model that I like first, but then I order the car on the Web. [6]It was less expensive, and I didn't have the hassle of dealing with a pushy salesperson.

[7]One of the best things about the electronic revolution, though, is the way it was changing the academic world. [8]My World Civilizations class meets online in a special chat room calls a MOO (for Multiple-user dungeon ObjectOriented), and we also will look at the various sites on the World Wide Web that showed pictures of archaeological digs (like the one on the Mayans), architecture, and so on. [9]Taking a history class this way makes it lived for me. [10]It also makes my Shakespeare class more interesting. [11]I will look at the William Shakespeare pages on the World Wide Web and can find comments that famous scholars will make and citations to books and articles that helped me understanding the plays better. [12]I don't think I will have taken the time to go to the library for the same material—and it wouldn't have been as much fun to look at, either.

Mechanics

Chapter 8 Document Design

This chapter contains information on presenting your writing so that it is as readable as possible. As the volume of information grows, so does the importance of its delivery—the visual design that gives readers the cues that lead them to the information they require and enable them to read it efficiently.

Visual design sends messages to readers. A dense, tightly packed page with narrow margins signals difficult material. Ample white space signals openness and availability. White space frames the material on the page, preventing it from seeming oppressive and burdensome, and so contributes to ease in reading regardless of the difficulty of the content. But too much white space can send a negative message: For instance, a triple-spaced term paper with huge margins announces that the writer has little to say.

Because the way you design your documents tells a reader much about you, a well-designed letter of application and résumé can mean the difference between being hired and not being hired. Similarly, a well-designed term paper can make a difference in how favorably a professor regards the quality of your work.

8a Using the proper materials enhances readability.

(1) Paper and binding

Use good 20-pound white 8½-by-11-inch paper (neither onionskin nor erasable bond); this kind of paper is suitable for use with typewriters, word processors, and most printers linked to a computer. If your printer requires continuous sheets, choose paper that allows clean removal of pin-feed strips and separation of sheets. If you write your papers by hand, use regular 8½-by-11-inch lined white notebook paper and follow your instructor's recommendations.

Use a paper clip or a staple to fasten pages; do not fasten them by folding down one corner. Unless your instructor tells you differently, do not use folders of any kind.

(2) Electronic documents

If you submit your work electronically (by electronic or e-mail, on a bulletin board, in a Web document, or on disk), follow your instructor's directions exactly. If you use a disk, make sure that you use the proper size, density, and format. Most machines now accept only 3½″ high-density disks, but if your reader uses a machine that reads only double-density disks, you must accommodate that restriction. Macintosh disks will not work on PCs unless they are specifically reformatted. Label disks clearly. If you submit your work using e-mail or a bulletin board, use the subject line correctly and ensure that your work is error free before you send it. Whatever the requirements, the computing facilities to meet them are likely to be available on campus at no cost.

(3) Type, fonts, and justification

Although laser and ink jet printers can print different typesizes and -styles (fonts) on a single page, most academic papers should be printed using a font that looks like typewriter type, such as Courier 10 or 12, or a simple proportional font such as 10- or 12-point Times Roman. Using a variety of fonts detracts from the content. Resist the impulse to justify (make straight) your right margins. Unless your printer has proportional spacing, it justifies the right margin by inserting spaces between words so that every line is the same length; the irregular spacing within the line can be distracting and at times misleading to readers. Because college classes often simulate professional writing situations and since publishers and editors of learned journals generally request that manuscripts not be justified, it is usually inappropriate to justify the right margin of academic documents even if the printer has proportional spacing. Justification may be appropriate if a document will not be reformatted before being printed, as is the case with some business documents or documents intended for desktop publishing.

Pages from a good ink jet or laser printer are always acceptable. If you have a dot-matrix printer, you can set the program (or the printer) for letter-quality or near-letter-quality print; readers find print that shows separate dots hard to read. Further, before you start, make sure that the printer cartridge has enough ink or toner to complete your document. If you use a typewriter or dot-matrix printer, the ribbon must be fresh enough to type clear, dark characters. If your instructor accepts handwritten papers, write in blue or black ink on one side of the paper only.

8b Clear and orderly arrangement contributes to ease in reading.

The advice here follows the guidelines in the *MLA Handbook for Writers of Research Papers,* fourth edition (New York: MLA, 1995). If you are using another style manual, check the most recent edition. (See the list of style manuals, pages 438–39.)

(1) Layout

Follow your instructor's directions about margins and other formatting. Word processing software can be set to lay out pages exactly to your specifications: It can number your pages, print a certain number of lines per page, and incorporate appropriate word divisions. Software also allows you to vary the spacing between lines, but unless your instructor agrees to different spacing, observe the conventions of academic writing and double-space all papers except those you write by hand. Generally, leave margins of one inch (or no more than one and one-half inches) on all sides of the text to give your reader room for comments and to prevent a crowded appearance. The ruled vertical line on notebook paper marks the left margin for handwritten papers. You can adjust the margin control on a typewriter to provide the margins you need.

(2) Indention

The first lines of paragraphs should be uniformly indented. You can set your word processing software to indent the first lines of all paragraphs one-half inch. (Indent five spaces on a typewriter, or one inch if writing by hand.) Indent block quotations one inch from the left margin (ten spaces on the typewriter). (See 16b.)

(3) Paging

Place Arabic numerals—without parentheses or periods—at the right margin, one-half inch from the top of each page. Unless you are using a format that requires running titles (e.g., APA), put your last name immediately before the page number in case a page gets misplaced.

The first page

Unless your instructor requests a title page, place your name, your instructor's name, the course and section number, and the date in the top left-hand corner (one inch from the top and one inch from the left edge of the page), double-spacing after each line. You should also double-space between the lines of a long title and center all titles.

Begin your first paragraph on the second line below the title (first double-spaced line). (See the models in chapters 33, 38, and 39.) Most research papers do not require a title page, but if you use one, follow your instructor's directions about the form.

Subsequent pages

Place your name and the page number in the upper right-hand corner, one-half inch from the top. Begin text at the left margin, one inch from the top and double-space throughout.

(4) Headings

Headings can make a long document easier to read. They can highlight the organization of a long block of information or make it easy to combine several brief statements to avoid choppiness. If you use headings, make them consistent throughout your document, and if you have two levels of headings, treat all occurrences of each level alike. For instance, headings in this book follow a pattern similar to that of an outline. The main rules are identified by a number and letter set against the left margin and followed by subdivisions marked by numbers in parentheses. Further subdivisions are set flush with the left margin and, depending on the level of the division, appear in bold type of various sizes.

8c The appropriate form for electronic documents can vary.

Electronic documents may be published on the Internet, on your campus network, on a class or organization's electronic bulletin board, or even on a disk that you hand to your instructor or fellow student. Electronic documents, which are usually easy to modify, permit new kinds of collaboration and use of materials.

(1) Electronic mail

E-mail is a new medium for communication. E-mail is much less formal than a letter or a memo, but more enduring than conversation in that it can be edited, saved, and filed. It also fosters very speedy communication and offers more convenience than either postal mail (called "snail mail" by those who use e-mail frequently) or voice mail. E-mail uses a format like that of an interoffice memo, with "TO" and "SUBJECT" lines for entering the address of the person you are writing to and the topic of your message. (See also 39b(1).)

Using e-mail puts concern for audience in the foreground and requires special care to communicate ideas clearly. Experienced users have developed guides (humorously referred to as netiquette) to help new users avoid some common hazards. Some standard advice appears below.

Checklist for Bulletin Board Postings and Electronic Mail ✓

1. Keep line length short. Because some users have monitors that display only 40 characters in a line, it is considerate to keep your messages concise, your paragraphs short, and your subject focused.
2. Make the subject line descriptive of your message so your reader(s) can find and file your message easily.
3. Use a signature line at the end of each message. Your signature should include three things: your name, your position and affiliation (if any), and your e-mail address. It can also include your postal address and telephone number if you wish, but it should not be longer than four lines.
4. Use capitals as you would in an ordinary typewritten document; that is, use mixed upper- and lowercase letters. Full capitals in electronic communications is understood as shouting. If you wish to stress a word, you can enclose it in asterisks, but do so *sparingly*.
5. Use good sense regarding what you write about others. Like a bulletin board, e-mail is neither private nor secure, and while it is unlikely that anyone would snoop in your mail messages, it is possible that a recipient might forward your message without your knowledge, embarrassing you—or even making you liable. Regular Internet users advise, "If you wouldn't like to see it on the evening news, don't put it in e-mail."
6. Similarly, respect the privacy of others. Just as you would not distribute photocopies of personal notes or post them on a campus bulletin board, don't forward personal messages without the writer's permission. (And don't perpetuate chain letters. They use up electronic resources that may already be strained.)

continued

continued from previous page

7. Respect copyright. Anything not specifically designated as public domain is copyrighted, including messages from friends that you got in your electronic mailbox. Credit any quotations, references, and sources. (See also 37g.)
8. Sarcasm and irony are frequently misunderstood in messages posted to bulletin boards, and even in personal e-mail. These strategies depend in large part on facial expression and tone of voice, so your joke may be seen as criticism, and what is meant to be irony is frequently confused with straightforward statement.
9. Consider carefully before you use emoticons or Internet jargon. Although people often follow an ironic statement with an emoticon to emphasize that it isn't to be taken seriously, others find those little faces (or *smileys*) constructed out of punctuation marks annoying (:–>). And although acronyms are widely used in informal electronic communication, it can be confusing and annoying to the uninitiated, who may not understand a statement such as BTW for "by the way" or "sorry for the flame" as an apology for antagonistic criticism.

(2) The World Wide Web

Whereas electronic mail is a new kind of correspondence, the World Wide Web is similar to a newspaper or magazine. It contains **pages** that a reader can view using a **browser.** (A browser is a computer program that fetches the text and graphic images that make up a Web document—a page—and enables the user to view them.) Web pages can be dynamically linked to other Web pages to form a new sort of document set. It is as different from a book as a book is from an ancient papyrus scroll, but it can contain much the same information, just presented differently. Instructors increasingly ask students to construct

Web pages in lieu of submitting papers. While the details of such construction are beyond the scope of this handbook, a few tips might be helpful.

Checklist for Designing Web Pages ✓

1. Write the page so that it can be viewed with or without pictures. While graphics greatly enhance the experience of moving from page to page, many people lack a connection that will allow them to receive graphics.
2. Use graphics sparingly. Graphic files are typically very large and take a long time to transfer. Unless a reader has very fast equipment, he or she may well abandon your beautiful, graphics-rich document for one that is less lovely but faster to access.
3. Don't crowd your page with text. Just as books with narrow margins and dense type can be intimidating, so can a similarly constructed Web page. Set pages up so that they can be read on a single screen and provide a link to other screens.
4. Understand the difference between a paper page and a Web page. Each has its advantages and disadvantages. Quick access to dozens or even hundreds of topics is easier with a Web browser than with a book, but few would care to curl up with a video monitor. Take advantage of the capabilities of the tool you are using.

8d Proofreading provides quality control.

Proofreading is different from revising or editing. (See 33b–d.) **Revising** requires you to reconsider and possibly reorganize your ideas. **Editing** makes sure your prose is as clear, accurate, and stylistically consistent as possible and pays particular attention to the conventions of grammar, mechanics, punctuation, and spelling. **Proofreading** checks for and corrects errors of layout, spelling, punctuation, and mechanics, and serves as a final check to make sure all necessary revising and editing have been done. Proofreading can be done manually or with a word processing program; doing both is insurance against error.

If you are using a word processing program, it is a good idea to print out a draft of your document so that you can check it carefully on paper and make any necessary changes before you print the final copy. If you have typed or handwritten your document, make any necessary corrections by neatly drawing a single line through the incorrect material, placing a caret (^) where the correct material is to be inserted, and writing the correct information clearly above the typed or handwritten line or, if long, to the side with a line drawn to the caret.

To use the proofreading checklist that follows, you should first make sure your paper is properly formatted as specified in 8b (or by your instructor). Then you might try reading your paper backward, sentence by sentence, out loud, checking for accuracy as recommended in each of the other sections of the list. Read the words slowly, looking at and pronouncing each syllable carefully. Some people find it more efficient to read through the paper several times this way, checking for a different set of items on each pass. It helps to refer to the chapters and sections cross-referenced in this handbook and also to keep your dictionary handy (19a, chapter 18) to look up any words you are uncertain about as you proofread.

Checklist for Proofreading a Text ✓

Layout

- Have you used proper margins? For paper documents, are all margins one inch wide or according to your instructor's specifications? For electronic documents, are margins consistent throughout the document? Are paragraphs formatted consistently?

continued

continued from previous page

✓

- Is each page numbered?
- Does the first page have the appropriate title and heading?
- Is the first line of each paragraph indented five spaces (or one inch if handwritten)?
- Is the print (or type or handwriting) dark, clean, clear, and legible?
- Are the lines double-spaced?
- Are all listed items numbered sequentially?

Spelling (18)

- Are all words spelled correctly? Have you run a spell checker program?
- Have you double-checked the words you frequently misspell or any the spell checker might have missed (e.g., homonyms or misspellings that still form words, such as *form* for *from*)?
- Have you consistently used the American spelling of words that have more than one option (*theater/theatre*)?
- Have you double-checked the spelling of all foreign words?

Punctuation (12, 13, 14, 15, 16, 17)

- Does each sentence have appropriate closing punctuation, and have you used only one space after each period (17a)?
- Is all punctuation within sentences appropriately used and correctly placed (comma, 12; semicolon, 14; apostrophe, 15; other internal marks of punctuation, 17; hyphen, 18f)?
- Are quotations carefully and correctly punctuated (16, 37h)?

Capitalization and italics (9 and 10)

- Does each sentence begin with a capital letter (9e)?
- Are all proper names, people's titles, and titles of published works correctly capitalized (9a–c)?
- Are quotations capitalized properly (16a, 37h(2))?
- Are italics used properly (10)?

Chapter 9 Capitals

Capital letters denote such things as proper names, peoples and their languages, geographical names, and certain organizations. Different conventions for capitalization have prevailed in different eras, and some conventions continue to vary. The following guidelines will help in specific cases, however. When special problems arise, consult a good, recent dictionary (**19a**). Dictionaries list not only words and abbreviations that begin with capitals but also acronyms (**11e**) that use full capitals.

Tom Cruise, Italians, Alabama, Federal Express, Rev., NASA

A recent dictionary is also useful when the capitalization of a word depends on a given meaning: "*mosaic* pictures" but "*Mosaic* Laws," "on *earth*" but "the planet *Earth*."

A style manual for the discipline in which you are writing is another useful guide for capitalization. (For a list of such manuals, see pages 438–39.)

When capitalizing something is optional, be consistent in your use of the option you choose:

sunbelt OR Sunbelt, blacks OR Blacks, a.m. OR A.M.

9a Proper names are capitalized and so usually are their abbreviations and acronyms.

As you study the following examples, observe that common nouns like *college, company, park,* and *street* are capitalized when they are essential parts of proper names.

(1) Names and nicknames of persons or things and trademarks

Zora Neale Hurston, John Paul II, Buffalo Bill, Skylab, Flight 224, Pepsi, Nike, Academy Award, Honda Accord, Polaroid picture, Scotch tape

(2) Peoples and their languages

African Americans, Asians, Eskimos, Latinos, Poles, Sikhs, English, Korean, Spanish, Swahili, Urdu

(3) Geographical names

Arctic Circle, China, Ellis Island, Grand Canyon, Havana, Iowa, Lincoln Memorial, Middle West, Mississippi River, New Jersey, Nigeria, Seventh St., Yellowstone National Park

(4) Organizations, government agencies, institutions, and companies

B'nai B'rith, Congress for Racial Equality, International Red Cross, Phi Beta Kappa, Internal Revenue Service, National Endowment for the Arts, Howard University, Museum of Modern Art, Chicago Cubs, Ford Motor Company

(5) Days of the week, months, and holidays

Wednesday, August, Tet, Thanksgiving, Fourth of July, Veterans Day

The names of the seasons—spring, summer, fall, winter—are not capitalized.

(6) Historical documents, periods, events, and movements

Declaration of Independence, Stone Age, the Renaissance, Gulf War, Impressionism

(7) Religions and their adherents, holy books, holy days, and words denoting the Supreme Being

Christianity, Hinduism, Islam, Judaism
Christian, Hindu, Muslim, Jew
Bible, Book of Mormon, Koran, Talmud
Easter, Ramadan, Yom Kippur
Allah, Buddha, God, Vishnu, Yahweh

Some writers always capitalize pronouns referring to the Deity (except *who, whom, whose*). Others capitalize such pronouns only when the capital is needed to prevent ambiguity, as in "The Lord commanded the prophet to warn *His* people."

(8) Personifications

Then into the room walked Death. [COMPARE His death shocked everyone.]

Her heart belonged to Envy. [COMPARE She frequently experienced envy.]

(See also page 225.)

(9) Words derived from proper names

Americanize [verb]; Marxism [noun]; Orwellian [adjective]

When a proper name and its derivatives become the name of a general class of objects or ideas, it is no longer capitalized.

zipper [originally a capitalized trademark]

blarney [derived from the Blarney stone, said to impart skill in flattery to those who kiss it]

When in doubt about whether a proper name or derivative has become a general class, consult a dictionary. Many such words can be treated with or without capitalization.

French windows OR french windows, Roman numeral OR roman numeral

When you have the option to capitalize or not, it is important to follow one option consistently.

(10) Abbreviations and acronyms or shortened forms of capitalized words

AMEX, AT&T, B.A., CBS, CST, JFK, L.A., NFL, OPEC, UNESCO, Y.M.C.A. [words derived from the initial letters of capitalized word groups]

(See also chapter **11** and **17a(2)**.)

9b Titles of persons that precede the name are capitalized but not those that follow it or stand alone.

Governor Christine Todd Whitman, Captain Machado, Uncle Verne

Christine Todd Whitman, the governor; Machado, our captain; Verne, my uncle

President Lincoln, the president of the United States

Words denoting family relationships are usually capitalized when serving as substitutes for proper names:

Tell **M**other I'll write soon. [COMPARE "My mother wants me to write."]

9c In titles and subtitles of books, plays, essays, and other titled works, the first and last words are capitalized, as well as most other words.

All words in titles and subtitles are capitalized, except articles, coordinating conjunctions, prepositions, and the *to* in infinitives (unless they are the first or last word). The articles are *a, an, the;* the coordinating conjunctions are *and, but, or, nor, for, so, yet.* (Formerly, longer prepositions like *before, between,* or *through* in titles were capitalized; MLA style, however, favors lowercasing prepositions, whatever the length.) (See 38a.)

The Scarlet Letter
"Why Women Are Paid Less Than Men"
"What It Takes to Be a Leader"
Autobiography of a Face
From Here to Eternity
Men Are from Mars, Women Are from Venus

In a title, capitalize the first word of a hyphenated compound. As a rule, capitalize the word following the hyphen if it is a noun or a proper adjective or if it is equal in importance to the first word.

The Building of the H-Bomb [noun]
The Arab-Israeli Dilemma [proper adjective]
Stop-and-Go Signals [words of equal importance]

Usage varies with respect to the capitalization of words following such prefixes as *anti-, ex-, re-,* and *self-:*

Overcoming Self-Destructive Behavior OR *Overcoming Self-destructive Behavior*

In all cases, use the style appropriate to your discipline, or ask your instructor. (See 16c, 10a, and 38a and b.)

9d The pronoun *I* and the interjection O are capitalized.

> If I forget thee, O Jerusalem, let my right hand forget her cunning. —PSALMS

The interjection *oh* is not capitalized except when it begins a sentence.

9e The first word of every sentence (or of any other unit written as a sentence) and of directly quoted speech is capitalized.

> Procrastination is one of my specialties.
>
> Oh, really! Do you want to become more efficient? Not right now.
>
> Experienced cooks are usually ready to try something new. (You can learn from them.) [a parenthetical sentence]
>
> Beth got out of the car and shouted, "Home at last!"
>
> He says, "Stop dieting and start exercising."
> OR "Stop dieting," he says, "and start exercising."
> OR "Stop dieting," he says. "And start exercising."
>
> One thing is certain: We are still free. [an optional capital after the colon—see also 17d]

For the treatment of directly quoted written material, see chapter 16.

9f Capitals sometimes indicate emphasis.

Occasionally, a common noun is capitalized for emphasis or clarity.

The motivation of many politicians is Power.

If you overuse this strategy, it will not achieve its purpose. There are alternative methods for achieving emphasis. (See chapter 29.)

9g Unnecessary capitals are distracting.

Do not capitalize common nouns preceded by the indefinite articles *a* and *an* or by such modifiers as *every* or *several.*

a speech course in theater and television [COMPARE Speech 324: Theater and Television]

a university, **several** high schools [COMPARE University of Michigan, Hickman High School]

However, always capitalize proper nouns, even when preceded by *a* or *an* or by modifiers like *every* or *several.* In such cases, capitalized nouns name one or many of the members of a class: *a* St. Bernard, *every* Virginian, *several* Canadians.

STYLE SHEET FOR CAPITALIZATION

Capitals	No Capitals
Revolutionary War	an eighteenth-century war
a Chihuahua, a Ford tractor	a poodle, a farm tractor
Washington State University	a state university
Declaration of Independence	a declaration of independence
May, Memorial Day	spring, holiday
the South, Southerners	to drive south, the southern regions
German, Italian, Japanese	the language requirement
the P.T.A. [OR the PTA]	an organization for parents and teachers

Parkinson's disease	flu, asthma, leukemia
the U.S. Army	a peacetime army
two Democratic candidates	democratic procedures
Dr. Catherine Kadohata	every doctor, my doctor

Exercise 1

Write brief sentences using each of the following words correctly.

1. president
2. President
3. company
4. Company
5. west
6. West
7. avenue
8. Avenue
9. republican
10. Republican

Exercise 2

Supply capitals wherever needed.

[1]my first semester in college was overwhelming. [2]i failed economics and almost failed spanish and chemistry. [3]one problem was that i was putting in too many hours at the bavarian inn, where i worked as assistant manager. [4]the restaurant is popular because it is on the east side right across the street from the convention center. [5]richard gross, the manager, was never around, and i usually had to work sundays and holidays as well as weekday nights. [6]when other students were relaxing over thanksgiving, i was working overtime. [7]my advisor finally told me, "this schedule isn't working for you. [8]you should reduce the number of classes you're taking at dixon college or cut back your hours at the restaurant." [9]when my grades came in january, i quit my job and took a special course on improving study habits. [10]i got a lot out of our textbook *focusing attention: how to manage time and improve concentration.* [11]next year I may transfer to metropolitan community college in minneapolis so that I can live closer to home.

Chapter 10 Italics

When using a word processing program, you can follow the conventions of professional typesetters who use italics to indicate certain titles—and also, occasionally, for other purposes. In handwritten or typewritten papers, you can indicate italics by underlining. In most situations, either italicizing or underlining is acceptable. If in doubt, follow your audience's preference. (See 32a(2).)

It was on *60 Minutes*. It was on <u>60 Minutes</u>.

10a Italics identify the titles of separate publications.

A separate publication is a work published as a whole rather than as part of a larger published work. A newspaper, for example, is a separate publication but an editorial in that newspaper is not. So different conventions are used for indicating the title of the newspaper and the title of the editorial. (See 16c.) Following these conventions helps readers gauge the size of a work and the relation between one work and another.

Have you seen Russell Baker's "Disturbers of the Peace" in today's *New York Times*?

I especially enjoyed "The Politics of Paradise" in Ellen Pagel's *Adam, Eve, and the Serpent.*

In addition to newspapers, the titles of books, magazines, pamphlets, plays, and films are usually italicized. Italics also indicate the titles of television and radio programs, entire recordings, works of art, long poems, comic strips, genera, species, and software programs.

Books	*Beloved*	*The Journey Home*
Magazines	*Wired*	*National Geographic*
Newspapers	*USA Today*	*Wall Street Journal*
Plays, Films	*Othello*	*Forest Gump*
Recordings	*Unforgettable*	*Great Verdi Overtures*
Works of Art	*Mona Lisa*	*The Last Supper*
Long Poems	*Paradise Lost*	*The Divine Comedy*
Comic Strips	*Peanuts*	*Doonesbury*
Genera, Species	*Homo sapiens*	*Rosa setigera*
Software	*VirusScan*	*WordPerfect*

Neither italics nor quotation marks are used in references to major historical documents or religious texts.

The Magna Carta marked a turning point in English history.

Matthew, Mark, Luke, and John are the first four books of the New Testament.

A title is not italicized when it stands at the beginning of a book or article. Accordingly, the title at the top of a paper or report (unless it is also the title of a book or includes the title of a book) should not be italicized. (See also 9c.)

10b Italics identify foreign words and phrases in the context of an English sentence.

> I tell her I know Chinese. "*Beyeh fa-foon,*" I say. "*Shee-veh, Ji nu,*" meaning "Stop acting crazy. Rice gruel, Soy sauce."
> —GISH JEN

> What I can't push as successfully out of sight are my own immigrant childhood fears of having a *gringa* stepmother with foreign tastes in our house. —JULIA ALVAREZ

Countless words borrowed from other languages are a part of the English vocabulary and are therefore not italicized. The more familiar the word becomes, the less likely it is to be italicized.

cliché (French)	pizza (Italian)	versus (Latin)
bayou (Choctaw)	patio (Spanish)	karate (Japanese)

10c Italics identify the names of legal cases.

Andrews v. City of Philadelphia

Roe v. Wade

Italics also indicate the shortened name of a case.

> As *Andrews* demonstrates, employers can be held responsible for offensive speech in the workplace.

Italics are not used when referring to a case by other than its official name.

> I think the media gave too much attention to the O.J. Simpson case.

10d Italics identify the names of specific ships, satellites, and spacecraft.

U.S.S. *Picking* the space shuttle *Challenger*

The names of trains and the names of a general class or a trademark are not italicized: Orient Express, PT boat, Boeing 747, Telstar, ICBMs.

10e Italics indicate words, letters, or figures spoken of as such or used as illustrations, statistical symbols, or the variables in algebraic expressions.

Finally he told my mother to put an *H* in that blank. "For *human* race," he said. —ELIZABETH GORDON

$c = r^2$

In APA style, volume numbers in reference lists are italicized. (See 38d.)

Memory & Cognition, 3, 635–647.

10f When used sparingly, italics indicate emphasis.

If they take offense, then that's *their* problem.

These *are* the right files.

Overuse of italics for emphasis (like overuse of the exclamation point) defeats its own purpose. If you tend to rely on italics to stress ideas, study chapter 29 and try substituting more specific or forceful words for those you are tempted to underline.

Exercise 1

Underline all words that should be italicized in the following sentences.

1. NotaBene is a word-processing program designed especially for use in colleges and universities.
2. I looked up the New Yorker in the library in order to read Mousetrap, a story by Jane Shapiro.
3. Carlos enjoys watching classic films like Casablanca.
4. I like to find appropriate quotations in The New Quotable Woman.
5. The New York Times reported that another attempt has been made to explore the ruins of the Britannic, sister ship of the Titanic.

Chapter 11

Abbreviations, Acronyms, and Numbers

Abbreviations and numbers are used in tables, notes, and bibliographies and in some kinds of special or technical writing. In formal writing, follow the principles outlined in this section. The first time abbreviations or acronyms are used in a paper, they should be spelled out.

> Behaviors that rate high on the Sensation Seeking Scale (SSS) include engaging in risky sports, occupations, or hobbies; seeking variety in sexual and drug experiences; behaving fearlessly in common phobic situations; and preferring exotic foods.

Traditionally abbreviations are marked with periods; acronyms are not.

11a Designations such as *Ms., Mr., Mrs., Dr.,* and *St.* appear before a proper name, and those such as *Jr., Sr.,* and *II* appear after.

Mrs. Adrienne Marcus	Mr. Julio Rodriguez
Dr. Sonya Allen	Ms. Gretel Lopez
P.T. Lawrence, III	Mark Ngo, Sr.
St. Paul	Erika C. Scheurer, Ph.D.

Avoid redundant titles.

> Dr. Carol Ballou or Carol Ballou, M.D. [NOT Dr. Carol Ballou, M.D.]

Most abbreviations form plurals by adding *-s* alone, without an apostrophe: *IRAs, CODs.*

Use abbreviations such as *Prof., Sen., Capt.,* or *Rev.* only before initials or full names. In formal writing, *Reverend* or *Rev.* and *Honorable* are adjectives and are preceded by *the* and followed by title, full name, or initials.

> the Reverend Dr. Campbell OR the Reverend George Tyler Campbell OR the Honorable G.T. Campbell

ESL Other cultures sometimes use *the* before titles. American English omits *the* except when using *Reverend* or *Honorable.*

> ~~the~~ Dr. Sonya Allen ~~the~~ Professor Rodriguez

11b The names of states, countries, continents, months, days of the week, and units of measurement are not abbreviated when they appear in a sentence.

> On a Tuesday in June, we drove ninety-nine miles to Columbia, Missouri; the next day we flew to Texas.

For addresses in correspondence, however, use appropriate postal abbreviations. (No period follows the abbreviation.)

POSTAL ABBREVIATIONS

AL	Alabama	MT	Montana
AK	Alaska	NE	Nebraska
AZ	Arizona	NV	Nevada
AR	Arkansas	NH	New Hampshire
CA	California	NJ	New Jersey
CO	Colorado	NM	New Mexico
CT	Connecticut	NY	New York
DE	Delaware	NC	North Carolina
DC	District of Columbia	ND	North Dakota
FL	Florida	OH	Ohio
GA	Georgia	OK	Oklahoma
GU	Guam	OR	Oregon
HI	Hawaii	PA	Pennsylvania
ID	Idaho	PR	Puerto Rico
IL	Illinois	RI	Rhode Island
IN	Indiana	SC	South Carolina
IA	Iowa	SD	South Dakota
KS	Kansas	TN	Tennessee
KY	Kentucky	TX	Texas
LA	Louisiana	UT	Utah
ME	Maine	VT	Vermont
MD	Maryland	VA	Virginia
MA	Massachusetts	VI	Virgin Islands
MI	Michigan	WA	Washington (state)
MN	Minnesota	WV	West Virginia
MS	Mississippi	WI	Wisconsin
MO	Missouri	WY	Wyoming

11c Words such as *Street, Avenue, Road, Park,* and *Company* are abbreviated only when they appear in addresses.

Thompson Avenue is south of Hollywood Park.

When used as part of an address in correspondence, such words can be either written out or abbreviated: **Thompson Ave.**

11d The words *volume, chapter,* and *page* are written out when they appear in sentences but abbreviated when they appear in bibliographies and reference lists.

I read pages 82–89 of chapter 10 in volume 3 for my sociology course.

Following is a list of abbreviations commonly used in documenting research papers.

abr.	abridged, abridgment
Acad.	Academy
anon.	anonymous
app.	appendix
Apr.	April
Assn.	Association
Aug.	August
biog.	biography, biographer, biographical
bk., bks.	book, books
bull.	bulletin
c.	circa, "about" (for example, "c. 1960")
cf.	compare
ch., chs.	chapter, chapters
col., cols.	column, columns
Coll.	College
comp.	compiled by, compiler
Cong. Rec.	*Congressional Record*
cont.	contents OR continued
DAB	*Dictionary of American Biography*
Dec.	December
dept.	department
dir.	directed by, director
diss.	dissertation
div.	division
DNB	*Dictionary of National Biography*

ed., eds.	edition(s) OR editor(s)
enl.	enlarged (as in "rev. and enl. ed.")
et al.	et alia, ("and others")
Feb.	February
fig.	figure
fwd.	foreword, foreword by
gen. ed.	general editor
govt.	government
GPO	Government Printing Office
HR	House of Representatives
illus.	illustrated by, illustrator, illustration
inc.	incorporated OR including
Inst.	Institute, Institution
intl.	international
introd.	[author of] introduction, introduced by
Jan.	January
jour.	journal
l., ll.	line, lines (omitted before line numbers unless the reference would be unclear)
mag.	magazine
Mar.	March
ms., mss.	manuscript, manuscripts
n, nn	note, notes (used immediately after page number: 6n3)
natl.	national
n.d.	no date [of publication]
no., nos.	number [of issue], numbers
Nov.	November
n.p.	no place [of publication] OR no publisher
n. pag.	no pagination
Oct.	October
P	Press (used in documentation; see "UP")
p., pp.	page, pages (omitted before page numbers unless the reference would be unclear)
pref.	preface, preface by
pseud.	pseudonym
pt., pts.	part, parts
rept.	reported by, report

rev.	revision, revised, revised by OR review, reviewed by
rpt.	reprinted, reprint
sec., secs.	section, sections
Sept.	September
ser.	series
sic	thus, so; reproduced exactly as written
Soc.	Society
supp.	supplement
trans.	translated by, translator, translation
U	University (used in documentation; see "UP")
UP	University Press (used in documentation; Wesleyan UP)
vol., vols.	volume, volumes (omitted before volume numbers unless the reference would be unclear)

The following kinds of abbreviations and acronyms are commonly used in writing.

(1) Clipped forms of some words

A clipped form is an abbreviation that can be pronounced as a word; it is not marked with a period.

Some clipped forms—such as rep, exec, or info—are avoided in formal writing. Others—such as exam, lab, Cal Tech, and math—are so common that they are becoming acceptable.

(2) Certain words used with dates or figures

82 B.C. [OR B.C.E.]	A.D. 95 [OR 95 C.E.]
7:40 a.m. [OR A.M.]	4:52 EST [OR E.S.T.]
No. 19	85 MPG [OR mpg]

(3) The abbreviations for the District of Columbia (DC) and the United States (U.S.) when used as adjectives

Washington, DC; the U.S. Navy [COMPARE "The District of Columbia has many monuments."]

(4) The names of some organizations, agencies, countries, persons, or things commonly referred to by their capitalized initials

FDA	VCR	NFL	PC	NBC
IQ	TV	MIT	ABC	JFK

(5) Certain common Latin expressions (with the English equivalent spelled out in brackets here)

cf.	[compare]	etc.	[and so forth]
e.g.	[for example]	i.e.	[that is]
et al.	[and others]	vs. OR v.	[versus]

11e When unfamiliar with an acronym, readers benefit from seeing it spelled out the first time it is used.

Acronyms are words formed from the initial letters of other words or from the combination of syllables of other words: *AIDS* (acquired immunodeficiency syndrome), *sonar* (sound navigation ranging).

FEMA (the Federal Emergency Management Administration) was criticized for its slow response to the victims of Hurricane Andrew.

OR

The Federal Emergency Management Administration (FEMA) was criticized. . . .

Your reader will probably be familiar with such terms as NATO, NASA, radar, laser, and SAT but perhaps not with VAT or ROM.

Exercise 1

Strike out any form that is inappropriate in formal writing.

1. after 8 P.M.; after eight in the P.M.
2. on November 15; on Nov. 15
3. in Calif. and Ill.; on TV; 85 mph
4. for Jason Ross, Jr.; for Jr.
5. Mr. Robert Lyons; a prof.
6. on Eastwood Ave.; on Eastwood Avenue

11f Numbers are written in different ways depending on the size of the numbers and the frequency with which they appear.

When you use numbers infrequently in a piece of writing, you can spell out those that can be expressed in one or two words and use figures for the others. When you use numbers frequently, spell out those from one to nine and use figures for all others. Very large numbers can be expressed by a combination of words and figures.

Always over three inches

But one-half of a foot

Always after 124 days

But after thirty-three days OR after 33 days

Always 758 students

But seven hundred students OR 700 students

Eleven million customers, 11,000,000 customers, or 11 million customers

In a discussion of related items containing both single- and double- or triple-digit numbers, use figures for all numbers.

Lana ate 7 cookies but Julio ate 12.

If a sentence begins with a number, spell out the number.

Two hundred twenty-five contestants competed in the talent show.

Some numbers follow special usages.

Specific time of day

4 p.m. OR 4:00 p.m. OR four o'clock in the afternoon

9:30 a.m. OR half-past nine in the morning

Dates

November 8, 1962 OR 8 November 1962 (NOT November 8th, 1962)

December fourth OR the fourth of December OR December 4

the fifties OR the 1950s

the fourteenth century

in 1362   in 1320–21 OR the winter of 1320–21

from 1330 to 1335

ESL Many languages invert the numbers for the month and the day. For *September 18, 1997,* they would use the numbers **18/9/97**. In American practice, the numbers would read **9/18/97**.

Addresses

25 Arrow Drive, Apartment 1, Columbia, Missouri 78209

OR 25 Arrow Dr., Apt. 1, Columbia, MO 78209

21 Second Street

459 East 35 Street OR 459 East 35th Street

Identification numbers

Channel 10   Interstate 40   Edward III   Room 222

Pages and divisions of books and plays

page 15   chapter 8   part 2

in act 2, scene 1 OR in Act II, Scene I

Decimals and percentages

a 2.5 average   12½ percent   0.853 metric tons

Large round numbers

forty million dollars OR $40 million OR $40,000,000

[Figures are often used for emphasis.]

Repeated numbers (in legal or commercial writing)

The lawyer's fee will exceed two million (2,000,000) dollars. OR The lawyer's fee will exceed two million dollars ($2,000,000).

ESL Languages differ in their use of the period and comma with numbers.

American English marks any amount smaller than one with a decimal point (period) and uses a comma to divide larger numbers into more understandable units. Starting at the left of the decimal you should place a comma between every third and fourth number to separate thousands.

10,000	(ten thousand)
7.65	(seven point six five OR seven and sixty-five one hundredths)
7,000.65	(seven thousand and sixty-five one hundredths)

In some other cultures, the decimal and the comma are reversed.

10.000	(ten thousand)
7,65	(seven point six five OR seven and sixty-five one hundredths)

Exercise 2

Using accepted abbreviations and figures, change each item to a shortened form.

1. in the first scene of the second act
2. four o'clock in the afternoon
3. on the seventh of April
4. Doctor Maria Roberto
5. ten thousand two hundred sixty-three students

Punctuation

Chapter 12 The Comma

Punctuation lends to written language a flexibility that facial expressions, pauses, and variations in voice pitch give to spoken language. For instance, a pause after *sister* in the first example below makes it clear that the spoken sentence refers to only two people—the *sister* and a person named *Mary Ellen*. In the second example, a pause after *Mary* lets us know that the sentence refers to three people—the *sister*, *Mary*, and *Ellen*. In written language, a comma creates this pause.

When my sister called, Mary Ellen answered.

When my sister called Mary, Ellen answered.

If you understand the following four principles, you will see through most of the mystery surrounding commas and find them easier to use consistently.

Commas

- come before coordinating conjunctions when they link independent clauses.
- follow introductory adverb clauses and, usually, introductory phrases.
- separate items in a series (including coordinate adjectives).
- set off nonrestrictive and other parenthetical elements.

12a Commas come before a coordinating conjunction that links independent clauses.

INDEPENDENT CLAUSE,	CONJUNCTION	INDEPENDENT CLAUSE.
Subject + predicate,	and / but / or / for / nor / so / yet	subject + predicate.

The minutes would pass, and then suddenly Einstein would stop pacing as his face relaxed into a gentle smile.

—BANESH HOFFMANN

Fanny Lou Hamer was a Black woman who pioneered civil rights organizing in the South, but few Americans know of Hamer's work. —META GAIL CARSTARPHEN

Justice stands upon Power, or there is no Justice.

—WILLIAM S. WHITE

From one point of view their migration was the fruit of an old prophecy, for indeed they emerged from a sunless world.

—N. SCOTT MOMADAY

I am not complaining, nor am I protesting either.

—RALPH ELLISON

I wanted to be as they were telling me I should be, so I had ceased to exist; I had renounced my soul's private obligations. —ROSARIO FERRÉ

There was no voice apart from his, yet he appeared to be chatting in friendly, excited tones with some other person.

—WOLE SOYINKA

When a sentence contains multiple clauses, a comma comes before each coordinating conjunction.

> I chose to follow in the footsteps of my unconventional Aunt Esther, and I have never regretted my choice, but I think my mother was jealous of Aunt Esther, and I fear she never approved of me.

When the clauses are short, the comma can be omitted before *and, but,* or *or,* but not usually before *for, nor, so,* or *yet*. (See also page 37.)

> I liked the haircut and it made me actually look forward to my future fame. —AMY TAN

Sometimes a semicolon separates independent clauses, especially when the second one contains commas or when it reveals a contrast. (See also **14a**.)

> Most people, according to my mother, skip cleaning in the corners; on the other hand, she used to say, they don't skip payday.

Not all coordinating conjunctions, however, are preceded by commas. A common slip is to place one before the *and* linking the parts of a compound predicate.

> He snapped the locker door open and kicked his shoes off without sitting. —REGINALD McKNIGHT [compound predicate—no comma before *and*]

Especially when a sentence is long, writers occasionally use a comma to emphasize a distinction between the parts of the predicate, as in E. M. Forster's "Artists always seek a new technique, and will continue to do so as long as their work excites them."

Exercise 1

Follow **12a** as you insert commas before conjunctions linking independent clauses in these sentences. (Remember that not all coordinating conjunctions link independent clauses and that *but, for, so,* and *yet* do not always function as coordinating conjunctions.)

1. A physician is accused of performing unnecessary surgery. Another hospital investigation is launched.
2. Families can choose to have their elderly relatives live with them at home. They may choose to house them in retirement centers.
3. Everyone in our class was assigned to an editing group. Only three of the groups could work together efficiently.
4. There are many customs for us to learn about. Our society has finally begun to appreciate its diversity.
5. We had not seen a bear before we went to Yellowstone. We had not seen a moose, either.

12b A comma usually follows introductory words, phrases, and clauses.

(1) Adverb clauses before independent clauses

ADVERB CLAUSE, INDEPENDENT CLAUSE.

When you write**,** you make a sound in the reader's head.
—RUSSELL BAKER

The safest automobile on the road is expensive**,** but if I consider the protection it offers**,** I cannot find the cost unreasonable. [adverb clause preceding the second independent clause]

If the omission does not make reading difficult, writers may omit the comma after an introductory adverb clause, especially when the clause is short.

If you look to the history of Europe you find that homelessness first appears (or is first acknowledged) at the very same moment that bourgeois culture begins to appear.

—PETER MARIN

A comma is usually unnecessary when the adverb clause follows the independent clause.

I should have no difficulties establishing my citizenship in the tribe because my grandmother's name can be found on the Dawes roll. [*Because,* a subordinating conjunction, introduces an adverbial clause.]

If an adverb clause does not affect the meaning of the independent clause, a comma can precede it.

Women must be able to take their birth names from their mothers and keep them after marriage**,** if they wish to be truly equal.

(2) Introductory phrases before independent clauses

INTRODUCTORY PHRASE, INTRODUCTORY WORD,	} subject + predicate.

Prepositional phrases

From the deck**,** I could not see my father, but I could see my mother facing the ship, her eyes searching to pick me out.

—JAMAICA KINCAID

If the comma after an introductory prepositional phrase is not necessary to prevent misreading, it can be omitted:

For safety the university installed call boxes linked directly to campus security.

Other types of phrases

Having traveled nowhere, she believed the rest of the world was like her own small town; having read little, she had no sense of how other people think. [participial phrases before both independent clauses—see also 1d and 1e]

The language difference aside, life in Germany doesn't seem much different from life in America. [absolute phrase—see also 12d(7)]

Introductory words

Furthermore, the person responsible for breaking or damaging university equipment will be fined. [transitional expression—see the lists on pages 41–42]

Well, move the ball or move the body.

—ALLEN JACKSON [interjection]

Yes, I bought my tickets yesterday. No, I didn't pay cash. [introductory *yes* or *no*]

Commas are not used after phrases that begin inverted sentences. (See also 29f.)

With the hurricane came the tornadoes. [COMPARE "Tornadoes came with the hurricane."]

Of far greater concern than censorship of bad words is censorship of ideas. —DONNA WOOLFOLK CROSS

Exercise 2

Insert a comma where needed in the following sentences. Explain why each comma is necessary. Put a check mark before any sentence in which a comma is not needed.

1. If you are counting on a tax refund to give you a small nest egg you'd better have a backup plan.
2. As far as he is concerned all politicians are corrupt.

3. At the same time we understand why they can't always keep a campaign promise.
4. Before noon on Saturday the checkout lines at the discount grocery were thirty feet long.
5. While passing three gravel trucks going downhill Felicia lost control of her car.
6. Trying to make the best product possible used to be the main concern of almost every company.
7. With one hand on the wheel and the other on the gear shift Dick guided the Jeep expertly down the narrow winding mountain trail.
8. Under the desk she keeps a small electric heater as well as some unused computer equipment.
9. The meal far from over the children began to demand dessert.
10. When you can talk to someone more knowledgeable than you are.

12c Commas separate items in a series (including coordinate adjectives).

A series contains three or more parallel elements. (See chapter 26.) The punctuation of a series depends on its form:

> The melon was *pink*, *sweet*, and *juicy*. [**a**, **b**, and **c**—a preferred comma before *and*]
>
> The melon was *pink*, *sweet* and *juicy*. [**a**, **b** and **c**—an acceptable omission of the comma before *and* when there is no danger of misreading; compare "Leila was my mother's sister, my aunt and my friend," a compound appositive indicating two elements: **a**, **a** and **b**]
>
> The melon was *pink*, *sweet*, *juicy*. [**a**, **b**, **c**]

(1) Words, phrases, and clauses in a series

A pet should be affectionate, trusting, obedient, and intelligent. [words in a series]

My job requires me to start work at 7 a.m., to drive to three different towns every day, and to carry heavy repair equipment upstairs. [phrases in a series]

My idea of a great vacation spot is one where no telephone rings, someone else fixes me great food, and I sit on the porch in the cool shade all day and read mystery novels. [clauses in a series]

If items in a series contain internal commas, you can make the meaning clear by separating the items with semicolons. (See **14b**.)

For special emphasis, writers sometimes use commas to slow the pace when coordinating conjunctions link all the items in a series.

We cannot put it off for a month, or a week, or even a day.

The melon was *pink* and *sweet* and *juicy*. [**a** and **b** and **c**]

(2) Coordinate adjectives

Coordinate adjectives are two or more adjectives that modify the same noun or pronoun. One test for coordinate adjectives is to switch them; another is to put *and* between them. If the meaning does not change, the adjectives are coordinate. Commas separate coordinate adjectives not linked by a coordinating conjunction.

It is a waiting, silent, limp room. —EUDORA WELTY [*Waiting, silent*, and *limp* all modify *room*. COMPARE "It is a silent, limp waiting room."]

Walking along the rushing, shallow creek, I slipped on a rock and sank above my boot tops into a small, still pool.

[*Rushing* and *shallow* modify *creek* and *small* and *still* modify *pool.*]

Exercise 3

Using commas as needed, write sentences supplying coordinate adjectives to modify any five of the following ten word groups.

EXAMPLE
metric system *Most countries use the familiar, sensible metric system to measure distances.*

1. onion bagel
2. classical music
3. cheddar cheese
4. metal sculpture
5. computer software
6. community college
7. baseball parks
8. office buildings
9. sports car
10. state highway

12d Commas set off nonrestrictive and other parenthetical elements, as well as contrasted elements, items in dates, and so on.

Nonrestrictive clauses or phrases give nonessential information about a noun or pronoun. They can be omitted without changing the meaning.

To set off a nonrestrictive word or word group, use two commas, unless the element is placed at the beginning or the end of the sentence. (Expressions that come at the beginning of a sentence are also treated in 12b.) Of course, not all words preceded and followed by commas are nonrestrictive.

> Most single people in their twenties, according to my brother, prefer to live at home where Mom and Dad pay the big bills. [COMPARE "According to my brother, most single people . . ." and ". . . Mom and Dad pay the big bills, according to my brother."]

Restrictive clauses or phrases follow and limit the words they modify. They are essential to the clear identification of the word or words they refer to.

(1) Adjective clauses or phrases

Adjective clauses that describe the noun they modify are nonrestrictive, but those that limit the noun are restrictive. In the first example below, the proper name "Marilyn Greer" identifies which woman at the bank the sentence is describing. As a result, the sentence requires no additional information unless there are two Marilyn Greers. "The woman," however, could be any woman, not just the bank manager, and so needs a modifier that limits it to someone in particular.

Nonrestrictive	Restrictive or Essential
Clauses	
I spoke with Marilyn Greer, who manages the bank.	I spoke to the woman who manages the bank.
We climbed Mt. Rainier, which is over 15,000 feet high.	We climbed a mountain that is over 15,000 feet high.
Phrase	
The new Saturn, covered in mud, looks worn out.	The new car covered in mud looks worn out.

Sometimes only the omission or use of commas indicates whether a modifier is restrictive or nonrestrictive and thus signals the writer's exact meaning. Although many writers prefer to use *that* at the beginning of restrictive clauses, *which* has become acceptable if it does not cause confusion.

I like to drive a car that [or which] has fast acceleration and nimble handling.

(2) Appositives

Appositives can supply additional but nonessential details about a noun or pronoun (nonrestrictive), or else they limit the meaning of a noun or pronoun by indicating which one—or ones—is meant (restrictive).

Nonrestrictive	Restrictive or Essential
Even Zeke Thornbush, **my friend,** let me down.	Even my friend **Zeke Thornbush** let me down.
Voyager photographed Saturn, **the ringed planet.**	Voyager photographed the planet **Saturn.**

Abbreviations after names are treated as nonrestrictive appositives: "Was the letter from Frances Evans, **Ph.D.,** or from F. H. Evans, **M.D.?**"

Exercise 4

Set off nonrestrictive adjective clauses or phrases and nonrestrictive appositives with commas. Put a check mark after any sentence that needs no commas.

1. I was able to take a class from Dr. Thompson who teaches Shelley and Keats.
2. I was able to take a class from the Dr. Thompson who teaches Shelley and Keats.
3. Lilacs which have a beautiful fragrance are my favorite flower.
4. Few people around here have ever heard of my home town a little place called Bugtussle.
5. Charles M. Duke Jr. and astronaut John W. Young landed the lunar vehicle near Plum Crater.

(3) Contrasted elements

Human beings, **unlike oysters,** frequently reveal their emotions. —GEORGE F. WILL

Some writers put a comma before *but* and *not* in such sentences as the following, while others do not.

> Other citizens who disagree with me base their disagreement, not on facts different from the ones I know, but on a different set of values. —RENÉ DUBOS

> Today the Black Hills are being invaded again, not for gold but for uranium. —PETER MATTHIESSEN

(4) Geographical names, items in dates, and addresses

> Nashville, Tennessee, is the largest country and western music center in the United States.

> I had to write to Ms. Melanie Hobson, 2873 Central Avenue, Orange Park, FL 32065. [no comma between the state abbreviation and the ZIP code]

> Hunter applied for the job on Wednesday, June 12, 1996, but turned it down on June 14 because it paid only minimum wage.

> **OR**

> Hunter applied for the job on Wednesday 12 June and turned it down on Friday 14 June because it paid only minimum wage. [Commas are omitted when the day of the month precedes rather than follows the month.]

(5) Parenthetical expressions

> Language, **then,** sets the tone of our society. —EDWIN NEWMAN

> Much of the court and, **thus,** a good deal of the action are often invisible to a basketball player, so he needs more than good eyesight. —JOHN McPHEE

When they cause little or no pause in reading, expressions such as *also, too, of course, perhaps, at least, therefore,* and *likewise* need not be set off by commas.

Our ideas about gender roles have **perhaps** changed in recent decades. —LAWRENCE SACHS

I'm trying to keep my spending to a minimum **at least** until I finish my degree.

(6) Mild interjections and words used in direct address

Ah, that's my idea of a good meal. [interjection]

Now is the time, **animal lovers**, to protest. [direct address]

(7) Absolute phrases

His temper being what it is, I don't want a confrontation.

He was thumping at a book, **his voice growing louder and louder.** —JOYCE CAROL OATES

12e Commas are occasionally needed for ease in reading.

Some commas are necessary to prevent misreading. Without them the following sentences would confuse the reader, if only temporarily.

Still, water must be transported to dry areas. [COMPARE "Still water. . . ."]

The day before, I had talked with her on the phone. [COMPARE "I had talked with her the day before."]

Someone predicted that by the year 2000, 3.5 million employees would be on the federal payroll. [COMPARE "Someone predicted that by the year 2000 3.5. . . ."]

The earth breathes, in a certain sense. —LEWIS THOMAS [COMPARE "The earth breathes in moisture."]

Sometimes a comma replaces a clearly understood word or group of words.

Politicians sometimes make controversial remarks; bureaucrats, never. —MARGARET McCARTHY

Exercise 5

Explain the reason for each comma used, and point out which commas are optional and which are a matter of stylistic preference.

1. When I was six, we moved closer to civilization, but by then the twig had been bent. —MARGARET A. ROBINSON
2. My guess is that as the family breaks down, friendships will grow in importance. —SUSAN LEE
3. Whatever she planted grew as if by magic, and her fame as a grower of flowers spread over three counties. —ALICE WALKER
4. But alas, I do not rule the world and that, I am afraid, is the story of my life—always a godmother, never a god. —FRAN LEBOWITZ
5. If all else fails, try doing something nice for somebody who doesn't expect it. —GEORGE BURNS

Exercise 6

For humorous effect the writer of the following paragraph deliberately omits commas that can be justified by the rules in this chapter. Identify where commas might be inserted to contribute to ease in reading. Compare your version with someone else's and comment on any differences you find.

> [1]The commas are the most useful and usable of all the stops. [2]It is highly important to put them in place as you go along. [3]If you try to come back after doing a paragraph and stick them in the various spots that tempt you you will discover that they tend to swarm like minnows into all sorts of crevices whose existence you hadn't realized and before you know it the whole long sentence becomes immobilized and lashed up squirming in commas. [4]Better to use them sparingly, and with affection precisely when the need for one arises, nicely, by itself.
>
> —LEWIS THOMAS, *The Medusa and the Snail*

Exercise 7

Explain each comma in the following paragraph (from *Time* magazine).

[1]Yet punctuation is something more than a culture's birthmark; it scores the music in our minds, gets our thoughts moving to the rhythm of our hearts. [2]Punctuation is the notation in the sheet music of our words, telling us when to rest, or when to raise our voices; it acknowledges that the meaning of our discourse, as of any symphonic composition, lies not in the units, but in the pauses, the pacing and the phrasing. [3]Punctuation adjusts the tone and color and volume till the feeling comes into perfect focus. . . . [4]A world which has only periods is a world without inflections. It is a world without shade. [5]It has a music without sharps and flats. [6]It has a jackboot rhythm. [7]Words cannot bend and curve. . . . [8]A comma, by comparison, catches the gentle drift of the mind in thought, turning in on itself and back on itself, reversing, redoubling and returning along the course of its own sweet river music; while the semicolon brings clauses and thoughts together with all the silent discretion of a hostess arranging guests around her dinner table. . . . [9]Punctuation, then, is a matter of care. [10]Care for words, yes, but also, and more important, for what the words imply. —PICO IYER

Chapter 13

Superfluous Commas

Although a comma ordinarily signals a pause, not every pause calls for a comma. As you read the following sentence aloud, you may pause naturally at several places, but no commas are necessary.

> The authorities of [the] College have suggested that for me to speak longer than 20 minutes would be regarded as cruel and inhuman punishment and that . . . several strong men will mount this platform and forcibly remove me.
>
> —RUSSELL BAKER

To avoid using unnecessary commas, observe the following guidelines.

13a Commas do not separate the subject from its verb or the verb from its object.

Remove the circled commas.

> Most older, married students(,) must hold a job in addition to going to school. [separation of subject (*students*) and verb (*must hold*)]
>
> The lawyer said(,) that I could appeal the speeding ticket. [separation of verb (*said*) and direct object (a noun clause: *that I could . . .*)]

13b Commas do not follow coordinating conjunctions, and they immediately precede them only when they link independent clauses. See chapter 3 and 12a.

Remove the circled commas.

> I fed the dog, and put it out for the night. [separation of compound verbs (*fed* . . . and *put out*)]
>
> For three decades the Surgeon General's office has warned us about the dangers of smoking, but, millions of people still smoke. [separation of the conjunction (*but*) and the subject of the clause (*millions of people*)]

13c Commas set off only those words and short phrases that are clearly parenthetical.

Remove the circled commas.

> Martha was born, in Miami, in 1976.
>
> Perhaps, the valve is not correctly calibrated.

13d Commas do not set off restrictive (necessary) clauses, phrases, or appositives. See 12d.

Remove the circled commas.

> Everyone, who owns an automobile, needs to have collision insurance.

With strains of bagpipes in the background, crowds watched two men(,) carrying lances as they charged each other on horseback.

13e Commas do not precede the first or follow the last item of a series (including a series of coordinate adjectives).

Remove the circled commas.

Field trips were required in a few courses, such as(,) botany, geology, and sociology.

I've always wanted a low-slung, fast, elegant(,) convertible.

Exercise 1

Study the structure of the following sentences, then answer the question that follows by giving a specific reason for each item. Be prepared to explain your answers in class.

[1]At the age of eighty my mother had her last bad fall, and after that her mind wandered free through time. [2]Some days she went to weddings and funerals that had taken place half a century earlier. [3]On others she presided over family dinners cooked on Sunday afternoons for children who were now gray with age. [4]Through all this she lay in bed but moved across time, traveling among the dead decades with a speed and ease beyond the gift of physical science.

—RUSSELL BAKER

Why is there no comma after the following words: (1) *eighty,* (2) *and* (sent. 1), (3) *that* (sent. 1), (4) *weddings,* (5) *and* (sent. 2), (6) *others,* (7) *dinners,* (8) *this* (sent. 4), (9) *bed,* and (10) *and* (sent. 4)?

Exercise 2

Change the structure and punctuation of the following sentences according to the pattern of the examples.

EXAMPLE
A fishing boat saw their distress signal, and it stopped to offer aid. [an appropriate comma: see 12a]
A fishing boat saw their distress signal and stopped to offer aid. [The second main clause is reduced to a part of the compound predicate, so the comma is no longer needed.]

1. Our employers gave us very good annual evaluations, and they also recommended us for raises.
2. Much modern fiction draws on current psychological knowledge, and it presents very believable characters.
3. Kim has several jobs to put herself through college, and she works hard at all of them.

EXAMPLE
If a person suffers physical abuse, he or she should notify the police. [an appropriate comma: see 12b(1)]
Any person who suffers physical abuse should notify the police. [The introductory adverb clause is converted to a restrictive clause, so the comma is no longer needed.]

4. When people make requests rather than give orders, they generally get cooperation.
5. If older folks want younger folks to take advice, they would do well to listen to what the young people say.

Chapter 14

The Semicolon

The semicolon has two uses: First, it links closely related independent clauses.

> Luverne walked slowly down the street; Hugh ran as fast as he could.

Second, by acting as a stronger mark of punctuation than the comma, it separates sentence elements that contain internal commas.

> Watching stupid, sentimental, dull soap operas; eating junk food like french fries, cheeseburgers, and milkshakes; and just doing nothing are my favorite vices.

14a Semicolons connect independent clauses not linked by a coordinating conjunction.

Two or more related independent clauses can be linked by a semicolon, connected by coordinating conjunctions (*and, but, for, or, nor, so, yet*), or punctuated as separate sentences.

> Some french fries are greasy; others are not; I like them all.
>
> Some french fries are greasy, **and** others are not, **but** I like them all.
>
> Some french fries are greasy. Others are not. I like them all.

The semicolons indicate a close connection between the ideas, the conjunctions indicate a less close connection, and the periods separate the ideas. Note the different intonation patterns when you read the above sentences aloud.

This principle also applies in compound-complex sentences. (See also 14b.)

> When you discover yourself lying on the ground, limp and unresisting, head in the dirt, and helpless, the earth seems to shift forward as a presence; hard, emphatic, not mere surface but a genuine force—there is no other word for it but *presence*. —JOYCE CAROL OATES

Sometimes a semicolon (instead of the usual comma) precedes a coordinating conjunction when a sharp division between the two independent clauses is desired. (See also 12a, page 138.)

> Politicians may refrain from negative campaigning for a time; but when the race gets close, they can't seem to resist trying to dredge up personal dirt to use on their opponents.

Occasionally, a comma separates short, very closely related main clauses.

> We are strengthened by equality, we are weakened by it; we celebrate it, we repudiate it. —THOMAS GRIFFITH [A semicolon is used between pairs of independent clauses joined by commas.]

A semicolon precedes conjunctive adverbs only when they come between independent clauses. (See 3b and the list on p. 41.)

> Some french fries are greasy; **however**, others are not. I like them any way you fix them.

After a conjunctive adverb or transitional expression, the comma is often omitted when the adverb is not considered parenthetical or when the comma is not needed to prevent misreading.

> New Orleans is unique among American cities; indeed in many ways it is scarcely American. —PHELPS GAY

When the second main clause explains or amplifies the first, a colon is sometimes used between main clauses. (See 17d(1), page 177.)

> Problems for residents of our inner cities are increasing: These include expanding unemployment, uninhibited crime, an intensification of racism.

The semicolon is characteristic of very formal or literary writing. It is often better to revise compound sentences using a subordinate construction or sentence punctuation. (See chapter 24.)

14b Semicolons separate elements that themselves contain commas.

> I subscribe to several computer magazines that include reviews of new, better-designed hardware; descriptions of inexpensive commercial software programs; advice from experts; and actual utility programs that make keeping track of my files easier.

Exercise 1

Substitute a semicolon for any comma that could result in misreading.

1. A large number of today's popular authors include politicians and their advisers, experts in the social sciences, such as psychologists and sociologists, and physicists and geologists.
2. In her research paper, Brigitte cited Noam Chomsky, the father of transformational linguistics, Bertrand Russell, the famous logician, philosopher, and pacifist, and Carl Rogers, a clinical psychologist interested in counseling.

14c Semicolons do not connect parts of unequal grammatical rank.

Semicolons do not connect clauses and phrases. (See 1d and 1e.)

> I admired Mr. Grimes; the repair wizard.
>
> We drove two cars to Colorado; it being perhaps the most spectacular state in the country.

Semicolons do not connect a main clause and a subordinate clause.

> I learned that she had lost her job; which really surprised me.
>
> This suit is really too tight; although I can still wear it.

Exercise 2

Find the semicolons used between parts of unequal rank and punctuate appropriately. Do not change properly used semicolons.

1. I like to put two things in my hot tea; a spoonful of honey and a slice of lemon.
2. Elaine always bought her pants and shirts at thrift stores; no expensive trendy fashions for her; then she put together some of the most outrageous outfits I have ever seen.
3. Walking late at night; holding hands with my boyfriend; just listening to the street sounds; are what I would rather be doing than anything else.
4. Many times I've had to run for the morning bus; after I've arrived at the bus stop only a minute late; those buses keep a very strict schedule.
5. Although he knows he should finish his homework first; he still wants to go to the movies right now.

Chapter 15 The Apostrophe

Apostrophes show possession (except for personal pronouns), mark omissions in contractions, and form certain plurals.

15a The apostrophe shows possession for nouns and indefinite pronouns (*everyone, everybody*).

The possessive case shows ownership: Tonya's car. The possessive case of nouns and of indefinite pronouns is indicated by the use of *'s*—see 15a(1)—or by the apostrophe alone—see 15a(2).

Al's pie someone's car

Occasionally, the possessive is indicated by both an *of* phrase and *'s* (often called a **double possessive**):

that book of LaShonda's [LaShonda owns or wrote the book.]

that book of LaShonda [The book describes LaShonda.]

A possessive can follow the word it modifies:

Is that new computer Ana's or Kim's? [COMPARE Ana's or Kim's computer.]

(1) Singular nouns, indefinite pronouns, and acronyms add the apostrophe and *-s*.

Nona's house   anyone's computer   NASA's goal

When the *'s* results in the awkward repetition of an *s*, *x*, or *z* sound, the *-s* is omitted: *Moses' city*.

(2) Plural nouns ending in *-s* add only the apostrophe.

the boys' game   the babies' toys

Plurals not ending in *-s* add the apostrophe and *-s*.

men's lives   women's cars

(3) Compounds and expressions that show joint ownership add the apostrophe and *-s* to the last word only.

Olga and Nadia's house [COMPARE Olga and Nadia's houses—they jointly own more than one house.]

her mother-in-law's telephone

Walter Bryan, Jr.'s edited version [To avoid confusion, no comma follows *Jr.'s* although *Jr.* is often set off by commas.]

(4) Individual ownership is indicated by adding the apostrophe and *-s* to each name.

Tamiko's and Sam's apartments

(5) Sometimes a relationship comparable to ownership adds the apostrophe, especially in time relationships, in academic titles, or before gerunds. (See 1d(2).)

an hour's delay   in a week's time

Bachelor's degree   Asa's dancing

Luverne's having to be there seemed unnecessary.

Proper names (organizations, geographical locations, and so on) sometimes do not use the apostrophe or the apostrophe and *-s*. Follow local usage.

Devil’s Island   Devils Tower   Devil Mountain

Exercise 1

Change the modifier after the noun to a possessive form before the noun, following the pattern of the examples.

EXAMPLES

proposals made by the committee	the committee’s proposals
poems written by Keats	Keats’s poems OR Keats’ poems

1. the mansion of Elvis Presley
2. a hat belonging to somebody else
3. shoes for children
4. the glossary of that book
5. an error made by the math professor
6. the desires of the employer
7. the coat belonging to Maurice Champaign, Jr.
8. the sounds of the video game and dishwasher
9. the apartment inhabited by Jonette
10. the aspirations of my brother
11. worth 50 cents
12. paintings by Picasso
13. a paper written by David and Jennifer
14. the description of the child
15. the friends of Mary and Jonette

15b The apostrophe marks omissions in contractions and numbers.

don’t   they’ll   class of ’98

ESL Since contractions are seldom used in academic writing, you can safely write out the two words in question and omit contractions altogether: *do not, they will.*

15c The apostrophe and *-s* form certain plurals.

The apostrophe and *-s* are used for the plural forms of lowercase letters and of abbreviations followed by periods.

his *p*'*s* and *q*'*s*.

When needed to prevent confusion, *'s* shows the plural of capital letters and of words referred to as words.

too many A's three minus's

When no confusion would result, either *'s* or *-s* forms such plurals as the following:

the 1900's OR the 1990s his 7's OR his 7s
her and's OR her ands the VFW's OR the VFWs
the &'s OR the &s

Who's is the contraction of *who is*. *Whose* is the possessive form of the relative pronoun *who*.

Who's [Who is] responsible? **Whose** responsibility is it?

CAUTION An *'s* is not used to indicate plurals of words: The Smiths are home.

15d Personal pronouns and plural nouns that are not possessive do not take an apostrophe.

A personal pronoun (*I, we, you, he, she, it, they*) has its own form to show possession (*my, mine, our, ours, your, yours, his, her, hers, its, their, theirs*).

A friend of **theirs** knows a cousin of **yours**.

CAUTION Do not confuse *it's* with *its*. *It's* is a contraction for *it is*. *Its* is the possessive form of *it*. Used with a personal pronoun, *'s* always indicates a contraction.

Its motor is small.	**It's** [it is] a small motor.
The dog enjoys **its** bone.	**It's** [it is] the dog's bone.
The board made **its** plan.	**It's** [it is] the board's plan.
It's mine.	**It is** mine.

Exercise 2

Insert apostrophes where needed. Indicate sentences that need no revision by a check mark.

1. Pictures of the class of 97 fill Marks photo album.
2. There are two is and two ls in *illustrious*.
3. NASAs space flights still capture many peoples imaginations.
4. My fathers unexpected mood swings are making me nervous.
5. Many peoples beliefs had changed by the 1960s.
6. Upon graduation, several of my brothers friends received gifts from their grandparents.
7. Cherise likes fencing; its technical dimensions intrigue her.
8. “Its just one MDs diagnosis, right?” Jomol inquired.
9. Theres a big gap between Lonas age and theirs.
10. People often mistake my car for someone elses.

Chapter 16 Quotation Marks

Quotation marks are always used in pairs. They enclose direct quotations (except those in indented blocks), some titles, and words used in a special sense. The first mark indicates the beginning of the quotation, and the second indicates the end. Any other marks associated with the quotation follow the rules explained below.

16a Quotation marks set off direct quotations and dialogue.

Double quotation marks set off direct quotations, but not indirect ones. Single quotation marks enclose a quotation within a quotation.

(1) Direct quotations

> "People are trapped in history," writes James Baldwin, "and history is trapped in them." [Quotation marks enclose only the quotation, not expressions like *she said* or *he replied*. Place the period within the quotation marks—see 16f.]

(2) Indirect quotations

> James Baldwin claims that people cannot escape history and that history cannot exist without people. [Quotation marks are not used for indirect quotations.]

(3) Quotations within quotations

"Jennifer keeps telling me to 'get a life,' " Mark complained. [The comma appears in the quotation within a quotation; the period goes at the end of the sentence. See page 167 for how to punctuate a quotation within a quotation presented as an indented block.]

ESL British English and some other languages reverse the use of single (') and double (") quotation marks. It is important to learn the correct system to use in American writing. (See also 16f.)

Other usage: The police officer said, 'When I saw the thief running away, I shouted, "Stop! You are under arrest." '

American English: The police officer said, "When I saw the thief running away, I shouted, 'Stop! You are under arrest.' "

In direct quotations, reproduce all quoted material exactly as it appears in the original, including capitalization and punctuation. If the quoted material contains an error, insert "sic" within brackets immediately after the error. (See 17g.) If the quoted material contains a reference that would be unclear once the material is taken out of context, explain the reference in one or two words immediately after the reference. (See 37f(2).) Indicate an omission within a quotation by the use of ellipsis points. (See 17i.)

(4) Dialogue

Dialogue is directly quoted conversation. When quoting conversation, write what each person says, no matter how short, as if it were a separate paragraph. It helps to include expressions such as *he said,* as well as closely related bits of narrative, in the same paragraph as the direct quotation.

> Through an interpreter, I spoke with a Bedouin man tending nearby olive trees.
>
> "Do you own this land?" I asked him.
>
> He shook his head. "The land belongs to Allah," he said.
>
> "What about the trees?" I asked. He had just harvested a basket of green olives, and I assumed that at least the trees were his.
>
> "The trees, too, are Allah's," he replied.
>
> I marveled at this man who seemed unencumbered by material considerations . . . or so I was thinking when, as if in afterthought, he said, "Of course, I own the *olives*."
>
> —HARVEY ARDEN

When quoting more than one paragraph by a single speaker, put quotation marks at the beginning of each new paragraph. There is only one set of closing quotation marks, at the end of the last paragraph.

(5) Thoughts

Double quotation marks set off thoughts, as if they were stated.

> "I won't make that mistake again," I thought.

16b Long quotations are indented.

Indention sets off long quotations of prose and poetry, but short quotations are run in to the text.

(1) Prose

When using the Modern Language Association (MLA) style of documentation (38a), set off any quotation consisting of more than four lines by indenting all lines ten spaces. When using the American Psychological Association (APA) style (38d), set off quotations of more than forty words by indenting all lines five spaces. When using either MLA or APA style, double-space the lines in the block.

If you quote one or more complete paragraphs, indicate the beginning of each paragraph by indenting its first line an additional three spaces in MLA style and an additional five spaces in APA style. If you quote only part of a paragraph, do *not* indent its first line the additional spaces.

A colon usually introduces a long quotation. Use internal quotation marks only if they appear in the original.

> Metal coins replaced bartering. Then paper money became more convenient to use than metal coins not only because it is easy to handle but also because, as Cetron and O'Toole say in *Encounters with the Future,* it has other advantages:
>
> > Printing more zeros is all it takes on a bill to increase its value. Careful engraving makes it easy to recognize and difficult to counterfeit. The fact that private individuals cannot create it at will keeps it scarce. Karl Marx once said that paper money was valued "only insofar as it represents gold" but that may never have been true. (188)
>
> Today, checks and credit cards are even more convenient than paper money.

(2) Poetry

Except for very special emphasis, enclose a quotation of three (or fewer) lines of poetry in quotation marks and run it in to the text as you would a short prose quotation. Indicate the divisions between lines by a slash with a space on each side. (See 17h.) Passages of more than three lines should be set off—double-spaced and indented ten spaces unless unusual spacing is part of the poem. Use quotation marks only if they appear in the original. Numbers in parentheses placed two spaces after the close of the quotation can be used to indicate line numbers of the poem.

> In "London" William Blake expressed his horror of institutional callousness:
>
> How the Chimney-sweeper's cry
> Every black'ning Church appalls;
> And the hapless Soldier's sigh
> Runs in blood down Palace walls. (9–12)

16c Quotation marks enclose the titles of short works such as stories, essays, poems, songs, episodes of a radio or television series, articles in periodicals, and subdivisions of books.

> Lon Otto's *Cover Me* contains such wonderful stories as "Winners" and "How I Got Rid of That Stump." [short stories]
>
> "Nani" is my favorite of the poems by Alberto Rios that we studied this semester. [poem]
>
> I always want to laugh when I hear "Big Girls Don't Cry." [song]
>
> Coral Browne starred in "An Englishman Abroad," part of the *Great Performances* series. [episode in a television series]
>
> Did you read William Gibson's "Disneyland with the Death Penalty" when it appeared in *Wired*? [article in a periodical]

Use double quotation marks to enclose a secondary title appearing in a longer italicized (underlined) title. Use single marks for a title within a longer title enclosed in double quotation marks.

Interpretations of "The Secret Sharer"

"Cynicism in Hardy's 'Ah, Are You Digging on My Grave?' "

16d Used sparingly, quotation marks may enclose words intended in a special or ironic sense.

His "gourmet dinner" tasted as if it had come out of a grocer's freezer. [COMPARE His so-called gourmet dinner tasted as if it had come out of a grocer's freezer. The use of *so-called* eliminates the need for quotation marks.]

And I do mean good and evil, not "adjustment and deviance," the gutless language that so often characterizes modern discussions of psychological topics. —CAROL TAVRIS

Either quotation marks or italics can be used in definitions. (See also 10e.)

Ploy means "a strategy used to gain an advantage."

Ploy means *a strategy used to gain an advantage.*

16e Overusing quotation marks detracts from readability.

Quotation marks are not needed in the following cases:

(1) To call attention to a cliché (See 20c.)

Highlighting a cliché in this way emphasizes an unwillingness to think of a fresh expression.

A good debater does not beat around the bush.

(2) To enclose *yes* or *no* in indirect discourse

I have to learn to say no to people who ask me to do more than I should.

(3) To indicate questionable diction

A wimp can't say no to anyone. [Neither *wimp,* a slang term, nor *no* is set off with quotation marks.]

16f Follow American printing conventions for using various marks of punctuation with quoted material.

(1) Comma and period

Generally speaking, commas go inside the closing quotation marks; so do periods if the quotation ends the sentence.

"Lou," she said, "let's go someplace after class."

Aaron declared, "I'm nearly finished with 'The Machine Stops.' "

The period goes at the end of the sentence if other words follow the end of the quotation.

"I don't know why my CD player doesn't work," she said.

The period goes after a parenthetical citation when it follows a quotation that ends a sentence. For example, in MLA-style documentation, a page number in parentheses follows a quotation. (See **38a(1)**.)

In their biography of Bill Gates, *Hard Drive,* Wallace and Erickson explain, "What sustained the company was not

Gates’ ability to write programs, to ‘crank code’. . . ; Gates sustained Microsoft through tireless salesmanship” (152). [The first ellipsis mark appears outside the single quotation mark to show that only a part of the original sentence is quoted. The final period comes after the parenthetical citation.]

For block quotations, see pages 166–67.

(2) Semicolon and colon

Semicolons and colons always go outside the quotation marks.

She spoke of “the gothic tale”; I immediately thought of “The Dunwich Horror”: H. P. Lovecraft’s masterpiece is the epitome of “gothic.”

(3) Question mark, exclamation point, and dash

When a question mark, an exclamation point, or a dash applies only to the quoted matter, it goes inside the quotation marks. When it does not, it goes outside.

Inside the quotation marks:

Pilate asked, “What is truth?”

Gordon replied, “No way!”

“Achievement—success!—” states Heather Evans, “has become a national obsession.”

Why do children keep asking “Why?” [a question within a question—one question mark inside the quotation marks]

Outside the quotation marks:

What is the meaning of the term “half-truth”?

Stop whistling “All I Do Is Dream of You”!

The boss exclaimed, "No one should work for the profit motive!"—no exceptions, I suppose.

Exercise 1

Write a page of dialogue between two friends who are disagreeing about songs or stories. Punctuate the quotations carefully.

Exercise 2

Insert quotation marks where they are needed and change any direct quotations to indirect, any indirect quotations to direct.

1. Have you read Amy Tan's essay Mother Tongue?
2. I was disturbed by the article Who Owns the Law?
3. Andy said, Have people ever asked me Do you revise what you write? Yes, lots of times, and when they do, I tell them that my motto is A writer's work is never done.
4. Here, stoked means fantastically happy on a surfboard.
5. Although running keeps me trim, Claudia claimed, it also gives me energy.
6. In a short story called Everyday Use, Alice Walker explores the meaning of family heritage.
7. Luis explained that he enjoys music the most when he can listen to it when he is alone.
8. Connie said that she thought Mike really lived according to the saying, All I want is more than my share.
9. *Women's Ways of Knowing* begins with a chapter entitled To 21.
10. I recently heard a song titled HTML, a hilarious parody of the old song, YMCA, by the Village People.

Chapter 17

The Period and Other Marks

Periods, question marks, exclamation points, colons, dashes, parentheses, brackets, slashes, and ellipsis points are important in writing and in transferring meaning from spoken to written language. (For use of the hyphen, see 18f.) In the sentences below, the marks in color signal meaning and intonation.

> The days are dark. Why worry? The sun never stops shining!
>
> In *Lady Windermere's Fan* (1892) is this famous line: "I [Lord Darlington] can resist everything except temptation."
>
> According to *Consumer Reports,* "The electronic radio/clock . . . is extremely complicated—enough so to require five pages of instruction in the owner's manual."

Current practice, as dictated in contemporary style manuals (MLA, APA) allows for only one space following all punctuation marks: the period, the question mark, the exclamation point, the colon, the ending parenthesis and bracket, and each of the dots in ellipsis points. No spaces precede or follow the hyphen or dash.

17a Periods punctuate certain sentences and abbreviations.

(1) Use the period to mark the end of a declarative or a mildly imperative sentence.

We are first and foremost fellow human beings. [declarative]

Respect your ethnic heritage. [mild imperative]

"Go home," he ordered. [declarative sentence containing an imperative]

She asks how people can belittle the ethnic heritage of others. [declarative sentence containing an indirect question]

"How can people belittle the ethnic heritage of others?" she asked. [declarative sentence containing a direct quotation]

"I'm as good as you are!" he shouted. [declarative sentence containing an exclamation]

(2) Use periods after some abbreviations.

Dr., Jr.   a.m., p.m.   vs., etc., et al.

Periods are not used with all abbreviations (for example, *MVP, mph, FM*—see chapter 11). When in doubt about whether to punctuate an abbreviation, consult a desk dictionary. Dictionaries often list options, such as *USA* or *U.S.A., CST* or *C.S.T.*

Use only one period after an abbreviation that ends a sentence:

The study was performed by Ben Werthman et al.

17b The question mark occurs after direct (but not indirect) questions.

What in the world is Jennifer doing? [direct question]

They want to know what Jennifer is doing. [indirect question]

Did you hear them ask, "What is Jennifer doing?" [A direct question within a direct question is followed by one question mark inside the closing quotation mark: see chapter 16.]

What is Jennifer doing? dancing? playing? [A series of questions having the same subject and verb can be treated as elliptical; that is, only the first item need include both the subject and verb.]

Declarative sentences sometimes contain direct questions:

He asked, "Did Cisneros publish a collection of stories in 1991?" [Put a question mark inside quotation marks when it concludes a direct question—see 16f(3).]

When we ask ourselves, Why does evil happen? we seek a logical explanation for the irrational. [A question mark follows the interpolated question not enclosed in quotation marks. Capitalize the word beginning a formal question.]

A question mark within parentheses expresses the writer's uncertainty about the correctness of the preceding word, figure, or date.

Chaucer was born in 1340 (?) and died in 1400.

CAUTION Do not write an indirect question as a direct question.

She asked him ~~would~~ he go. [handwritten edits: "if" inserted after "him", "would" inserted after "he"]

17c The exclamation point occurs after an emphatic interjection and after other expressions to show strong emotion, such as surprise or disbelief.

Wow! That was so cool! Amazing!

The comma or period that normally follows a direct quotation is omitted when the quotation has an exclamation point.

"Get off the road!" he yelled.

He yelled, "Get off the road!"

Use the exclamation point sparingly; overuse diminishes its value. A comma is better after mild interjections, and a period is better after mildly exclamatory expressions and mild imperatives.

Oh, look at that cracked windshield.

How quiet the lake was.

Exercise 1

Illustrate the chief uses of the period, the question mark, and the exclamation point by composing and punctuating brief sentences of the types specified.

1. a declarative sentence containing a quoted exclamation (**17a**, **17c**)
2. a mild imperative (**17a**)
3. a direct question (**17b**)
4. a declarative sentence containing an indirect question (**17b**)
5. a declarative sentence containing a direct question (**17b**)

17d The colon calls attention to what follows and separates time and scriptural references and titles and subtitles.

(1) A colon directs attention to what follows: an explanation or summary, a series, or a quotation.

> Surprisingly enough, my first impression of Nairobi was that it was just like any American city: skyscrapers, movie theaters, discos, and crime. —JAY FORD

The colon can introduce a second independent clause that explains or amplifies the first independent one.

> For I had no brain tumor, no eyestrain, no high blood pressure, nothing wrong with me at all: I simply had migraine headaches, and migraine headaches were, as everyone who did not have them knew, imaginary. —JOAN DIDION

Similarly, a colon occasionally follows one sentence to introduce the next.

> The sorrow was laced with violence: In the first week of demolition, vandals struck every night. —*SMITHSONIAN*

Style manuals vary in their instructions on whether to capitalize a complete sentence after a colon. MLA permits the use of a lowercase letter, but APA does not. All style manuals, however, use a capital letter to begin a quoted sentence that follows a colon.

> Claire Safran points out two of the things that cannot be explained: "One of them is poltergeists. Another is teenagers."

Be especially careful not to use an unnecessary colon between a verb and its complement or object, between a preposition and its object, or after *such as*.

Unnecessary Colon The winners were: Asa, Vanna, and Jack.

Use Instead There were three winners: Asa, Vanna, and Jack.

OR

The winners were as follows: Asa, Vanna, and Jack.

OR

The winners were Asa, Vanna, and Jack.

Unnecessary Colon Many vegetarians do not eat dairy products, such as: butter and cheese.

Use Instead Many vegetarians do not eat dairy products, such as butter and cheese.

(2) Use the colon between figures in time references and between titles and subtitles.

We are to be there by 11:30 a.m.

I just read *Women's Ways of Knowing: The Development of Self, Voice and Mind.*

Many writers prefer to use a colon in scriptural references: He quoted from Psalms 3:5. MLA recommends periods (Psalms 3.5), and recent biblical scholarship follows this practice.

(3) Use a colon after the salutation of a business letter.

Dear Dr. D'Angelo: Dear Faustine:

The colon also appears in bibliographic data. (See chapter 38.)

Exercise 2

Punctuate the following sentences by adding colons or semicolons. Put a check mark after those sentences that require no revision.

1. Sandy's difficult semester had a positive effect she enjoyed her summer vacation even more than usual.
2. Only a few of the old houses remain on Starr Street; perhaps none of them do.
3. While visiting my aunt, I met Ronielda and Sarah for the first time we eventually became the best of friends.
4. She found the main character arrogant, insensitive, and extremely interesting.
5. While surfing the Internet, I looked for on-line versions of each of the following books *Always Coming Home, The Dispossessed,* and *The Left Hand of Darkness.*
6. Four cities noted for their tourist appeal are these Paris, Rome, New York, and London.
7. By 730 p.m. he had watched three movies: *First Knight, Casablanca,* and *Raiders of the Lost Ark.*
8. For months she has argued with her parents over this concept animals have the right to live full, pain-free lives.
9. Some students were truly interested in the material others were simply fulfilling a degree requirement.
10. The medication the doctor prescribed caused Mario to experience one negative side effect it made him sleepy.

17e The dash marks a break in thought, sets off a parenthetical element for emphasis or clarity, and sets off an introductory series.

On a keyboard, indicate a dash by two hyphens with no spaces; in handwriting, by an unbroken line the length of two hyphens.

CAUTION Use dashes sparingly, not as easy or automatic substitutes for commas, semicolons, or end marks.

(1) A dash marks a sudden break in thought, an abrupt change in tone, or faltering speech.

A hypocrite is a person who—but who isn't?

—DON MARQUIS

When I was six I made my mother a little hat—out of her new blouse. —LILY DACHÉ

But perhaps Miss—Miss—oh, I can't remember her name—she taught English, I think—Miss Milross? She was one of them. —GARRISON KEILLOR

(2) A dash sets off a parenthetical element for emphasis or (if it contains commas) for clarity.

Local governments—with the encouragement of cable operators—have thrown up nearly insurmountable barriers to the entry of more than one firm into each market.

—JOHN MERLINE

Sentiments that human shyness will not always allow one to convey in conversation—sentiments of gratitude, of apology, of love—can often be more easily conveyed in a letter.

—ARISTIDES

(3) A dash occurs after an introductory list or series.

In the main part of the following sentence, *all* points to or sums up the meaning of the list.

Keen, calculating, perspicacious, acute and astute—I was all of these. —MAX SHULMAN

17f Parentheses set off nonessential matter and enclose characters used for enumeration.

Use parentheses to set off parenthetical, supplementary, or illustrative matter and to enclose figures or letters used for enumeration within a sentence.

> Through the use of the Thematic Apperception Test (TAT) they were able to isolate the psychological characteristic of a *need to achieve*. —MATINA HORNER [first-time use of an acronym in an article: see 11e and the Glossary of Terms]

> Bernard Shaw once demonstrated that, by following the rules (up to a point), we could spell fish this way: ghoti.
> —JOHN IRVING [an explanatory parenthetical expression]

> In contrast, a judgment is subject to doubt if there is any possibility at all (1) of its being challenged in the light of additional or more accurate observations or (2) of its being criticized on the basis of more cogent or more comprehensive reasoning. —MORTIMER J. ADLER [In long sentences especially, enumeration highlights the points.]

In the next example the entire sentence is parenthetical. (See also 9e.)

> If we refuse to talk "like a lady," we are ridiculed and criticized for being unfeminine. ("She thinks like a man" is, at best, a left-handed compliment.) —ROBIN LAKOFF

Use parentheses sparingly; the elements they enclose should still read smoothly in the sentence as a whole.

Dashes, parentheses, commas are all used to set off parenthetical matter, but they express varying degrees of emphasis. Dashes set off parenthetical elements sharply and usually emphasize them:

> But in books like Piri Thomas's *Down These Mean Streets* and Pedro Pietri's *Puerto Rican Obituary,* there was suddenly a literature by Puerto Ricans, in English and decidedly in—and against—the American grain. —JUAN FLORES

Parentheses usually deemphasize the elements they enclose:

> But in books like Piri Thomas's *Down These Mean Streets* and Pedro Pietri's *Puerto Rican Obituary,* there was suddenly a literature by Puerto Ricans, in English and decidedly in (and against) the American grain.

Commas separate elements, usually without emphasizing them:

> But in books like Piri Thomas's *Down These Mean Streets* and Pedro Pietri's *Puerto Rican Obituary,* there was suddenly a literature by Puerto Ricans, in English and decidedly in, and against, the American grain.

17g Brackets set off interpolations in quoted matter and replace parentheses within parentheses. (See also 16a(3).)

> The *Home Herald* printed the beginning of the mayor's speech "My dear fiends [sic] and fellow citizens." [A bracketed *sic*—meaning "thus"—tells the reader that the error appears in the original.]
>
> Deems Taylor has written, "Not for a single moment did he [Richard Wagner] compromise with what he believed, with what he dreamed." [An unclear pronoun reference is explained by the bracketed material.]
>
> Not every expert agrees. (See, for example, Malachi Martin's *Rich Church, Poor Church* [New York: Putnam's, 1984].)

17h The slash occurs between terms to indicate that either term is applicable and also marks line divisions in quoted poetry.

A slash is used unspaced between terms, but with a space before and after it between lines of poetry.

> Equally rare is a first-rate adventure story designed for those who enjoy a smartly told tale that isn't steeped in blood and/or sex. —JUDITH CHRIST

> When in "Mr. Flood's Party" the hero sets down his jug at his feet "as a mother lays her sleeping child/Down tenderly, fearing it may awake," one feels Robinson's heart to be quite simply on his sleeve. —WILLIAM H. PITCHARD

Extensive use of the slash to indicate that either of two terms is applicable (as in *and/or, he/she*) can make writing choppy.

Exercise 3

Punctuate each of the following sentences by supplying commas, dashes, parentheses, brackets, or slashes. Prepare to explain the reason for all marks you add, especially those you choose for setting off parenthetical matter.

1. Loyalty, courtesy, and courtly love these were the most important concepts for chivalric knights.
2. In the ten years between 1960 and 1970, two of the city's biggest buildings were erected downtown The Tower of Freedom 1961 and the Municipal Auditorium 1967.
3. A car's optional features an automatic transmission instead of a standard one a CD player instead of a factory radio power windows instead of manually operated ones can increase its price.

4. Many Italian sauces for example pizza sauce and marinara sauce require tomatoes and garlic as ingredients.
5. Two of my favorite programs news and sports round-up were shown on Friday night at 7:00 p.m. and 8:00 p.m. respectively.
6. This strange vague statement appeared in the entertainment section of the local newspaper: Because of an unforeseen technical problum sic this evening's main feature will be delayed by one hour.
7. She's a woman who has it all a job, a family, and an education.
8. What I really hate about this job she began but she stopped when the boss stepped into the room.
9. A trip to the dentist which many people fear can be a relatively painless experience.
10. It was Shakespeare or was it his character Polonius who said "To thine own self be true."

17i Ellipsis points (three equally spaced periods) mark an omission from a quoted passage or a reflective pause or hesitation.

(1) Ellipsis points mark an omission within a quoted passage.

Original To bring rowing to minorities, it's important to first understand why they aren't rowing. The first clue is that not long ago programs spent as much energy keeping minorities out of rowing as they now expend to attract them.

—TINA FISHER FORDE

Omission within a quoted sentence

> Noting that "programs spent . . . energy keeping minorities out of rowing," Tina Fisher Forde explains one reason for the small numbers of minorities in rowing.

Omission at the beginning or end of a quoted sentence

Neither ellipsis points (nor capitals) are used at the beginning of a quotation, whether it is run in to the text or set off in a block.

An omission at the end of the quoted sentence that coincides with the end of your sentence requires a period in addition to the three ellipsis points, with no space immediately after the last word in the sentence. In a parenthetical reference, the period comes after the second parenthesis instead.

> Tina Fisher Forde claims that in the past rowing programs worked hard at "keeping minorities out of rowing. . . ." [OR rowing . . ." (19).]

Omission of a sentence or more

A period before ellipsis points (that is, four dots) marks omissions within a quoted passage if a complete sentence stands on either side of the ellipsis. Also, a period before ellipsis points marks the omission of a sentence or more (even a paragraph or more) within a quoted passage. If the quoted material ends with a question mark or exclamation point, three ellipsis points are added and the mark is retained.

Original There's an uncertainty in our minds about the engineering principle of an elevator. We've all had little glimpses into the dirty, dark elevator shaft and seen the greasy cables passing each other. They never look totally safe. The idea of

> being trapped in a small box going up and down on strings induces a kind of phobia in all of us.
> —ANDREW A. ROONEY

Of the common fear of riding in an elevator, Andrew A. Rooney writes, "We've all had little glimpses into the dirty, dark elevator shaft. . . . The idea of being trapped in a small box going up and down on strings induces a kind of phobia in all of us." [Thirteen words have been omitted from the original, but a sentence comes before and after the period and ellipsis points.]

Andrew A. Rooney writes about the fear of riding in an elevator: "We've all had little glimpses into the dirty, dark elevator shaft and seen the greasy cables passing each other. . . . The idea of being trapped in a small box going up and down on strings induces a kind of phobia in all of us." [Five words have been omitted from the original, all in a single sentence.]

To indicate the omission of a full line or more in quoted poetry, use spaced periods covering the length either of the line above it or of the omitted line.

> I love people who harness themselves, an ox to a heavy cart,
> who pull like water buffalo, with massive patience,
> . . . .
> who do what has to be done, again and again.
> —MARGE PIERCY

(2) Although ellipsis points can mark a reflective pause or hesitation, they should not be overused.

Love, like other emotions, has causes . . . and consequences. —LAWRENCE CASTER

Ellipsis points to show a pause can also come after the period at the end of a sentence:

All channels are open. The meditation is about to begin. . . .
—TOM ROBBINS

Exercise 4

Punctuate the following sentences by supplying appropriate end marks, commas, colons, dashes, and parentheses. Do not use unnecessary punctuation. Be prepared to explain the reason for each mark you add, especially when you have a choice of correct marks (for example, commas, dashes, or parentheses).

1. I keep remembering what my father used to say jokingly "Some day you'll grow up and have kids who will treat you the way you treat me"
2. For his birthday Matthew requested the following gifts a Spider Man action figure a water gun some new athletic shoes
3. "Good and" can mean "very" "I am good and mad" and "a hot cup of coffee" means that the coffee not the cup is hot
4. Many small country towns are very similar a truck stop a gas station a crowded diner
5. Gretchen, Jordan's best friend, sat at the back of the church where she wouldn't be seen and cried quietly and softly through the entire wedding
6. As my grandmother used to say "Love trust and considerate behavior are all necessary for a good marriage"
7. I imagine that the tickets will seem expensive to all my friends employed or unemployed who want to go to the Lollapalooza concert
8. "Is he is he okay" I stammered
9. She believed the best way to age gracefully was to look at the world through a child's eyes not to act like a child
10. "Mark" I yelled "Mark how could you have done such a thing" I tried to hurry out the door before he could respond but he caught up with me

Spelling and Diction

Chapter 18

Spelling, the Spell Checker, and Hyphenation

Spelling problems are highly visible, and misspellings may make a reader doubt whether the writer can present information clearly and correctly. Therefore, always proofread to detect misspellings or typographic errors. (See 33d.)

People often feel that they no longer need to worry about spelling since computers have spell checkers to correct errors. While a spell checker can be helpful, it does not solve all spelling problems. For example, the computer cannot tell when you confuse such words as *principal* and *principle* because it cannot know which meaning is called for.

In addition, there are times when you will be writing in-class papers or essay exams. Spelling errors in such situations can give your reader a poor initial impression and cause your work to be taken less seriously, or your grade to be lowered. So a basic knowledge of spelling is always important.

One way to improve spelling is to record the words you have misspelled and study them. Another way is to develop your own tricks to help you remember. For example, you might remember the spelling of "separate" by reminding yourself that it has "a rat" in it or the spelling of "attendance" by remembering that it includes "dance."

If you have doubts about spelling, consult your dictionary. Watch for restrictive labels such as *British* or *chiefly British*. In general, use the American form.

American	theater	fertilize	color	connection
British	theatre	fertilise	colour	connexion

In ordinary writing, do not use spellings labeled *obsolete* or *archaic, dialectal* or *regional, nonstandard* or *slang.*

Not	afeard	heighth	chaw	boughten
But	afraid	height	chew	bought

If your dictionary lists two unlabeled alternatives, either form is correct—for example, *fulfill* or *fulfil, symbolic* or *symbolical.* The first option listed is usually the more common form.

18a Spelling often does not reflect pronunciation.

Many words in English are not spelled as they are pronounced, so we often cannot rely on pronunciation for correct spelling. One trick you might use is to be aware of how the word would sound if it were pronounced as it is spelled. Following is a list of such words with the trouble spots boldfaced.

accident**al**ly	congra**tu**lations	gover**n**ment	**per**spire
a**th**lete	Feb**r**uary	mod**er**n	re**al**tor
can**d**idate	gen**er**ally	nu**cle**ar	stren**gth**

Many unaccented syllables have acquired a neutral vowel sound, usually an indistinct *uh* sound in spoken English, although the spelling can use any one of the vowels (*a*, *e*, *i*, *o*, *u*). In your dictionary, this neutral vowel sound is represented by a special symbol /ə/ called a *schwa,* as in *confidence,* /'kän-fə-dən(t)s/.

It is sometimes helpful to think of the spelling of the root word as a guide to correct spelling.

confidence, confide	exultation, exult
different, differ	indomitable, dominate

A word that is difficult to spell, such as *often,* sometimes has alternate pronunciations (ôf'ən, ôf'tən). Of these, one might be a better guide to spelling. Here are examples of other such words.

everybody	literature	veteran
interest	sophomore	which

CAUTION Words like *and, than,* and *have* are often not stressed in speech and are thus misspelled. A spell checker will not catch these misspellings.

> I would ~~of~~ *have* preferred fish rather ~~then~~ *than* soup ~~an~~ *and* salad.

18b When words sound alike but have different meanings, the spelling determines the meaning.

Words such as *forth* and *fourth* or *sole* and *soul* are homophones: They sound alike but have vastly different meanings and spellings. Be careful to choose the right word for your context. A spell checker will not catch such errors.

Many frequently confused spellings can be studied in groups.

(1) Contractions and possessive pronouns

It's my turn next.	Each group waits **its** turn.
You're next.	**Your** turn is next.
There's no difference.	**Theirs** is no different.

(See 15b and 15d.)

(2) Single words and two-word phrases

A number of words function both as single words and as two-word phrases with different meanings. The following are examples of such words.

He wore **everyday** clothes.	He wears them **every day**.
Maybe we will go.	We **may be** going.
You ran **into** my car.	We can run **in to** check it.
Nobody was there.	The police found **no body**.

Other examples are *anymore, any more; awhile, a while; everybody, every body; everyone, every one*.

CAUTION *A lot* and *all right* are still spelled as two words; *alot* and *alright* are considered incorrect, although *alright* is often used in journalistic and business writing. (See the Glossary of Usage.)

(3) Singular nouns ending in *-nce* and plural nouns ending in *-nts*

Assistance is available.	I have two **assistants**.
For **instance**, *Jack can go.*	*They arrived* **instants** *ago.*
My **patience** *is frayed.*	*Some* **patients** *waited for hours.*

The following list contains words that sound exactly alike (*break/brake*), ones that sound alike in certain dialects (*horse/hoarse*), and ones that are similar in sound, especially in rapid speech (*believe/belief*), but are different in meaning. The spell checker cannot identify words that are correctly spelled but wrongly used. In general, the words listed here present common spelling rather than usage problems. You probably understand the distinction in meaning between the terms in most of the following pairs but sometimes confuse the spelling because they sound so much alike. If you are unsure about the difference in meaning between any pair of words, consult the Glossary of Usage, the Index, or your dictionary.

WORDS WHOSE SPELLINGS ARE FREQUENTLY CONFUSED

accept, except
access, excess
adapt, adopt
advice, advise
affect, effect
aisles, isles
alley, ally
allude, elude
already, all ready
altar, alter
altogether, all together
always, all ways
amoral, immoral
angel, angle
ante-, anti-
ascent, assent
ask, ax
assistance, assistants
baring, barring, bearing
began, begin
believe, belief
board, bored
break, brake
breath, breathe
buy, by, bye
canvas, canvass
capital, capitol
censor, censure, sensor
choose, chose
cite, site, sight
clothes, cloths
coarse, course

complement, compliment
conscience, conscious
council, counsel
cursor, curser
dairy, diary
decent, descent, dissent
desert, dessert
device, devise
discreet, discrete
dominant, dominate
dyeing, dying
elicit, illicit
emigrate, immigrate
envelop, envelope
fair, fare
faze, phase
fine, find
formerly, formally
forth, fourth
forward, foreword
gorilla, guerrilla
have, of
hear, here
heard, herd
heroin, heroine
hole, whole
holy, wholly
horse, hoarse
human, humane
idea, ideal
instance, instants
its, it's
knew, new
later, latter
lay, lie (see 7b)
lead, led
lessen, lesson
lightning, lightening
lose, loose
marital, martial
maybe, may be
midst, mist
minor, miner
moral, morale
of, off
passed, past
patience, patients
peace, piece
persecute, prosecute
personal, personnel
perspective, prospective
plain, plane
pray, prey
precede, proceed
predominant, predominate
presence, presents
principle, principal
prophecy, prophesy
purpose, propose
quiet, quit, quite

raise, rise (see 7b)
respectfully, respectively
right, rite, write
road, rode
sat, set (see 7b)
sense, since
shown, shone
stationary, stationery
straight, strait
than, then
their, there, they're, there're
threw, through, thorough
throne, thrown
to, too, two
tract, track
waist, waste
weak, week
weather, whether
were, wear, where, we're
which, witch
who's, whose
your, you're

18c Adding a prefix to a base word changes the meaning.

Prefixes are added to the beginning of the base word, called the root.

necessary, unnecessary   moral, immoral

No letter is added or dropped when a prefix is added. These misspellings are usually detected by a spell checker.

18d Adding a suffix may require changing the spelling of the base word.

Suffixes are added to the end of the base word.

resist, resistant   beauty, beautiful

Spelling, however, is irregular and follows certain conventions. These misspellings are usually detected by a spell checker.

(1) Dropping or retaining a final unpronounced *e*

A word ending in an unpronounced *e* drops the final *e* before a suffix beginning with a vowel.

bride, brid**al**	combine, combin**ation**
come, com**ing**	prime, prim**ary**

A word ending in an unpronounced *e* retains the final *e* before a suffix beginning with a consonant.

rude, rude**ness**	entire, entire**ly**
sure, sure**ly**	place, place**ment**

Some exceptions are *likable, ninth, truly, duly, awful, wholly*.

To keep the /s/ sound in *ce* or the /j/ sound in *ge*, do not drop the final *e* before *-able* or *-ous*:

notice**able** manage**able** courage**ous**

(2) Doubling a final consonant before a suffix

Double the final consonant before a suffix beginning with a vowel if (a) the consonant ends a one-syllable word or a stressed syllable and (b) the consonant is preceded by a single vowel.

drop, dro**pping**	BUT	droop, drooping
admit, admi**tted**	BUT	figure, figured

(3) Changing or retaining a final *y* before a suffix

Change the *y* to *i* before suffixes—except *-ing*.

defy: defies, defied, defiance BUT defying
modify: modifies, modifier, modified BUT modifying

Most verbs ending in *y* preceded by a vowel do not change the *y* before *-s* or *-ed*: *stay, stays, stayed*. Similarly, nouns like *joys* or *days* retain the *y* before *-s*. The following irregularities in spelling are especially troublesome: *lays, laid; pays, paid; says, said*.

(4) Retaining a final *l* before *-ly*

usual, usually real, really cool, coolly
formal, formally

Exercise 1

Add the designated suffixes to the following words.

EXAMPLES

-er, -ness, -ly: late	*later, lateness, lately*
-ing, -ed: rebel	*rebelling, rebelled*
-ing: lose, guide, rise	*losing, guiding, rising*

1. -ous: courage, continue
2. -ly: like, sure, safe
3. -ing, -ed, -ance: admit
4. -ment, -ed, -ing: manage
5. -able: notice, manage, desire
6. -ed, -ing, -ment: conceal
7. -ing, -ed, -ful: care, use, hope
8. -ing, -ed, -er: play, jog
9. -ed, -ing, -ly: complete
10. -ed, -ing: pay, plan

(5) Adding *-s* or *-es* to form the plural of nouns

Form the plural of most nouns by adding *-s* to the singular.

toys scientists tables

the Smiths [proper names], sisters-in-law [chief word pluralized]

For nouns ending in an *f* or *fe,* change the ending to *ve* before adding *-s* when the plural changes from an *f* sound to a *v* sound: *thief, thieves; life, lives;* BUT *roof, roofs.*

For nouns ending in *s, z, ch, sh,* or *x,* add *-es* when the plural adds another syllable.

box, boxes peach, peaches crash, crashes

the Rodriguezes

For nouns ending in *y* preceded by a consonant, add *-es* after changing the *y* to *i*:

company, companies ninety, nineties

Although usage varies, for most nouns ending in *o* preceded by a consonant, add *-es*. Consult a dictionary if you have a question.

echoes heroes potatoes vetoes [*-es* only]

autos memos pimentos pros [*-s* only]

Some words, like *nos/noes*, *mottos/mottoes*, and *zeros/zeroes*, can add *-s* or *-es*.

Certain irregular nouns, including retained foreign spellings, do not add *-s* or *-es* to form the plural. Again, the dictionary will answer your questions.

Singular	woman	goose	analysis	datum	species
Plural	women	geese	analyses	data	species

Singular	criterion	alumnus	alumna
Plural	criteria	alumni	alumnae

Exercise 2

Supply plural forms (including any optional spellings) for the following words. If a word is not covered by the rules, use your dictionary.

1. half	6. theory	11. passer-by	16. bush
2. speech	7. radius	12. halo	17. hero
3. phenomenon	8. bath	13. tomato	18. Kelly
4. woman	9. story	14. leaf	19. church
5. potato	10. genius	15. scarf	20. life

18e *Ei* and *ie* are often confused.

When the sound is /ē/ (as in *me*), write *ie* except after *c*, in which case write *ei*.

chief yield priest
[BUT after *c*] receive perceive conceit

When the sound is other than /ē/, you should usually write *ei*:

eight heir rein their weight foreign

Some exceptions include *either, neither, friend,* and *species.*

18f Hyphens both link and divide words.

Hyphens link, or make a compound of, two or more words that function as a single word and divide words at the end of a line.

(1) Linking two or more words to form a compound that functions as a single word

Nouns We planted forget-me-nots and Johnny-jump-ups.

Verbs He speed-read the paper. I double-checked.
He hard-boiled the egg.

Some compounds are conventionally connected with hyphens (*eye-opener, cross-examine*), others are written separately (*eye chart, cross fire*), and still others are written as one word (*eyewitness, crossbreed*). When in doubt, consult your dictionary.

CAUTION Do not confuse the hyphen with the dash, which is keyboarded as a double hyphen with no spaces before and after. (See 17c.)

Hyphenate two or more words serving as a single adjective before a noun. (See also 1c(2).)

a well-built house [COMPARE a house that is well built]

He has that get-it-done, make-it-happen attitude.

In a series, hyphens can carry over from one item to the next.

eighteenth- and nineteenth-century houses

Omit the hyphen in the following cases.

(a) after an adverb ending in *-ly* (*quickly frozen foods*),
(b) in chemical terms (*sodium chloride solution*), and
(c) in a modifier using a letter or numeral as the second element (*group C homes, type IV virus*).

Hyphenate spelled-out fractions and compound numbers from twenty-one to ninety-nine (or twenty-first to ninety-ninth).

one-eighth eighty-four twenty-third

Also hyphenate combinations of figures and letters (*mid-1990s*) as well as ZIP codes that include the additional four digits (Dallas, TX *75392-0041*).

Hyphenate to avoid ambiguity or an awkward combination of letters or syllables between a prefix and root or a suffix and root.

re-sign the petition [COMPARE "resign the position"]

Hyphenate the prefixes *ex-* ("former"), *self-*, and *all-;* the suffix *-elect;* and a prefix with a capitalized word.

president-elect   ex-husband   all-important   self-made
non-British   anti-American   mid-August

Exercise 3

Refer to **18f(1)** and to your dictionary as you convert each phrase (or words in each phrase) to a compound or to a word with a prefix. Use hyphens when needed.

EXAMPLES

a movie lasting two hours	a two-hour movie
glasses used for water	water glasses

1. an antique couch covered in velvet
2. a brush for teeth
3. diplomats who solve problems
4. in the shape of an O
5. a house twenty years old
6. a garage for three cars
7. a holiday lasting four days
8. a light used at night
9. a highway with four lanes
10. light bulbs costing ten dollars

(2) Breaking a word at the end of a line with a hyphen

If you must divide a word at the end of a line, use a hyphen to separate syllables. In dictionaries, dots usually divide words into syllables: **re · al · ly, pre · fer, pref · er · ence, sell · ing, set · ting.** But not every division between syllables is an appropriate place for dividing a word. The following principles are useful guidelines.

Do not divide abbreviations, initials, capitalized acronyms, or one-syllable words.

p.m. [NOT p.-m.]   USAF [NOT US-AF]

UNESCO [NOT UNES-CO]   through [NOT thr-ough]

Do not create one-letter syllables by putting the first or last letter of a word at the end or beginning of a line.

omit   able   boa

~~o-mit~~   ~~a-ble~~   ~~bo-a~~

Do not put the last two letters of a word at the beginning of a line.

dated   doesn't   safely   gravel   taxis

~~dat-ed~~   ~~does-n't~~   ~~safe-ly~~   ~~grav-el~~   ~~tax-is~~

Divide hyphenated words only at the hyphen.

mass-| produce

father-| in-law   OR   father-in-| law

Divide words between two consonants that come between vowels—except when the division does not reflect pronunciation.

pic-| nic   dis-| cuss   thun-| der   BUT   co-| bra

Divide words between those consonants that you double when adding *-ing*.

set-| ting   jam-| ming   plan-| ning

[COMPARE sell-| ing]

Exercise 4

Write a list of five cues that help you remember certain difficult spellings. Share your devices with other members of the class.

Exercise 5

Edit the following paragraph for misspellings and correct usage of the hyphen.

[1]My friends and I recently watched *First-Knight,* a movie that is principly located in the make believe city of Camelot. [2]Of course, we had all heard the story of Lancelot and Guinevere, too of the most famous lovers in all of fiction, and their troubled relationship with King Arthur. [3]Despite this fact, we liked the movie because it successfully communicatid the various phenomena associated with the conflict between love and loyalty. [4]One scene in which this conflict is most readyly apparent occurs after Guinevere marries Arthur. [5]When her former home is attacked, Guinevere becomes concerned for her family's safety and, not surprisingly, both men come to her rescue: Arthur, because Guinevere is his wife and because he loves her; and Lancelot, because Arthur is his king and because he also loves Guinevere. [6]Fortunately, Arthur's military strategies and Lancelot's individual prowess lead to the invaders' defeat, even if only temporarily, proving that victory depends not on the sighs of an army, but on its skill and cooperation. [7]In fact, all of the issues concerning love and loyalty portrayed in the movie's storyline are timeless ones and will be as important in the twenty first century as they were in the eighth. [8]Nevertheless, although the film maker did a good job of conveying such significant issues, some of my friends didn't like the fact that the costumes worn by the actors and actresses were historically inaccerate.

Chapter 19 Good Usage

There is a difference between the words used in informal writing and conversation (colloquialisms) and the more formal language appropriate for college and business writing. In speech, you use dialect words or words that only persons from your own area, profession, or generation might understand. In writing, select words that are meaningful to the members of your audience.

A thesaurus, which alerts you to possible synonyms, is an important aid to writing. A dictionary, however, is indispensable to alert you to subtle differences in meaning. In addition to furnishing the meaning of a word, a dictionary also provides its pronunciation, its part of speech, and the forms of plurals and verb tenses. Although a dictionary includes words appropriate for both speech and formal writing, it also includes usage labels and short usage paragraphs to distinguish between the two. Words labeled **dialect**, **slang**, or **non-** or **substandard**, as well as words no longer in common use labeled **archaic** or **obsolete**, are usually inappropriate for edited American English. If a word has no label, it is acceptable. (See the **Glossary of Usage**.)

Dictionaries

It helps to have ready access to a good, recent desk dictionary such as one of those listed below. The date is important because language is constantly changing. Many desk dictionaries are available either in paperback or on CD-ROM, both of which usually include the same information. The pocket version, which is useful for spelling and a quick definition, omits important information on usage and derivation.

The American Heritage Dictionary

Funk & Wagnalls Standard College Dictionary

The Random House Dictionary

Webster's New World Dictionary

Merriam Webster's Collegiate Dictionary

Occasionally you may need to refer to an unabridged or a special dictionary.

Unabridged dictionaries

The Oxford English Dictionary. 2nd ed. 20 vols. 1989–.

Webster's Third New International Dictionary of the English Language. 1986.

Special dictionaries

Bryson, Bill. *The Facts on File Dictionary of Troublesome Words*. 1985, 1987.

Cowie, A. P., and R. Mackin. *Oxford Dictionary of Current Idiomatic English*. Vols. 1–2. 1975, 1983.

Follett, Wilson. *Modern American Usage: A Guide*. 1966.

Morris, William, and Mary Morris. *Harper Dictionary of Contemporary Usage*. 2nd ed. 1985.

Onions, C. T. *Oxford Dictionary of English Etymology*. 1966.

Partridge, Eric. *Dictionary of Catch Phrases*. Rev. ed. 1986.

———. *Dictionary of Slang and Unconventional English*. 8th ed. 1984.

Roget's International Thesaurus. 4th ed. 1977.

Webster's Collegiate Thesaurus. 1976.

Webster's Dictionary of English Usage. 1989.

ESL The following dictionaries are recommended for nonnative English speakers.

Longman Dictionary of Contemporary English, 1987. (*Longman Dictionary of American English*, 1983, is the American abridgment.)

Longman Dictionary of English Language and Culture, 1992.

The Newbury House Dictionary of American English, 1996.

Oxford Advanced Learner's Dictionary, 1989. (*Oxford ESL Dictionary*, 1994, is the American edition.)

Two excellent resources for ESL students are the following:

Longman Language Activator, 1993. (This book supplies definitions, usage, and sample sentences: a cross between a dictionary and a thesaurus.)

Swan, Michael. *Practical English Usage*, 1995. (This is a practical reference guide to problems encountered by users of English as a second language.)

Inexpensive collections that include a dictionary, thesaurus, usage guide, and certain other reference works are beginning to be available on a single CD-ROM disk.

CAUTION Most word processing programs also include a thesaurus. When using a computer thesaurus, do not merely substitute one word for another without understanding subtle differences in meaning. In listing synonyms, dictionaries often point out such distinctions.

19a Dictionaries provide information beyond the definition of a word.

Reading the introductory material and noting the meaning of any special abbreviations will help you understand the information your dictionary provides. The following sample entry from the 10th edition of *Merriam Webster's Collegiate Dictionary* provides important information. Almost all desk dictionaries provide the same information, although possibly in a different order. *Answer* is listed twice in the following entries—first as a noun and then as a verb.

Part of speech — Pronunciation — Syllabication — Origin — Spelling — Date of first occurrence — Usage of definition #3 — vb. forms

[1]**an·swer** \'an(t)-sər\ *n* [ME, fr. OE *andswaru* (akin to ON *andsvar* answer); akin to OE *and-* against, *swerian* to swear — more at ANTE-] (bef. 12c) **1 a** : something spoken or written in reply to a question **b** : a correct response **2** : a reply to a legal charge or suit : PLEA; *also* : DEFENSE **3** : something done in response or reaction ⟨his only ~ was to walk out⟩ **4** : a solution of a problem **5** : one that imitates, matches, or corresponds to another ⟨television's ~ to the news magazines⟩

[2]**answer** *vb* **an·swered; an·swer·ing** \'an(t)s-riŋ, 'an(t)-sə-\ *vi* (bef. 12c) **1** : to speak or write in reply **2 a** : to be or make oneself responsible or accountable **b** : to make amends : ATONE **3** : to be in conformity or correspondence ⟨~*ed* to the description⟩ **4** : to act in response to an action performed elsewhere or by another **5** : to be adequate : SERVE ~ *vt* **1 a** : to speak or write in reply to **b** : to say or write by way of reply **2** : to reply in rebuttal, justification, or explana-

tion 3 a : to correspond to ⟨~*s* the description⟩ b : to be adequate or usable for : FULFILL 4 *obs* : to atone for 5 : to act in response to ⟨~*ed* the call to arms⟩ 6 : to offer a solution for; *esp* : SOLVE—**an·swer·er** \'an(t)-sər-ər\ *n*

syn ANSWER, RESPOND, REPLY, REJOIN, RETORT mean to say, write, or do something in return. ANSWER implies the satisfying of a question, demand, call, or need ⟨*answered* all the questions⟩. RESPOND may suggest an immediate or quick reaction ⟨*responded* eagerly to a call for volunteers⟩. REPLY implies making a return commensurate with the original question or demand ⟨an invitation that requires you to *reply*⟩. REJOIN often implies sharpness or quickness in answering ⟨"who asked you?" she *rejoined*⟩. RETORT suggests responding to an explicit charge or criticism by way of retaliation ⟨he *retorted* to the attack with biting sarcasm⟩.

Synonyms and distinctions with usage examples

Spelling, syllabication, and pronunciation

The dictionary describes both written and spoken language. You can check spelling and word division (syllabication) as well as pronunciation of unfamiliar words. A key to sound symbols appears at the bottom of the entry pages and also in the introduction. Alternative pronunciations usually represent regional differences.

Parts of speech and inflected forms

The dictionary also labels the possible uses of words in sentences—for instance, *tr. v., adj*. It identifies the various ways that nouns, verbs, and modifiers change form to indicate number, tense, and comparison.

Word origin/etymology

The origin of a word—also called its derivation or etymology—can be useful in understanding its meaning and in realizing the many cultures that have influenced, and continue to influence, the English language.

Date of first occurrence

The date (*bef. 12c*) in parentheses in the above sample is the first known occurrence of the word in written English.

Definitions

Definitions are listed in different order in different dictionaries. The sample above lists the oldest meaning first. Often they are ordered according to how common they are.

Usage

Most dictionaries give guidance on usage through discussion and quotations showing how the word has been used in context.

Synonyms

Dictionaries always list synonyms, sometimes with detailed explanations of subtle differences in meaning. When discussions such as the one in the above sample are used in conjunction with a thesaurus, they are extremely helpful. The entry for the word *answer* lists five one-word synonyms. The entry for each one-word synonym has a cross-reference to the entry for *answer*.

Exercise 1

Study the pronunciations of the following common words in your dictionary and determine how you might pronounce them in your own region. Be prepared to discuss your pronunciations with your classmates, whose pronunciations may differ.

1. news 2. which 3. either 4. wash 5. orange

Exercise 2

Study the definitions for the following pairs of words, and write a sentence for each pair to illustrate the subtle differences in meaning.

1. clemency-mercy
2. provoke-excite
3. vampire-necrophile
4. ingenuous-innocent
5. putrefy-rot
6. courageous-fearless
7. charm-charisma
8. practicable-viable
9. liberate-free
10. sensuous-sensual

19b Colloquial or informal

Words labeled **colloquial** or **informal** are common to speech and used by writers in dialogue and informal writing. Such words may be used for special effect in college writing, but in general unlabeled words are preferred.

Informal	dopey	belly button
Formal	stupid	navel

Although contractions, such as *it's* and *aren't,* are common in English, they are sometimes considered inappropriate for academic writing.

ESL If you are confused about the correct form of contractions, it is acceptable not to use them.

19c Slang

Slang is usually defined as words belonging to a particular age group, locality, or profession. Slang, in fact, covers a wide range of words that are variously considered breezy, racy, excessively informal, facetious, or taboo. Sometimes they are newly coined or highly technical. Slang is usually avoided in college writing, however, because it can easily become dated or is meaningless to your readers.

19d Regionalisms

Regional or dialectal usages are normally avoided in writing outside the region where they are current since their meaning may not be widely known. Speakers and writers can safely use regional words known to the audience they are addressing, however.

19e Nonstandard and substandard

Words and expressions labeled nonstandard or substandard should not be used in formal writing, except possibly in direct quotations. For example, *ain't* should not be used for *am not*, nor should "He done ate" be used for "He has already eaten."

19f Archaic and obsolete

All dictionaries list words (and meanings for words) that have long since passed out of general use. Such words as *rathe* (early) and *yestreen* (last evening) are still found in dictionaries because they occur in our older literature and so must be defined for the modern reader.

A number of obsolete or archaic words—such as *worser* (for *worse*) or *holp* (for *helped*)—are still in use but are now nonstandard.

19g Technical words

In writing for the general reader, avoid all unnecessary technical language. The careful writer will not refer to an organized way to find a subject for writing as a *heuristic* or a need for bifocals as *presbyopia*. Of course, the greater precision of technical language makes it desirable when the audience can understand it, as when one physician writes to another.

Jargon is technical language tailored specifically for a particular occupation. Technical language can be an efficient shortcut for specialized concepts, but you should use jargon only when you can be sure that both you and your readers understand it.

19h A clear, straightforward style is preferable to an ornate one.

An ornate or flowery style makes reading slow and calls attention to your words rather than your ideas. Although different styles are appropriate for different situations—depending, for example, on purpose, audience, and occasion (32a)—you should usually keep your writing simple and straightforward.

Ornate The majority believes that the approbation of society derives primarily from diligent pursuit of allocated tasks.

Simple Most people believe that success results from hard work.

ESL American rhetoric derives many of its principles from the work of philosophers in classical Greece and Rome who advocated a plain, straightforward style. In other cultures shaped by different traditions, being direct and straightforward might be considered rude, but this is not the case in the United States. If you feel that you are being rude when you write straightforward English, consider your word choice and your tone (33a). By making careful choices, it is possible to be both straightforward and polite.

Exercise 3

Rewrite the following passages for a friendly audience that likes a simple, straightforward style.

1. Expert delineation of the characters in a work of fiction is a task that is difficult to facilitate.
2. In an employment situation, social pleasantries may contribute to the successful functioning of job tasks, but such interactions should not distract attention from the need to complete all assignments in a timely manner.
3. Commitment to an ongoing and carefully programmed schedule of physical self-management can be a significant resource for stress reduction.
4. The Center for Automotive Maintenance recommends regular monitoring of fluids necessary for internal combustion vehicles and increasing the allocation level of such fluids when necessary.
5. Students troubled by dysfunctions in interpersonal relationships can receive support from information specialists in the counseling division of health services.

19i Inclusive language

Making language inclusive (that is, avoiding sexist language) means treating men and women equally. For example, many feel that women are excluded when *man* is used to refer to both men and women.

Man's achievements in the twentieth century are impressive.

Also, avoid stereotyping sex roles—for example, assuming that all nurses are women and all doctors are men.

Inappropriate	**Appropriate**
authoress	author
the common man	the average person, ordinary people
lady doctor	doctor
male nurse	nurse
mankind	humanity, human beings, people
policeman	police officer
weatherman	meteorologist, weather forecaster
Have your *mother* send a snack.	Have your **parent** send a snack.
The law should prohibit someone with a drinking problem from driving *his* car.	The law should prohibit someone with a drinking problem from driving **a** car.
My *girl* will call the members.	My **assistant** will call the members.
The professors and their *wives* attended.	The professors and their **spouses** attended.

Exercise 4

Make the following sentences inclusive by eliminating all sexist language.

1. She was a published authoress as well as a fine actress.
2. The reporter interviewed President Berrier and his secretary, Rosa Gonzales.
3. Both Louise, a skilled pianist, and Erik, a handsome man, played with the local symphony last Friday night.
4. The ladies took a tour of the city while the executive managers met for a business conference.
5. The repairman came to fix the refrigerator.
6. My uncle has never married and his sister is a spinster.
7. Rosalind is a stay-at-home mom.
8. The guest list included the corporate executives and their wives.
9. If everyone realizes his personal potential, society will prosper.
10. These students are particularly interested in studying mankind and his technological advancements.

Exercise 5

Make a list of ten words or phrases that you would ordinarily consider informal and prepare for a class discussion on whether you would use them (a) in a job interview, (b) in a conversation with a friend, (c) in a conversation with one of the deans, (d) in a letter of application, or (e) in an essay. Check your dictionary to see how each word is labeled.

Exercise 6

Rewrite the following paragraph in standard English appropriate for a paper in an English composition class. Consult the **Glossary of Usage** or a dictionary to determine appropriate usages.

[1]I've been blessed by having a large amount of friends throughout my life, but as far as friends go, Melinda is one of the best. [2]We've had alot of fun together through

the years. [3]Several years ago, however, I found a job where I could move up the ladder of success, so I moved away, knowing that Melinda and myself would keep in touch. [4]Even though my leaving saddened us both, it didn't effect our basic friendship at all. [5]We write to each other most every week, and not long ago, I made a surprise visit to her, and I stayed for a week. [6]If she had known I was arriving that afternoon, she would have taken off of work to meet me at the airport. [7]Even though we stay in touch, I still miss her; hopefully we'll be able to see each other again soon.

Chapter 20

Exactness

Good writing often consists of short, familiar words precisely used. When drafting (chapter 32), choose words that express your ideas and feelings. When revising (chapter 33), make those words exact, idiomatic, and fresh. Use the words you already know effectively, but add to your vocabulary to increase your options for choosing the exact word that suits your purpose, audience, and occasion. Make new words your own by mastering their denotations and connotations and by writing clear definitions.

20a Accurate and precise word choice conveys meaning efficiently.

(1) Accuracy is essential.

The **denotation** of a word indicates what it names, not what it suggests. For example, the noun *beach* denotes a sandy or pebbly shore, not suggestions of summer fun. Inaccurate usage misstates your point, inexact usage diminishes it, and ambiguous usage confuses your reader. Select words that state your point exactly.

> The figures before me ~~inferred~~ implied that our enrollment had increased significantly this year. [*Infer* means "to draw a conclusion from evidence." For example: From the figures before me, I inferred that our enrollment had increased significantly

this year. *Imply* means "to suggest," so *implied* is the exact word for the sentence as drafted.]

Jennifer spends too much money on clothes, ~~and~~ but she earns it herself. [*And* adds or continues; *but* contrasts. In this case, negative and positive information are contrasted.]

The lecture will focus on ~~inspiring~~ motivating athletes. [*Inspiring* is ambiguous in this context because the lecture could be about "how to inspire athletes" or "athletes who are inspiring."]

Exercise 1

The italicized words in the following sentences are inaccurate, inexact, or ambiguous. Replace these words with exact ones.

1. Luis worked hard to *obtain* a higher position in the company.
2. Have you decided to *except* his proposal?
3. That movie was very *unique*.
4. She has based her campaign on four basic *principals*.
5. Tom likes good food, *but* he frequently tries new restaurants.
6. I cried at the end of the movie because it was so *sentimental*.
7. We need to consider how this change will *effect* our budget.
8. Let's hire a consultant so that we can get an *uninterested* opinion.
9. There were *little* people in the store.
10. After I write my first draft, I always like to *proofread* it.

(2) Connotations enrich meaning.

The **connotation** of a word is what the word suggests or implies. *Beach,* for instance, may connote natural beauty, warmth, surf, water sports, fun, sunburn, crowds, or even gritty sandwiches. Context has much to do with the connotations a word evokes; in a treatise on shoreline management, *beach* has scientific, geographic connotations, whereas in a fashion magazine it evokes images of bathing suits. In addition to being influenced by context, most readers carry with them a wealth of personal associations that can influence how they respond to the words on the page. The challenge for writers is to choose the words that are most likely to evoke the appropriate connotations.

> One of the reasons I am recommending Mr. Krueger for this job is that he is so ~~relentless~~ persistent. [*Relentless* has negative connotations that are inappropriate for a recommendation.]
>
> I love the ~~odor~~ aroma of freshly baked bread. [Many odors are unpleasant; *aroma* sounds more positive, especially in association with food.]
>
> He gets into trouble sometimes because he is so ~~innocent~~ naive. [*Innocent* suggests virtue; *naive* suggests a lack of judgment.]

ESL Your ability to understand connotations will improve as your vocabulary improves. When you learn a new word that seems to mean exactly what another word means, ask a native speaker if these words have different connotations.

(3) Specific and concrete words are usually stronger than general and abstract ones.

A **general** word is all-inclusive, indefinite, and sweeping in scope. A **specific** word is precise, definite, and limited in scope.

General	Specific	More Specific/Concrete
food	fast food	cheeseburger
prose	fiction	short stories
place	city	Cleveland

An **abstract** word deals with concepts, with ideas, with what cannot be touched, heard, or seen. A **concrete** word signifies particular objects, the practical, what can be touched, heard, or seen.

Abstract democracy, loyal, evil, hate, charity

Concrete mosquito, spotted, crunch, grab

Some writers use too many abstract or general words, leaving their writing vague and lifeless. As you select words to fit your context, you should be as specific and concrete as you can. For example, instead of the word *bad,* consider using a more precise adjective.

bad planks: rotten, warped, scorched, knotty, termite-eaten
bad children: rowdy, rude, ungrateful, perverse, spoiled
bad meat: tough, tainted, overcooked, contaminated

To test whether or not a word is specific, you can ask one or more of these questions about what you want to say: Exactly who? Exactly what? Exactly when? Exactly where? Exactly how? As you study the following examples, notice what a difference specific, concrete words can make in expressing an idea and how specific details can expand or develop ideas.

Vague She has kept no reminders of performing in her youth.

Specific She has kept no sequined costume, no photographs, no fliers or posters from that part of her youth. —LOUISE ERDRICH

Vague A big bug got stuck in my candle and died.

Specific A golden female moth, a biggish one with a two-inch wingspread, flapped into the fire, dropped abdomen into the wet wax, stuck, flamed, and frazzled in a second. —ANNIE DILLARD

Vague When I was younger, I could eat more without getting fat.

Specific When I worked on farms as a boy, loading hay bales onto wagons and forking silage to cows, shoveling manure out of horse barns, digging postholes and pulling barbed wire, I could eat the pork chops and half-dozen eggs my neighbors fed me for breakfast, eat corn bread and sugar in a quart of milk for dessert at lunch, eat ham steaks and mashed potatoes and three kinds of pie for supper, eat a bowl of hand-cranked ice cream topped with maple syrup at bedtime, and stay skinny as a junkyard dog.

—SCOTT RUSSELL SANDERS

As these examples show, sentences with specific details are often longer than sentences without them. But the need to be specific does not necessarily conflict with the need to be concise. (See chapter 21.) Simply substituting one word for another can often make it far easier to see, hear, taste, or smell what you are hoping to convey.

> I ~~had an accident~~ *fell out of the canoe* while trying to ~~catch a fish~~ *land a muskie*.

Occasionally, a skillful writer can achieve a dramatic effect by mixing concrete and abstract terms, as in the following example:

> We inhaled those nice big fluffy fumes of human sweat, urine, effluvia, and sebaceous secretions. —TOM WOLFE

And all writers use abstract words and generalizations when these are vital to communicating their ideas, as in the following sentence:

> The romantic principles of Existentialism in its broadest, most vernacular sense have much to do with one's volition and one's will in creating oneself as an ethical being by way of a chosen action. —JOYCE CAROL OATES

Abstract words are exact when they are used to express abstractions—words like "immortal," "inexhaustible," "soul," "spirit," "compassion," "sacrifice," and "endurance." When you use abstract words and generalizations, make sure you do so deliberately and with good reason.

Exercise 2

Replace the general words and phrases in italics with specific ones.

1. You can't believe what you read in the *media*.
2. *Everyone in today's society* seems concerned about staying fit.
3. Cities have *a lot of problems* today.
4. When my family gets together, we fall into *old routines*.
5. I thought about *the numerous advantages* of my major.
6. The police searched *the whole area* thoroughly.
7. No matter how often she gets hurt, she keeps going out with *the same kind of guy*.
8. I've got to have the freedom *to do what I need to do*.
9. That girl needs *a complete makeover*.
10. You'll love this program because it offers such *a spiritual experience*.

(4) Figurative language can contribute to exactness.

Commonly found in nonfiction prose as well as in fiction, poetry, and drama, figurative language uses words in an imaginative rather than a literal sense. Simile and metaphor are the chief **figures of speech**. A **simile** is the comparison of dissimilar things using *like* or *as*. A **metaphor** is an implied comparison of dissimilar things not using *like* or *as*.

Similes

He was like a piece of rare and delicate china which was always being saved from breaking and finally fell.
—ALICE WALKER

The thick blood welled out of him like red velvet, but still he did not die. —GEORGE ORWELL

She sat like a great icon in the back of the classroom, tranquil, guarded, sealed up, watchful. —REGINALD McKNIGHT

For the canyon traps light, rehearses all the ways a thing can be lit: the picadors of light jabbing the horned spray of the Colorado River; light like caramel syrup pouring over the dusky buttes; the light almost fluorescent in the hot green leaves of seedlings. —DIANE ACKERMAN

Metaphors

His money was a sharp pair of scissors that snipped rapidly through tangles of red tape. —HISAYE YAMAMOTO

We refuse to believe that the bank of justice is bankrupt.
—MARTIN LUTHER KING, JR.

It was gurgling out of her own throat, a long ribbon of laughter, like water. —SANDRA CISNEROS [a metaphor and a simile]

Single words are often used metaphorically:

These roses must be **planted** in good soil. [literal]

Keep your life **planted** wherever you can put down the most roots. [metaphorical]

We always **sweep** the leaves off the sidewalk. [literal]

He seems likely to **sweep** her right off her feet. [metaphorical]

Similes and metaphors are especially valuable when they are concrete and point up essential relationships that cannot otherwise be communicated. (For faulty metaphors, see 23c.) Similes and metaphors can also be extended throughout a comparison paragraph. (See 31d(5).)

Other common figures of speech include **personification** (attributing to nonhumans characteristics possessed only by humans), **paradox** (a seemingly contradictory statement that actually makes sense when you think about it), and **irony** (a deliberate incongruity between what is stated and what is meant). In addition, experienced writers often enjoy using **overstatement, understatement, images,** and **allusions.** Figures such as these can contribute to lively, memorable writing even if they do not always contribute to exactness. (For a discussion of these figures, see 39a(4).)

20b Exact word choice requires an understanding of idioms.

An **idiom** is an expression whose meaning is peculiar to the language or differs from the individual meanings of its elements. Be careful to use idiomatic English, not unidiomatic approximations. *She talked down to him* is idiomatic. *She talked under to him* is not. Occasionally the idiomatic use of prepositions proves difficult. If you do not know which preposition to use with a given word, check the dictionary. For instance, *agree* may be followed by *about, on, to,* or *with*. The choice depends on the context. Writers sometimes have trouble with expressions such as these:

accuse **of** perjury
bored **by** it
comply **with** rules
conform **to/with** standards
in accordance **with** policy
independent **of** his family
inferior **to** ours
happened **by** accident
jealous **of** others

Many idioms—such as *all the same, to mean well, eating crow, raining cats and dogs*—cannot be understood from the individual meanings of their elements. Some like *turning something over in one's mind* are metaphorical. Such expressions cannot be meaningfully translated word for word into another language. Used every day, they are at the very heart of the English language. As you encounter idioms that are new to you, master their meanings just as you would when learning new words.

ESL When learning how to use idioms, study how writers use them. The context in which idioms appear will often help you understand their meaning. For example, if you read, "I never eat broccoli because I can't stand it," you would probably understand that *not to be able to stand something* means *to dislike something*. As you learn new idioms from your reading, try using them in your own writing. If you are confused about the meaning of an idiom, check an idiom dictionary.

Exercise 3

Write sentences using each of the following idioms correctly. Use your dictionary when necessary.

1. hang up, hang out
2. differ from, differ with
3. wait on, wait for
4. get even with, get out of hand
5. on the go, on the spot

20c Fresh expressions are more distinctive than worn-out ones.

Such expressions as *bite the dust, breath of fresh air,* or *smooth as silk* were once striking and effective. Excessive use, however, has drained them of their original force and made them **clichés**. Some **euphemisms** (pleasant-sounding substitutions for more explicit but possibly offensive words) are not only trite but wordy or awkward—for example, *correctional facility* for *jail* or *pre-owned* for *used.* Many political slogans and the catchy phraseology of advertisements soon become hackneyed. Faddish or trendy expressions like *whatever, impacted, paradigm, input,* or *be into* (as in "I am into dieting") were so overused that they quickly became clichés.

Nearly every writer uses clichés from time to time because they are so much a part of the language, especially the spoken language. But experienced writers often give a fresh twist to an old saying.

> I seek a narrative, a fiction, to order days like the one I spent several years ago, on a gray June day in Chicago, when I took a roller-coaster ride on the bell curve of my experience.
>
> —GAYLE PEMBERTON
>
> [COMPARE frequent references elsewhere to being on "an emotional roller-coaster."]

Variations on familiar expressions from literature or the Bible, many of which have become part of everyday language, can often be used effectively in your own writing.

> Now is the summer of my great content.
>
> —KATHERINE LANPHER
>
> [COMPARE Shakespeare's "Now is the winter of our discontent. . . ."]

Good writers, however, do not rely too heavily on the words of others; they choose their own words to communicate their own ideas.

Exercise 4

From the following list of trite expressions, select ten that you often use or hear and replace them with carefully chosen words or phrases. Use five of them in sentences.

EXAMPLES
beyond the shadow of a doubt: *undoubtedly*
slept like a log: *slept deeply*

1. a crying shame
2. after all is said and done
3. at the crack of dawn
4. bored to tears/death
5. to make a long story short
6. drop a bombshell
7. hoping against hope
8. in the last analysis
9. flat as a pancake
10. over and done with
11. hard as nails
12. avoid like the plague
13. swam like a fish
14. smell a rat
15. stick to your guns
16. the agony of defeat
17. the powers that be
18. in this day and age
19. the bitter end
20. the bottom line

Exercise 5

Choose five of the ten items below as the basis for five original sentences containing figurative language, exact denotations, and appropriate connotations.

1. the look of her hair
2. a hot summer day
3. studying for an exam
4. your favorite food
5. buying a car
6. an empty street
7. college athletes
8. a heavy rain
9. a traffic jam
10. the way he talks

Exercise 6

Study the following paragraphs and prepare to discuss in class your response to the authors' choice of words—their use of exact, specific language to communicate their ideas.

[1]One morning in Stockholm, after rain and just before November, a mysteriously translucent shadow began to paint itself across the top of the city. [2]It skimmed high over people's heads, a gauzy brass net, keeping well above the streets, skirting everything fabricated by human arts—though one or two steeples were allowed to dip into it, like pens filling their nibs with palest ink. [3]It made a sort of watermark over Stockholm, as if a faintly luminous river ran overhead, yet with no more weight or gravity than a vapor. —CYNTHIA OZICK

[1]A single knoll rises out of the plain of Oklahoma, north and west of the Wichita range. [2]For my people, the Kiowas, it is an old landmark, and they gave it the name Rainy Mountain. [3]The hardest weather is there. [4]Winter brings blizzards, hot tornadic winds arise in the spring, and in summer the prairie is an anvil's edge. [5]The grass turns brittle and brown, and it cracks beneath your feet. [6]There are green belts along the rivers and creeks, linear groves of hickory and pecan, willow and witch hazel. [7]At a distance in July or August the steaming foliage seems almost to writhe in fire. [8]Great green and yellow grasshoppers are everywhere in the tall grass, popping up like corn to sting the flesh, and tortoises crawl about on the red earth, going nowhere in plenty of time. . . .

—N. SCOTT MOMADAY

Chapter 21

Conciseness: Avoiding Wordiness and Needless Repetition

Using words economically is fundamental to writing clearly because unnecessary words or phrases distract readers and blur meaning. Good writers know how to make their points concisely.

Wordy In the early part of August, a hurricane was moving threateningly toward Houston.

Concise In early August, a hurricane threatened Houston.

Wordy This excellent baker makes excellent bread.

Concise This baker makes excellent bread.

In some situations, repetition of a word or phrase can be useful. (See 26b, 29e, and 31b(3).) But in most cases, repetition is a sign of inefficiency.

21a Every word should count; words or phrases that add nothing to the meaning should be omitted.

(1) Redundancy

Restating a key point in different words can help readers understand it. (See 37h(4).) But there is no need to explain the meaning of readily understood terms by using different words that say the same thing. If you use additional words to convey meaning already conveyed by the words you've written, your work will suffer from redundancy: being repetitious for no good reason.

> Ballerinas auditioned ~~in the tryouts~~ for *The Nutcracker*.
>
> Each actor has a unique talent. ~~and ability that he or she uses in his or her acting.~~

In the common phrases listed below, useless words appear in brackets.

yellow [in color]	circular [in shape]
at 9:45 a.m. [in the morning]	return [back]
[basic] essentials	rich [and wealthy] nations
bitter[-tasting] salad	small[-size] potatoes
but [though]	to apply [or utilize] rules
connect [up together]	[true] facts
because [of the fact that]	was [more or less] hinting
[really and truly] fearless	by [virtue of] his authority
fans [who were] watching TV	the oil [that exists] in shale

Avoid grammatical redundancy, such as double subjects (*my sister* [*she*] *is*), double comparisons ([*more*] *easier than*), and double negatives (*could*[*n't*] *hardly*).

(2) Unnecessary words

> ~~In the event that~~ If taxes are raised, expect complaints ~~on the part of the~~ from voters.

One or two words can replace expressions such as these:

at all times	**always**
at this point in time	**now**

by means of	**by**
for the purpose of	**for**
in an employment situation	**at work**
in spite of the fact that	**although**
on account of the fact that	**because**
somewhere in the neighborhood of $2,500	**about $2,500**

One exact word can say as much as many inexact ones. (See also 20a.)

spoke in a low and hard-to-hear voice	**mumbled**
persons who really know their particular field	**experts**

(3) Expletives

There followed by a form of *to be* is an *expletive*—a word that signals that the subject will follow the verb. (See also 29f.) Because expletives shift emphasis away from the subject, they can result in the use of unnecessary words.

> ~~There were~~ T three children play~~ing~~ ed in the yard.

It is also an expletive when it lacks an antecedent and is followed by a form of *be*.

> Learning to ski
> ~~It~~ is easy ~~to learn to ski.~~

The *it* construction is necessary only when there is no logical subject. For example: It is going to snow.

Exercise 1

Substitute one or two words for each of the following phrases.

1. in this day and age
2. has the ability to sing
3. was of the opinion that
4. in a serious manner
5. prior to the time that
6. did put in an appearance
7. located in the vicinity of
8. has a tendency to break
9. during the same time that
10. involving too much expense

Exercise 2

Revise each of the following sentences to make them more concise.

1. There are three possible dates that they might release the film on.
2. During our trip to Seattle, many ridiculous things happened that were really funny.
3. It looked to me as if the bridge could be dangerous because it might not be safe.
4. Many seriously ill patients in need of medical attention were diagnosed by physicians on the medical staff of the hospital.
5. In the frozen wastes of the southernmost continent of Antarctica, meteorites from outer space that fell to earth thousands of years ago in the past were exposed to view by erosion by the deteriorating ice.

21b Combining sentences or simplifying phrases and clauses can eliminate needless words.

Note the differences in emphasis as you study the following examples.

A carpet of blue-green grass
~~The grass was like a carpet. It~~ covered the whole playing field.

~~The color of the grass was blue green.~~

cheating
Some ~~phony~~ unscrupulous brokers are ~~taking money and savings from elderly~~ old people ~~who need that money because~~
out of their *s*
~~they planned to use it as a retirement~~ pension.

21c Repetition is useful only when it improves emphasis, clarity, or coherence. (See also 26b, 29e, and 31b(3).)

~~Your teacher is unlike my teacher.~~ Your teacher likes teaching better than mine ~~does.~~

She hoped he understood that *her comment* ~~the complaint she made was~~ *did not reflect her real feelings* ~~not the way that she really felt about things.~~

We will not rest until we have pursued every lead, inspected every piece of evidence, and interviewed every suspect. [In this case, the repetition of *every* is useful because it emphasizes the writer's determination.]

21d Pronouns and elliptical constructions can eliminate needless repetition. (See chapter 28.)

Instead of needlessly repeating a noun or substituting a clumsy synonym, use a pronoun. If the reference is clear (28b), several pronouns can refer to the same antecedent.

The hall outside these offices was empty. *It* ~~The hall~~ had dirty floors, and *its* ~~the~~ walls ~~of this corridor~~ were covered with graffiti.

An **elliptical construction** (the omission of words that will be understood by the reader without being repeated) helps the writer of the following sentence be concise.

Speed is the goal for some swimmers, endurance [is the goal] for others, and relaxation [is the goal] for still others.

Sometimes, as an aid to clarity, commas mark omissions that avoid repetition.

> My family functioned like a baseball team; my mom was the coach; my brother, the pitcher; and my sister, the shortstop.

As these examples show, parallelism facilitates elliptical constructions. (See chapter 26.)

Exercise 3

Revise the following sentences to eliminate wordiness and needless repetition.

1. The bricks on our new house are red in color and in spite of the fact that they are new the look of these bricks is a used, beat-up appearance.
2. America has two main kinds of business. Americans need to pay attention to getting justice for all, and they also need to be sure that everyone is treated alike.
3. Because of the fact that my parents thought my fiancé was really a terrific guy, I put a lot of effort into trying to work through my conflicts with him.
4. I couldn't understand her response to my paper because of the illegible handwriting that could not be read.
5. Our skating coach made the recommendation saying that my pairs partner and I should put more time into our practicing.

Chapter 22

Clarity and Completeness

In rapid speech we often seem to omit words because our listeners simply do not hear them. These words are necessary in writing, however, to make the meaning clear. For example, instead of "We had better study hard" a listener might hear "We better study hard." Although *had* is often not heard in speech, it must be included in writing.

22a Articles, pronouns, conjunctions, or prepositions are sometimes necessary for clarity and completeness.

(1) Use of articles

Review material on count and noncount nouns. (See 1c(2).)

ESL Indefinite articles

The indefinite articles *a* and *an* are used with singular countable nouns in the following situations:

with descriptive or general nouns

a house **an** orange

with something mentioned for the first time

Our history professor assigned **an** exam for next Monday.

with the meaning of *one*, not *more*

I chose **a** piece of fruit from the basket.

with reference to a member of a group

a novel

Use *a* before a consonant sound: **a** yard, **a** university. Use *an* before a vowel sound: **an** *apple,* **an** *hour.*

Plural count nouns use words such as *some* or *any*. (See 6a(7).)

some magazines **any** books

Definite articles

The definite article *the* is used with singular or plural noncount nouns to indicate a specific person, place, or thing in the following situations:

when the noun has been previously introduced or when you and the reader know what you are referring to

We must leave **the** building now.

We will have a quiz tomorrow. **The** quiz will cover chapters 1 and 2.

when the noun is unique

the Vietnam Memorial

when an ordinal number (fourth, sixth) or superlative (least, best) comes before the noun

the eighth day of the month

the least expensive

Omission of the article

The article is omitted entirely in a number of cases and is optional in others. Some general directions for omitting the article follow:

with another determiner

Sign up for this new course.

before a noncount noun

Let's have ice cream and cake.

before a plural countable noun that does not refer to a specific item

Buy oranges and apples.

before a plural noun that has a general meaning

Everyone wants benefits.

The article is omitted in certain common expressions: go to school, go to class, go to college, go to bed

Confusion with omitted articles

The sentence in the following example is ambiguous. Unless edited, the person "standing nearby" could be either one person or two.

A friend and ^a^ helper stood nearby.

(2) Omitted conjunctions or prepositions

In the following example, the *of* is often omitted in speech but is added in writing.

We had never tried that type ^of^ film before.

Although often omitted in speech, two prepositions may be required after different verbs to make the meaning clear.

I neither believe ^in^ nor approve of those attitudes.

In the following sentences, use a comma when the conjunction *and* is omitted.

Habitat for Humanity built the house, (**and**) then later painted it.

22b Verbs and auxiliaries that are sometimes omitted in speech are necessary in writing to avoid awkwardness or to complete meaning.

The revision eliminates the awkwardness in the following sentence.

> Voter turnout has never ‸been and will never be 100 percent.

Although *is* may not be heard in speech, it is included in writing.

> Lamont ‸is strong and very tall.

In sentences such as the following, omitting or including the second verb is optional.

> The storm was fierce and the thunder (**was**) deafening.

22c Complete comparisons are needed in writing to complete the meaning if it is not suggested by the context.

> He is taller *than his brother.*
>
> Most people think television is more violent *than it used to be.*

Comparisons can be completed by other words or phrases in the sentence, by other sentences in the paragraph, or by the context.

> In the next century, people will need more education.

22d The intensifiers *so, such,* and *too* need a completing phrase or clause.

In informal writing, a completing phrase is often omitted after intensifiers such as *so, such,* and *too* when they are used for emphasis.

My hair is **so** long.

Julian has **such** a hearty laugh.

It is just **too** much.

In formal writing, intensifiers are followed by a completing phrase or clause.

My hair is **so** long **that I must get it cut today.**

Julian has **such** a hearty laugh **that it makes everyone feel good.**

It is just **too** much **for me to try to do.**

Exercise 1

Supply the words needed for formal writing in the following verb phrases and comparisons.

1. They always have and always will go to the coast for vacation.
2. Cars with standard transmissions are better.
3. Rogelio likes his hardcover books better.
4. The airline passengers better pay attention to the safety guidelines.
5. Siobhan been trying to make her research paper more persuasive.

Exercise 2

Insert words where needed.

1. The snow in the plains region is as heavy as the mountains.
2. Chris stronger than my father.
3. The auditorium was already packed with people and still coming.
4. I had an unusual party my last birthday.
5. The students are angered and opposed to the administration's attempts to change university policy.

Effective Sentences

Chapter 23

Sentence Unity: Consistency

Good writing is unified and sticks to its purpose. It does not contain unrelated ideas, mixed constructions, or faulty predication. It is consistent throughout, with no shifts in grammatical structure, tone, style, or viewpoint.

23a Making the relationship of ideas in a sentence immediately clear helps the reader.

Unrelated	Alaska has majestic glaciers, but most Americans must travel great distances. [unity thwarted by a gap in thought]
Related	Alaska has majestic glaciers, but **to see them** most Americans must travel great distances.

Exercise 1

All the sentences below contain apparently unrelated ideas. Adding words when necessary, rewrite each sentence to indicate a logical relationship between the ideas. If you cannot establish a close relationship, put the ideas in separate sentences.

1. The coffee at the diner is incredibly bad, and most of the customers seem to buy it often.
2. Dr. Roberts has an unusual and innovative teaching style, and I was unable to attend her class last week.

3. Her friends ski on the mountain in the winter, and in the summer earn money by working at odd jobs they avoid doing the rest of the year.
4. Enrique gave his mother a new coat for Christmas, and she went to dinner with his father.
5. There are lots of problems with the new supervisor at work, but I like to avoid them and talk to her one-on-one.

23b Arranging details in a clear sequence makes your point clear.

The first sentence below has excessive detail. Although detail usually makes writing more interesting, too much can be distracting. Do not include details that are not necessary to develop the point that you are making.

Excessive	When I was only sixteen, I left home to attend a college that was nearby and that my uncle had graduated from twenty years earlier.
Clear	I left home when I was only sixteen to attend a nearby college. [If the detail about the uncle is important, include it in another sentence. If not, delete it.]

When getting rid of excessive details, remember that length alone does not make a sentence ineffective. Sometimes you may need a long sentence in which every detail contributes to the central thought. Parallel structure (see chapter 26), balance, rhythm, effectively repeated connectives, and careful punctuation can make even a paragraph-length sentence coherent.

> The rediscovery of fresh air, of home-grown food, of the delights of the apple orchard under a summer sun, of the swimming pool made by damming the creek that flows

through the meadow, of fishing for sun perch or catfish from an ancient rowboat, or of an early morning walk down a country lane when the air is cool—all of these things can stir memories of a simpler time and a less troubled world.

—CASKIE STINNETT, *The Wary Traveler*

Exercise 2

Revise each sentence in the following passage to eliminate excessive detail.

[1]I have never seen a place that was as filled with history that had been passed along by various family members who cherished every moment of it. [2]Finally I returned to the place where I had lived for years which had been built decades before my birth.

[3]The old farm, considered a model of technological advances only 30 years before, but then in need of paint and repairs, as is so often the case with places long inhabited, had to be renovated for future use. [4]Because of this, when I was eight years old, sleeping in the bedroom at the far north corner of the main house, because the larger bedrooms were occupied by my older brothers and sisters, my parents decided that they wanted to move us to a more modern home located in the suburbs of the city. [5]The renovation of the old farm lasted only a few years, which really seemed much longer than that but made us appreciate our history, as many fail to do, until it is too late.

23c Mixed metaphors and mixed constructions are illogical.

(1) Mixed metaphors

A **mixed metaphor** combines different images, creating an illogical comparison.

Mixed Her climb up the ladder of success was nipped in the bud.

Revised She slipped on her climb up the ladder of success.

OR

Before her career could blossom, it was nipped in the bud.

(2) Mixed constructions

A sentence that begins with one kind of construction and shifts to another is a **mixed construction**. (See also 23d and 27.) Mixed constructions often omit the subject or the predicate.

Mixed When Win plays the accordion attracts the audience's attention. [adverb clause + predicate; no subject]

Revised When Win plays the accordion, she attracts the audience's attention. [adverb clause + main clause]

OR

Win's playing of the accordion attracts the audience's attention. [subject + predicate]

Mixed It was an old ramshackle house but that was quite livable.

Revised It was an old ramshackle house, but it was quite livable. [main clause + independent clause]

OR

It was an old ramshackle house that was quite livable. [noun + adjective clause]

23d Faulty predication can lead to problems.

Faulty predication occurs when the subject and predicate do not fit together logically.

Faulty One book I read believes in eliminating subsidies. [A person, not a thing, believes.]

Revised The author of one book I read believes in eliminating subsidies.

Faulty An example of discrimination is an apartment owner, especially after he has refused to rent to people with children. [The refusal, not the owner, is an example of discrimination.]

Revised An example of discrimination is an apartment owner's refusal to rent to people with children.

23e Unnecessary shifts are disconcerting.

(1) Faulty *is . . . when, is . . . where,* or *is . . . because* constructions

Constructions combining *is* with *when, where,* or *because* are often illogical since forms of *to be* signify identity or equality between the subject and what follows.

Faulty The reason the package arrived so late is because he didn't mail it soon enough.

Revised The package arrived so late because he didn't mail it soon enough.

(2) Definitions clarify the precise meaning of words.

A short dictionary definition may be adequate when you need to define a term or a special meaning of a word that may be unfamiliar to the reader.

Here *galvanic* means "produced as if by electric shock." [See also 16d.]

Giving a synonym or two may clarify the meaning of a term. Such synonyms are often used as appositives.

> A *dolt* is a dullard, a blockhead.
>
> *Magendo,* or black-market corruption, is flourishing.
>
> —KEN ADELMAN

Writers frequently show—rather than tell—what a word means by giving examples.

> Many homophones (*be* and *bee, in* and *inn, see* and *sea*) are not spelling problems.

Words often have a number of meanings. It must be clear to the reader which meaning you are using.

> If this paper, I use the word *communism* in the Marxist sense of social organization based on the holding of all property in common.

By stipulating your meaning in this way, you set the terms of the discussion.

You can also formulate your own definitions of the concepts you wish to clarify.

> Questions are windows to the mind.
>
> —GERARD I. NIERENBERG
>
> Clichés are sometimes thought of as wisdom gone stale.
>
> —JOSEPH EPSTEIN

A formal definition first states the term to be defined and puts it into a class, then differentiates the term from other members of its class.

> A phosphene [term] is a luminous visual image [class] that results from applying pressure to the eyeball [differentiation].

Exercise 3

Define any two of the following terms in full sentences using first (a) a short dictionary definition, then (b) a synonym, and finally (c) an example.

1. neurotic
2. humanism
3. bowie knife
4. integrity
5. uncanny
6. wetlands
7. racism
8. liberal
9. peer

Chapter 24

Subordination and Coordination

Subordination and **coordination** establish clear structural relationships between ideas. Subordinate structures—phrases, appositives, or subordinate clauses—make the ideas they express appear less important than ideas expressed in main independent clauses. In the following sentence, the subordinate clause is italicized; the main clause containing the main idea is boldface.

Since it was pouring rain, **the game was canceled.**

When two ideas in a sentence are equal, they are expressed in coordinate structures (**SUBJECT** + **PREDICATE**, and **SUBJECT** + **PREDICATE**). In the following example, ideas of equal importance are expressed in coordinate structures—two main clauses.

They did their best, and they ran the course.

Coordination in words and phrases also gives equal structural emphasis to equal ideas.

a **stunning** and **unexpected** conclusion [coordinating adjectives]

in the attic or **in the basement** [compound prepositional phrases]

(See **1d** and **1e** for an explanation of the difference between phrases and clauses and between subordinate and main clauses.)

24a Careful subordination can combine a series of related short sentences into longer, more effective units.

Choppy I was taking eighteen hours of course work. I wanted to graduate in three years. It turned out to be too much. I also had a full-time job at the newspaper. I just couldn't do both. I needed the money. I needed the extra course in order to graduate early. I felt bad about the whole thing. I had to drop one of my courses. I had to have the money from my job. I had to pay my tuition.

Revised I was taking eighteen hours of course work, because I wanted to graduate in three years, but it turned out to be too much. Since I already had a full-time job at the newspaper, I just couldn't do both. I needed the money, but I needed the extra course in order to graduate early. Even though I felt bad about the whole thing, I had to drop one of my courses because I had to have the money from my job in order to pay my tuition.

When combining a series of related sentences, select the main idea, express it in the structure of a base sentence (**SUBJECT** + **PREDICATE**) and use some of the following subordinate structures to relate less important ideas to the main one.

(1) Adjectives and adjective phrases

Choppy The limbs were covered with ice. They sparkled in the sunlight. They made a breathtaking sight.

Better **Sparkling in the sunlight**, the **ice-covered** limbs made a breathtaking sight. [participial phrase and hyphenated adjective]

(2) Adverbs and adverb phrases

Choppy Season the chicken livers with garlic. Use a lot of it. Fry them in butter. Use very low heat.

Better **Heavily** season the chicken livers with garlic, and **slowly** fry them in butter. [coordination]

OR

After heavily seasoning the chicken livers with garlic, slowly fry them in butter. [subordination]

Choppy His face was covered with white dust. So were his clothes. The man looked like a ghost.

Better **His face and clothes white with dust,** the man looked like a ghost. [The first two sentences are combined in an absolute phrase.] (See **absolute phrase** in the Glossary of Terms.)

(3) Appositives and contrasting elements

Choppy Her comments were uncalled for and unnecessary. They were mean. And everyone noticed them.

Better Everyone noticed her mean, unnecessary, and uncalled-for comments.

(4) Subordinate clauses

Subordinate clauses are linked and related to main clauses by markers (subordinating conjunctions and relative pronouns) that signal whether a clause is related to the base sentence by **time** (*after, before, since, until, when, while*), **place** (*where, wherever*), **reason** (*as, because, how, so that, since*), **condition** (*although, if, unless, whether*), or **additional information** (*that, which, who, whose*). (See page 25 for a list of these markers.)

Choppy The blizzard ended. Then helicopters headed for the mountaintop. It looked dark and forbidding.

Better **As soon as the blizzard ended,** helicopters headed for the mountaintop, **which looked dark and forbidding.** [adverb clause and adjective clause]

24b Using subordination and coordination is preferable to stringing several main clauses together.

Do not overuse coordinating connectives like *and, but, or, so, then, however,* and *therefore*. For ways to revise stringy or loose compound sentences, see 30c. Methods of subordination that apply to combining two or more sentences (24a) also apply to revising faulty or excessive coordination in a single sentence.

(1) Subordinate structures for ideas that are less important than main ideas

In the following example, the main idea, expressed in the main clause, is boldface; the less important idea, expressed in the subordinate clause, is italicized.

Since he already had a job, **Jim didn't really mind losing the election.**

(2) Coordinate structures for ideas of equal importance

The dam broke, and the town was destroyed.

(3) Logical connection of ideas by subordinate and coordinate structures

The gasoline tank sprang a leak, ~~when~~ so all hope of winning the race was lost.

On your way
~~You can walk~~ to school, ~~and~~ you can mail the letter.

CAUTION Do not use *but* or *and* before *which, who,* or *whom* when introducing a single adjective clause.

Leela is a musician ~~and~~ who can play several instruments.

24c Faulty or excessive subordination can confuse the reader.

Faulty Chen was only a substitute pitcher, winning half of his games.

Better Although Chen was only a substitute pitcher, he won half of his games. [*Although* establishes the relationship between the ideas.]

Excessive Some people who are not busy and who are insecure when they are involved in personal relationships worry all the time about whether their friends truly love them.

Better Some insecure, idle people worry about whether their friends truly love them. [two subordinate clauses reduced to adjectives]

Exercise 1

Observing differences in emphasis, convert each pair of sentences below to (a) a simple sentence, (b) a compound sentence consisting of two main clauses, and (c) a complex sentence with one main clause and one subordinate clause. Be prepared to discuss the most effective revision.

1. Mara likes to take a small afternoon nap after finishing her homework. She is a dedicated and talented student.
2. The house was very ancient and gloomy. It was a grand Victorian home on the edge of town.
3. David was driving to San Francisco. On the way there, his truck broke down.

4. After the guests left the party the hosts cleaned the living room. Then they washed the dishes before going to bed.
5. The kids couldn't concentrate in the living room studying their Spanish homework that they had to finish. They stopped their studying and went outside.

Exercise 2

Revise the following passage using effective subordination and coordination.

[1]Bennett Hall is a residence unit at our college and it is an old building. [2]It is nearer to my classes than the other dorm rooms would be since it is only a five-minute walk to the center of campus. [3]It has large, spacious bedrooms. [4]It is a good distance away from the football stadium and it offers a great deal of privacy to its residents. [5]There's little noise. [6]My room is on the far corner of the building. [7]It faces east. [8]It has a balcony overlooking the yard below. [9]There are dark green shrubs that are covered with small white flowers. [10]The place is comfortable and I enjoy living there.

Chapter 25

Coherence: Misplaced Parts and Dangling Modifiers

Keeping related parts of the sentence together and avoiding dangling modifiers makes meaning clearer to your reader.

25a Placing modifiers near the words they modify clarifies meaning.

The meaning of the following sentences changes according to the position of the modifiers.

> Natasha went out with **just** her coat on.
> Natasha **just** went out with her coat on.
> **Just** Natasha went out with her coat on.
>
> The man **who drowned** had tried to help the child.
> The man had tried to help the child **who drowned**.

(1) In formal English, place modifiers such as *almost, only, just, even, hardly, nearly,* and *merely* immediately before the words they modify for emphasis and clarification of meaning.

The truck only costs $2,000.

He even works during his vacation.

(2) Place a modifying prepositional phrase to indicate clearly what the phrase modifies.

in the first paragraph
Arne says ^ that he means to leave the country ^ ~~in the first paragraph~~.

(3) Place adjective clauses near the words they modify.

that I had recently purchased
I put the chair ^ in the middle of the room ^ ~~that I had recently purchased~~.

(4) Revise "squinting" constructions—modifiers that may refer to either a preceding or a following word.

I agreed the next day to help him.

(5) Revise awkward constructions that split an infinitive.

Jim failed to early enough study for the exam.

However, splitting an infinitive is sometimes not only natural but desirable.

He forgot to **completely** close the gate. [COMPARE: He forgot **completely** to close the gate.]

Exercise 1

Revise the following sentences, placing the modifiers in correct relation to the words they modify.

1. Mark and Judy returned yesterday from their trip to Europe by plane.
2. Olivia wore her favorite coat almost until the sleeves were threadbare.
3. The tornado only destroyed two buildings.

4. My sister decorated the walls of her kitchen with pictures from the covers of *The New Yorker.*
5. Mark neglected to, because he was forgetful, set his alarm.
6. Sandy promised when she was going to the theater to see the latest summer hit.
7. The sitcom appearing on last night's television schedule which is new is really funny.
8. Nelda said last week that she had arrived.
9. Jack went to work in his restaurant uniform on the bus.
10. At the coffee house the employees serve steaming coffee to customers in big coffee cups.

25b There are several ways to revise dangling modifiers.

Dangling modifiers Dangling modifiers are primarily verbal phrases that do not clearly refer to other words or phrases in the sentence, although any misplaced word, phrase, or clause can be said to dangle. The words in the sentence can be rearranged, or words can be added, to make the meaning clear.

(1) Revise dangling participial phrases. (See 1d.)

Dangling *Taking our seats,* the game started. [no clear word for the phrase to refer to]

Revised *Taking our seats,* **we** started the game. [word supplied—participants]

OR

Taking our seats, **we waited** for the game to start. [words supplied—observers]

Placed after the basic sentence, the participial phrase in the revision below refers to the subject.

Dangling The evening passed very pleasantly, *munching* popcorn and *watching* a late movie. [no clear reference]

Revised **We** passed the evening very pleasantly, *munching* popcorn and *watching* a late movie. [reference supplied]

(2) Revise dangling phrases containing gerunds or infinitives. (See 1d(1).)

Dangling On *entering* the stadium, the size of the crowd surprised Theo. [no clear subject]

Revised On *entering* the stadium, **Theo** was surprised at the size of the crowd. [subject supplied]

Dangling *To write* well, good books must be read. [no clear subject]

Revised *To write* well, **I** must read good books. [subject supplied]

(3) Revise dangling elliptical adverb clauses. (See 1e(2).)

Elliptical clauses imply some words that are not stated.

Dangling *When only a small boy,* my father took me with him to Chicago.

Revised *When* **I was** *only a small boy,* my father took me with him to Chicago.

Sentence modifiers (see the **Glossary of Terms**) are considered standard usage, not danglers. (See also 1c(4).)

First, I will learn to dance.

I just don't care, **frankly.**

Exercise 2

Revise the following sentences to eliminate dangling modifiers. Put a check mark after any sentence that needs no revision.

1. Dusk having fallen, the kids went inside.
2. Our conversation ended by exchanging phone numbers and promising a visit in the near future.
3. Leaving the house, the front door was locked.
4. To paint memorable pictures, the colors should be vivid.
5. Having repeated their vows, the minister married the couple.
6. By following the rules of the road, accidents are less likely to happen.
7. In determining an appropriate college, considering the degrees offered is important.
8. After working on assignments for three hours, the rain began.
9. Knowing how to drive is necessary before getting a driver's license.
10. Even though expecting a large reward, the money wasn't the main motive.

Chapter 26

Parallelism

Ideas in parallel grammatical form express ideas parallel in meaning. Parallelism contributes to ease in reading by making ideas that are parallel in meaning parallel in structure. It also provides clarity and rhythm. Parallel elements regularly appear in lists or series, in compound structures, in comparisons, in comparisons using *than* or *as,* and in contrasting elements.

> I like to swim, to dance, and ~~having~~ *to have* fun.
>
> **OR**
>
> I like swimming, dancing, and ~~to have~~ *having* fun.

Many parallel elements are linked by a coordinating conjunction (such as *and, or, but*) or by correlatives (such as *neither . . . nor, whether . . . or*). Others are not. In the following examples, verbals used as subjects and complements are parallel in form.

> **To define** flora is **to define** climate. —NATIONAL GEOGRAPHIC
>
> **Seeing** is **believing.**

Parallel structures are also used in outlines to indicate elements of equal importance. (See 31b(3), page 307.)

> We are not so much what we eat as ~~the thoughts~~ *what* we think.
>
> **OR**
>
> We are not so much ~~what~~ *the food* we eat as the thoughts we think.

If elements are not parallel in thought, rather than trying to make them parallel in grammatical structure, rethink the sentence.

> We can choose ~~ham, tuna salad~~ *to eat ham or tuna salad*, or *we can watch* television.

26a Similar grammatical elements need to be balanced.

For parallel structure, balance nouns with nouns, prepositional phrases with prepositional phrases, and clauses with clauses. In the examples that follow, repetition emphasizes the balanced structures.

(1) Parallel words and phrases

The Africans carried with them a pattern of kinship
that emphasized || **collective survival,**
mutual aid,
cooperation,
mutual solidarity,
interdependence,
and || **responsibility for others.**

—JOSEPH L. WHITE

She had || **no time to be human,**
no time to be happy. —SEAN O'FALLON

(2) Parallel clauses

I remember Iyatiku's sister, Sun Woman,
|| **who held so many things in her bundle,**
who went away to the east. —PAULA GUNN ALLEN

(3) Parallel sentences

When I breathed in, I squeaked.
When I breathed out, I rattled. —JOHN CARENEN

Exercise 1

Write three sentences: one containing parallel words, one containing parallel phrases, and one containing parallel clauses. Use the examples in **26a** as models.

26b Parallels need to be clear to the reader.

Repeating a preposition, an article, the *to* of the infinitive, or the introductory word of a phrase or clause can make parallel structure clear.

For about fifteen minutes I have been sitting chin in hand in front of the typewriter,
trying to be honest with myself,
trying to figure out why writing this seems to be so dangerous an act. —ADRIENNE RICH

The reward rests not **in** the task
but **in** the pay.
—JOHN KENNETH GALBRAITH

I was happy in the thought
that our influence was helpful
and **that** I was doing the work I loved
and **that** I could make a living out of it. —IDA B. WELLS

26c Correlatives can be used with parallel structures.

With the correlatives (*both . . . and, either . . . or, neither . . . nor, not only . . . but also, whether . . . or*), parallel structures are required.

Whether at home or at work, he was always busy.

The team not practices

~~Not~~ only ~~practicing~~ at 6 a.m. during the week, but ~~the team~~ also scrimmages on Sunday afternoons.

OR

does the team practice it

Not only ~~practicing~~ at 6 a.m. during the week, but ~~the team~~ also scrimmages on Sunday afternoons.

Exercise 2

Make the structure of each sentence parallel.

1. He uses his computer for writing and to play games.
2. She was praised by her supervisor and her secretary admired her.
3. I started swimming, running, and lifted weights.
4. My mother said that she wanted me to pick up some things from the store and for me to be home by dinner.
5. The student was not only diligent but also enjoyed having fun.
6. I couldn't decide whether to buy the new car or take a vacation.
7. She really enjoys going to the movies and to watch television.
8. Her true pleasure is playing the piano rather than in the library.
9. He is intelligent but a coward.
10. She found that her son had more time to do his work and it was better quality.

Chapter 27

Consistency: Avoiding Shifts

Avoid abrupt, unnecessary shifts—for example, from past to present, from singular to plural, from formal diction to slang, or from one perspective to another. Such inconsistencies make reading difficult and obscure the meaning.

27a Consistent tense, mood, and person

> Arlo **believed** in nuclear power while Mary ~~**believes**~~ *believed* in solar power. [both verbs in the past tense]

> If I **were** not so stupid and he ~~**was**~~ *were* not so naive, we would have known better. [both verbs in the subjunctive mood]

> I had to exercise daily and *I especially despised* the rowing **machine**. ~~was especially despised.~~ [persons made consistent]

When using the literary or historical present, avoid slipping from the present into the past tense. (See the Glossary of Terms.)

> Romeo and Juliet **fall** in love at first sight, **marry** secretly, and ~~**died**~~ *die* together in the tomb within the same hour. [verbs in present tense]

27b Consistent person and number (See also 28.)

If ~~a person is~~ you are going to improve, you should work harder. [Both subjects are in the second person.]

The team is counting on winning ~~their~~ its game. [Both *team is* and *its* are singular.]

27c Shifts between direct and indirect discourse (See also 26a.)

Janet wondered how the thief got the computer out and why ~~didn't he~~ he didn't steal the TV.

Her assistant said, "She's out," and "would ~~I~~ you please wait?"

27d Consistent tone and style

It seemed to Romeo, as he gazed up at the balcony, that Juliet's face was as white as ~~the underbelly of a fish~~ a lily.

27e Consistent perspective and viewpoint

Standing in the valley, I could see our troops at the crest of the hill and~~,~~ later, standing on the other side of the ridge, I could see the enemy in full retreat.

Exercise 1

Correct all unnecessary shifts. Put a check mark after any sentence that needs no revision.

1. First sauté the garlic in olive oil and then you should add the crushed tomatoes.
2. The kids put away their toys and run to the dinner table.
3. Barney likes reading but eating is also liked by him.
4. If there are any complaints, you might inquire, "Why should they be complaining?" and ask that they adopt a better attitude.
5. Marguerite spent her evenings reading popular novels and her days were devoted to studying.
6. Even though his mother may not approve, he used to go visit his friends anyway.
7. They had reached a point where it is difficult for one to stop.
8. Like a shark through the waves, our distinguished gray-haired hostess glided through the throngs of people on the ballroom dance floor.
9. Drive the car to the auto mechanic's garage, and then it should be left there for repairs.
10. My sister asked me if I had met my friend at the airport and will she be staying with us while she's in town.

Exercise 2

Revise the following paragraph to eliminate all unnecessary shifts.

[1]She was an honest young woman, it always seemed to me. [2]She has an astonishingly open manner, and her face suggests a wisdom beyond her years. [3]She said that I always try to speak my mind but tried to be diplomatic. [4]Nevertheless she will let it be seen that she is not voicing her entire opinion. [5]Take these observations and use them wisely; it may help one in interpreting this woman's true thoughts.

Chapter 28

Pronoun Reference

Pronouns refer to the nouns immediately preceding them. Each boldfaced pronoun below clearly refers to its italicized antecedent, which can be a single word or a word group:

> Perhaps it is the same survival instinct that makes *women* amenable to change that also tends to make **them** vulnerable.
> —ROSE M. NOLEN

> A cow-calf operation keeps *cattle* year-round in the same pastures where **they** are bred, born, and raised.

> Thus, *being busy* is more than merely a national passion; **it** is a national excuse. —NORMAN COUSINS

Without any loss of clarity, a pronoun can often refer to a noun that follows it:

> Unlike **their** predecessors, today's *social workers* cannot exclusively seek middle-class, home-owning, two-parent, one-career families for the children they want to place.
> —MARSHA TRUGOT

The meaning of each pronoun should be immediately obvious. To avoid any confusion, repeat the antecedent, use a synonym for it, or recast your sentence.

28a Clear antecedents

When a pronoun could refer to either of two possible antecedents, the reader is confused. Recasting the sentence or replacing the pronoun with a noun makes the antecedent clear.

> Juan told Peter that he had made a mistake. [Whom does *he* refer to?]
>
> The books were standing on the shelf that needed sorting. [Did the books or the shelf need sorting?]

A pronoun may sometimes clearly refer to two or more antecedents.

> Jack and Jill met **their** Waterloo.

28b Clear references

If a pronoun is too far away from its antecedent, the reader may have to backtrack to get the meaning. A pronoun that refers to a modifier can also obscure meaning. Recasting the sentence to bring a pronoun and its antecedent closer together or substituting a noun for the obscure pronoun will clarify the meaning.

Remote The *sophomore* found herself the unanimously elected president of a group of animal lovers, *who* was not a joiner of organizations. [*Who* is too far removed from the antecedent *sophomore*. (See also 25a(3).)]

Better The **sophomore, who** was not a joiner of organizations, found herself the unanimously elected president of a group of animal lovers.

Obscure Before Ellen could get to the jewelry store, *it* was all sold. [reference to a modifier]

Better Before Ellen could get to the jewelry store, all the **jewelry** was sold.

28c Broad or implied references

Pronouns such as *it, this, that, which,* and *such* may refer to a specific word or phrase or to the sense of a whole clause, sentence, or paragraph.

Specific Reference The glow was enough to read by, once my eyes adjusted to it. —MALCOLM X [*It* refers to *glow.*]

Broad Reference Some people think that the fall of man had something to do with sex, but that's a mistake. —C. S. LEWIS [*That* refers to the sense of the whole clause.]

When used carelessly, broad references can make writing unclear.

Avoid broad references to an expressed idea.

When class attendance is compulsory, some students feel that education is being forced on them. This is not true. [*This* has no antecedent.]

Make the antecedent explicit rather than implicit.

Lois said that she would stay in Yuma for at least a year. This remark suggests that she is happy there. [*This* has no expressed antecedent.]

My father is a music teacher. ~~It~~ Teaching music is a profession that requires much patience. [*It* has no expressed antecedent.]

28d Awkward use of *it* or *you*

Awkward It was no use trying.

Revised **There was** no use trying.

OR

Trying was useless.

In an informal context, the use of the impersonal, or indefinite, *you* is both natural and acceptable. It is also becoming more acceptable in academic writing. In the following example, *you* is equivalent in meaning to "people in general" or "the reader."

> The study of dreams has become a significant and respectable scientific exploration, one that can directly benefit **you**.
>
> —PATRICIA GARFIELD

You in this sense is generally still not appropriate in very formal writing.

Avoid the awkward placement of *it* near another *it* with a different meaning.

Awkward It would be unwise to buy the new model now, but it is a superior machine. [The first *it* is an expletive (see **Glossary of Terms**). The second *it* refers to *model.*]

Revised Buying the new model now would be unwise, but it is a superior machine.

Exercise 1

Revise the following sentences as necessary to make all references clear. Put a check mark after any sentence that needs no revision.

1. Sandra did not buy a season ticket, which turned out to be a mistake.
2. If you are taken to the courthouse, they will fine you.

3. When the termite eggs are hatched, they grow wings and fly around the country in swarms.
4. In the book it says that the author dislikes anteaters.
5. Sherry decided not to go to the movie, which she came to regret.
6. Everyone has trouble writing, but this is not true when you are excited about your subject.
7. Collette told Li that she was a good friend.
8. Marilyn decided not to attend the reunion which was a disappointment for our grandparents.
9. When building railroads, the engineers planned embankments for fear that flooding would cover them and make them useless.
10. The increase in tuition discouraged students which seemed unreasonably high.

Chapter 29

Emphasis

You can emphasize ideas by using subordination and coordination (24), parallelism (26), and exact word choice (20) and also by writing concisely (21). This chapter presents additional ways to emphasize material.

29a Words at the beginning or end of a sentence receive emphasis.

Because words at the beginning or end of a sentence—especially the end—receive emphasis, place important words in these positions whenever possible.

> ~~In today's society, most~~ G ~~g~~ood jobs today require a college education. ~~as part of the background you are supposed to have.~~
>
> ~~I could hear the roar of~~ T ~~t~~raffic roared outside my hotel room in Chicago. ~~when I was there.~~

As these examples show, you can often make your sentences more concise (chapter 21) by revising them so that important words occur at the beginning or end. Sometimes, however, you may need to add a few words to make a sentence emphatic.

Because the semicolon (see chapter 14) is a strong punctuation mark when used between main clauses, the words placed immediately before and after a semicolon tend to be emphasized.

The colon and the dash often precede an emphatic ending. (See also 17d and 17e.)

> In short, the freedom that the American writer finds in Europe brings him, full circle, back to himself, with the responsibility for his development where it always was: in his own hands.
>
> —JAMES BALDWIN

> Until fairly recently, the pattern was that the father and sons worked, and, to whatever extent their earnings allowed, the mothers and daughters were supposed to display culture, religion, luxury, and other assorted fine feelings of society—in addition to seeing that the housework got done.
>
> —JUDITH MARTIN

Exercise 1

Placing important words carefully, revise the following sentences to improve emphasis.

1. A computer has become essential to write with.
2. Marsha is very successful and a tireless worker, in my opinion.
3. They say Woodbury has decided to spend more money on schools; soon its surrounding towns may invest more in education also.
4. There was a sign in the motel office announcing that there was a state park about a mile away, more or less.
5. In a sense, music has the power to unleash the imagination for us.

29b When surrounded by cumulative sentences, a periodic sentence receives emphasis.

In a **cumulative sentence**, the main idea (the independent clause or sentence base) comes first; less important ideas or details follow. In a **periodic sentence**, however, the main idea comes last, just before the period.

Cumulative	History has amply proved that large forces can be defeated by smaller forces superior in arms, organization, morale, and spirit.
Periodic	That large forces can be defeated by smaller forces superior in arms, organization, morale, and spirit has been amply proved by history.
Cumulative	Memory operates by way of the senses, by way of detail, which is the stuff of fiction, the fabric of good stories. —DAVID HUDDLE
Periodic	In a day when movies seem more and more predictable, when novels tend to be plotless, baggy monsters or minimalist exercises in interior emotion, it's no surprise that sports has come to occupy an increasingly prominent place in the communal imagination. —MICHIKO KAKUTANI

Both types of sentences can be effective. Because cumulative sentences are more common, however, the infrequently used periodic sentence is often the more emphatic.

29c When ideas are arranged from least important to most important, the most important idea receives the most emphasis.

In the following examples, the ideas are arranged in an order that places the writer's most dramatic or important idea last.

> They could hear the roar of the artillery, the crash of falling timbers, the shrieks of the wounded.

Benefiting from much needed rest, moderate medication, and intensive therapy, he eventually recovered from despair.

The applicants relaxed when they saw that she was charming, friendly, and kind.

The violation of this principle can achieve a humorous effect when a writer shifts suddenly from the dignified to the trivial or from the serious to the comic. This effect is appropriate only when a writer intends to be humorous.

Contemporary man, of course, has no such peace of mind. He finds himself in the midst of a crisis of faith. He is what we fashionably call "alienated." He has seen the ravages of war, he has known natural catastrophes, he has been to singles bars. —WOODY ALLEN

Exercise 2

Arrange the ideas in the following sentences in order of what you consider the least important to the most important.

1. Juan was known for his wisdom, humor, and efficiency.
2. She majored in communications because she wanted to understand people, inspire them, and influence them.
3. Unless we rebuild downtown, the city will become dangerous, unattractive, and unlivable.
4. I bought my share of supplies for the picnic: ribs, mustard, paper plates, and pickles.
5. Alcoholism destroys families, ruins health, and leads to erratic behavior.

29d Forceful verbs can make sentences emphatic.

(1) The active is more emphatic than the passive voice.

Active voice emphasizes the *doer* of the action by making the doer the subject of the sentence. **Passive voice** emphasizes the *receiver* of the action, minimizes the role of the doer, and results in wordier sentences. One sign of passive construction is that a form of the verb *to be* is added to the action conveyed by another verb in the sentence.

Active Sylvia won the race.

Passive The race was won by Sylvia.

Active All citizens should insist on adequate medical care.

Passive Adequate medical care should be insisted on by all citizens.

Because whoever or whatever is responsible for the action in the sentence is no longer the subject, sentences in the passive voice are often less precise. It is grammatically correct but stylistically undesirable to write "The race was won." Such a sentence leaves unanswered the question of who did the winning. Politicians sometimes favor the passive voice because it allows them to avoid assigning responsibility—hence constructions like "a meeting has been called" or "your taxes have been raised."

The passive voice is appropriate, however, when the doer of an action is unknown or unimportant.

Passive The television set was stolen. [The thief is unknown.]

Passive We couldn't watch the Super Bowl because our television had been stolen. [The identity of the thief is unimportant, given the emphasis of the sentence.]

When reporting research or scientific experiments, writers often choose to use the passive voice to preserve their objectivity and to emphasize the work being done on a project rather than who is doing it.

Passive The experiment was conducted under carefully controlled conditions over several months.

Unless they have a strong reason to use the passive voice, good writers prefer the active voice because it is clearer and more emphatic.

(2) Action verbs and forceful linking verbs are more emphatic than forms of *have* or *be*.

Forms of *have* or *be*, when used without an action verb, rob your writing of energy and forcefulness. The real action often lies in a verbal phrase or in the object or complement.

Our college is always ~~the winner of~~ the conference. [The subject complement—*winner*—contains the real action more forcefully conveyed by the verb *win*.]

The meat ~~has a~~ rotten ~~smell~~. [Action is in the direct object—*smell*. Used as a verb, *smell* conveys the action.]

You can ~~be more effective at solving~~ a problem ~~by~~ understand~~ing~~ the problem first. [The objects of the prepositions (*solving*, *understanding*) contain the action more forcefully conveyed by verbs.]

Exercise 3

Make each sentence more emphatic by substituting active voice for passive or by substituting a more forceful verb for a form of *have* or *be*.

1. A motion was made to expel you from school.
2. Every weekday afternoon, questionable values are taught by soap operas and talk shows.

3. The sales manager is responsible for supervising a staff of fifteen.
4. A bowl was broken when the dishes were being washed.
5. Every worker has the desire for respect.

29e Repeating important words gives them emphasis.

Although good writers avoid unnecessary repetition (chapter 21), they also understand that deliberate repetition emphasizes key terms.

> We forget all too soon the things we thought we could never forget. We forget the loves and the betrayals alike, forget what we whispered and what we screamed, forget who we are.
>
> —JOAN DIDION

When you decide to repeat a word for emphasis, make sure that it is a word worth emphasizing, that it conveys an idea central to your purpose.

29f Inverting the standard word order of a sentence gives it emphasis.

> At the feet of the tallest and plushiest offices lie the crummiest slums. —E. B. WHITE [COMPARE "The crummiest slums lie at the feet of the tallest and plushiest offices."]
>
> Basic to all the Greek achievement was freedom.
>
> —EDITH HAMILTON
>
> [COMPARE "Freedom was basic to all the Greek achievement."]

When you invert standard word order for emphasis, you should make sure your sentence has not become so awkward or artificial that it is difficult to read.

29g Balanced sentence construction provides emphasis.

A sentence is balanced when grammatically equal structures—usually main clauses with parallel elements—express contrasting (similar) ideas. (See chapter 26a.) A balanced sentence emphasizes the contrast (or similarity) between parts of equal length and movement.

> Love is positive; tolerance negative. Love involves passion; tolerance is humdrum and dull. —E. M. FORSTER

29h A short sentence following one or more long ones is emphasized.

> In the last two decades there has occurred a series of changes in American life, the extent, durability, and significance of which no one has yet measured. No one can. —IRVING HOWE

Exercise 4

Revise each sentence for emphasis. Be prepared to explain why your revision provides appropriate emphasis in the context you have in mind.

1. I gave him the letter, two weeks ago, when he asked me.
2. Scouting develops a person morally, mentally, and physically.
3. The tornado devastated Iowa on a hot and humid day.
4. As the station is reached, the train is seen coming around the bend.
5. In college she devoted herself to studying hard, making new friends, going to parties, and working part-time.
6. He thought about the children, he considered the budget, he reflected on past experience, and a decision was reached by him.

7. Lots of angry protestors were all around us for a while.
8. It is usually required by the state that cars be inspected before their registration can be renewed each year.
9. We will give our hearts, we will donate our money, and we will share our time.
10. The paintings in the exhibit were unoriginal, but the use of color was appealing in them.

Chapter 30

Variety

Varying the kinds of sentences you use can make your writing lively and distinctive. Many writers tend to rely too heavily on a few familiar structures, and the result often seems predictable. If you experiment with sentence structure, you increase the chance of readers' paying attention to what you write.

Compare the two paragraphs below. Both express the same ideas in virtually the same words, both use acceptable sentence patterns, and both are grammatically correct. Variety in sentence structure and length, however, gives one paragraph a stronger rhythm than the other.

Not Varied

This account is *about* television only in part. I don't mean to cast it as an evil appliance. I will be describing phenomena that appear on television often, but they are also on the radio and in magazines and everywhere else. They are parts of modern life. Television covers an extraordinary amount of territory in twenty-four hours. I could find fifty references to any topic. [six sentences: five simple, one compound; all starting with the subject; three starting with *I*]

Varied

But only in part is this account *about* television, which I don't mean to cast as an evil appliance. Often I will be describing phenomena that appear on television, but they are also on the radio and in magazines and everywhere else, because they are parts of modern life. The amount of territory that television covers in twenty-four hours is extraordinary—I could find fifty references to any topic that interested me.

[three sentences: one complex, one compound-complex, and one compound; first sentence subject/verb order reversed; four dependent clauses] —THE *NEW YORKER*

If you have difficulty distinguishing various types of structures, review the fundamentals treated in chapter 1, especially 1b.

30a A series of short, simple sentences sounds choppy. (See also 29h.)

To avoid the choppiness produced by a series of short, simple sentences, you can lengthen some sentences by showing how the ideas are subordinate or coordinate. (See chapter 24.)

Choppy The Maine coast and the Oregon coast look very much alike. The houses by the water, however, are different. It's a matter of architectural style.

Effective Although the Maine coast and the Oregon coast look very much alike, the architectural style of the houses by the water is different. [use of subordination to combine sentences]

Choppy Some people study everything on the menu. Next they ask about how various dishes are made. Then they think things over for a few minutes. Finally they order exactly what they had the last time. The idea is to look interested in food without taking any risks.

Effective To look interested in food without taking any risks, some people study everything on the menu, ask how various dishes are made, think things over, and end up ordering exactly what they had the last time. [use of coordination to combine sentences]

Occasionally, as the example below illustrates, a series of brief, subject-first sentences can be used for special effect:

> Although it had been an easy enough day, much like any other, something seemed wrong just before dinner. I felt hot. My chest hurt. The room began to tilt. [The feeling of a heart attack is conveyed by a series of abrupt sentences.]

Exercise 1

Convert the following series of short, simple sentences into single sentences. Use no more than one coordinating conjunction in each.

1. It was the bottom of the ninth inning. The score was tied. Bases were loaded. There were two outs.
2. Eileen bought a laptop. She chose a Toshiba. It has plenty of memory. She is still getting used to the keyboard.
3. He made an interesting argument. Employers should offer flexible working hours. Giving people more flexibility will improve morale.
4. My car needs new tires. It also needs a brake job. I should probably get it tuned up also.
5. Shopping for clothes can be fun. You have to have time to try things on. Otherwise you might make mistakes.

30b Writing sounds monotonous when too many sentences begin the same way.

Most writers begin more than half their sentences with the subject—far more than any other construction. Although this pattern is normal for English sentences, relying too heavily on it can make your writing monotonous. Experiment with the following alternatives for beginning sentences.

(1) Begin with an adverb or an adverbial clause.

Suddenly a hissing and clattering came from the heights around us. —DOUGLAS LEE [adverb]

Even though baseball is essentially the same, the strategy of play then and now is different.
—JAMES T. FARRELL [adverbial clause]

When you first start writing—and I think it's true for a lot of beginning writers—you're scared to death that if you don't get that sentence right that minute it's never going to show up again. —TONI MORRISON [adverbial clause]

(2) Begin with a prepositional phrase or a verbal phrase.

Out of necessity they stitched all of their secret fears and lingering childhood nightmares into this existence.
—GLORIA NAYLOR [prepositional phrase]

To be really successful, you will have to be trilingual: fluent in English, Spanish, and computer.
—JOHN NAISBITT [infinitive phrase]

Looking out of the window high over the state of Kansas, we see a pattern of a single farmhouse surrounded by fields, followed by another single homestead surrounded by fields.
—WILLIAM OUCHI [participial phrase]

(3) Begin with a sentence connective—a coordinating conjunction, a conjunctive adverb, or a transitional expression.

In the following examples, each sentence connective shows the relationship between the ideas in each set of sentences. (See also 31b(4).)

Many restaurants close within a few years of opening. **But** others, which offer good food at reasonable prices, become well established. [coordinating conjunction]

Difficulty in finding a place to park is one of the factors keeping people from shopping downtown. **Moreover,** public transportation has become too expensive. [conjunctive adverb]

This legislation will hurt the economy. **In the first place,** it will cost thousands of jobs. [transitional expression]

(4) Begin with an appositive, an absolute phrase, or an introductory series. (See 24a.)

A town of historic interest, Sante Fe also has many art galleries. [appositive]

His fur bristling, the cat attacked. [absolute phrase]

Light, water, temperature, minerals—these affect the health of plants. [introductory series—see 17e(3)]

Exercise 2

Rewrite each sentence so that it begins with an appositive, an absolute phrase, or an introductory series.

1. Customers were waiting an hour before the store opened because advertisements had convinced them that the best merchandise would go fast.
2. A field full of abandoned cars stretched before them.
3. He began to write poetry using scraps of paper while he was in prison.
4. *Gilligan's Island,* a mindless series from the sixties, illustrates a number of stereotypes that are strangely enduring.
5. The printer at my office works twice as fast as the one I have at home and provides a greater variety of fonts.

30c Stringing simple sentences together to make compound sentences is less effective than experimenting with sentence structure.

Although compound sentences are often useful, some are ineffective. If you normally write short, simple sentences, and then revise your sentence structure by just linking simple sentences with *and* or *but*, your writing will still lack variety. Remember that subordination is as important as coordination. (See chapter 24.) To revise an ineffective compound sentence, you can use one of the following methods.

(1) Make a compound sentence complex.

Compound Seafood is nutritious, and it is low in fat, and it has become available in a greater variety.

Complex Seafood, which is nutritious and low in fat, has become available in a greater variety.

(2) Use a compound predicate in a simple sentence.

Compound She caught the bird expertly, and next she held it so its feet were still, and then she slipped a numbered yellow band around its left leg.

Simple She caught the bird expertly, held it so its feet were still, and slipped a numbered yellow band around its left leg.

(3) Use an appositive in a simple sentence.

Compound J. T. Nichols was an old-fashioned naturalist, and he spent his life studying birds and turtles on Long Island.

Simple J. T. Nichols, an old-fashioned naturalist, spent his life studying birds and turtles on Long Island.

(4) Use a prepositional or verbal phrase added to a simple sentence.

Compound The rain was torrential, and we could not see where we were going.

Simple Because of the torrential rain, we could not see where we were going.

Compound I checked into the hotel about 4:30, and then I called the office about my return flight.

Simple After checking into the hotel about 4:30, I called the office about my return flight.

Compound The town is near the interstate, and it attracted commuters, and its population grew rapidly.

Simple The town, located near the interstate, attracted commuters and grew rapidly in population.

(5) Use additional conjunctions to increase the compounds in a sentence.

Experienced writers sometimes achieve interesting effects by exaggerating what could be considered a flaw. By using a number of conjunctions in close succession, you can slow the pace and dignify material that might otherwise seem unremarkable.

> I was on Fire Island when I first made that sauerkraut, and it was raining, and we drank a lot of bourbon and ate the sauerkraut and went to bed at ten, and I listened to the rain and the Atlantic and felt safe. —JOAN DIDION

Exercise 3

Using the methods illustrated in 30c, revise these compound sentences.

1. My sister became frustrated in her job, so she quit after a few months, and now she is collecting unemployment and feeling that she made a mistake.
2. Annuals can add color to your garden, and many of them are inexpensive, but you have to do a lot of replanting.
3. First semester was difficult, and I almost dropped out of school, but I learned how to plan my time, and then my grades improved.
4. Greg is always talking about taking a vacation, but he never does it, and he is overworking himself.
5. Coffee shops are popular meeting places, and they have improved the standard of coffee served in town, but there are too many of them, and I wonder how they can all stay in business.

30d Occasionally using words or phrases to separate subject and verb can vary the conventional subject-verb sequence.

Although it is usually best to keep the subject next to the verb so that the relationship between the two is clear, breaking this pattern on occasion can lead to variety. In the following examples, subjects and verbs are in boldface.

Subject-Verb **Great Falls was** once a summer resort, but **it has become** a crowded suburb.

Varied	**Great Falls,** once a summer resort, **has become** a crowded suburb.
Subject-Verb	The **crowd applauded** every basket and **cheered** the team to victory.
Varied	The **crowd,** applauding every basket, **cheered** the team to victory.

An occasional declarative sentence with inverted word order can also contribute to sentence variety. (See **29f**.)

Exercise 4

Using the methods illustrated in **30d**, vary the conventional subject-verb sequence in these sentences.

1. The video store is across from the high school, and it attracts many students.
2. His ability to listen is an acquired skill that makes him a good counselor.
3. Mark was hurrying to get home before the storm broke, but he flooded the engine of his car.
4. The manager identified with the employees, so she supported their decision to ask for shorter hours.
5. The customers were frustrated by the lack of service and walked out of the restaurant.

30e When surrounded by declarative sentences, a question, an exclamation, or a command adds variety.

What was Shakespeare's state of mind, for instance, when he wrote *Lear* and *Antony and Cleopatra*? It was certainly the state of mind most favourable to poetry that there has ever existed. —VIRGINIA WOOLF [Woolf's answer follows the initial question.]

Now I stare and stare at people, shamelessly. Stare. It's the way to educate your eye. —WALKER EVANS [A one-word imperative sentence provides variety.]

Exercise 5

Prepare for a class discussion on the sentence variety in the following paragraph.

[1]It is too much that with all those pedestrian centuries behind us we should, in a few decades, have learned to fly; it is too heady a thought, too proud a boast. [2]Only the dirt on a mechanic's hands, the straining vise, the splintered bolt of steel underfoot on the hangar floor—only these and such anxiety as the face of a Jock Cameron can hold for a pilot and his plane before a flight, serve to remind us that, not unlike the heather, we too are earthbound. [3]We fly, but we have not "conquered" the air. [4]Nature presides in all her dignity, permitting us the study and the use of such of her forces as we may understand. [5]It is when we presume to intimacy, having been granted only tolerance, that the harsh stick falls across our impudent knuckles and we rub the pain, staring upward, startled by our ignorance. —BERYL MARKHAM

Larger Elements

Chapter 31 Working with Paragraphs

Although they are an essential unit of thought in writing, paragraphs rarely stand alone. They stand in relation to and in the context of all the other paragraphs that surround them in a composition. It is, however, occasionally useful to view them separately to observe how a single paragraph is organized and why it is or is not effective. Furthermore, many of the development patterns and strategies described in this chapter as paragraph strategies also apply to writing the whole essay. As you work through this chapter, you should keep in mind that the flow of information in your essay is one of your most important considerations and that you may want to revise paragraphs to support and reflect that flow.

Good paragraphs are **unified**, **coherent**, and **well developed**, and they can be said to contribute to the development of the main idea of a paper in ways similar to those in which sentences contribute to the development of an idea in a paragraph. (See 31c and d.) Sentences and paragraphs are integral parts of the larger units—that is, the paragraphs and the essays—to which they belong. The beginning of a paragraph is indented to signal the reader that a new idea or a new direction for an idea follows. (Indention is also used in dialogue, as discussed in 16a(4).)

In paragraph 1, observe how the sentences relate to a single main idea (showing unity), how ideas progress easily from sentence to sentence (showing coherence), and how specific details support the main idea (showing development). (For easy reference, the paragraphs in this section are numbered—except for those needing revision. The topic sentences in paragraphs 1 to 6 are indicated by italics.)

1 *But those Levi's marked more than my move from little-girl clothes to big-brother clothes.* Indeed, they were the only hand-me-downs ever handed down. Instead, those old ratty pants marked my move to freedom, freedom from the conventional girl-stuff my mother had so carefully fostered only one year earlier. Maybe my mother—who was learning the difference between roofing nails and wood screws, who was learning to mix paint in the vise-gripping shake-machine bolted to the floor in the back room of the hardware store, who would later teach me to cut glass, make keys, and clean Surge milk pumpers—wanted me to know what she was learning about women's work and men's work. I don't know. I just know that those Levi's—old, worn, with a difficult-to-manage button fly—meant the world to me, at least the limited world offered by my neighborhood.

—MARILYN SCHIEL, "Levi's"

Paragraphs have no set length. Typically, they range from 50 to 250 words and average perhaps 100 words. Paragraphs in books are usually longer than those in newspapers and magazines.

Although one-sentence paragraphs are occasionally used for emphasis, short paragraphs often indicate inadequate development. Long paragraphs, too, can reveal problems in your writing, especially if they exhaust one point or combine too many points.

Transitional paragraphs (page 313) as well as introductory and concluding paragraphs (chapter 32) serve other purposes.

ESL Some cultures find the directness and brevity valued in U.S. academic and business writing inelegant or even rude. If your culture values indirection, you may have trouble adjusting to this kind of directness. However, if you will be writing for readers in U.S. academic and business circles, it is important to learn to be direct. (See also chapter 21.)

31a Paragraphs should be unified.

In a unified paragraph, each sentence helps develop the main idea or the gist of the paragraph. Stating the main idea in a single sentence (often called a topic sentence), will help you achieve unity.

(1) Main idea and topic sentences

Writers usually convey the main idea of a paragraph in a topic sentence, which may appear at any point in the paragraph. For example, the topic sentence of paragraph 2 (in italics) announces the idea that rumors can be classified by how people react to them. It also suggests the approach of the paragraph by establishing an expectation that the writer will explain the two categories of rumors.

2 *Rumors basically deal with people's anxieties and uncertainties, Rosnow says, and he divides them into two types: wish rumors that we hope are true, and dread rumors that we pray are false.* Your company is giving a year-end bonus, property taxes are going down, there's not going to be a final exam. These are examples of wish rumors. Dread rumors are on the darker side: there are going to be layoffs at work, a fare increase is on the way, your company is going to be moving.

—ROBIN WESTEN,
"The Real Slant on Gossip" *Psychology Today*

The main idea of a paragraph is frequently stated at or near the beginning, as in paragraph 2. It is sometimes also restated at the end to emphasize its importance, particularly in introductory paragraphs. In paragraph 3, compare "Americans do not achieve this status until" with the final statement, "we often meander through an analogous rite of passage."

3 *In most cultures, adulthood is equated with self-reliance and responsibility, yet often Americans do not achieve this status until we are in our late twenties or early thirties—virtually the entire average lifespan of a person in a traditional non-Western society.* We tend to treat prolonged adolescence as a warm-up for real life, as a wobbly suspension bridge between childhood and legal maturity. Whereas a nineteenth-century Cheyenne or Lakota teenager was expected to alter self-conception in a split-second vision, we often meander through an analogous rite of passage for more than a decade—through high school, college, graduate school.

—MICHAEL DORRIS, "Life Stories"

Occasionally, the topic sentence is stated near the end of the paragraph, especially when the writer progresses from specific examples to a generalization as in paragraph 4.

4 Sisters have been taking in other people's children since the days when Pharaoh's daughter had a maiden scoop Moses out of the bullrushes. *In modern times, as efforts to recruit Black adoptive parents have accelerated, Black single women and men have heeded the call.* —CHERYL EVERETTE, "Going Solo: Singles Open Their Lives to Adoption" *Emerge*

A single topic sentence can serve for a sequence of two or more paragraphs.

5 *The world has always been divided into two camps: those who love garlic and onions and those who detest them.* The first camp would include the Egyptian pharaohs who were entombed with clay and wood carvings of garlic and onions

to ensure that meals in the afterlife would be well seasoned. It would include the Jews who wandered for 40 years in the Sinai wilderness, fondly remembering "the fish which we did eat in Egypt so freely, and the pumpkins and melons, and the leeks, onions and garlic." It would include Sydney Smith, the 19th-century essayist, whose "Recipe for Salad" includes this couplet: "Let onion atoms lurk within the bowl, / And, scarce-suspected, animate the whole."

6 The camp of the garlic and onion haters would include the Egyptian priests who, according to Plutarch, "kept themselves clear of the onion. . . . It is suitable neither for fasting nor festival, because in the one case it causes thirst, and in the other tears for those who partake it." The camp would include the ancient Greeks, who considered the odor of garlic and onions vulgar and prohibited garlic and onion eaters from worshiping at the Temple of Cybele. It would include Bottom, who in *A Midsummer Night's Dream* instructs his troupe of actors to "eat no onions nor garlic, for we are to utter sweet breath."

—ERIC BLOCK, "The Chemistry of Garlic and Onions"

Occasionally, a paragraph contains no topic sentence because the details unmistakably imply the main idea. For example, the idea that perceptions change as people change, although never explicitly stated, is clearly the central idea of the following paragraph.

7 Everything Chuck did that summer was kind, and helped me to grow normally. I would love to meet him now and thank him for all the strength I took from him. Every person probably encounters these "saints" again and again in his lifetime, without understanding their importance or being grateful. If I saw him now, the way he was then, I wonder if I would even appreciate Chuck. He was fresh out of the army, starting college on the GI Bill, had a cautious way of speaking, not much book culture. What hurts in all this is knowing that I probably would have condescended to someone like him at college, barely eight years after looking up to him as everything. —PHILIP LOPATE, "Summer Camps"

Exercise 1

Photocopy a page or two from a piece of writing you like and mark the topic sentences. Be prepared to share your work in class.

Exercise 2

Write a paragraph with a topic sentence at the beginning, another with the topic sentence at the end, and a third with the topic sentence at the beginning and restated at the end.

If you get stuck, here are a few suggestions to get you started.

1. Two benefits of peer editing are . . . .
2. You know you are in trouble when . . . .
3. Discrimination can be defined as . . . .
4. Before speaking in front of others . . . .

(2) Main idea and paragraph unity

The most common way to unify a paragraph is to make each sentence support the main idea. In paragraph 8, each sentence shows exactly what the writer means by the curious experiences referred to in the topic sentence.

8 The beat spirit was wry, lighthearted and macabre at the same time. Beats celebrated the breaking down of barriers between life and art. Beats celebrated the everyday, down-and-out and ephemeral. They embraced be-bop music and other inventions of black culture. They were early performance artists. They crossed over from one art form to another. They experimented with collage, assemblage and stream of consciousness. —MICHAEL KIMMELMAN,
"Celebration of Beat Culture (Sandals and All)"
New York Times

Each sentence in paragraph 9 supports the main idea that the media are not friendly to change, and each sentence also contributes to the **unity** of Crichton's essay as a whole by pointing toward the main idea of the next paragraph—that the media pass off outworn and discredited ideas as truth.

> 9 This polarization of the issues has contributed greatly to our national paralysis, because it posits false choices which stifle debate essential to change. It is ironic that this should happen in a time of great social upheaval, when our society needs more than ever to be able to experiment with different viewpoints. But in the media world, a previously established idea, like a previously elected politician, enjoys a tremendous advantage over any challenger.
>
> —MICHAEL CRICHTON, "The Mediasaurus" *Wired*

As you check your paragraphs for unity, revise or eliminate any information that does not clearly relate to the main idea. If the relationship between the main idea and the details is obvious to you but not to your reader, add a phrase or a sentence to make their relevance clear. If more than one major idea appears in a single paragraph, either refocus your main idea or develop each idea in a separate paragraph.

Exercise 3

Note how each sentence in the following paragraph expresses a different major idea. Select one sentence and use it as a topic sentence to develop a unified paragraph with specific details and examples.

[1]People don't always understand how hard it is to go to college while you're trying to support yourself and your kids. [2]After the divorce, I had to get a different kind of job to support my kids, but jobs with the right hours are hard to find if you don't have any real education, so I had to take a job as a cook. [3]My mom keeps the kids during the day while

I go to school, but I have to get a sitter to take care of them while I work the dinner shift. [4]I try to study in between when I get home from school and when I have to go to work, but the kids are usually all over me wanting attention. [5]So, what I don't get done then I have to do after I get off work which is pretty late in the evening. [6]Then, I have to be up to get the kids fed before I go to class. [7]It doesn't leave much time for study or for my kids either.

31b Clearly arranged ideas and effective transitions foster paragraph coherence.

A paragraph is coherent when the relationship among the ideas is clear and the progression from one sentence to the next is easy for the reader to follow. To achieve this goal, arrange ideas in a clearly understandable order. If your paragraph emphasizes the main idea as paragraph 10 does, make sure that each sentence refers to the subject of the topic sentence. If your paragraph moves along like paragraph 11, the subject of each sentence should echo the predicate of the previous one. In either instance, link the sentences by effective use of pronouns, repetition, conjunctions, transitional phrases, and parallel structure. These transitional devices also ease the transitions between paragraphs.

(1) Patterns of coherence

Different kinds of writing use different patterns to establish coherence. In the humanities, the primary pattern establishes links between the subject of the topic sentence and all subsequent sentences in the paragraph, as the following diagram suggests.

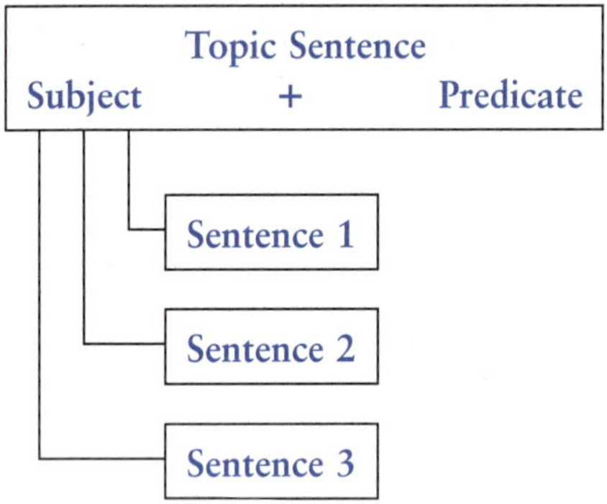

10 Women from all classes protested these abusive and discriminating practices. These protesters banded together and marched through the streets of their country demanding equality with men. And these women were labeled feminists. They wanted the right to vote, they wanted the right to fair working conditions and fair wages, and they wanted the right to live their lives in the manner they chose without ostracism from society. Yes, these women (and a few like-minded men) were called feminists.

—CAROL JOHNSON, "What Is a Feminist?"

The pattern that dominates in the natural and social sciences links each sentence, chain-like, to the predicate of the preceding one, as in paragraph 11 and the diagram that follows.

11 A spider's muscles can curl its legs. But to straighten their legs, spiders have to pump fluids into them. If the spider hasn't gotten enough water, its legs will curl up and cannot be straightened.

—MARRIETTA DICHRISTINA, "Come into My Parlor" *Popular Science*

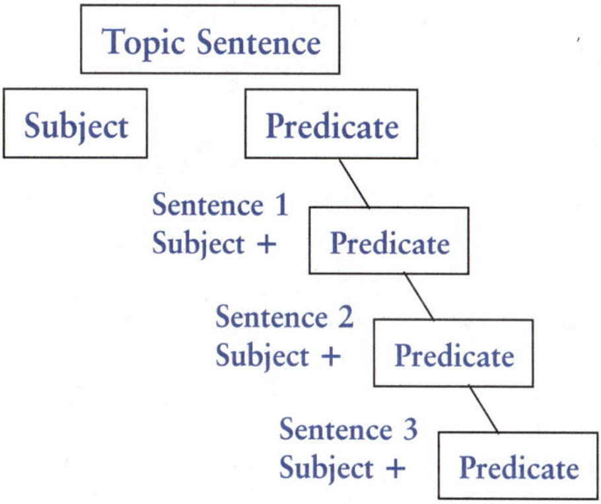

But writers generally match the pattern they use to the writing they do. Writers in the humanities who wish to move quickly over material are likely to use a chaining pattern. Similarly, writers in the sciences who wish to explain a single idea in depth will generally use the focused pattern.

(2) Order of ideas

One of the simplest ways to arrange ideas in a paragraph is to use **chronological order.**

12 Standing in line at the unemployment office makes you feel very much the same as you did the first time you ever flunked a class or a test—as if you had a big red "F" for "Failure" printed across your forehead. I fantasize myself standing at the end of the line in a crisp and efficient blue suit, chin up, neat and straight as a corporate executive. As I move down the line I start to come unglued and a half hour later, when I finally reach the desk clerk, I am slouching and sallow in torn jeans, tennis shoes and a jacket from the Salvation Army,

carrying my worldly belongings in a shopping bag and unable to speak.

—JAN HALVORSON, "How It Feels to Be Out of Work"

Descriptive passages are often arranged in **spatial order**. Starting from a single point of reference, the description can move from north to south, from near to distant, from left to right, and so on. Note the movement from the top of the plateau to the bottom of the gorge in paragraph 13.

13 The highway, without warning, rolled off the plateau of green pastures and entered a wooded and rocky gorge; down, down, precipitously down to the Kentucky River. Along the north slope, man-high columns of ice clung to the limestone. The road dropped deeper until it crossed the river at Brooklyn Bridge. The gorge, hidden in the tableland and wholly unexpected, was the Palisades. At the bottom lay only enough ground for the river and a narrow strip of willow-rimmed floodplain. —WILLIAM LEAST-HEAT MOON, *Blue Highways*

Another useful arrangement is **order of importance** (climactic), from most to least important or from least to most important. (See also 29c.) In paragraph 14, the author focuses on a hierarchy of intelligence, moving from lower to higher forms of life.

14 An ant cannot purposefully try anything new, and any ant that accidentally did so would be murdered by his colleagues. It is the ant colony as a whole that slowly learns over the ages. In contrast, even an earthworm has enough flexibility of brain to enable it to be taught to turn toward the left or right for food. Though rats are not able to reason to any considerable degree, they can solve such problems as separating round objects from triangular ones when these have to do with health or appetite. Cats, with better brains, can be taught somewhat more, and young dogs a great deal. The higher apes can learn by insight as well as by trial and error.

—GEORGE RUSSELL HARRISON, *What Man May Be*

Sometimes the movement within the paragraph is from **general to specific** or from **specific to general.** A paragraph may begin with a general statement or idea, which is then supported by particular details, as in paragraph 14 above, or it may begin with a striking detail or series of details and conclude with a climactic statement as in paragraph 15, or a summarizing statement as in paragraph 16.

15 It was not the only disappointment my mother felt in me. In the years that followed, I failed her so many times, each time asserting my own will, my right to fall short of expectations. I didn't get straight As. I didn't become class president. I didn't get into Stanford. I dropped out of college.

—AMY TAN, "Two Kinds"

16 To bring back some excitement to concertgoing—and some emotions other than nostalgia and/or pity—the music industry has turned to festivals. Not stationary, one-time events like Woodstocks I and II, but massive, carnival-like musical tours that feature at least half a dozen acts as well as food booths, souvenir stands and more. This summer several festivals are touring the land, each with a distinct character vying for a hold on the pop-culture imagination and wallet.

—CHRISTOPHER FARLEY, "Where the Moshers Are"

One common form of the general-specific pattern is **topic-restriction-illustration**, in which the writer announces the topic, restricts it, and illustrates the restricted topic. In paragraph 17, the writer announces the topic—the oddest artificial language—restricts it in the second sentence by giving a reason and then illustrates it with examples.

17 One of the oddest artificial languages ever was Solresol, invented by François Sudre in 1827. The Frenchman reasoned that since music was the universal language, the seven notes of the musical scale were the perfect building blocks for an

international vocabulary. Single notes were reserved for simple words (*do* for "no," *re* for "and"), double notes for pronouns, triple notes for everyday words (*do-re-la* for "year"), and longer combinations for more uncommon terms. In addition, opposites were expressed whenever possible by reversing the order of the notes: *do-mi-sol* for "God" means that "Satan" must be *sol-mi-do*. Sudre tinkered with the language for 45 years, but was never able to overcome the fundamental flaw: people would rather speak a conversation than whistle it.

—GAVIN EDWARD, "Dejpu'bogh Hov rur qabllj! (Your Face Looks Like a Collapsed Star)" *Wired*

In the **question-answer** pattern, the first sentence asks a question that the supporting sentences answer.

18 What's wrong with the student-union book shop? Everything. It's interested in selling sweatshirts and college mugs rather than good books. Its staff often is incompetent and uncivil. The manager may not be intelligent enough even to order a sufficient number of copies of required textbooks for the beginning of a term. As for more lively books—why, there are masses of paperbacks, perhaps, that could be procured at any drugstore; there are a few shelves or racks of volumes labeled "Gift Books," usually lavishly illustrated and inordinately costly, intended as presents to fond parents, but there are virtually no book books, of the sort that students might like to buy.

—RUSSELL KIRK, "From the Academy: Campus Bookshops"

Another common paragraph arrangement is the **problem-solution** pattern, in which the first sentence or two state the problem and the rest of the paragraph suggests the solution, as illustrated by paragraph 19.

19 That many women would be happier not pursuing careers or intellectual adventures is only part of the truth. The whole truth is that many people would be. If society had the clear

sight to assure men as well as women that there is no shame in preferring to stay non-competitively and non-aggressively at home, many masculine neuroses and ulcers would be avoided, and many children would enjoy the benefit of being brought up by a father with a talent for the job instead of by a mother with no talent for it but a sense of guilt about the lack. —BRIGID BROPHY, "Women"

Paragraphs 12 through 19 illustrate eight of the many possible types of arrangement within the paragraph. Any order or combination of orders is satisfactory as long as the sequence of ideas is logical and clear.

Exercise 4

Find examples of three different kinds of paragraph development. Identify the coherence pattern of each and its order of ideas (chronological, spatial, climactic, general to specific, specific to general, topic-restriction-illustration, question-answer, problem-solution). Explain in writing how each paragraph follows the pattern and organization you have identified.

Exercise 5

Examine paragraphs from your own writing in other projects and find two examples of subject-focused paragraphs and two of chaining paragraphs. Revise each paragraph, converting the focused paragraphs to chaining paragraphs and vice versa. What difficulties do you encounter? What happens to each paragraph?

(3) Transitional devices: pronouns, repetition, transitional words and phrases, and parallel structures

Many of the same kinds of transitions link sentences within paragraphs and paragraphs within a paper: pronouns, repetition of key words or ideas, conjunctions and other transitional phrases, and parallel structures. (See also chapters 23 and 26.)

Pronouns

In paragraph 20, the writer links sentences by using the pronouns *their* and *they*. Although these same two pronouns are used repeatedly, their referent, "easy victims," is always clear.

20 Several movements characterize easy victims: their strides were either very long or very short; they moved awkwardly, raising their left legs with their left arms (instead of alternating them); on each step, they tended to lift their whole foot up and then place it down (less muggable sorts took steps in which their feet rocked from heel to toe). Overall, the people rated most muggable walked as if they were in conflict with themselves; they seemed to make each move in the most difficult way possible. —CARIN RUBENSTEIN, "Body Language That Speaks to Muggers"

Repetition of words, phrases, or ideas

In paragraph 21, the repetition of the key word *wave* links the sentences. The repetition also provides emphasis. (See 29e.)

21 The weekend is over, and we drive down the country road from the cottage to the pier, passing out our last supply of waves. We wave at people walking and wave at people riding. We wave at people we know and wave at people who are strangers.

—ELLEN GOODMAN, "Waving Goodbye to the Country"

Conjunctions and other transitional expressions

Conjunctions and transitional phrases demonstrate the logical relationship between ideas. Notice the subtle changes in the relationship between two clauses linked by different conjunctions in the following sentences.

He laughed, and she frowned.

He laughed while she frowned.

He laughed because she frowned.

He laughed, so she frowned.

He laughed; later, she frowned.

Here is a checklist of some frequently used transitional connections arranged according to the kinds of relationships they establish.

Checklist of Transitional Connections ✓

• **Alternative and Addition**	or, nor, and, and then, moreover, besides, further, furthermore, likewise, also, too, again, in addition, even more important, next, first, second, third, in the first place, in the second place, finally, last
• **Comparison**	similarly, likewise, in like manner
• **Contrast**	but, yet, or, and yet, however, still, nevertheless, on the other hand, on the contrary, conversely, even so, notwithstanding, in contrast, at the same time, although this may be true, otherwise, nonetheless
• **Place**	here, beyond, nearby, opposite to, adjacent to, on the opposite side
• **Purpose**	to this end, for this purpose, with this object
• **Result or Cause**	so, for, therefore, accordingly, consequently, thus, thereupon, as a result, then, because, hence
• **Summary**	to sum up, in brief, on the whole, in sum, in short
• **Repetition**	as I have said, in other words, that is, to be sure, as has been noted

continued

continued from previous page

• **Exemplification**	for example, for instance, in any event
• **Intensification**	in fact, indeed, to tell the truth
• **Time**	meanwhile, at length, soon, after a few days, in the meantime, afterward, later, now, then, in the past, while

Parallel structures

Parallelism is the repetition of a sentence pattern or of other grammatical structures. (See also chapter 26.) In paragraph 22, the first three sentences are structured the same way:

> When you're three years old . . . , that's expected.
>
> When you're six . . . , you deserve some credit. . . .
>
> When you're nine . . . , you should be applauded. . . .

Repeating this pattern emphasizes the close relationship of the ideas.

22 When you're three years old and stick mashed potatoes up your nose, that's expected. When you're six and make your bed but it looks like you're still in it, you deserve some credit for trying. When you're nine and prepare the family meal but the casserole looks worse than the kitchen, you should be applauded for your effort. But somewhere along the line, some responsible adult should say, "You're too old for this nonsense." —DAN KILEY, *The Peter Pan Syndrome: Men Who Have Never Grown Up*

Exercise 6

Revise the following paragraph so the thought flows smoothly from one sentence to the next. Add pronouns and linking devices, and revise sentences to create parallel structure and to repeat key phrases.

23 [1]The Internet offers a number of benefits to businesses and consumers. [2]Internet presence allows businesses to introduce their new products in a timely fashion. [3]They can more effectively beat their competition to sales. [4]Their presence on the Internet offers businesses a cheap and effective method of advertising. [5]They save money on printing and mailing advertisements and can reach consumers worldwide. [6]Corporations can link their catalogs on their Web sites. [7]People can order the products through the Internet. [8]The consumers save time and money by browsing the Internet catalogs and ordering products directly from the companies. [9]The use of the Internet by businesses and consumers saves time and money. [10]It strengthens the relationship between businesses and consumers.

(4) Transitions between paragraphs

Transitions between paragraphs are as important as transitions between sentences and are achieved by many of the same devices—repetition of words or ideas, conjunctions and other transitional expressions, and parallel structures. Such devices are usually evident in the first sentence of a paragraph. (The italics in each of the following examples were added.)

You can repeat a word or idea from the last paragraph in the first sentence of the new one, as in paragraphs 24 and 25. (See also **31b**.)

24 For those who pray or chant with great perseverance, there is the suggestion that their *waiting* has been converted into purposefulness.

25 Of course, we do not just *wait* for love; we *wait* for money, we *wait* for the weather to get warmer, colder; we *wait* for the plumber to come and fix the washing machine. . . .

—EDNA O'BRIEN, "Waiting"

In paragraphs 26 and 27, Grace Paley picks up the idea of sentencing as a transition to her second paragraph.

26 I was in jail. I had been sentenced to six days in the Women's House of Detention, a fourteen-story prison right in the middle of Greenwich Village, my own neighborhood. This happened during the American War in Vietnam, I have forgotten which important year of the famous sixties. The civil disobedience for which I was paying a small penalty probably consisted of sitting down to impede or slow some military parade.

27 I was surprised at the sentence. Others had been given two days or dismissed. I think the judge was particularly angry with me. . . .

—GRACE PALEY, "Six Days: Some Rememberings"

Paragraphs 28 and 29 show how you can use transitional words or phrases to connect paragraphs.

28 . . . America Online even banned the word "breast," leaving users with more colorful synonyms free to chat but making any discussions of breast cancer or breast exams impossible.

29 Another frightening aspect of the Decency Act is the imposition of the "community standards" clause concerning online communication. Given the right equipment, any site is reachable from any place on earth. . . .

—SANDY M. FERNANDEZ, "The Cybercops"

You can use parallel structures to demonstrate relationships between paragraphs, as in paragraphs 30 and 31.

30 I understood that when I graduated
  I would get a job at *Glamour* or *Mademoiselle*
    where I would meet a dashing young lawyer,
      fall in love,
      get married,
      have 2.5 children, and

play bridge all day
like my mother did.
But the Sixties gave me new goals.

31 I discovered that when I married,
I had to keep my job at *Rolling Stone*
where I met my unemployable poet-husband,
got promoted,
had 1 child, and
did the housework late at night
like my mother's maid had.

Sometimes a transitional paragraph serves as a bridge between two paragraphs. Ordinarily, such a paragraph is short (often consisting of only one sentence) because the writer intends it to be merely a signpost, as in paragraphs 32 through 34.

32 Now you are expecting me to describe how I saw the folly of my ways and came back to the warm nest, where prejudices are so often called loyalties, where pointless actions are hallowed into custom by repetition, where we are content to say we think when all we do is feel.

33 But you would be wrong. I dropped my hobby and turned professional.

34 If I were to go back to the headmaster's study and find the dusty statuettes still there, I would arrange them differently. I would dust Venus and put her aside, for I have come to love her and know her for the fair thing she is. But I would put the Thinker, sunk in his desperate thought, where there were shadows before him—and at his back, I would put the leopard, crouched and ready to spring.

—WILLIAM GOLDING, "Thinking as a Hobby"

31c Details and examples can develop paragraphs.

Many short paragraphs are adequately developed and supply enough information within the context of the essay to satisfy the reader. For example, the following paragraph, although only one sentence, contains considerable detail.

35 To have parents who are, as they say, dysfunctional—in this case, needy, infantile, self-indulgent, narcissistic, ruthlessly selfish hysterics who use up all the oxygen in the room and then gasp self-pityingly that they are having trouble breathing—is a maturing burden for a child, and a sad kind of discipline. —LANCE MORROW, "Childhood in a Fishbowl: Having Famous Parents Can Be So Embarrassing. How's a Kid Going to Cope?" *Time*

Sometimes short paragraphs can be combined if they deal with the same idea. More often, however, short paragraphs need to be developed with more specific details or examples.

(1) Developing with specific details

Notice how the series of details in paragraph 36 supports the topic sentence (italicized).

36 *I still go around tasting and smelling things the way I did when I was assaying the palatability of sheep feed; a handy skill, it turns out.* There's the funky tang of sage-like rotted lavender—beautiful or foul depending; and the tarry marvel of creosote bush in the summer after a rain, in the darkness, thunder still drumming the air, while the snakes are emerging, and the spadefoot toads come out to ring and blurt from transient pools. A thousand scents: the sweet headiness of desert mistletoe in dry Mojave canyons in January, the piss smell of the tiny white night-blooming flower called desert snow, the

cactus blooms that have a tang of tangerine or horehound, the mucilaginous beany taste of young nopales, and the scent of a salt spring, which is a little like death.

—DIANA KAPPEL-SMITH, "Salt"

(2) Developing with examples

Use appropriate and specific examples to clarify your ideas. The following definition may be unclear without the italicized example.

> A euphemism is the substitution of a pleasant expression for an unpleasant one, *such as "passed away" for "died."*

Paragraph 37 uses several closely related examples (as well as details) to explain why violence is both impractical and immoral.

37 Violence as a way of achieving racial justice is both impractical and immoral. It is impractical because it is a descending spiral ending in destruction for all. The old law of an eye for an eye leaves everybody blind. It is immoral because it seeks to humiliate the opponent rather than win his understanding; it seeks to annihilate rather than to convert. Violence is immoral because it thrives on hatred rather than love. It destroys community and makes brotherhood impossible. It leaves society in monologue rather than dialogue. Violence ends by defeating itself. It creates bitterness in the survivors and brutality in the destroyers. A voice echoes through time saying to every potential Peter, "Put up your sword." History is cluttered with the wreckage of nations that failed to follow this command.

—MARTIN LUTHER KING, JR., "Three Types of Resistance to Oppression"

You can also use one striking example, as in paragraph 38, to clarify your idea.

38 Glamour's lethal effect on the psyche is also caught in the language that commonly describes its impact: "dressed to

> kill," "devastating," "shattering," "stunning," "knockout," "to die." Perhaps it's not surprising that Rita Hayworth's famous pinup pose in which she's kneeling in a silk negligee on satin sheets was taped to the bomb that was dropped on Hiroshima.
>
> —JOHN LAHR, "The Voodoo of Glamour" *New Yorker*

Details and examples clarify and explain your point.

Exercise 7

Develop the following sentences with enough details and/or examples to make an interesting paragraph.

1. Many people wonder how _______ stays in shape.
2. It was the filthiest room I had ever seen.
3. The class was so boring I decided to cut.
4. I grew up in the friendliest neighborhood in the world.

Exercise 8

Examine your own writing and select a paragraph you think needs additional details or an appropriate example. Rewrite the paragraph.

31d Writers use various strategies to develop paragraphs.

You can learn to write good paragraphs by studying the various techniques professional writers use to develop ideas. All the strategies for developing paragraphs discussed in the following pages are useful for developing whole compositions. (See also chapters 32 and 33.)

The more you read, the more you will find that most paragraphs are developed by a combination of methods. Some good paragraphs almost defy analysis. Because these development strategies reflect the ways people think, we tend to use them in combination with each other. For example, the formal definition can be developed through both classification and contrast, or narration can be developed by using descriptive details. The important consideration is not that a specific method is used to develop the paragraph, but that the development is clear, complete, and appropriate. No one method or combination is better than another. Use the one—or ones—that best suit your purpose. As you study the following illustrations of good paragraphs, notice how each main idea is developed.

(1) Narrating a series of events

A narrative discusses a sequence of events, normally in the order in which they occur, that develop the point you are making. This form often uses time markers such as *then*, *later*, or *at a later date*. (Longer narratives often begin in the middle of a sequence of events and contain flashbacks to earlier events.) The narrative must be closely related to your main idea and must develop that idea. The writer in paragraph 39 uses narrative to develop the main idea stated in the last sentence in the paragraph.

39 Contrary to popular opinion, it is not easy to write country songs. One guy who never made it is Robin Dorsey from Matador, Texas. He went to Tech and had a girlfriend from Muleshoe about whom he wrote the love song "Her Teeth Was Stained but Her Heart Was Pure." She took offense and quit him over it, which caused him to write the tragedy-love song "I Don't Know Whether to Commit Suicide Tonight or Go Bowlin'." —MOLLY IVINS, "Honky Tonking"

(2) Describing to make a point

Focus your description according to your purpose. In describing your car, you would emphasize certain features to a prospective buyer, others to a mechanic who is going to repair it, and still others to a friend who wants to borrow it.

Descriptive details should be clearly ordered—from near to far, from general to particular, from right to left, from top to bottom—thus providing an orderly scheme for the reader. In paragraph 40, Thomas Merton uses a near-far perspective to enable the reader to share his experience as he approached the monastery that was to become his home. Notice also his use of metaphors ("a barrier and a defense against the world"), similes ("as gray as lead"), and personification ("The tires sang"). (See figurative language in 20a(4).)

40 I looked at the rolling country, and at the pale ribbon of road in front of us stretching out as gray as lead in the light of the moon. Then suddenly I saw a steeple that shone like silver in the moonlight, growing into sight from behind a rounded knoll. The tires sang on the empty road and breathless I looked at the monastery that was revealed before me as we came over the rise. At the end of an avenue of trees was a big rectangular block of buildings, all dark, with a church crowned by a tower and a steeple and a cross: and the steeple was as bright as platinum and the whole place was as quiet as midnight and lost in the all-absorbing silence and solitude of the fields. Behind the monastery was a dark curtain of woods and over to the west was a wooded valley and beyond that a rampart of wooded hills, a barrier and a defense against the world. —THOMAS MERTON, *The Seven Storey Mountain*

Descriptions can appeal to more senses than just sight. Kathleen Murphy in paragraph 41 makes her description of Clint Eastwood's *High Plains Drifter* character vivid by blending visual and auditory images and suggesting images of touch.

41 His gait is that of a ghost or a predator, his poncho'd torso remaining strangely still, propelled ahead by the long legs, as

though swimming upright in slow motion. Paradoxically, the hands of the remorseless gunfighter are those of a musician or a painter: elegant, long-fingered, with graceful wrists. In these formative stages of the Eastwood persona, his often nearly whispered vocal tones seem too pressured for ordinary speech. The silky, then increasingly abrasive sibilance of his drawl, like sand or gravel shifting in water, works best for epigrams, cryptic ripostes, up-close seduction.

—KATHLEEN MURPHY, "The Good, the Bad, and the Ugly: Clint Eastwood as Romantic Hero" *Film Comment*

(3) Explaining a process

Process paragraphs, in explaining how something is done or made, often use both description and narration. You might describe the items used in the process and then narrate the steps chronologically, as in paragraph 42.

42 The best of all scientific tricks with an egg is the well-known one in which air pressure forces a peeled hard-boiled egg into a glass milk bottle and then forces it out again undamaged. The mouth of the bottle must be only slightly smaller than the egg, and so you must be careful not to use too large an egg or too small a bottle. It is impossible to push the egg into the bottle. To get the egg though the mouth you must heat the air in the bottle. That is best done by standing the bottle in boiling water for a few minutes. Put the egg upright on the mouth and take the bottle off the stove. As the air in the bottle cools it contracts, creating a partial vacuum that draws the peeled egg inside. To get the egg out again invert the bottle so the egg falls into the neck. Place the opening of the bottle against your mouth and blow vigorously. This will compress the air in the bottle. When you stop blowing, the air expands, pushing the egg through the neck of the bottle and into your waiting hands.

—MARTIN GARDNER, "Mathematical Games"

(4) Showing cause and effect

A paragraph that explores a cause raises the question Why? and must answer that question to the satisfaction of the reader. Be sure to avoid the fallacy of assuming that since one event precedes another it is necessarily the cause of that event. (See **35h(8)**, false cause.) Paragraph 43 provides several reasons for the development of machismo.

43 Where did machismo come from? From 500 years of total suppression by a dominant culture that spoke of honor but which extended no honor to the colonized people of South and Central America, and which acted dishonorably toward them. Caught between survival realities and powerlessness, further constricted by the dictates of the church, the Latino male became a silent cauldron of unexpressed, justifiable anger. As literal colonialism gave way to economic imperialism, the difficulties of meeting family responsibilities in concert with race hatred turned Latino men inward to internalized self-hatred. Activist poet and former gangsta Luis J. Rodriguez describes it like this: "The patriarchal Mexican culture helped build a wide breach between my father and me. The silent and strong man—vestiges of deceit—was revered. Waited on. Accepted." This persona is lethal.

—RAY GONZALEZ,
"Machismo: Silence, the Lethal Weapon" *Sí*

Paragraphs can also demonstrate effects, as in paragraph 44, which discusses some results of protecting the endangered alligator.

44 The alligator's turnaround since that time has made national news. Protection and strict controls on interstate shipment of gator hides have worked: the animals have come back strong. Every so often, one will eat a poodle or take up residence in the water hazard on the sixteenth hole. Fish-and-game people are then called out to lasso the uncomprehending reptile and move it to an out-of-the-way place. There is even some limited commerce again in the skins. At least one entre-

preneur is ranching alligators, just as though they were cattle or mink. Not long ago, someone in Florida was killed by an alligator in what I suspect must have been a well-deserved attack. —GEOFFREY NORMAN, "Gators"

(5) Comparing and contrasting to develop an idea

A **comparison** points out similarities; a **contrast** points out differences. A comparison or a contrast can be organized in either of two ways (or a combination of them), the choice depending on the writer's purpose. Writers often use both methods for the sake of variation. Arthur L. Campa uses the **part-by-part method** in paragraph 45, in which he analyzes cultural differences between the Spanish and the English colonizers by looking first at the effects of geography on the English, then on the Spanish, and next at the effects of demographics on first the English and then the Spanish.

45 Cultural differences are implicit in the conceptual content of the languages of these two civilizations, and their value systems stem from a long series of historical circumstances. Therefore, it may be well to consider some of the English and Spanish cultural configurations before these Europeans set foot on American soil. English culture was basically insular, geographically and ideologically; was more integrated on the whole, except for some strong theological differences; and was particularly zealous of its racial purity. Spanish culture was peninsular, a geographical circumstance that made it a catchall of Mediterranean, central European, and north African peoples. The composite nature of the population produced a market regionalism that prevented close integration, except for religion, and led to a strong sense of individualism. These differences were reflected in the colonizing enterprise of the two cultures. The English isolated themselves from the Indians physically and culturally; the Spanish, who had strong notions about *pureza de sangre* [purity of blood] among the nobility, were not collectively averse to adding one more

strain to their racial cocktail. Cortés led the way by siring the first *mestizo* in North America, and the rest of the conquistadores followed suit. The ultimate products of these two orientations meet today in the Southwest.

Campa switches in the next paragraph (46) to the **unit-by-unit method**, developing first the Anglo and then the Hispanic values.

46 Anglo-American culture was absolutist at the onset; that is, all the dominant values were considered identical for all, regardless of time and place. Such values as justice, charity, and honesty were considered the superior social order for all men and were later embodied in the American Constitution. The Spaniard brought with him a relativistic viewpoint and saw fewer moral implications in man's actions. Values were looked upon as the result of social and economic conditions.

—ARTHUR L. CAMPA, "Anglo vs. Chicano: Why?"

Two valuable kinds of comparisons are analogy and metaphor. A **metaphor** is a figure of speech. (See 20a(4).) An **analogy**, often used in argument, makes a point by comparing a complex or unfamiliar concept to a simple or familiar one or by comparing two familiar concepts that are not ordinarily thought to be similar. In paragraph 47, Nelson Mandela draws an analogy between leadership and gardening.

47 In some ways, I saw the garden as a metaphor for certain aspects of my life. A leader must also tend his garden; he, too, plants seed, and then watches, cultivates, and harvests the result. Like the gardener, a leader must take responsibility for what he cultivates; he must mind his work, try to repel enemies, preserve what can be preserved, and eliminate what cannot succeed.

—NELSON MANDELA, "Raising Tomatoes and Leading People"

However, it is important that you do not assume that because two things are alike in some ways they are alike in all ways. (See 35h(6), false analogy.)

(6) Classifying and dividing to develop an idea

To classify is to categorize things in large groups that share certain common characteristics. **Classification** is a way to understand or explain a large or diverse subject and discover the relationships within it. When you classify chocolate pudding as a dessert, you tell your reader that, like most desserts, it is probably sweet and high in calories. **Division**, in contrast, breaks objects and ideas into parts that are smaller and examines the relationships among them. A store manager might group books according to publisher for her own inventory or according to types—biography, science fiction, mystery, and so forth—for her customers.

Classification and division represent two different perspectives; ideas can be put into groups (classification) or split into subclasses (division) on the basis of a dividing principle. Classification and division most often work together because once you have placed something in a class, the next logical step is to explain the characteristics of that class, which is division. So you may find yourself using both classification and division to approach your subject. They work together to give a view that places the subject in a context and develops it in detail. Notice how Russell Baker first establishes his classifications in paragraph 48 and then explains them in paragraph 49.

> 48 Inanimate objects are classified scientifically into three major categories—those that break down, those that get lost, and those that don't work.

> 49 The goal of all inanimate objects is to resist man and ultimately to defeat him, and the three major classifications are based on the method each object uses to achieve its purpose. As a general rule, any object capable of breaking down at the moment when it is most needed will do so. The automobile is typical of the category.
>
> —RUSSELL BAKER, "The Plot against People"

Analysis, like division, breaks an object or idea into its elements. In paragraph 50, Aaron Copland analyzes three ways to listen to music.

50 We all listen to music according to our separate capacities. But, for the sake of analysis, the whole listening process may become clearer if we break it up into its component parts, so to speak. In a certain sense we all listen to music on three separate planes. For lack of a better terminology, one might name these: (1) the sensuous plane, (2) the expressive plane, (3) the sheerly musical plane. The only advantage to be gained from mechanically splitting up the listening process into these hypothetical planes is the clearer view to be had of the way in which we listen.

—AARON COPLAND, "How We Listen to Music"

(7) Formulating a definition

Paragraphs of definition explain the meaning of a concept, a term, or an object. Sometimes we define arbitrarily: "They use the term 'pony' to refer to an equine of any size." Or we may define by describing how something works: "A security system is supposed to hinder burglars." The effect of definition is to put a concept, a term, or an object into a class and then differentiate it from other members of the class: "A concerto [the term] is a symphonic piece [the class] performed by one or more solo instruments and orchestra [the difference]." The **difference** distinguishes the **term** from all other members of the **class**. Paragraph 51 defines volcanos by putting them in a class ("landforms") and by distinguishing them ("built of molten material") from other members of that class. The definition is then clarified by examples.

51 Volcanos are landforms built of molten material that has spewed out onto the earth's surface. Such molten rock is called *lava*. Volcanos may be no larger than small hills, or

> thousands of feet high. All have a characteristic cone shape. Some well-known mountains are actually volcanos. Examples are Mt. Fuji (Japan), Mt. Lassen (California), Mt. Hood (Oregon), Mt. Etna and Mt. Vesuvius (Italy), and Paricutín (Mexico). The Hawaiian Islands are all immense volcanos whose summits rise above the ocean, and these volcanos are still quite active. —JOEL AREM, *Rocks and Minerals*

Definitions can be clarified and extended by details, as in paragraph 51, or by examples, synonyms, or etymology (the history of the word). Synonyms are often only one or two words enclosed in commas immediately following the term.

> Sophomores, *second-year students,* derive their name from two Greek words meaning "wise fool."

31e Editing can improve paragraph logic and effectiveness.

At some point in the process of writing your essay, you may stop to assess the logic and effectiveness of a paragraph. Although this activity is a normal part of revising and editing, it can also occur at almost any time during your writing, and it can be repeated as frequently as necessary. When you rework paragraphs, you should consider the points in the following checklist.

Checklist for Revising Paragraphs ✓

- Do all the ideas in the paragraph belong?
- Are any necessary ideas left out?
- Is the paragraph coherent? Do the sentences focus on the topic? Do they link to previous sentences? Is the order of sentences logical?

continued

continued from previous page

✓

- Are sentences connected to each other with easy, effective, and natural transitions? Is the paragraph linked to the preceding and following paragraphs?
- Is the paragraph adequately developed? If there are problems, can analyzing the strategy used to develop the paragraph help solve the problem?

Exercise 9

Prepare for a class discussion of the following paragraphs (52, 53, and 54) by identifying main ideas (**31a**), transitions (**31b**), and methods of development (**31c** and **31d**).

52 Tigger began by staring at the white door of the refrigerator for several minutes before stepping up to one of the saucers at its base and carefully brushing his paw pads lightly over the surface of the thick paint it contained. Then, perfectly balanced on his hind legs, he reached up and made the most delicate comma-like swirl of blue just below the handle. He repeated the motif three more times in different colors, one below the other, and then, with scarcely a glance at what he'd done, nonchalantly walked outside to wash his paws. The whole operation lasted only a few minutes but had been performed with such casual grace it appeared as if nothing unusual had occurred at all.

—HEATHER BUSCH and BURTON SILVER, *Why Cats Paint: A Theory of Feline Aesthetics*

53 The strain of not relating is what provokes the bloodshed, and some people will kill each other for love, particularly during the holidays when we're supposed to love each other to death. But perhaps the reason it's so hard to relate is because it's so hard to be disappointed, to know that the schizoids, compulsive cleaners, alcoholics, and dullards, all the relatives who come home to roost, are not so different from us.

—PHYLLIS THEROUX, "Fear of Families"

54 Just as I meant "shimmer" literally I mean "grammar" literally. Grammar is a piano I play by ear, since I seem to have been out of school the year the rules were mentioned. All I know about grammar is its infinite power. To shift the structure of a sentence alters the meaning of that sentence, as definitely and inflexibly as the position of a camera alters the meaning of the object photographed. Many people know about camera angles now, but not so many know about sentences. The arrangement of the words matters, and the arrangement you want can be found in the picture in your mind. The picture dictates the arrangement. The picture dictates whether this will be a sentence with or without clauses, a sentence that ends hard or a dying-fall sentence, long or short, active or passive. The picture tells you how to arrange the words and the arrangement of the words tells me what's going on in the picture. *Nota bene* [note well].

—JOAN DIDION, "Why I Write"

Exercise 10

Write paragraphs using any of the strategies of development described in **31d**. Start with one of the following topic sentences.

1. The (largest, ugliest, most unusual, oldest, etc.) building I ever saw . . . .
2. When we were ten years old . . . .
3. I like the kind of (car/truck/van, computer, camera, etc.) I have now better then the last (specific car/truck/van, computer, camera, etc.) I had because . . . .
4. Let me explain why I can't stand . . . .
5. My job is the very definition of (stress, pleasure, frustration, gratification, challenge, stupidity).

Chapter 32

Planning and Drafting Essays

Whenever you write an essay, you engage in a process of developing an appropriate topic (32b) for a certain audience. You often need to explore various possibilities to discover what you want to write (32c(1)), how to focus your subject (32c(2)), how to form a thesis (32d), and how to develop an appropriate plan of organization (32e). Your writing will benefit if you write more than one draft, rethinking and restructuring what you have written. If you try to engage in all of these activities simultaneously, you may become frustrated. Experienced writers understand that writing is a process, a process that usually requires a considerable investment of time.

As you move through this process, you may need to return to a specific activity several times. For example, drafting may help you see that you need to go back and collect more ideas, change your thesis, or even start over with a new one. Rather than seeing repeated effort as a sign of failure, experienced writers consider it an indication of commitment. Writing effective essays requires serious work, but the effort is worthwhile. Although the process of writing essays is seldom neat or straightforward, working out your ideas and making them clear to readers will help you gain new insights and enjoy a sense of genuine accomplishment.

32a Writers must understand their purpose, audience, and occasion.

Effective writers have a clear sense of purpose, audience, and occasion.

Purpose	What a writer hopes to achieve in a piece of writing
Audience	Who will read the piece in question
Occasion	Where and when the exchange between writer and audience takes place

Your purpose should be appropriate for both the audience and the occasion. Consider, for example, how your speech changes depending on the audience and the occasion. You would not talk to a prospective employer the way you talk to your closest friend. Nor would you speak the same way to your friend regardless of the occasion—which means not only the immediate time and place an exchange takes place, but also how context influences that time and place. Meeting a friend for coffee when she is excited about getting a new job would generate words different from the ones you would say to her the first time you see her after she has suffered a serious loss. You should demonstrate similar flexibility when making appropriate choices for different essays. The combination of purpose, audience, and occasion is called your **rhetorical situation**. Assess your rhetorical situation when you are planning an essay and remember it when you are revising (chapter 33) your drafts.

(1) Purpose means why you are writing.

The clearer your purpose, the better your writing is likely to be. To clarify your purpose, or why you are writing, it helps to ask yourself if you want to

- express how you feel about something
- report information to readers
- explain the significance of information
- persuade readers to agree with you
- convince readers to undertake a specific action
- amuse or entertain readers

When classified according to purpose, nonfiction writing is often described as expressive, expository, or persuasive.

Expressive writing emphasizes the writer's feelings and reactions to the world—to people, objects, events, and ideas. Personal letters and journals are often expressive, as are many essays. The following example comes from an essay designed to convey how the author feels about the relationship he had with his father.

> At just about the hour when my father died, soon after dawn one February morning when ice coated the windows like cataracts, I banged my thumb with a hammer. Naturally I swore at the hammer, the reckless thing, and in the moment of swearing I thought of what my father would say: "If you'd try hitting the nail it would go in a whole lot faster. Don't you know your thumb's not as hard as that hammer?" We were both doing carpentry that day, but far apart. He was building cupboards at my brother's place in Oklahoma; I was at home in Indiana putting up a wall in the basement to make a bedroom for my daughter. By the time my mother called with the news of his death—the long distance wires whittling her voice until it seemed too thin to bear the weight of what she had to say—my thumb was swollen. A week or two later a white scar in the shape of a crescent moon began to show

> above the cuticle, and month by month it rose across the pink sky of my thumbnail. It took the better part of a year for the scar to disappear, and every time I noticed it I thought of my father.
>
> —SCOTT RUSSELL SANDERS, "The Inheritance of Tools"

Expository writing, or referential writing as it is sometimes called, focuses the reader's attention on the objective world—the objects, the events, and the ideas themselves—rather than on the writer's feelings about them. Textbooks, news accounts, scientific reports, and encyclopedia articles are often expository, as are many of the essays students are expected to write in college. When you report, explain, clarify, or evaluate, you are practicing exposition. The following paragraph comes from a book discussing how our culture came to be concerned about age.

> This preoccupation with age came about because modern technological society radically changed the conditions of growing up and the entire human life cycle. As modern societies developed age-graded institutions, age came to matter in new ways: our birthdates came to determine when we must go to school and when we can leave school, when we can vote, or work full time, drive, marry, buy liquor, enter into contracts, run for public office, retire, and receive Social Security.
>
> —ARLENE SKOLNICK, *The Psychology of Human Development*

Persuasive writing is intended to influence the reader's attitudes and actions. Most writing is to some extent persuasive; through the choice and arrangement of material, even something as apparently straightforward as a résumé can be persuasive. However, writing is usually called persuasive if it is clearly arguing for or against a position.

When you write persuasively, you need the critical and rhetorical skills discussed in chapter 35. Persuasion depends on both rational and emotional appeals. The reader's perception of a writer's honesty, fair-mindedness, and goodwill is as crucial as the writer's presentation of evidence and rational arguments. In turn, the writer needs to respond to a reader's concerns and doubts. In the opening paragraph of his "Letter from Birmingham Jail," Martin Luther King, Jr., establishes his own patience and good sense while confirming that his readers are persons "of genuine good will."

> MY DEAR FELLOW CLERGYMEN:
>
> While confined here in Birmingham city jail, I came across your recent statement calling my present activities "unwise and untimely." Seldom do I pause to answer criticism of my work and ideas. If I sought to answer all the criticisms that cross my desk, my secretaries would have little time for anything other than such correspondence in the course of the day, and I would have no time for constructive work. But since I feel that you are men of genuine good will and that your criticisms are sincerely set forth, I want to try to answer your statement in what I hope will be patient and reasonable terms.
>
> —MARTIN LUTHER KING, JR., "Letter from Birmingham Jail"

In addition to writing to express themselves, inform others, or persuade others, some people write primarily because they find satisfaction in the imaginative use of language. This purpose is often evident in fiction, poetry, and drama. (See 39a.) It can also be found in nonfiction writing, such as the following example from an essay describing a sudden encounter with a wild animal.

> Our look was as if two lovers, or deadly enemies, met unexpectedly on an overgrown path when each had been thinking of something else: a clearing blow to the gut. It was also a bright blow to the brain, or a sudden beating of brains, with all the charge and intimate grate of rubbed balloons. It emptied our lungs. It felled the forest, moved the fields, and drained the pond; the world dismantled and tumbled into that black hole of eyes. If you and I looked at each other that way,

> our skulls would split and drop to our shoulders. But we don't. We keep our skulls. So.
>
> —ANNIE DILLARD, "Living like Weasels"

Writing that emphasizes the imaginative use of language is sometimes described as **literary** writing, whether it takes the form of a poem, an essay, or a joke.

Writers frequently have more than one purpose, choosing to write humorously, for example, to persuade readers to change a certain behavior. There is nothing wrong with having more than one purpose. The challenge is to be sure that you *have* a purpose. If you have more than one purpose, you should be using one to help you achieve another—which is very different from writing without a purpose or simply losing sight of your original purpose.

Exercise 1

Select one of the following subjects and write a description of how you would approach this subject if you were writing an essay that would be primarily (a) expressive, (b) expository, (c) persuasive, and (d) literary.

1. summer	4. computers	7. working
2. children	5. rain	8. music
3. cars	6. fast food	9. housing

(2) Audience means who will read your writing.

Understanding your audience will help you decide on the length and depth of your essay, the kind of language to use, and the examples that will be the most effective. Audiences vary considerably, and so do writers. Some writers like to plan and draft essays with a clear sense of audience already in mind; others like to focus on the audience primarily when they are revising their work (chapter 33). At some point, however, you must think clearly about who will be reading your writing and ask yourself if your choices are appropriate for this audience.

Specialized audiences

A **specialized audience** has considerable knowledge of the subject you are writing about and a keen interest in it. For example, if your subject is a new skiing technique, a group of ski instructors would obviously constitute a specialized audience. So would readers of *Ski* magazine, although in writing for this audience you would allow for a greater variation in the knowledge and interest of the reader.

When writing for specialized audiences, you need to consider how much and what kinds of information, as well as what methods of presentation, are called for. You can adjust your tone and the kind of language you use as you tailor your presentation to their expertise and attitudes. (See 19g.) The average reader would probably find the following example impenetrable, but it is written for a specialized audience of experts who understand linguistics and are familiar with the terminology.

> The notions of illocutionary force and different illocutionary acts involve really several quite different principles of distinction. . . . So we must not suppose what the metaphor of "force" suggests, that the different illocutionary verbs mark off points on a single continuum. Rather, there are several different continua of "illocutionary force," and the fact that the illocutionary verbs of English stop at certain points on these various continua and not at others is, in a sense, accidental. For example, we might have had an illocutionary verb "rubrify," meaning to call something "red." Thus, "I hereby rubrify it" would just mean "It's red." Analogously, we happen to have an obsolete verb "macarize," meaning to call someone happy.
>
> —J. R. SEARLE, "Speech Acts: An Essay in the Philosophy of Language"

Many of the papers you write in college are for a specialized audience. When you write an essay for a college course, you can assume that your instructor is already well informed about the material. No one is ever entirely expert, however, and a specialized audience is usually pleased to learn something new. However, writing for a specialized audience does not necessarily demand that you know more than specialists in that field. At times it may be sufficient to demonstrate that you understand the material and can use appropriate language to discuss it. Moreover, a specialized audience for one subject would be a general audience for another.

General audiences

A **general audience** consists of readers not expert on your topic but presumably willing to read what you have to say about it. It is possible to identify certain characteristics even in a general audience so that you can shape your presentation accordingly. When writing essays, you can usually assume that your readers have many interests different from your own but share a willingness to learn about new material if it is presented clearly and respectfully. This assumed audience is not very different from the one articles in a general encyclopedia are written for. Consider how the following description from an introductory linguistics textbook explains a concept that the author of the comparable passage on page 334 assumed to be already understood by a specialized audience.

> The study of how we do things with sentences is the study of **speech acts**. In studying speech acts, we are acutely aware of the importance of the *context of the utterance*. In some circumstances *There is a sheepdog in the closet* is a warning, but the same sentence may be a promise or even a mere statement of fact, depending on circumstances. We call this purpose—a warning, a promise, a threat, or whatever—the **illocutionary force** of a speech act.
>
> —VICTORIA FROMKIN and ROBERT RODMAN, *An Introduction to Language*

General audiences may be of quite different kinds and require some adjustment of subject matter and diction. For example, the author of an advanced textbook can assume an audience already familiar with basic concepts in the field, so one approach to envisioning a general audience is to think in terms of education level. You could ask yourself, for example, whether the audience you are writing for is composed of college sophomores or college graduates who majored in a field different from yours. An upper-division textbook in linguistics presents a somewhat more complete approach to speech acts than an introductory text:

> Every speech act has two principal components: the utterance itself and the intention of the speaker in making it. First, every utterance is represented by a sentence with a grammatical structure and a meaning; this is variously called the **locution** or the utterance act. Second, speakers have some intention in making an utterance, something they intend to accomplish; that intention is called an **illocution**, and every utterance consists of performing one or more illocutionary acts.
>
> —EDWARD FINEGAN and NIKO BESNIER, *Language: Its Structure and Use*

You could also envision a general audience defined by some other common ground—such as readers of the same gender. If you look through popular magazines, you can easily find articles written for either men or women. However, when writing for a gender-specific audience, do not make the mistake of thinking that all men—or all women—think the same way or share the same values. Further, there is a big difference between consciously choosing to write for a gender-specific audience and accidentally ignoring gender differences when writing for an audience that includes both men and women.

Sometimes you may not know much about your audience. When this is the case, you can often benefit from imagining a thoughtful audience of educated adults. Such an audience is likely to include people with different backgrounds and cultural values, so be careful not to assume that you are writing for readers who are exactly like you. A useful technique, in this case, is to imagine yourself in conversation with a small group of specific persons who have diverse backgrounds but nevertheless share an interest in your topic.

Multiple audiences

Writers often need to address multiple audiences. At work, for example, you might need to write a memo or a letter that will be read not only by the person to whom it is addressed but also by other people who receive copies. The readers in a multiple audience can have distinctly different expectations. If, for example, you are asked to evaluate the performance of an employee you supervise and send copies to both that person and your own boss, one part of your audience is probably looking for praise while the other is looking to see if you are a competent supervisor.

When writing essays in college, you may find yourself writing for multiple audiences. The most common example is drafting an essay that will be discussed in a small group of fellow students and read by your instructor. If you choose to write an essay for a general audience and submit it to a college professor who is a specialist on your subject, you are, in effect, writing for multiple audiences. Writing effectively for multiple audiences requires you to consider a variety of attitudes and positions. (See 36c.) You can benefit from doing so when planning your essay and also by reading what you have drafted from different points of view as you prepare to revise it. (See chapter 33.)

Exercise 2

Choose a recent class and write a description of it that would be read by (a) a member of your family, (b) the teacher of the class, or (c) the dean of your school. Then write a second description that would be read by all three of these audiences.

(3) Occasion means the circumstances under which writers and readers communicate.

Occasion is the context in which the writing occurs, the circumstances under which the exchange between a writer and a reader takes place: time, place, and climate. A letter written on the occasion of a friend's marriage is likely to differ from a letter written on the occasion of her divorce. A message sent by e-mail—see 8c(1) and 39b(1)—is seldom written with precisely the same care as a letter sent to the same person. An essay written outside class may be very different from an essay written in a classroom even if both are written for the same audience and with the same purpose. Moreover, either of these essays could be influenced by climate or social context—whatever is happening in the writer's world. Students taking the same exam for the same teacher are to some extent influenced by external events. For example, a national economic crisis could either distract their attention or improve their motivation.

When you read the work of other writers, you will sometimes find examples in which the occasion is specifically stated, as in the following passage.

> In the twenty-second month of the war against Nazism we meet here in this old Palace of St. James, itself not unscarred by the fire of the enemy, in order to proclaim the high pur-

> poses and resolves of the lawful constitutional Governments of Europe whose countries have been overrun; and we meet here also to cheer the hopes of free men and free peoples throughout the world.
>
> —WINSTON CHURCHILL, "Until Victory Is Won"

Often, however, the occasion must be inferred. Whether or not you choose to state your occasion when writing an essay, it is essential that you consider it. For example, your instructor may have higher expectations for your final essay in a course than for your first. The occasion is different because the time and climate are different.

32b Writers need to find appropriate subjects.

If you are assigned a subject or if your situation clearly dictates one, you can move directly to considering the particular aspect of it you will emphasize (32c(2)), the expectations of your audience (32a(2)), and the method of organization best suited for your discussion (32e). If you must choose your own subject, you should consider not only your own interests but also your rhetorical situation. Of the various subjects that appeal to you, which would be the best for your purpose on this occasion for this audience?

When you are free to choose a subject, you can write an appealing paper on almost anything that interests you. Often the best subject is one drawn from your own experience—your personal knowledge, interests, and beliefs. Do you play a musical instrument? Enjoy sports? Like to travel? Do you have a job? Can you think of a particular place that is important to you? An interesting person you know? What ambitions do you have for yourself? What strong convictions do you hold? The challenge, of course, is to make what interests you interesting to your readers. Whether your purpose is to express, inform, or persuade, take this opportunity to share something that is important to you so that others will recognize its value.

College students are often asked to write essays about subjects outside their own experience. For instance, you may have to write a paper for a microbiology course. Although you are free to choose your subject, your purpose is to write an expository essay demonstrating your command of information (see page 331) rather than an expressive paper revealing how you feel about microbes. (See page 330.) Just as you do when you write about personal experience, however, you should make an effort to find material of interest to you. Look in your textbook, particularly in the sections listing suggestions for further reading and study. Go through your lecture notes and examine the annotations you made in whatever you read for the course. (See chapter 37f(2).) Ask yourself if there are any aspects of your subject that you feel certain about and any others about which you would like to learn more. Writing about a subject is one of the best ways to learn about it, so use this assignment not only to satisfy your audience but also to satisfy yourself.

Finding a subject can be difficult, and some writers become frustrated at this stage of the writing process. (See 34b.) Do not be afraid to talk with your instructor or with other students. Discussing ideas with other people can help you generate new ones and decide on those likely to yield good essays.

Exercise 3

1. Choose a personal experience that might be an appropriate subject. Write a paragraph describing why you think it would be useful to share this experience with others. Identify your audience and write a second paragraph describing how much information you would need to include so that this audience would understand your experience. Then, for your own reference, set some limits for yourself by making a separate list of anything about this experience that you do not want to include because you wish to protect your privacy or avoid embarrassing your audience.
2. Select an academic subject from one of your college courses and write a paragraph describing how you would approach this subject if you were writing for the instructor of that course and how you would approach the same material if you were writing for ninth graders.

32c By exploring subjects, you can focus on a topic.

When you are free to choose your own subject, you can use a number of different methods to discover the best subject for your essay. If you already have one in mind, the same methods can be used to explore possibilities for focusing and developing it. As you explore, you will probably discover a number of paths that look as if they could take you where you want to go and others that you will choose not to follow.

(1) There are several ways to search for a subject.

If you have a hard time finding subjects to write about, try journaling or freewriting. If you have a subject in mind but are unsure of how to develop it, try listing, questioning, and applying perspectives. Use whatever methods produce results for you. Different methods may work best for different subjects; if you run out of ideas when using one method, switch to another. Sometimes, especially for an assigned subject remote from your own interests and knowledge, you may need to try several methods.

Journaling

Keeping a journal is a proven way to generate subjects for essays. Although there are many different kinds of journals, students often benefit from writing daily in a personal journal or a writer's notebook.

In a **personal journal**, you reflect on your experience. Instead of simply listing activities, meals, or weather reports, you use writing to explore how you feel about what is happening in your life. You might focus on external events, such as what you think about a book or a film, or focus on your inner life by exploring changes in mood or attitude. Writers who keep a personal journal usually write for their own benefit; they are their own audience and do not share what they write with others. But in the process of writing this journal—or reading it—they discover subjects that can be used for essays.

Like a personal journal, a **writer's notebook** also includes responses to experience. In this case, however, the emphasis is on sorting through what you are learning. Students often benefit from keeping a writer's notebook in which they respond exclusively to what they are reading. They record quotations that seem especially meaningful, evaluate the strengths and weaknesses of a particular text, summarize the material (37f), note points they agree with, and jot down questions they would like to raise in class or pursue in an essay. In addition to helping you discover subjects for essays, a writer's notebook can help you become a better reader.

Some writers keep both a personal journal and a writer's notebook. Others keep only one—or create a combination of the two. In either case, they feel free to write quickly without worrying about spelling, grammar, or organization.

Freewriting

When freewriting, writers put down on paper without stopping whatever occurs to them during a limited period of time—often no more than ten minutes or so. They do not worry about whether they are repeating themselves or getting off the track; they simply write to see what comes out. No matter how bad the writing may be, the process helps them discover ideas they did not realize they had. The entries in a personal journal or writer's notebook may be freewritten, but freewriting is not limited to journaling. You can take out a sheet of paper and freewrite whenever you have a few minutes to spare. Some writers use different-colored marking pens to identify different topics generated by this activity.

In directed freewriting, writers begin with a general subject area and record whatever occurs to them about this subject during the time available. When asked by his English teacher to write about whatever he remembered about high school, Peter Geske wrote the following example of directed freewriting during five minutes of class time. This was the first step toward drafting the essay that appears later in this chapter (pages 368–70), the final version of which appears in chapter 33 (pages 385–88).

Write about high school? I can't believe this topic. Does he think we're all eighteen? I can hardly remember high school and what I remember isn't too good. That's why I didn't go to college right away. Now look at me. A good five years older than anyone in the class and stuck in a dead-end job. Working forty hours a week and borrowing money so that I can go back to school part time and write about some of the worst years in my life. All those stupid cliques and teachers who were real losers. Rodriguez was O.K. At least he listened and didn't treat us like convicts. Maybe that's why I'm still interested in history. But forget the rest of them. Kleinberg had so little control that the kids were flashing knives right in front of him and he never said a thing. No wonder I'm lousy in math. And that zombie who taught chemistry. All she ever did was read from the book. She never even looked at us. Maybe she was afraid to see how many kids were strung out. I don't see how I would've made it except for football. Reynolds wouldn't let us get away with anything. A real tough guy but he really cared about us.

As the color coding shows, this freewrite generated at least four possible writing topics about high school: cliques, unqualified teachers, the importance of football, and positive influences. Some of these topics overlap. Football, for example, could be combined with positive influences; or a good teacher might be contrasted with a poor teacher. However, the focus could also be narrowed to a single teacher or even to a single aspect of that teacher's performance—such as the inability to control the class. Within a few minutes, this writer has discovered that he has more to say than can be addressed in a single essay.

Listing

One way to gather ideas about your writing topic is to make an informal list. The advantage to listing is that, like an outline, it lets you see individual items at a glance rather than having to pick them out of a block of writing. It also encourages the establishment of relationships. Jot down any ideas that come to you while you are thinking about your subject. Do not worry if the ideas come without any kind of order, and do not worry about the form in which you write them down; grammar, spelling, and diction are not important at this stage. Devote as much time as necessary to making your list—perhaps five minutes, perhaps an entire evening. The point is to collect as many ideas as you can.

Peter made the following list after he had decided to focus his essay on the quality of the education he received at his high school.

geometry with Kleinberg
sophomore English with Mrs. Sullivan
American history with Mr. Rodriguez
out-of-date books
a terrible library
out-of-control classes
failing chemistry
good grades in English and history

blow-off courses
    social problems
    sex education
    speech

partying throughout senior year

too many students in each class

useless computers

This list may appear chaotic, but earlier items suggest later ones, and a review of the whole list may suggest items that need to be added. As you look through the list, you will find some ideas that are closely related and might be grouped together. For instance, items about school facilities can easily be grouped together, as can items concerning specific courses. Toward the end of his list, Peter began to establish some relationships by developing a sublisting of courses he found useless. Order and direction are beginning to emerge.

For an example of a list written and revised under pressure, see page 394.

Questioning

Explore a subject by asking yourself questions. There are two structured questioning strategies you might use—journalists' questions and a similar approach known as the pentad that encourages seeing relationships. The **journalists' questions** ask *Who? What? When? Where? Why?* and *How?;* they are easy to use and can help you discover ideas about any subject. Using journalists' questions to explore the subject of high school education could lead you to think about *who* goes to public high school and *who* teaches there, *what* courses are offered, *when* education improved or deteriorated, *why* some classes get overcrowded and *why* funds are short, *where* funding comes from and *where* teachers get their training, *how* education stimulates or *how* it fails.

The **pentad** considers the five dramatic aspects of a subject: the *act* (what happens), the *actor* (who does it), the *scene* (the time, place, and conditions under which the event occurred), the *agency* (the method or circumstances facilitating the act), and the *purpose* (the intent or reasons surrounding the act). This method differs from journalists' questions by suggesting relationships among the various aspects of the subject. For instance, what relationships can be explored between failing chemistry (the act) and the people involved in this act—the actors, in this case the student and the teacher. Or a writer could explore the relationship between the act and the scene by describing overcrowded classes and out of date equipment, both of which are conditions under which the act occurred.

Applying perspectives

Sometimes it is helpful to consider a subject in three quite different ways—as static, dynamic, and relative. A **static perspective** would focus your attention on what a high school education is. You might define it, describe the standard curriculum and school year, analyze its components, or use a specific school to provide an example.

The **dynamic perspective** focuses on action and change. You might examine the history of high school education, how it has changed over the years, or how your education changed you.

The **relative perspective** focuses on systems and relationships. You could examine the relationship between a public and private high school education or between funding for public education and economic conditions in your area, or you could compare secondary school education in the United States with secondary education in another country.

(2) Writers need to focus on specific material.

Exploring the subject will suggest not only productive strategies for development but also a direction and focus for your writing. Some ideas will seem worth pursuing; others will seem inappropriate for your purpose, audience, or occasion. You will find yourself discarding ideas even as you develop new ones. A simple analogy will help explain. When you want a picture of a landscape, you cannot photograph all that your eye can take in. You must focus on just part of that landscape. As you aim your camera, you look through the viewfinder to make sure the subject is correctly framed and in focus. At this point you may wish to move in closer and focus on one part of the scene or to change your angle, using light and shadow to emphasize some features of the landscape over others. You can think of your writing the same way—focusing and directing your ideas just as you focus and direct the lens of your camera—moving from a general subject to a more specific one.

For example, "high school" is too large and general a subject to make a good writing topic. However, some of the items that emerged in freewriting about this subject (page 344) and in the list that it elicited (pages 345–46) can be grouped to form a topic that is both interesting and manageable. Or a single item, if well chosen, could lead to a sharply focused essay of some depth. When you compare the draft of Peter Geske's essay on high school education (pages 368–70) and the final version of it (pages 385–88), you will see how drafting and revising can sharpen a writer's focus.

Strategies for development, which are discussed in 31d as ways to develop paragraphs, are natural thinking processes that are especially useful for shaping ideas about a subject. Remember that purpose, audience, and occasion, as well as the subject, must be considered when selecting a guiding strategy. Often the strategy emerges as you explore or draft; do not impose an inappropriate strategy. Refer to the explanations and examples in 31d as you work through the various strategies. Here are questions that you might ask yourself.

a. *Narration* What happened to me in high school? What is the story of my high school education?
b. *Process* How do teachers teach? How do students spend their days? What was my learning process like?
c. *Cause and effect* Why did I hate high school? How was I influenced by peers? Would I have done better in a different school district?
d. *Description* What did my high school look like? What did a typical class look like? What was it like to be in study hall, the cafeteria, or the gym?
e. *Definition* What is education? What is a good school? How demanding should a high school education be?
f. *Classification and division* How could I classify the students or teachers in my high school? What is the significance of dividing students by year rather than by accomplishment? What group did I belong to?
g. *Example* What was a typical day like? Who was my best teacher and who was my worst?
h. *Comparison and contrast* How did my school compare with a rival school? How does going to a public high school differ from going to a private high school? What did my two best teachers have in common?

The following introductory sentence suggests a focus on comparison and contrast:

> When I think of my last two English teachers, I can see how a teacher who cares about students differs from someone who is bored by them.

This sentence suggests cause and effect:

> The poor quality of the high school I attended can be traced to a shrinking tax base, a lack of parental interest, and an administrative failure to hold the school accountable to state standards.

Essays frequently combine several of these strategies to achieve yet another strategy. Yi-Fu Tuan narrates, describes, and defines in the process of comparing Chinese place and American space.

> Americans have a sense of space, not of place. Go to an American home in exurbia, and almost the first thing you do is drift toward the picture window. How curious that the first compliment you pay your host inside the house is to say how lovely it is outside his house! He is pleased that you should admire his vistas. The distant horizon is not merely a line separating earth from sky, it is a symbol of the future. The American is not rooted in his place, however lovely; his eyes are drawn by the expanding space to a point on the horizon which is his future.
>
> —YI-FU TUAN, "American Space, Chinese Place"

In the following introduction, Desmond Morris suggests the overall organization of a classification-division essay, but in the essay itself he uses definition, narration, and description to develop his discussion of the three kinds of territory he names in the opening.

> A territory is a defended space. In the broadest sense, there are three kinds of human territory: tribal, family, and personal. —DESMOND MORRIS, "Territorial Behavior"

The exact focus you finally choose will be determined by your purpose, your audience, and the time and space available.

Exercise 4

Explore one of the subjects from Exercise 3 by writing down your answers to the journalists' questions (Who? What? When? Where? Why? and How?). Next use the three perspectives to explore by writing answers to the questions What is it? How does it change? and What is it related to (part of, different from, or like)? Finally, explore the subject by writing questions appropriate to the various development strategies. How would you limit your subject? What would you focus on?

32d A clearly stated thesis conveys your main idea.

If you have limited and focused your subject, you have gone a long way toward developing an idea that controls the content you include and the approach you take. Your controlling idea, or thesis, ensures that decisions you have made about purpose, audience, and occasion, fit together.

(1) Essays usually include a thesis statement.

In academic and many other kinds of writing you will be expected to state your main idea succinctly. This **thesis statement** contains a single idea, clearly focused and specifically stated, that grows out of your exploration of a subject. A thesis statement can be thought of as a central idea phrased in the form of an assertion. It is basically a claim (see 35b)—that is, it indicates what you claim to be true, interesting, or valuable about your subject.

An explicitly stated thesis statement helps you keep your writing on target. It identifies the topic you are writing about, the approach you are taking, and in some cases the plan of development you are using. Note how the thesis statements below do all of these. The first is from an expressive essay:

> By the time that his children were growing up the great days of my father's life were over.
>
> —VIRGINIA WOOLF, "Leslie Stephen"

With this apparently simple statement, the author has established that the topic is her father and indicated that she will discuss both early accomplishments and later decline while focusing primarily on his life within the family.

The following thesis statement for an expository essay divides "discipline" into three kinds.

> A child, in growing up, may meet and learn from three different kinds of disciplines.
>
> —JOHN HOLT, "Kinds of Discipline"

The main idea in a persuasive essay usually carries a strong point of view—an argumentative edge.

> Nothing better illustrates the low regard that the NCAA has often had for the rights of student-athletes than its random drug-testing policy.
>
> —ALLEN L. SACK, "Random Tests Abuse Dignity"

You will probably try out several thesis statements as you explore your subject. Rather than starting with a preconceived thesis that you must then rationalize, let it develop out of your thinking and discovery process. (See 32c.) Your goal should be a claim that is neither self-evident nor too broad.

A clear, precise thesis statement will help unify your paper; it will guide many decisions about what details to keep and what to toss out. You can also use the thesis to guide your search for additional information you may need to strengthen your point. But it is important to allow your essay to remain flexible in the early stages. If you have information about your subject that is interesting but does not really help you make your point, including it in your early drafts might lead you to a better essay by indicating a more profitable focus. As you write, check your thesis statement frequently to see if you have drifted away from it. Do not hesitate to change your thesis, however, if you find a more productive path or one you would rather pursue. Make whatever adjustments you need to ensure a unified essay. When you revise (chapter 33), test everything you retain in your essay against the thesis you have finally decided on—your original or a new version you have developed—and scrupulously discard any information that does not contribute.

In some cases a thesis might be stated in more than one sentence, but it is more often stated in a declarative sentence with a single main clause (1e)—that is, in either a simple or a complex sentence. If your thesis statement announces two or more coordinate ideas, as a compound sentence does, be sure you are not in danger of having your paper lose direction and focus. If you wish to sharpen the thesis statement by adding information that qualifies or supports it, subordinate such material to the main idea.

Beware of vague qualifiers such as *interesting, important,* and *unusual.* Often such words signal that you have chosen a subject that does not interest you much; you would do better to rethink your subject to come up with something you care about. In a thesis statement such as "My education has been very unusual," the vague word *unusual* may indicate that the idea itself is weak and that the writer needs to find a stronger subject. However, this kind of vague thesis may disguise an idea of real interest that simply needs to be made specific: "Our family grew closer after my parents decided to teach me at home." Sometimes thesis statements containing vague words can be made more effective by simply replacing the bland words with other, more meaningful ones. The following examples show ways to focus, clarify, and sharpen vague thesis statements.

Vague I have trouble making decisions.

Better Making decisions is difficult for me, especially when money is involved and most of all when such decisions affect other people.

Vague Summer is an interesting season.

Better Summer is the best season for losing weight.

Thesis statements appear most often in the introductory paragraph, although you can put them anywhere that suits your purpose—occasionally even in the conclusion. The advantage of putting the thesis statement in the first paragraph, however, is that your reader knows from the beginning what you are writing about and where the essay is going. Especially appropriate in academic writing, this technique helps readers who are searching for specific information to locate it easily. If the thesis statement begins the introductory paragraph, the rest of the sentences in the paragraph usually support or clarify it with more specific information.

> America is suffering from overwork. Too many of us are too busy, trying to squeeze more into each day while having less to show for it. Although our growing time crunch is often portrayed as a personal dilemma, it is in fact a major social problem that has reached crisis proportions over the past 20 years. —BARBARA BRANDT, "Less Is More"

> In many ways a pool is the best place to do real swimming. Free water tends to be too tempestuous, while in a pool it is tamed and imprisoned; the challenge has been filtered out of it along with the bacteria.
>
> —JOHN KNOWLES, "Everybody's Sport"

ESL American readers are accustomed to finding a clearly stated thesis statement early in an essay. If you introduce your ideas more gradually—which is the custom in some cultures—you may confuse American readers. Stating your main idea early will help Americans understand what you write in English.

(2) A main idea is necessary even when a thesis statement is not required.

Some kinds of writing do not require a formulated thesis statement, but they do contain a main, or controlling, idea. A memoir, for example, or a journal—such as the record you might keep of a camping trip—is a focused piece of writing preserving your reflections and observations. In the example below, notice how Edward Abbey uses the quality of light and air in Death Valley as a controlling idea for focusing the reader's attention.

> The glare is stunning. Yet also exciting, even exhilarating—a world of light. The air seems not clear like glass but colored, a transparent, tinted medium, golden toward the sun, smoke-blue in the shadows. The colors come, it appears, not simply from the background, but are actually present in the air itself—a vigintillion microscopic particles of dust reflecting the sky, the sand, the iron hills.
>
> —EDWARD ABBEY, *The Journey Home*

Expressive writing is sometimes characterized by a spirit of inquiry in which the writer plays with possibilities without necessarily coming to a conclusion or making a specific point. Rather than approaching his topic as a definition, Joseph Epstein establishes his essay as an inquiry, inviting the reader to consider the subject from various angles.

> What's vulgar? Some people might say that the contraction of the words *what* and *is* itself is vulgar. On the other hand, I remember being called a stuffed shirt by a reviewer of a book of mine because I used almost no contractions. I have forgotten the reviewer's name but I have remembered the criticism. Not being of that category of writers who never forget a compliment, I also remember being called a racist by another reviewer by observing that failure to insist on table manners in children was to risk dining with Apaches. The larger criticisms I forget, but, oddly, these goofy little criticisms stick in the teeth like sesame seeds. Yet that last trope—is it, too, vulgar? Ought I really to be picking my teeth in public, even metaphorically? —JOSEPH EPSTEIN, "What Is Vulgar?"

Writing without a thesis statement is especially common when the main thrust of the development is narrative or descriptive. And reports of information, whether research papers (chapter 38) or business documents (39b), frequently do not require a thesis. Even in persuasive writing the thesis is sometimes implicit rather than explicit. Yet, even when your thesis is implied, your readers should be able to sense a clear direction and focus in your paper. You can make sure they will by articulating your main idea for yourself and then checking that your writing stays focused on it.

CAUTION Many college teachers expect every essay to have a clear thesis statement.

32e Arranging ideas requires choosing an appropriate method or combination of methods.

Many writers need a working plan to direct their ideas and keep their writing on course. Some follow a formal arrangement pattern; others use informal written lists or formal topic or sentence outlines. Such plans are especially helpful for lengthy papers and for writing under pressure. (See chapter 34.) Whatever method you choose for planning your writing, remember that you can always change your plan to suit any new direction your writing takes. The point is to have a means for directing your effort toward fulfilling your purpose.

(1) Informal working plans

An informal working plan need be little more than an ordered list that grows out of a collection of ideas. Look at the informal working plan that Peter Geske made as he prepared to write on the quality of his high school education.

Before he started to write his first draft, Peter reexamined his freewriting (page 344) and his first list of ideas (pages 345–46). He decided that he was right to focus on evaluating the quality of the education he had received—passing over other topics such as cliques and football. Reviewing the items on his list, he noticed that his concerns could be grouped into three categories: facilities and supplies, curriculum, and teachers. He then formulated a tentative thesis and made an ordered list to chart the direction of his essay:

THESIS: Academic facilities and standards were so low at my high school that I learned very little while I was there and became discouraged about school.

1. **Physical description of the school**
2. **Textbooks, computers, and other supplies**
3. **Class size**
4. **Courses that were a waste of time**

```
5. Bad teachers
6. A few bright spots
```

When you make such a list, ideas might overlap. For example, it may not be possible to separate "courses that were a waste of time" from "bad teachers." Some ideas may drop out, and others may occur as you draft. But you have the beginning of a plan that can guide you.

As Peter continued to work on his essay, he made several changes in his original plan. For example, he decided to discuss class size before discussing textbooks and other supplies, added a conclusion, and then wrote an entirely different conclusion. Because writing is a process, changes of this sort are natural.

(2) Outlines

Writers sometimes find themselves required to follow a plan of organization that has been determined for them. The ancient Greeks, for example, developed a method of arrangement that helped audiences follow whatever a speaker was saying because certain aspects of a speech almost always occurred in the same sequence. Even today, this **classical arrangement** proves useful for many writers—especially writers trying to persuade. For a description of classical arrangement, see page 432.

Often, however, outlines grow out of the writing. Some writers can develop an excellent plan early in their writing process, turning a working list into a formal outline. Others discover that they need to rethink their original plan after they have actually done some writing. But whether it is written before the first draft or after it, a formal outline is often helpful when analyzing a draft and preparing to revise it. For example, if an outline shows only one subgroup under a heading, that section of the draft might need rethinking.

A structured outline uses indention and numbers to indicate various levels of subordination. Thus it is a kind of graphic scheme of the logic of your paper. The main points form the major headings, and the supporting ideas for each point form the subheadings. An outline of Peter's paper might begin as follows:

```
THESIS: Academic facilities and standards were
so low at my high school that I learned very
little while I was there and became
discouraged about school.
 I. Physical description of the school
    A. The building itself
       1. Run-down
          a. Exterior
          b. Interior
       2. Overcrowded
          a. Hallways
          b. Classrooms
    B. Facilities
       1. Terrible library
          a. Few books
          b. Useless computers
       2. Inadequate labs
          a. Chemistry lab
          b. Biology lab
II. Courses I took
```

A decimal system can also be used:

```
1. Physical description of the school
   1.1. The building itself
        1.11. Run-down
        1.12. Overcrowded
```

```
   1.2. Facilities
        1.21. Terrible library
        1.22. Inadequate labs
2. Courses I took
```

The types of outlines most commonly used are the topic outline and the sentence outline. The headings in a **topic outline** are expressed in grammatically parallel phrases, while a **sentence outline** presents headings in complete and usually parallel sentences. A topic outline has the advantage of brevity and highlights the logical flow of your paper; a sentence outline forces you to think through your ideas more thoroughly. Here is how a sentence outline for Peter's essay might begin:

```
THESIS: Academic facilities and standards were
so low at my high school that I learned very
little while I was there and became
discouraged about school.
I. The school building hindered learning.
   A. The building was an eyesore.
      1. It was run-down and covered with
         graffiti.
      2. It was so overcrowded that it
         couldn't be kept clean.
   B. Facilities were inadequate.
      1. The library was terrible.
      2. Laboratories lacked equipment.
```

The headings in a sentence outline can often serve as topic sentences when you draft.

Regardless of what type of outline you choose, you will need enough major headings to develop your subject fully within the boundaries established by your thesis. Outlines are also useful for summarizing the main ideas of lectures and reading material when you want to communicate ideas to other people in a brief, readily accessible form. When drafting an essay, however, do not let your outline become a straitjacket. If new ideas occur to you as you are writing, put them down as they occur. You may find that these ideas enrich your paper even though they did not appear in the outline. If you later find that you strayed off track, you can eliminate the digressive material as you revise.

32f Your first draft will not be your final draft.

Put your ideas on paper quickly. Matters such as spelling, punctuation, and usage are not as important in the first draft as they are in the final draft. Your first draft may be sloppy and tentative, but it gives you something you can improve on in another draft. Keep your plan in mind as you draft. If you find yourself losing track of where you want to go, stop writing and reread what you have. You may need to revise your plan, or you may simply need to reorient yourself. If you are stuck and do not know what to write next, referring to your plan can help.

You may prefer to write chunks or blocks of your essay without worrying about the final order of those chunks. Many writers do. For example, if you have trouble writing the introduction, start with a supporting idea you feel sure of, and write until you reach a stopping point. When you are actually writing, you will probably think more efficiently. You can then move on to another part that will be easy to write—another supporting idea paragraph or even the introduction or conclusion. What is important is to begin writing, to write as quickly as you can, and to save your early work so that you can refer to it during revision.

(1) Introductions must be effective.

An effective introduction arouses the reader's interest and indicates the subject and tone of the essay. (See 32a and 33a.) For long or complex essays especially, a good introduction also charts the direction the essay will follow so that readers know what to expect.

The introduction often contains the thesis statement. (See 32d.) Introductions have no set length; they can be as brief as a couple of sentences or as long as a couple of paragraphs or more. Although introductions appear first in the essay, experienced writers may compose them at any time during the writing process—even after they have drafted the rest of the paper.

You can arouse the interest of your audience by writing introductions in a number of ways.

a. Start with an interesting fact or unusual detail that catches the reader's attention.

> A new Census Bureau report predicts that there will be 383 million Americans in the year 2050. That's 128 million more than there are now, and 83 million more than the bureau was predicting just four years ago, when it appeared that the U.S. population would peak and stabilize at around 300 million. —MICHAEL KINSLEY, "Gatecrashers"

b. Use an intriguing statement to lure the reader into continuing.

> After smiling brilliantly for nearly four decades, I now find myself trying to quit. Or, at the very least, seeking to lower the wattage a bit.
>
> —AMY CUNNINGHAM, "Why Women Smile"

c. Engage the reader's attention with an anecdote.

As I walked out the street entrance to my newly rented apartment, a guy in maroon high-tops and a skateboard haircut approached, making kissing noises and saying, "Hi, gorgeous." Three weeks earlier, I would have assessed the degree of malice and made ready to run or tell him to bug off, depending. But now, instead, I smiled, and so did my four-year-old daughter, because after dozens of similar encounters I understood he didn't mean me but *her*.

—BARBARA KINGSOLVER, "Somebody's Baby"

d. Begin with a question your essay will answer.

In a series of futuristic commercials, AT&T paints a liberating picture of your not-too-distant life, when the information superhighway will be an instrument of personal freedom and a servant to your worldly needs and desires. But is the future of cyberspace really so elegant, so convenient? Or does it represent a serious threat to your privacy and your freedom? —ERIK NESS, "BigBrother@cyberspace"

e. Start with an appropriate quotation.

When the Reverend Jerry Falwell learned that the Supreme Court had reversed his $200,000 judgment against *Hustler* magazine for the emotional distress he had suffered from an outrageous parody, his response was typical of those who seek to censor speech: "Just as no person may scream 'Fire!' in a crowded theater when there is no fire, and find cover under the First Amendment, likewise, no sleazy merchant like Larry Flynt should be able to use the First Amendment as an excuse for maliciously and dishonestly attacking public figures, as he has so often done."

—ALAN DERSHOWITZ, "Shouting 'Fire!'"

f. Open with an illustration.

Libby Smith knows what it is like to be a victim of gay bashing. First, there were the harassing telephone calls to her home. Then, one evening last March as she went to get her book bag out of a locker at the University of Wisconsin at Eau Claire, she was attacked by two men.

—MARY CRYSTAL CAGE, "Gay Bashing on Campus"

g. Begin with general information about the subject or show how you came to choose it.

Anyone new to the experience of owning a lawn, as I am, soon figures out that there is more at stake here than a patch of grass. A lawn immediately establishes a certain relationship with one's neighbors and, by extension, the larger American landscape. Mowing the lawn, I realized the first time I gazed into my neighbor's yard and imagined him gazing back into mine, is a civic responsibility.

—MICHAEL POLLAN, "Why Mow? The Case Against Laws"

h. Simply state your thesis.

Even today, when the American landscape is becoming more and more homogeneous, there is really no such thing as an all-American style of dress. A shopping center in Maine may superficially resemble one in Georgia or California, but the shoppers in it will look different, because the diverse histories of these states have left their mark on costume.

—ALISON LURIE, "American Regional Costume"

Whatever type of introduction you choose to write, use your opening paragraph to indicate your subject, engage readers' attention, and establish your credibility.

(2) An essay needs an effective conclusion.

The conclusion often summarizes the main points and may also encourage the reader to action or further thought on the subject. An essay should not merely stop; it should finish. Some suggestions follow.

a. Conclude by rephrasing the thesis.

Such considerations make it clear that it's time for schools to choose between real amateurism and real professionalism. They can't have a little of both. From now on, in college sports, it's got to be poetry or pros.

—LOUIS BARBASH, "Clean Up or Pay Up"

b. Direct the reader's attention to larger issues.

My antibody status does not matter to you. Certainly it matters—with absolute enormity—to me. But what I'd like you to remember is the blood on the subway, the click of the refrigerator door, the woman in black so elegant and uneasy, First Avenue at gritty, gorgeous dusk, the brilliance of that bad art in the examining room, the pores of the doctor's face—all of them declaring, by their very existence: As long and as well as you can, live, live.

—DAVID GROFF, "Taking the Test"

c. Encourage your readers to change their attitudes or to alter their actions.

Our medical care system is in trouble and getting worse. While the experts try to figure out how to achieve utopian goals at affordable prices, let's do something practical about the suffering on our doorsteps. Primary care is the most affordable safety net we can offer our citizens. By all means, let's continue the debate about universal, comprehensive insurance to cover all medical costs, but, in the meantime, let's provide primary health care to all uninsured Americans—now!

—GORDON T. MOORE, "Caring for the Uninsured and Underinsured"

d. Conclude with a summary of the main points covered.

All our giving carries with it messages about ourselves, our feelings about those to whom we give, how we see them as people and how we phrase the ties of relationship. Christmas giving, in which love and hope and trust play such an intrinsic part, can be an annual way of telling our children that we think of each of them as a person, as we also hope they will come to think of us.

—MARGARET MEAD and RHODA METRAUX, "The Gift of Autonomy"

e. Clinch or stress the importance of the central idea by referring in some way to the introduction.

Introduction I read *The National Enquirer* when I want to feel exhilarated about life's possibilities. It tells me of a world where miracles still occur. In the world of *The National Enquirer,* UFOs flash over the Bermuda Triangle, cancer cures are imminent, ancient film stars at last find love that is for keeps. Reached on The Other Side by spiritualists, Clark Gable urges America to keep its chin up. Of all possible worlds, I like the world of *The National Enquirer* best. . . .

Conclusion So I whoop with glee when a new edition of *The National Enquirer* hits the newsstands and step into the world where Gable can cheer me up from The Other Side.

—RUSSELL BAKER, "Magazine Rack"

Whatever strategy you choose, provide readers with a sense of closure. Bear in mind that they may be wondering, "So what?" Your conclusion gives you an opportunity to respond to that concern. If there is any chance readers may not understand your purpose, use your conclusion to clarify why you asked them to read what they have just read.

(3) A good title fits the subject and tone of an essay.

The title is the reader's first impression and, like the introduction, should fit the subject and tone of the paper.

Sometimes the title announces the subject simply and directly: "Grant and Lee" or "Civil Disobedience." Often a title uses alliteration to reflect the writer's humorous approach, as in "A Pepsi Person in the Perrier Generation," or a twisted cliché, as in "The Right Wrong Stuff." A good title may also arouse the reader's curiosity by asking a question, as does "Who Killed the Bog Men of Denmark? And Why?"

Some writers like to choose a title before they draft because they find that a good title helps clarify their direction. Others choose the title later in the writing process. Whenever you decide to title your paper, a good way to begin is to try condensing your thesis statement without becoming too vague or general. Reread your introduction and conclusion, and examine key words and phrases for possible titles. Try to work in some indication of your attitude and approach.

Exercise 5

Choose an article or chapter from a work you recently read and evaluate the introduction and conclusion. What writing strategies do they reveal, and how effective are they? Write an alternative introduction and conclusion using a significantly different strategy.

32g Studying a first draft helps writers to see how it can be improved.

As you read the following draft, remember that it is only the first draft. Two later drafts—including the final draft—are reprinted in chapter 33.

Peter Geske
English 101

School Daze

In today's society education is becoming more and more important. The children of today need education to get good jobs and keep up with this fast paced modern society. Nobody ever explained this to my teachers though. High school was the worst. The teachers at my school were losers and didn't know what they were doing. The building was falling apart also and their was alot of violence in it.

Central was built about a hundred years ago and that's probably the last time it got a coat of paint. The walls were cracked and we used to flick off loose paint chips all the time. On the outside it looked like a prison. It used to have big windows but they got bricked up to save energy. There was also graffiti all over the place. No trees anywhere but plenty of broken cement and crumbling asphalt.

The school had at least twice as many kids squeezed into it than it was designed for. Even with plenty of people cutting to party, every classroom was crowded. Sometimes at the beginning of the year there wasn't even a desk for everyone. Computers were a joke. We had about three for two thousand students and they were these old machines that you couldn't run good games or programs on.

Science equipment was also bad. I really hated my chemistry teacher but maybe she wouldn't of been so bad if we had a decent lab.

Once you got past your sophomore year you could do pretty much what you wanted to. You were supposed to take English every year and you had to take math and science too. You also had to take blow off courses you could sleep through like social problems where Mr. Thorp used to talk about the problems his kids were having and how students today aren't as good as they used to be. But juniors and seniors could take lots of electives and you could pass your English requirement by reading science fiction or taking a course where you did nothing but watch tapes on a VCR.

The teachers were the worst. They couldn't control their classes and everybody took advantage of that. Mr. Kleinberg was my geometry teacher. He wore these green socks everyday and I swear it was always the same pair. When you got close to him it was really gross he smelled so bad. Kids never paid attention to him and he would usually start screaming at one person while knives were being pulled in another corner and other kids were strung out on drugs. My chemistry teacher was just as bad. Her name was Mrs. Fiorelli and she was real skinny. All she would ever do was read from the text book. Her class was out of control also and when somebody would try to ask a question she would just keep on reading. She gave these killer tests though and I ended up flunking her course not that I need to know chemistry for anything.

It wasn't all bad though. Mr. Rodriguez taught American history and he was cool. My English teacher sophomore year was also ok.

```
This is just my opinion. There might be
other kids who had a good experience at
Central and maybe someday I'll laugh about it.
```

CAUTION The preceding paper is an early draft. Do not consider it a model essay. It is reprinted here so that you can see how it improved through revision. For later versions of this paper, see pages 382–85 and 385–88.

Here are some of the comments Peter received when he distributed this draft in a writing group.

I really liked your paper, especially the description of Mr. Kleinberg, because I could really picture him. I had a teacher just like that. His name was Mr. Percovich, and he couldn't control his class either. I had him for biology my junior year. I hated him!

Good paper! I think you should say more about science equipment though because that paragraph is so short. Also you mention your chemistry teacher in that paragraph and then talk about her again later on. Maybe you should keep the chemistry stuff together.

Great topic! I could really relate to your paper. I wouldn't change a thing.

The only thing that bothered me about your paper is how you mention teachers first and then the building in your first paragraph, but then you talk about the building first in your paper. Why not be consistent?

I like how you used your title to make a joke. So many titles are boring! I wish I could think of titles like that.

I loved your paper, except for the long paragraph about teachers. You make the important point that your math and chemistry teachers were poor, but when you pick on their personal appearance it makes you sound sarcastic. Also, I think you should add a thesis statement to the end of paragraph 1.

I was surprised by how angry you sound in this paper because you always seem so laid back in class. Does this paper sound the way you want it to sound? And if you really are angry, why back off in your conclusion? The last paragraph doesn't work for me because it sounds like you're apologizing for writing the paper.

Before revising this draft, Peter had to weigh these comments and decide for himself which were the most useful.

Exercise 6

Reread "School Daze" and the comments it received. Identify the comments that you think are the most useful and then add two of your own.

Chapter 33

Revising and Editing Essays

To **revise** means "to see again." This activity, which is at the heart of writing well, implies that you take a fresh look at your draft—rethinking what you have written and what you still need to write by distancing yourself from your work and evaluating it from a reader's point of view. To **edit** means to polish a piece of writing by making word choice more precise (20a), prose more concise (chapter 21), and sentence structure more effective (chapters 29 and 30), in addition to eliminating any errors in grammar, punctuation, and mechanics. Although these two activities can overlap, they are essentially very different. Inexperienced writers sometimes think they are revising when they are really editing. You need to do both, so be careful not to confuse one with the other.

Revising usually comes before editing, because you can waste time perfecting a paragraph that you later decide to delete. This does not mean that you cannot correct errors as you move along, especially if doing so makes you more confident or comfortable. But the more time and energy you invest in editing early on, the harder it may be to make major changes that would enrich your essay. When something looks perfect on the surface, it can be tempting not to touch it. Even if you do some editing as you draft, you should be willing to rearrange paragraphs and make significant cuts and additions as you revise.

33a Your tone reveals your attitude.

Tone reflects your attitude toward your subject and must be appropriate to your purpose, audience, and occasion, whether for a personal essay or a lab report. Although humor might well be suitable in a letter to a friend telling her of trouble with your new car, it would be inappropriate in a letter of complaint to the manufacturer. Consider the difference in tone between the following two writers, both of whom are trying to persuade people to support capital punishment. The first is from a successful journalist who amused and provoked readers of his newspaper column. The second is from a book by a university professor. Both are discussing what they learned from Aristotle about anger and revenge.

> A keeps a store and has a bookkeeper, B. B steals $700, employs it in playing at dice or bingo, and is wiped out. What is A to do? Let B go? If he does he will be unable to sleep at night. The sense of injury, of injustice, of frustration will haunt him like pruritus. So he turns B over to the police, and they hustle B to prison. Thereafter A can sleep. More, he has pleasant dreams. He pictures B chained to the wall of a dungeon a hundred feet underground, devoured by rats and scorpions. It is so agreeable it makes him forget his $700. He has got his *katharsis*. —H. L. MENCKEN, "The Penalty of Death"

> Anger is expressed or manifested on those occasions when someone has acted in a manner that is thought to be unjust, and one of its origins is the opinion that men are responsible, and should be held responsible, for what they do. Thus, as Aristotle teaches us, anger is accompanied not only by the pain caused by the one who is the object of anger, but by the pleasure arising from the expectation of inflicting revenge on someone who is thought to deserve it. . . . Anger is somehow

> connected with justice, and it is this that modern penology has not understood; it tends, on the whole, to regard anger as a selfish indulgence.
>
> —WALTER BERNS, *For Capital Punishment*

When Peter Geske revised the draft essay reprinted in chapter 32 (pages 368–70), he decided to change his tone after one of his readers commented that he sounded sarcastic and another commented on his anger. Although sounding angry or sarcastic might be appropriate in some rhetorical situations, Peter felt that he sounded harsher than he intended.

Exercise 1

1. Reread the passages by H. L. Mencken and Walter Berns and then write a short analysis of how these men sound. Be sure to identify specific words or phrases that led you to attribute this tone to them.
2. Study the draft of Peter Geske's essay (pages 368–70) and then study his final version (pages 385–88). Write a short essay comparing the tone of these two versions.

33b Revision is essential to writing well.

In one way or another you revise throughout the writing process. For example, even in the earliest planning stages, as you consider a possible subject and then discard it in favor of another, you are revising. Similarly, after choosing a subject, you might decide to change your focus or emphasize some new part of it. That, too, is a kind of revision. And, of course, you are revising when you realize that a sentence or a paragraph you have just written does not belong where it is, so you pause to strike it out or to move it elsewhere.

Nevertheless, experienced writers usually revise after they have completed a draft—no matter how much they may have revised while planning and drafting. They not only revise and develop paragraphs (chapter 31), they review the draft *as a whole*. Although some writers do so immediately after drafting, while their minds are still fully engaged by their topic, they usually benefit from setting the drafts aside for a time so that later they can see their work more objectively. What looks good when you are excited does not necessarily look good the morning after. Whenever possible, plan your writing process so that you can put a draft aside, at least overnight, and then see it later with fresh eyes.

Because revision is an ongoing process, writers often print several different versions when composing with a computer. By labeling each version—or at least dating each hard copy—you can keep track of how your work is evolving.

(1) Everything on the page benefits from reconsideration.

When you review your essay as a whole, ask yourself if the point of your essay comes through clearly and if you ever digress from it. Writers frequently get off the track as they generate ideas through the act of writing. Now is the time to eliminate those side trips. It is also wise to make sure that you are developing a point rather than simply repeating the same thing in different words—or, as sometimes happens, contradicting yourself by saying two very different things.

Revising also demands reconsidering your rhetorical situation (page 329). Have you provided examples or other details that will interest your audience? Are your ideas clearly expressed in language appropriate for your audience? Is your tone (33a) appropriate for this occasion?

Moreover, you should examine your paragraphs to make sure that they are unified, coherent, and well developed (chapter 31). Assess how well each paragraph leads to the next, whether you need to rearrange any, and whether your transitions are effective. (See 31b(4).)

CAUTION When you move paragraphs, check to see if your new arrangement works and if you need to write new transitions.

(2) What is not on the page can be even more important than what is there.

One of the most challenging tasks in revision is to look for what you have left out that your audience might expect or that would strengthen your paper as a whole. Your best ideas will not always surface in your first draft; you will sometimes have an important new idea only after you have finished your draft and taken a good look at it. No matter how good a draft looks, ask yourself if something is missing.

Inexperienced writers sometimes end an essay prematurely because they cannot think of anything else to say. One way to get past this block is to use such strategies as questioning (pages 346–47), listing (pages 345–46), and applying perspectives (page 347). Another way is to share your work with other readers and ask them to let you know if there is anything they find confusing or want to know more about. Providing readers with this kind of specific direction can get you a much more focused response than simply passing a paper to someone and asking, "What do you think?" When not given direction, some readers may keep reservations to themselves because they suspect they are being asked to approve a finished product.

Checklist for Revising Essays ✓

- Is the purpose of the work clear (32a(1))? Does the work stick to its purpose?
- Does the essay address the appropriate audience (32a(2))?
- Is the tone (33a) appropriate for the purpose, audience, and occasion?
- Is the subject focused (32c(2))?
- Does the essay make a clear point (32d)? Is this point well supported? Do the relationships expressed in the essay clearly relate to this point?
- Is each paragraph unified and coherent (31a–b)? Are the paragraphs arranged in a logical, effective order (32e)? (See the paragraph checklist on pages 325–26.)
- Does the essay follow an effective method or combination of methods of development (32e)?
- Is the introduction effective (32f(1))?
- Is the conclusion appropriate for the essay's purpose (32f(2))?

33c Editing improves your writing.

After you are satisfied with the revised structure of your paper and the content of your paragraphs, edit individual sentences for clarity, effectiveness, and variety. (See chapters 19 through 30.) Consider combining choppy or unconnected sentences and rework long, overly complicated ones. If you overuse some structures, say, introductory prepositional phrases, try to rework some of them into other patterns. Eliminate any needless shifts in grammatical structures, tone, style, or point of view.

Examine your diction, and make sure the words you have used are the best choices for this particular essay. If any words leap out as much more formal or informal than your language as a whole in the essay, replace them with words that are more consistent with your style. Eliminate any unnecessary words (chapter 21). If you have experimented with words new to your vocabulary, make sure that you have used them accurately.

Check whether your punctuation is correct and whether you have followed standard conventions for mechanics. Even if you have already used a spell checker (18a), use it again because new errors may have been introduced since you last checked. Remember also that such programs are never foolproof. Double-check that you are correctly using words like *there* and *their* or *who's* and *whose*—correctly spelled words that might be the wrong words in a specific context.

Checklist for Editing ✓

Sentences

- Are ideas related effectively through subordination and coordination (24)?
- Are all sentences unified (23)?
- Do any sentences contain misplaced parts or dangling modifiers (25)?
- Is there any faulty parallelism (26)?
- Are there any needless shifts in grammatical structures, in tone or style, or in viewpoint (27)?
- Are ideas given appropriate emphasis within each sentence (29)?

continued

continued from previous page

- Are the sentences varied in length and in type (30)? ✓
- Are there any fragments (2)? Are there any comma splices or fused sentences (3)?
- Do all verbs agree with their subjects (6a)? Do all pronouns agree with their antecedents (6b)?
- Are all verb forms appropriate (7)?

Diction

- Are any words overused, imprecise, or vague (20c, 20a)? Are all words idiomatic (20b)?
- Have all **unnecessary** words and phrases been eliminated (21)? Have any **necessary** words been left out by mistake (22)?
- Is the vocabulary appropriate for the audience, purpose, and occasion (19, 32a)?
- Have all technical words that might be unfamiliar to the audience been eliminated or defined (19g)?

Punctuation and mechanics

- Is all punctuation correct? Are any marks missing?
- Are all words spelled correctly (18)?
- Is capitalization correct (9)?
- Are titles identified by either quotation marks (16c) or italics (10a)?
- Are abbreviations (11) appropriate and correct?

33d Proofreading can help make your papers error-free.

Once you have revised and edited your essay, carefully format it (chapter 8). It is then your responsibility to proofread it. Proofreading means making a special search to ensure that the product you submit is error-free. Your proofreading may alert you to problems that call for further editing, but proofreading is usually the last step in the process of writing an essay.

Thanks to the computer, you can easily produce professional-looking documents with handsome fonts and perfect margins. Showing that you care about presentation indicates that you respect your audience and care about your work. Remember, however, that presentation is only one aspect of a successful project. A paper that looks good could still have problems. No matter how beautiful your paper looks when you print it out, proofread it carefully.

Be alert for minor errors that you could have missed—such as a misspelled word, a missing comma, or a book title that has not been italicized. Also watch for two common errors: accidentally leaving a word out or writing the same word twice. Errors of this sort are especially common now that so much writing is done on computers. A spell checker program can alert you to repeated words, but you have to proofread to see if deleting or moving material led to other errors. For example, when deleting a phrase you may have accidentally left one of its words in the text. Or when moving a sentence, you may have put it in the wrong spot.

Because the eye tends to see what it expects to see, many writers miss errors even when they think they have proofread carefully. It is usually wise to proofread more than once, and many writers find that they benefit from reading their work aloud as they proofread.

An extra pair of eyes can also be helpful, so you might ask a friend to help you. This is very different, however, from abdicating your own responsibility. If someone else helps you proofread, this check should be in addition to your own. Moreover, if you ask someone to proofread your work, remember that you are asking for only an error-check. If you want a more thoughtful response to your essay that could help you revise it, you need to ask for this kind of response at an earlier point in the process.

Use the Proofreading Checklist in chapter 8, pages 109–10, to check your format, spelling, punctuation, and mechanics. If your paper is to be in MLA or APA style, see chapter 38.

33e You can benefit from studying how other writers work.

After Peter Geske had time to reconsider the first draft of his essay evaluating his high school education and to think about the responses he received from readers, he made a number of changes in his second draft. Here is what his paper looked like midway through its revision.

Peter Geske

English 100

I need to add date and teacher's name

School Daze

~~In today's society education is becoming more and more important. The children of today need education to get good jobs and keep up with this fast paced modern society. Nobody ever explained this to my teachers though. High school was the worst. The teachers at my school were losers and didn't know what they were doing.~~ The building was falling apart also and their was alot of violence in it. Standards and facilities were so low that I

I nee a new intro!

learned very little and became discouraged about school.

Central was built about a hundred years ago and ~~that's probably the last time it got a coat of paint.~~ The walls were cracked and we used to flick off loose paint chips all the time. ~~On the outside~~ it looked like a prison. It used to have big windows but they got bricked up to save energy. There was also graffiti all over the place. No trees anywhere but plenty of broken cement and crumbling asphalt.

The school had at least twice as many kids squeezed into it than it was designed for. ~~Even with plenty of people cutting to party,~~ every classroom was crowded. Sometimes at the beginning of the year there wasn't even a desk for everyone. Computers were a joke. We had about three for two thousand students and they were these old machines that you couldn't run good games or programs on.

Science equipment was also bad. I really hated my chemistry teacher but maybe she would not have been so bad if we had a decent lab.

~~Once you got past your sophomore year you could do pretty much what you wanted to.~~ The curriculum was also a problem. You were supposed to take English every year, for example ~~and you had to take math and science too.~~ You also had to take blow off courses you could sleep through like social problems where Mr. Thorp used to talk about the problems his kids were having and how students today aren't as good as they used to be. But ~~juniors and seniors could take lots of electives and you could~~ it was possible to pass your English requirement by reading science fiction or taking a course where you did nothing but watch tapes on a VCR.

~~The~~ Many teachers ~~were the worst. They~~ couldn't control their classes and everybody took advantage of that. Mr. Kleinberg was my geometry teacher. ~~He wore these green socks everyday and I swear it was always the same pair. When you got close to him it was really gross he smelled so bad.~~ Kids never paid attention to him, and he would usually start screaming at one person while knives were being pulled in another corner and other kids were strung out on drugs. My chemistry teacher, ~~was just as bad. Her name was~~ Mrs. Fiorelli, ~~and she was real skinny. All she would ever do was~~ read from the textbook. ~~Her class was out of control also and~~ when somebody would try to ask a question she would just keep on reading. She gave these killer tests ~~though~~ and I ended up ~~flunking~~ her course ~~not that I need to know chemistry for anything~~.

never did anything except

But

failing

because I learned so little in it.

move up and link with line from p.1

It wasn't all bad though. Mr. Rodriguez taught American history and he was cool. My English teacher sophomore year was also ok.

say more about my good teachers earlier on so I don't sound like I'm whining.

~~This is just my opinion. There might be other kids who had a good experience at Central and maybe someday I'll laugh about it.~~

Too apologetic. What's the most important thing I still want to say?

33f The final draft reflects the care the writer took.

Peter Geske
English 101, Section 2
Professor Henrikson
12 March 1997

School Daze

Picture a run-down building that looks like a warehouse and feels like a prison. You approach through a sea of broken cement and crumbling asphalt. There are no trees near the building, although a few tufts of uncut grass struggle to grow in a yard of baked-down dirt. Many of the windows have been bricked in, and the ground floor is covered with graffiti. Inside, inadequate lights reveal old tiles, broken lockers, and flaking paint. The school is empty because it is only seven o'clock. Within an hour, however, it will be overcrowded with students who are running wild and teachers who don't know how to respond. You have entered Central High School, the institution where my education suffered because of poor facilities and low standards.

Built a hundred years ago, Central had a good reputation when the neighborhoods around it were prosperous. Now it is the worst high school in the city, and the school board seems to have given up on it. The more run-down it gets, the worse the morale gets, and as morale gets lower, the school goes further downhill.

After the condition of the building itself, the most obvious problem at Central is the overcrowding. Almost every classroom is filled to capacity, and the problem is so bad that you can't even count on finding a desk or a seat--especially at the beginning of the school year when most people are still showing up for school. The situation gets a little better by Columbus Day. That's when kids have figured out that one of the advantages of going to Central is that you can skip school without anybody caring.

Our textbooks were usually ten years out of date. And if more expensive supplies ever made it through the door, they didn't last long. We had only three or four computers for two thousand students, and they were old machines that couldn't run many programs. Science supplies were almost as bad. In the chemistry lab, for example, there was never enough equipment for individual experiments even when we were teamed with a lab partner. We were put in groups of four and had to wait half the class period before we got the chance to work. By then, most people had checked out. What usually happened is that one person would do the work, and the rest of the team would coast on those results.

My chemistry teacher, Mrs. Fiorelli, is a good example of another problem at Central: bad teachers. All she would ever do is read from the textbook. When somebody would try to ask a question, she would just keep reading. Then she would turn around every few weeks and give killer tests. It was like she hated us and wanted to punish us when she couldn't ignore us any longer.

I had many other teachers who were just as bad. Mr. Kleinberg, my geometry teacher, couldn't control the class. When we got out of control--which was every day--he would start screaming at one person (usually a girl who wasn't doing anything) while other students were flashing knives and plenty were nodding off from drugs. Would you be surprised to hear that I now have a problem with both science and math?

To be fair, I did have some good teachers at Central: Mr. Rodriguez, who taught American history; Mrs. Sullivan, who taught English composition; and Bob "The Ram" Reynolds, who coached the football team and taught Lifetime Fitness. But they were the exceptions. For every good teacher, there were at least three you wouldn't want to trust your children with. And for every course in which you might actually learn something, there were two blow-off courses in which all you had to do was read science fiction, watch tapes on a VCR, or listen to some guy talk about the problems he was having with his own kids.

As I look back at the four years I spent at Central, I am amazed that I learned anything at all. By the time I reached senior year, all I wanted to do was party. I'd lost interest in school--and that's one of the reasons why I've been working in a warehouse the past five years instead of having gone straight on to college. Now that I am here, I sure wish I were better prepared.

Exercise 2

Compare the two versions of "School Daze" reprinted in this chapter, and summarize how Peter revised his work. If he showed this paper to you before handing it in for a grade, what would you tell him?

Chapter 34

Writing under Pressure

Some writers feel under pressure no matter how much time they have because they suffer from writing anxiety. Strategies for reducing such anxiety include freewriting frequently (32c), making writing a normal part of the day by keeping a journal (32c), and learning that most writing situations allow time for a process (chapters 32 and 33) rather than a one-time chance at perfection. The focus of this chapter, however, is how to write well under the pressure of time constraints.

It is not always possible to engage in a writing process that stretches over a period of weeks or even days. Sometimes writers must quickly respond to e-mail (39b(1)) or prepare a proposal for presentation at a hastily convened meeting. Working students and single parents are sometimes unable to devote as much time as they would like to every writing assignment. And almost all students are faced, at some point, with essay examinations that must be written in two hours or less. The key to succeeding in such situations is to use whatever time you have as efficiently as possible.

34a Preparing ahead of time helps you succeed.

When required to write under pressure, bring knowledge to the situation by preparing ahead of time. Although an essay exam may not occur until midterm, preparation should begin on the first day of class. Decide what is most important about the material you are learning, and pay attention to indications that your instructor considers certain material especially important. Ask questions whenever you are uncertain.

In addition to knowledge, you can bring writing experience to potentially stressful situations. Plan your time so that you write frequently for your own benefit, even when you are not required to do so. By regularly exercising your writing ability, you will be able to write more fluently when forced to write quickly.

If you are faced with a specific task that must be completed in a relatively short time, invest a few minutes in making a schedule. If the time allowed for this assignment has already been specified, as is usually the case with an in-class essay, divide that time into blocks. Give yourself time to study the assignment, plan your response, and then draft your essay. Also, be sure to allow time for revising and proofreading.

If you are writing outside class, follow essentially the same process. The key difference is deciding how much time you can allot to this task and whether you want to complete it in a single block of time or in separate blocks stretched over an afternoon or evening in which you engage in other activities. If a writing task is important, even the busiest people usually manage to find time to complete it.

34b There are ways to overcome writer's block.

Writer's block can occur at any time to any writer, no matter how experienced. When time is not an issue, writers sometimes overcome their block by stepping away from the work and doing something else that does not require a lot of concentration. Completing a physical task, such as washing dishes or shoveling snow, can help writers by getting them away from their desks without making them forget the writing entirely. Activities such as these can be completed while the mind is still playing with writing possibilities. Good ideas often arise when the mind is only half focusing on how to resolve a particular problem.

When writing under pressure, however, you may not be able to leave your desk. If you fear that pressure will lead to writer's block, several strategies can help reduce the risk.

Checklist for Overcoming Writer's Block ✓

- Wear comfortable clothes. (If a particular pair of pants or shoes help you feel relaxed, this is a good time to wear them.)
- Use writing implements that work best for you. (Some pens feel better in the hand than others; if you are accustomed to using a computer, see if this is an option when writing away from your usual workplace.)
- Keep near you anything you are likely to need. (Even if you do not use your dictionary, for example, knowing that it is close at hand can help you avoid unnecessary stress.)
- Position yourself carefully. (If you are working at home, choose the place where you usually work most efficiently. If you are in a classroom with open seating, choose a seat that suits you. Some people feel safest when tucked in a corner, for example; others like to sit in the front row so they can shut out the rest of the class.)

Once you are actually writing, try not to stop prematurely. If you are following an abridged version of your regular writing process, you know that you can revise after you have drafted as much as you can. You can employ a process even when writing a fifty-minute in-class essay. By planning to save ten minutes at the end of the period for eliminating irrelevant points, clarifying others, and correcting errors, you can draft without becoming obsessed with whether or not you are making mistakes.

Exercise 1

Write an essay of approximately 500 words in which you describe your ideal working conditions for writing and identify which of these conditions you could create when writing an in-class essay.

34c Essay tests require special preparation.

(1) Read instructions and questions carefully.

Students who normally write well sometimes do poorly when writing in-class essays and essay exams because they are in such a rush to begin writing that they do not read the instructions carefully or adequately consider which question best suits them. Before you start writing, read the instructions carefully and note specific directions. For example, realizing that you must "answer questions A *and* B" is very different from believing that you must "answer question A *or* B." If you are responsible for more than one question, note how many points each is worth. When no points are specified, you can tell which questions are the most important if an instructor recommends spending more time on one than on another. If one question will count more heavily than the others, pace yourself with this fact in mind.

Invest a few minutes in studying the questions so that you do not make a false start and waste time. Most questions contain specific instructions about how, as well as what, you are to answer. Be alert for words like *compare, define, argue,* and *cause* that identify your task and provide cues for organizing your response. Other terms like *discuss* or *explain* are less specific, but they may be linked to words like *similar* or *differ* (which signal a comparison or contrast), *identify* (which signals definition or description), or *why* (which signals the need to identify causes). Also note language indicating whether you are being asked to report information or to offer your own views. Words like *think, defend,* and *opinion* signal that you are expected to frame a thesis (32d) and support it. When asked to answer more than one question, decide whether they are likely to overlap. If you accidentally drift into answering more than one question at a time, you might find yourself with nothing more to say when you get to the next section of your exam.

(2) Decide how to organize your response.

Although time constraints may keep you from creating an outline, you should always be able to find time to draft an informal working plan (32e). Identify the thesis you will offer, then list the most important points you plan to cover. These points might occur to you randomly, and you might subsequently decide to rearrange them, but the first step is to create a list that does justice to your topic. When you have finished the list, you can review it: Delete any points that seem irrelevant or not important enough to discuss in the time allowed. Then number the remaining points in a logical sequence determined by chronology (reporting events in the order in which they occurred), by causation (showing how one thing led to another), or by order of importance (going from the most important point to the least important). An alternative plan is to arrange your points in order of increasing importance, but this can be risky when writing under pressure: If you run out of time sooner than you expected, you may not get to your most important point.

Here is an example of an edited list quickly composed during the first few minutes of an essay exam. It was jotted down in response to the following question: "Some readers believe that *Huckleberry Finn* is racist. Discuss the treatment of race in this novel. Do you think the book is racist? If so, why? If not, why not?"

THESIS: Huckleberry Finn is not racist. The best character in the book is black, and a white boy comes to understand this.

tie together
5. use of racist language
1. treatment of Jim
4. Huck's go to hell speech
~~Jim in jail~~
6. reproducing authentic dialogue
3. Jim protects Huck in the storm — mention the snake bite
7. the scene where the slaves get sold ← if time allows
2. Jim as Huck's true father

The language of an assignment sometimes tells you how to organize it. For example, consider the following task.

> Discuss how the building of railroads influenced the development of the American West during the second half of the nineteenth century.

At first glance, this assignment might seem to state the topic without indicating how to organize a discussion of it. To *influence*, however, is to be responsible for certain consequences. In this case, the building of railroads is a cause and you are being asked to identify its effects (31d(4), 32e). Once you have recognized this, you might decide to discuss different effects in different paragraphs.

Here is another example:

> Consider the concept of the unconscious as defined by Freud and by Jung. On what points did they agree? How did they disagree?

The reference to two psychoanalysts, coupled with words like *agree* and *disagree,* indicates that your task is to compare and contrast. You could organize your response to this question by first discussing Freud's ideas and then discussing Jung's—preferably covering the same points in the same order. Or you could begin by establishing similarities and then move on to differences. There is almost always more than one way to organize a thoughtful response. Devoting at least a few minutes to planning your organization can help you demonstrate what you know.

(3) State main points clearly.

Instructors who read essay exams and in-class essays are usually looking to see how well students have understood assigned material. Stating your main points clearly will help them make that evaluation. In a weak essay, important points may be buried where they can be overlooked while minor or irrelevant points are prominent. Make your main points stand out from the rest of the essay by identifying them somehow. For instance, you can use transitional expressions such as *first, second, third;* you can underline each main point; or you can create headings to guide the reader. By the time you have drafted most of your essay, you should know what your key points are. Because the act of writing often generates new ideas, these points may differ from those you had planned to make. Use your conclusion to summarize your main points. If you tend to make points that differ from those you had in mind when you started, try leaving space for an introduction at the beginning of the essay and then drafting your introduction after you have drafted the rest.

(4) Stick to the question.

Always answer the exact question as directly as you can. Sometimes you may know more about a related question than the one assigned. Do not wander from the question being asked to answer the question you wish had been asked. Similarly, make sure that you follow your thesis as you answer the question; do not include irrelevant material. If you move away from your original thesis because better ideas have occurred to you as you write, go back and revise your thesis (32d). If you drift into including irrelevant material, draw a line through it.

(5) Revise and proofread.

Save a few minutes to reread your answer. Make whatever deletions and corrections you think are necessary. If time allows, think about what is not on the page by asking yourself if there is anything you have left out that you can still manage to include. Unless you are certain that your instructor values neatness more than competence, do not worry about making corrections. Doing so will allow you to focus on improving what you have written, whereas recopying your answer just to make it look neat can be an inefficient use of time (and possibly leave you with only half your essay recopied at the end of the exam). Make sure, however, that your instructor will be able to read your changes. Clarify any illegible scribbles. If you have added ideas in the margins, in each case draw a line to a caret (^) marking the exact place in the text where you want them to be placed. Finally, check spelling, punctuation, and sentence structure (33d).

Exercise 2

Write three questions that you might be asked on an essay exam for a course you are currently taking. Then choose the question you like best and write a description of how you would organize your response.

Exercise 3

Bring in an old exam from another course. If the exam posed any difficulties for you, be prepared to identify them and discuss how you responded. If you liked this exam, be ready to explain why.

Chapter 35

Reading and Thinking Critically

To read and think critically means to distinguish between ideas that are credible and those that are less so. In addition to reading for content by identifying the key points in a text, critical readers think about what they read and evaluate it. Critical thinking is essential for critical reading. It is also essential when writing arguments (chapter 36) and undertaking other types of writing (chapters 38 and 39).

Critical readers know that they cannot believe everything they are told. They understand that different writers discussing the same topic and drawing on the same evidence can reach significantly different conclusions. Instead of routinely agreeing with the writer who seems to reinforce reassuringly familiar beliefs, critical readers are likely to discover that different writers have each revealed a part of what may ultimately prove to be true. The challenge for readers, then, is to identify which ideas make more sense than others and to determine the extent to which those ideas are reliable and useful. In addition, critical readers study language carefully because they understand that writers influence readers by using a range of rhetorical strategies that may not be apparent at first glance.

Because thinking and reading critically involve making well-reasoned choices, these closely related skills are among the most valuable you can acquire. You can master them through practice, just as you have mastered other skills.

35a Previewing can help you read a text critically.

To **preview** reading means to orient yourself to a text by assessing how difficult it will be and what you are likely to learn from it. When you understand what a task demands, you are more likely to complete it successfully. Comprehending what you read is the first step toward reading critically. After all, you cannot determine the merits of a text without understanding its content.

When you page through a magazine looking for articles that seem interesting, you are, in a sense, previewing it. A simple preview of this sort can help you identify what you want to read, but it might also lead you to an article that disappoints you. A more systematic preview can give you better results, especially when you are undertaking serious reading in college.

To preview college reading assignments, ask yourself the following questions:

Checklist for Previewing a Text ✓

- How long is this work, and how long is its average paragraph? How much time will I need to read this piece carefully?
- What do I already know about this subject? Can I keep this knowledge in mind as I read so I can establish some immediate connections with this text?
- Do I have any strong feelings about this subject that could interfere with my ability to comprehend how it is treated in this text?
- Do I know anything about this author? If this author is already familiar to me, can I trust what he or she writes? If this author is unfamiliar to me, is there any biograph-

continued

continued from previous page

✓

ical information in this source that will help me assess his or her credibility? (See 35d.)

- What can I learn from the title? Is there a subtitle? If there are subheadings in the text, what do they reveal about the organization of this work?
- Does this book include a table of contents or an index? Does this article include an abstract? Are there graphs, figures, or other visual aids? If so, how can this material be useful to me?
- Is there a bibliography that will indicate how extensive and current the research is?
- Does the introduction or conclusion reveal the thesis of this piece?
- Has the author included a summary near the conclusion or at the end of any of the subsections?
- Would it be easier for me to understand this text if I read something else first?

In addition to asking yourself these questions, you can also benefit from scanning specific sentences and phrases. Although the central idea of a paragraph can occur anywhere within it (chapter 31), it often appears in the first or last sentence. By reading these sentences, you can get a sense of a work's content and organization. You can also scan for key phrases that writers use to signal important points. The phrase *in other words*, for example, signals that a writer is about to paraphrase (37h(4)) a point just made—probably because it is important. Other key phrases include *in the following article* (or chapter), which can signal a statement of the author's focus or purpose; and *in summary, in conclusion,* and *the point I am making,* which signal a restatement or clarification of the author's thesis. In addition, words like *therefore* and *thus* signal that a point is being made about the information just presented.

Previewing is a way to make reading easier and more meaningful. It can also help you select appropriate material when you do research (chapter 37). But remember that previewing a text is not the same as reading it fully and closely.

35b Critical readers distinguish between fact and opinion.

As you acquire information through reading, you may believe that you are acquiring **facts**—reliable pieces of information that can be verified through independent sources or procedures. Facts are valued because they are believed to be true. **Opinions** are assertions or inferences that may or may not be based on facts. When these ideas are widely accepted, they may seem to be factual when actually they are not.

Facts are not necessarily more valuable than opinions; a thoughtful opinion may have more merit than a page of random facts. But accepting opinions unsupported by facts can lead you to faulty conclusions that damage your credibility.

To distinguish between fact and opinion, ask yourself questions about what you have read: Can it be proved? Can it be challenged? How often is the same result achieved? (See 35c.) If a statement can consistently be proved true, then it is a fact. If it can be disputed, then it is an opinion.

Fact Spinach contains iron.

Opinion Americans should eat more spinach.

To say that spinach contains iron is to state a well-established fact; it can be verified by consulting published studies or by conducting laboratory testing. But to say that

Americans need to eat more spinach is to express an opinion that may or may not be supported by facts. When considering the statement "Americans should eat more spinach," a critical reader might ask, "What is spinach good for? How important is iron? Do *all* Americans suffer from iron deficiency? Is spinach the only source of iron?" Exploring any of these questions could lead to discovering differences of opinion as well as learning some facts.

Because the facts themselves can change, critical readers and thinkers need to remain flexible as they distinguish between fact and opinion. The erroneous belief that the sun revolves around the earth was once considered a fact, and Newtonian physics was once believed to be indisputably true. Describing what can easily happen in research, a distinguished physician writes that a good scientist must be prepared for the day when his or her life work is suddenly called into question:

> All the old ideas—last week's ideas in some cases—are no longer good ideas. The hard facts have softened, melted away and vanished under the pressure of new hard facts.
>
> —LEWIS THOMAS, "The Art of Teaching Science"

No matter how knowledgeable, a reader who is unwilling to assimilate new information and question old ideas cannot expect to meet the challenges of a rapidly changing world. The collapse of the Soviet Union, for example, necessitated that other countries devise new approaches to foreign policy. Or, to take another example, researchers studying AIDS must maintain their intellectual dexterity so they can adapt their work as new information becomes available.

Exercise 1

Determine which of the following statements are fact and which are opinion. Explain your decisions in writing and be prepared to discuss your choices in class.

1. Willa Cather won the Pulitzer Prize for fiction in 1923.
2. Women often earn less money than men holding the same position.
3. Women are more emotional than men.
4. You cannot write well unless you know how to write correctly.
5. A college diploma is necessary for jobs that pay well.
6. The capital of California is Sacramento.
7. Running is good for your health.
8. The United States won the Second World War.
9. Water freezes at 32 degrees Fahrenheit.
10. John F. Kennedy was assassinated by Lee Harvey Oswald.

35c Critical readers look for evidence.

Critical readers expect writers to support their claims with ample evidence consisting of facts and other data such as personal experience and observation. When you are reading a work that makes a specific point, ask yourself if the writer has provided evidence that is accurate, representative, and sufficient. Examine critically any information that writers present. Accurate information should be verifiable. Recognize, however, that a writer may provide you with data that are accurate but unreliable because they are drawn from an exceptional case or a biased sampling. If, for example, you are reading an argument about the death penalty that draws all its information from material distributed by a police association, the evidence cited is unlikely to represent the full range of data available on this topic.

Similarly, examine polls and other statistics carefully. How recent is the information, and how was it gathered? In 1936 a poll conducted by the *Literary Digest* predicted the election of Alf Landon, but Franklin D. Roosevelt won by a landslide. The poll was faulty because it was limited to people who owned cars or had personal telephone service. During one of the worst economic depressions in American history, Americans with cars and personal telephones were among the financially secure citizens most likely to vote against Roosevelt, who advocated increased government spending on domestic programs. Even with representative polls, statistics can be manipulated. Do not accept them uncritically.

To decide how much evidence is appropriate, consider the size and originality of the claim. As a general rule, a writer who takes an unusual position on an issue will need to provide more evidence than a writer who has taken a less controversial stand. But in either case, a surplus is usually better than a deficit. Be sure, however, to consider the quality and significance of the evidence.

Exercise 2

Study the evidence in the following two excerpts. How accurate and reliable is the evidence in each? Explain your opinion in writing.

> [1]The single most talked-about consequence of a global warming is probably the expected rise in sea level as the result of polar melting. [2]For the past several thousand years, sea level has been rising, but so slowly that it has almost been a constant. [3]In consequence, people have extensively developed the coastlines. [4]But a hundred and twenty thousand years ago, during the previous interglacial period, sea level was twenty feet above the current level; at the height of the last ice age, when much of the world's water was frozen at the poles, sea level was three hundred feet below what it is now. [5]Scientists estimate that the world's remaining ice cover contains enough water so that if it should all melt it would raise sea level more than two hundred and fifty feet.
>
> —BILL McKIBBEN, "The End of Nature"

> [1]Paradoxically, the historical records of temperature change do not jibe with the greenhouse theory. [2]Between 1880 and 1940, temperatures appeared to rise. [3]Yet between 1940 and 1965, a period of much heavier fossil-fuel use and deforestation, temperatures dropped, which seems inconsistent with the greenhouse effect. [4]And a comprehensive study of past global ocean records by researchers from Britain and M.I.T. revealed no significant rising temperature trends between 1856 and 1986. [5]Concludes Richard Lindzen of M.I.T.'s department of Earth, Atmospheric and Planetary Sciences, "The data as we have it does not support a warming."
>
> —ROBERT J. BIDINOTTO,
> "What Is the Truth about Global Warming?"

35d Readers must evaluate a writer's credibility.

Critical readers look for evidence that helps them determine if an author is well-informed and fair-minded. To determine how credible a writer is, ask yourself the following questions:

Checklist for Evaluating Credibility ✓

- Does the writer support claims with evidence?
- Does the writer reveal how and where evidence was obtained?
- Does the writer recognize that other points of view may be legitimate?
- Does the writer use sarcasm or make personal attacks on opponents?
- Does the writer reach a conclusion that is in proportion to the amount of evidence provided?
- Does the writer have credentials that invest the work with authority?

Thoughtful writers support their claims with evidence (35c, 36c) and reach conclusions that seem justified by the amount of evidence provided. They reveal how and where they obtained this evidence (38a, 38b, and 38d), and their tone (33a) is appropriate for their purpose, audience, and occasion (32a). Moreover, they show that they have given fair consideration to views with which they disagree (36c(2)). As you evaluate credibility, question any writer who seems entirely one-sided, but also question any writer who seems overly anxious to please.

Exercise 3

Evaluate the credibility of the following excerpt from an argument against gun control:

[1]The gun control issue, then, is never a question of what the government "allows" us to own. [2]The Constitution states that government has *no authority* over the firearms ownership of the people. [3]The people, not the government, possess an absolute right in the area of gun ownership. [4]If you or I want to own an AR-15 or any other gun, it is none of the government's business *why* we want it, and certainly none of its business to presume that we may be up to no good. [5]In a free society, the salient question is *never* whether the government can trust the people but always whether the people can trust their government. [6]The history of the Second Amendment makes this point ever so clear. [7]You could spend a lifetime studying the writings of the Founding Fathers and would never find among any of them the kinds of sentiments expressed by our 20th-century gun controllers—sentiments that reflect a profound distrust for a free people. [8]You would not find a single person among all the founders of our nation who was worried about firearms in the hands of the citizenry. [9]The very idea is preposterous.

—ROGER KOOPMAN, "Second Defense"

Exercise 4

Read a series of editorials or letters in a newspaper. Select one that is one-sided or inadequately supported; select another that is well supported and fair-minded. Your choices should be of similar length. Prepare to read them in class and to explain your evaluation of them.

35e Critical thinkers understand inductive reasoning.

When writers use **inductive reasoning**, they begin with a number of facts or observations and use them to draw a general conclusion. Inductive reasoning is commonly used in daily life. For example, if you get indigestion several times after eating sauerkraut, you might conclude that eating sauerkraut gives you indigestion. This use of evidence to form a generalization is called an **inductive leap**, and the leap should be in proportion to the amount of evidence gathered. It is reasonable to stop eating sauerkraut if it consistently makes you ill—especially if you had sampled sauerkraut from more than one source (since different preparations could change the effect). But if you conclude that no one should eat sauerkraut, your conclusion would be too general for the amount of evidence in question.

Because it involves leaping from evidence to interpreting it, inductive reasoning can help writers reach probable, believable conclusions, but not some absolute truth that will endure forever. Making a small leap from evidence to a conclusion that seems probable is not the same as jumping to a sweeping conclusion that could easily be challenged. Generally, the greater the evidence, the more reliable the conclusion.

Science's use of inductive reasoning is known as the scientific method. For instance, early medical studies equated diets high in fat with coronary disease. The scientific community reserved judgment since the early studies were based on small samplings, but later studies with broader sampling confirmed the early reports. Although all persons with coronary disease cannot be studied, the sampling is now large enough for scientists to draw the conclusion with more confidence. Nevertheless, a critical thinker would still examine the available evidence carefully and ask a number of questions about it. If the research had been conducted primarily on men, would the conclusions be equally applicable to women? Are the conclusions equally applicable to people of all races? To what extent have the researchers controlled all variables? Does the evidence support the conclusion that has been drawn, or should the conclusion be modified? Because they are critical thinkers who ask such questions, scientists are often motivated to do further research.

When used in persuasive writing (chapter **36**), inductive reasoning often employs examples. When you cannot cite all the instances that support your well-reasoned conclusion, one or a few examples closely related to the point you are making will provide evidence. (See **31c**.) In the following inductively organized paragraph, a number of examples support the last sentence.

> In Chicago last month, a nine-year-old boy died of an asthma attack while waiting for emergency aid. After their ambulance was pelted by rocks in an earlier incident, city paramedics wouldn't risk entering the Dearborn Homes project [where the boy lived] without a police escort. In Atlanta, residents of the Bankhead Courts project had their mail service suspended for two days last month after a postman nearly lost his life in the cross fire of a gun battle. Mail carriers wouldn't resume service until police accompanied them on

> their rounds. This is the day-to-day reality of life now in America's urban ghettos. Their residents, under siege by what are essentially organized drug terrorists, deserve the benefit of an unapologetic assault on drug-driven crime.
>
> —"Hot Towns," *Wall Street Journal*

How you organize your inductive reasoning varies with the situation. You may wish to provide your evidence first and then offer your conclusion. Or you may wish to reverse the order by stating the conclusion first, in the form of a topic sentence (31a(1)) or a thesis statement (32d), and then presenting the supporting examples.

35f Critical thinkers understand deductive reasoning.

When writers use **deductive reasoning,** they begin with generalizations (premises) and apply them to a specific instance to draw a conclusion about that instance. For example, if you know that all soldiers must complete basic training and that Martha has enlisted in the army, then you could conclude that Martha must complete basic training. This argument can be expressed in a structure called a **syllogism.**

Major Premise	All soldiers must complete basic training.
Minor Premise	Martha is a soldier.
Conclusion	Martha must complete basic training.

Sometimes premises are not stated.

> Martha has enlisted in the army, so she must complete basic training.

In this sentence, the unstated premise is that all soldiers must complete basic training. A syllogism with an unstated premise—or even an unstated conclusion—is called an **enthymeme.** Enthymemes are frequently found in arguments and can be very effective in writing, but they should be examined with care since the omitted statement may be inaccurate. "Samuel is from Louisiana, so he must like Cajun food" contains the unstated major premise that "Everyone from Louisiana likes Cajun food." This premise is unacceptable because there is no reason to assume that everyone from a particular region shares the same taste in food—even if the food in question happens to be a local specialty. As a critical reader, you must accept the truth of a writer's premises in order to agree with the writer's conclusion.

A deductive argument must be both true and valid. A **true** argument is based on generally accepted, well-backed premises. A **valid** argument is based on logical thinking. The conclusion in the following syllogism is valid because the conclusion follows logically from the major and minor premises, but it is not true because the major premise is not generally accepted.

Major Premise	All redheads are brilliant.
Minor Premise	Jane is a redhead.
Conclusion	Therefore Jane is brilliant.

The following deductively organized paragraph, from an argument on the welfare of children, draws on the premise stated in the first sentence.

> America cannot afford to waste resources by failing to prevent and curb the national human deficit, which cripples our children's welfare today and costs billions in later remedial and custodial dollars. Each dollar we invest in preventive health care for mothers and children saves more than $3 later. Every dollar put into quality preschool education like Head

> Start saves $4.75 later. It costs more than twice as much to place a child in foster care as to provide family preservation services. The question is not whether we can afford to invest in every child; it is whether we can afford not to. At a time when future demographic trends guarantee a shortage of young adults who will be workers, soldiers, leaders, and parents, America cannot afford to waste a single child. With unprecedented economic competition from abroad and changing patterns of production at home that demand higher basic educational skills, America cannot wait another minute to do whatever is needed to ensure that today's and tomorrow's workers are well prepared rather than useless and alienated—whatever their color.
>
> —MARIAN WRIGHT EDELMAN, *The Measure of Our Success*

According to the reasoning in this paragraph, America must invest more money in programs for the education and welfare of children. This conclusion rests on the premise "America cannot afford to waste resources." If children are resources for our country's future, and if current programs for children are failing "to ensure that today's and tomorrow's workers are well prepared," then it is logical to conclude that more money should be invested in those programs most likely to yield good results.

Exercise 5

Supply the missing premise in the following statements and determine if the reasoning is valid and true.

1. He must be a nice person. He smiles all the time.
2. She is a good writer. She is easy to understand.
3. It is going to rain tomorrow. There is a circle around the moon.
4. Omtronic Co. must be well managed. Its earnings have grown steadily during the past few years.
5. Dr. Kordoff must be a good teacher. Her classes always fill up quickly.

35g The Toulmin method is an alternative approach to reasoning.

Another way of using logic is through the method devised by Stephen Toulmin in *The Uses of Argument* (New York: Cambridge UP, 1964). To create a working logic suitable for the needs of writers, Toulmin drew on deductive reasoning but put less emphasis on the formal conventions of a syllogism. His approach sees argument as the progression from accepted facts or evidence (**data**) to a conclusion (**claim**) by way of a statement (**warrant**) that establishes a reasonable relationship between the two. For example, in the argument,

> Since soldiers are required to complete basic training, and since Martha is a soldier, Martha must complete basic training,

the claim is that Martha must complete basic training, and the data consists of the fact that she is a soldier. The warrant, that soldiers are required to complete basic training, ties the two statements together, making the conclusion follow from the data.

Data → **Claim (therefore)**

Martha is a soldier. → Martha must complete basic training.

Warrant (since)

Soldiers must complete basic training.

The warrant is often implied in arguments and, like the unstated premise in the syllogism, needs careful examination to be acceptable.

Of course, few arguments are as simple as this example. For instance, Martha may have been exempted from basic training because she has a special skill for which there is an urgent need. In such cases, writers can make allowances for exceptions. Qualifiers such as *usually, probably,* and *possibly* show the degree of certainty of the conclusion, and rebuttal terms such as *unless* allow writers to indicate exceptions.

> **Since** Martha is a soldier, she **probably** passed basic training **unless** an exception was made for her.

Notice that the boldfaced transitional words express logical relationships among ideas in the argument and corresponding elements in the sentence. Like inductive and deductive reasoning, the Toulmin model makes allowances for important elements of probability.

CAUTION Too many qualifiers can make an argument seem hesitant and unconvincing.

In the following paragraph, the writer claims that English should be "the official language of the United States." Her data is that English is the language of the government and the primary language of the media. Her warrant is "To be an effective citizen one ought to vote, and to do so intelligently one must be well informed."

> The movement to make English the official language of the United States is in no way a put-down of other languages or cultures. But it is the language used predominantly by the print and electronic media; it is the tongue in which government at every level is conducted. To be an effective citizen one

ought to vote, and to do so intelligently one must be well informed. Candidates, of course, present the issues and outline their platforms in English.

—YOLANDA DE MOLA, "The Language of Power"

Exercise 6

Analyze the argument in the following excerpt by asking yourself the following questions:

a. What is the conclusion or claim?
b. What data support the claim?
c. What is the warrant that underlies the argument?

[1]Whether in liquefied form, or used—as many recommend—as a substitute for oil or natural gas to produce electricity, coal is not so simple as it seems. [2]You don't just dig it out of the ground and burn it like waste paper. [3]It is a bulky commodity, and it has more than its share of disadvantages as a fuel.

[1]Railroad facilities and barge canals must be greatly expanded and pipelines constructed to carry the coal in dry or slurry form thousands of miles. [2]Underground mining is hazardous and expensive; open-pit, or strip, mining engenders stiff opposition because it threatens to scar the landscape—in the United States, some particularly beautiful Western landscapes would be an early target. [3]Burned under electric-generating boilers, coal leaves behind vast tonnages of residue, and the gasses it releases upon burning are heavy with contaminants. [4]Getting rid of coal's ashes—usually in the form of a fine powder, because coal must be pulverized before burning for maximum efficiency—is difficult. [5]Expensive scrubbers must be installed in new plants that burn coal with a high sulfur content to prevent the creation of "acid rain." [6]The huge quantities of carbon dioxide that would be released into the air by burning coal on a vastly expanded scale could raise further havoc with the earth's atmosphere.

—ROGER STARR, "The Case for Nuclear Energy"

35h Critical thinkers recognize logical fallacies.

Fallacies are lapses in logic that can result from misusing or misrepresenting evidence, from relying on faulty premises, or from distorting the issues. They can be the result of poor thinking, but they can also be a deliberate attempt to manipulate—as suggested by the origin of the term *fallacia,* which is Latin for "deceit." Fallacies are common, especially in persuasive writing. (See chapter 36.) Here are some of the major fallacies. Be alert for them in your reading, and try to avoid them in your thinking.

(1) Ad hominem: A personal attack on an opponent that draws attention away from the issues under consideration.

Faulty He is unfit to be governor because he drank too much when he was a college student. [Whether or not this candidate drank too much when he was young may reveal something about his character, but voters might decide that he now has political skills and principles that could benefit the state.]

(2) Appeal to tradition: An argument that says something should be done a certain way simply because it has been done that way in the past.

Faulty We should not allow women to join this club because we have never let women join before. [Times change; what was acceptable in the past is not necessarily acceptable in the present.]

(3) **Bandwagon:** An argument saying, in effect, "Everyone's doing or saying or thinking this, so you should too."

Faulty Everyone else is cheating, so why shouldn't you? [The majority is not always right.]

(4) **Begging the question:** A statement that assumes what needs to be proved.

Faulty We need to fire the thieves in the police department. [If there are thieves working in the police department, this point needs to be established.]

(5) **Equivocation:** An assertion that falsely relies on the use of a term in two different senses.

Faulty We know this is a natural law because it feels natural. [When first used, *natural* means principles derived from nature or reason; when used again, it means easy or simple because of being in accord with one's own nature.]

(6) **False analogy:** The assumption that because two things are alike in some ways, they must be alike in other ways.

Faulty Since the books are about the same length and cover the same material, one is probably as good as the other. [The length and coverage of the books cannot predict whether one is as good as the other.]

(7) **False authority:** The assumption that an expert in one field can be a credible expert in another.

Faulty The defense budget must be cut, as the country's leading pediatrician has shown. [Pediatric medicine is unrelated to economics or political science.]

(8) **False cause:** The assumption that because one event follows another, the first is the cause of the second. Sometimes called *post hoc, ergo propter hoc* ("after this, so because of this").

Faulty The new tax assessor took office last January, and crime in the streets has already increased 25 percent. [The assumption is that having a new tax assessor caused the increase in crime, an assumption unlikely to be true.]

(9) **False dilemma:** Stating that only two alternatives exist when in fact there are more than two (sometimes called the *either/or* fallacy).

Faulty We have only two choices: to build more nuclear power plants or to be completely dependent on foreign oil. [In fact, other possibilities exist.]

(10) **Guilt by association:** An unfair attempt to make someone responsible for the beliefs or actions of others.

Faulty Senator Barlow must be dishonest because she belongs to the same club as that judge who was recently disbarred. [People can belong to the same club—or live in the same neighborhood—without engaging in the same behavior.]

(11) **Hasty generalization:** A generalization based on too little evidence or on exceptional or biased evidence.

Faulty Ellen is a poor student because she failed her first quiz. [Her performance may improve in the weeks ahead.]

(12) **Non sequitur:** A statement that does not follow logically from what has just been said—a conclusion that does not follow from the premises.

Faulty Billy Joe is honest, therefore, he will get a good job. [Many honest people do not get good jobs.]

(13) **Oversimplification:** A statement or argument that leaves out relevant considerations about an issue to imply that there is a single cause or solution for a complex problem.

Faulty We can eliminate hunger by growing more food. [Increasing the amount of food produced does not guarantee that the hungry will have access to it.]

(14) **Red herring:** Dodging the real issue by drawing attention to an irrelevant issue (sometimes called *ignoring the question*).

Faulty Why worry about overcrowded schools when we ought to be trying to attract a professional hockey franchise? [Professional sports have nothing to do with overcrowded schoolrooms.]

(15) **Slippery slope:** The assumption that if one thing is allowed it will be only the first step in a downward spiral.

Faulty Handgun control will lead to a police state. [Handgun control has not led to a police state in England.]

Exercise 7

Identify the fallacies in the following statements. For each statement, write one or two sentences in which you explain the flaw in reasoning.

1. You should vote for Jonathan because everyone else is.
2. We must either build more prisons or crowd more prisoners into existing cells.
3. This car must be reliable; it's the kind my dentist drives.
4. If we censor pornography, we will ultimately lose freedom of speech.
5. I know that store is badly managed. One of the salespeople there was rude to me once.
6. If women dressed more conservatively, they wouldn't get raped.
7. You can't trust a guy like that; his brother was found guilty of tax evasion.
8. We should cut welfare because people on welfare are getting too many benefits.
9. The union is arguing for a cost-of-living raise, but its leaders are all a bunch of crooks.
10. Children would do a lot better at school if they didn't spend so much time watching television.

Exercise 8

Examine several recent magazine advertisements and study the claims the ads make. Look specifically for examples of logical fallacies. Choose one ad that seems especially illogical. Bring a copy of it to class, as well as a paragraph in which you explain why the ad is unconvincing.

Exercise 9

Read the following paragraph and identify the logical fallacies you find in it. Then, adopting the point of view of someone opposed to animal experimentation, write two or three paragraphs responding to the argument offered here.

[1]As the Oscar-winning director Scavan Kleck has argued, "Animal experimentation saves lives." [2]Isn't the life of a little girl more important than the life of a chimpanzee? [3]We have to choose: we can either experiment on animals to find cures for life-threatening diseases or we can stand by helplessly while thousands of children die. [4]Experimentation is necessary because research is important. [5]And why should we worry about what happens to animals in laboratories when the real problem is how people treat their pets? [6]Advocates of animal rights are a bunch of sentimental vegetarians who don't care what happens to children, and they will never be satisfied with banning painful experiments on animals. [7]If they succeed in getting legislation passed that restricts experimentation, it's only a question of time before the sale of meat is prohibited. [8]Just look at the trouble they've already caused. [9]The cost of research has soared since people started protesting against animal experimentation.

Chapter 36 Writing Arguments

When you are planning to write an argument, you begin by following the same process you use to write other essays. You consider your purpose, audience, and occasion (32a), find an appropriate subject (32b), explore that subject (32c), establish a thesis (32d), and organize your ideas (32e). In addition, you use logic (35), provide evidence to support your claims (35b), establish your authority to be writing on the subject you have chosen (35d), and determine whether it would be appropriate to appeal to the feelings of your audience (36d).

As you proceed, you should understand the importance of arguing ethically and treating your opponents with respect. Argument is a way to discover truth and negotiate differences. It should not be used to punish or ridicule people with whom you happen to disagree.

36a Different arguments have different purposes.

When writing an argument, you should consider your purpose. It may be to pursue the truth until you have formed an opinion that seems reasonable. It may be to convince an audience of readers that your position has merit. Or you might go farther and seek to persuade your audience to undertake a specific action that follows from the position you have taken. Just as important, your purpose could be to establish a consensus that brings people with differing views together. You can have a single purpose or more than one, but one purpose should predominate.

When you are writing to pursue the truth, you are writing **to inquire**. In conversation, you probably have ample experience with argument as a means of inquiry. When two or more people engage in conversation to explore what they think, they are engaging in inquiry. Two friends who meet to talk about a decision one of them needs to make are using argument as inquiry. Such an argument does not involve quarreling; it is shaped instead by the give-and-take of dialogue as different ideas are exchanged. Philosophers and rhetoricians call this kind of serious conversation **dialectic**. Many of the great works of ancient philosophy take the form of a dialogue written along these lines. You might practice dialectic by actually writing a dialogue between two speakers or by simply weighing the pros and cons of differing views until you arrive at a conclusion that seems true to you.

If you have already reached a conclusion to which you are committed, then your purpose is probably **to convince** other people to accept your position to some extent. This purpose can take at least four different forms. If there is little likelihood that you can convince an audience to change a strongly held opinion, you could be achieving a great deal by simply convincing them that your position deserves to be taken seriously. If the members of your audience are not firmly and absolutely committed to a position, then you might write in the hope of convincing them to agree with you. If they agree with you in principle, then you might convince them to undertake a specific action—such as voting for the candidate you are supporting. Finally, if there are fundamental differences within your audience, you might write to reduce the extent of their conflict by establishing common ground and negotiating a compromise.

Exercise 1

Study the following paragraph and decide what the author's purpose seems to be. Then write a paragraph stating that purpose and the grounds that led you to your conclusion.

> [1]I am not advocating the erection of a wall against immigration. [2]Instead a more generous immigration policy should go hand in hand with greater punishment of illegal entrants, including fines and possibly jail terms. [3]Greater legal immigration is not only desirable in its own right but would reduce the number who seek to enter illegally. [4]Not surprisingly, illegal entry generally expands when a country contracts the number of immigrants accepted.
>
> —GARY S. BECKER, "Illegal Immigration"

36b Argument assumes the existence of differing views.

If there are no differences, then there is no need to argue. The first step toward finding a subject for argumentation is to consider issues that inspire different opinions. If most people already share the same opinion—believing, for example, that it is nice to sit by a fireplace on a cold winter night—then there is little point in writing an argument espousing this view. Widely held opinions could become topics for expressive or informative essays (32a), such as "Why I Love Fireplaces" or "How to Build Your Own Fireplace," but they lack the element of controversy found in an appropriate topic for argumentation.

Behind any effective argument is a question that can generate more than one reasonable answer. If you ask "Is there poverty in our country?" almost anyone will agree that there is. But if you ask "Why is there poverty in our country?" or "What can we do to eliminate poverty?" you will hear very different answers. When you write an argument, you are either looking for an answer to a question or showing that you have found the answer. Choose a question that needs an answer, then focus (32c) on the part of this question that you will address in your essay.

A good subject may occur to you if you note how you respond to the views of others. Your response to a class discussion or material you have read for class could lead to a good essay. When you are free to choose your own subject, you should be able to think of many suitable ones if you stay abreast of current events by reading newspapers and magazines. Even if you are doing something as simple as listening to a television commentator, you might find yourself agreeing or disagreeing with what you hear, and a good essay could be developed from this response. To find a subject, you can also try freewriting and listing (32c(1)).

When you think you have found a suitable subject, you can benefit from asking yourself a series of questions:

Checklist for Evaluating a Subject ✓

- Is there more than one possible response? Would anyone be likely to disagree with me?
- Do I know enough about this subject? Can I find out what I need to know?
- Have I narrowed the subject so that I can do justice to it in the space I have available?
- Do I have a purpose in writing about this subject?
- Are the subject and purpose appropriate for my audience?

If you can answer "yes" to all these questions, you can feel confident about your subject and move farther into the writing process.

36c Argument requires development.

You will sometimes need to do research to find information on your subject. (See chapter 37.) At other times you will be able to write directly from your own experience and observations. In either case, you should explore your subject in enough depth to have a number of reasons to support your conclusion and enough evidence to support these reasons. In addition, you should consider the reasons why other people might disagree with you and be prepared to respond to them.

(1) Effective arguments are well-supported.

If you have an opinion or thesis (32d) that you wish to argue, you must have at least one reason for believing as you do. That reason must be established in your paper. Although it is possible to base your case on a single reason, doing so is usually risky. If your audience does not find this reason persuasive, you have no other support for your case. When you show that you have more than one reason for believing as you do, you increase the likelihood that your audience will find merit in your case. For example, suppose you believe in capital punishment and write an argument favoring it on the grounds that it deters crime. Readers who are aware of evidence showing that the death penalty does not deter crime could find your argument well written but dismiss it nevertheless. If you introduce other reasons for supporting the death penalty, then you make a more complex case that cannot be dismissed so readily.

When you are exploring your subject, make a list of the reasons that have led to your belief without trying to edit them. (See 32g(1).) When you are ready to begin drafting (32f), think critically (chapter 35) about the reasons on your list. Some may need to be eliminated because they overlap; some may need to be eliminated because you would have trouble supporting them or because they seem trivial compared with the others. You can then base your argument on the remaining reasons. If additional reasons occur to you as you draft, you can easily add them to your list or incorporate them immediately into your draft.

(2) Effective arguments respond to diverse views.

In addition to listing reasons for believing as you do, you should make a list of reasons why people might disagree with you. Good arguments are never one-sided. If you want to be persuasive, you must demonstrate that you are familiar with views other than yours. The most common strategy for doing so is to introduce reasons why others believe differently and then show why you do not find these reasons convincing. In classical rhetoric, this strategy is called **refutation**. By showing not only the reasons for your position but also the weakness of the objections that can be made against it, you bolster your case significantly.

As you consider opposing views, you are likely to discover some you cannot refute. Do not be surprised to discover that there is merit in other people's views. Issues are often controversial precisely because good arguments can be made by different sides. When you find yourself agreeing with a point raised on another side of the issue in question, you can benefit from offering a **concession**. By openly conceding that you agree with opponents on a specific point, you show that you are fair-minded (35d) and increase your credibility. Concessions also increase the likelihood that opponents will find merit in your case. It is hard to persuade people to agree with you if you insist that they are entirely wrong. If you admit that they are partially right, they are more likely to admit that you could be partially right as well.

ESL Although it is considered rude in some cultures to disagree openly with authority or to state your own views frankly, American readers are accustomed to such directness. Consider the expectations of your audience (**32a**) and write with these expectations in mind.

Exercise 2

The following paragraph is taken from an argument by Martin Luther King, Jr. in which he defended the struggle for civil rights against the public criticism of a group of prominent clergymen. Write a short analysis of this paragraph in which you note (a) an opposition argument to which he is responding, (b) a refutation that he offers to this argument, (c) a concession that he makes, and (d) any questions this excerpt raises for you.

> [1]You express a great deal of anxiety over our willingness to break laws. [2]This is certainly a legitimate concern. [3]Since we so diligently urge people to obey the Supreme Court's decision of 1954 outlawing segregation in the public schools, at first glance it may seem rather paradoxical for us consciously to break laws. [4]One may well ask: "How can you advocate breaking some laws and obeying others?" [5]The answer lies in the fact that there are two types of laws, just and unjust. [6]I would be the first to advocate obeying just laws. [7]One has not only a legal but a moral responsibility to obey just laws. [8]Conversely, one has a moral responsibility to disobey unjust laws. [9]I would agree with St. Augustine that "an unjust law is no law at all."
>
> —MARTIN LUTHER KING, JR., "Letter from Birmingham Jail"

36d Different kinds of appeal are often necessary.

If people were entirely rational, persuasion could be achieved through logic alone (chapter 35). But because people are often caught up in their own concerns, feel threatened by differences, or see argument as a kind of combat, they may not even hear what you are saying—no matter how logical it may be. Getting a fair hearing is essential if you want your views to be understood. Theories of argument, from the ancient world to the present, offer advice on how to gain this hearing.

(1) There are three classical appeals.

Aristotle and other important thinkers in the ancient world believed that persuasion is achieved through a combination of three appeals: ethos, logos, and pathos. **Ethos** means demonstrating that you are fair-minded and well-informed so that readers can trust what you say. **Logos** is the effective use of critical thinking (chapter 35) and the judicious use of information. It is what you employ when you support your claims, make reasonable conclusions, and avoid logical fallacies (35h). Both logos and ethos are essential to effective argumentation. **Pathos**, or using language that will stir the feelings of your audience, is also an option. Although it can be misused by people who wish to obscure thought, it can be effective when used to establish empathy. When you are trying to be persuasive, remember that human beings have feelings as well as thoughts. Appeal to these feelings if you can, but do not rest your entire case on them.

(2) Rogerian appeals emphasize showing other people that you understand them.

Rogerian argument derives from the work of Carl R. Rogers, a psychologist who believed that many problems are the result of a breakdown in communication. In his book *On Becoming a Person* (1961), Rogers argues that people often fail to understand each other because of a natural tendency to judge and evaluate, agree or disagree. He emphasizes the importance of listening carefully to what others say and understanding their ideas. His model calls for having the courage to suspend judgment until you are able to restate fairly and accurately what others believe. When each person in a conflict demonstrates this ability, the likelihood of misunderstanding is significantly reduced. One of the advantages of this model is that it can be initiated by a single person in a potentially explosive situation. Another advantage is that it can help foster personal growth. Skills such as paraphrasing and summarizing (37h) are essential to Rogerian argument. Although this model can be used to achieve a number of goals, it is especially useful when building consensus. An argument organized along Rogerian principles would begin with a careful restatement of other people's views, then offer concessions, and only then introduce the position the rest of the essay will support.

36e There are several ways to organize an argument.

To organize your argument, you can begin by outlining or by writing your first draft and then deciding how to better organize it as you revise (chapter 33). In either case, you can organize your argument deductively (35f) by working to a conclusion that is entailed by your premise or inductively (35e) by moving toward a conclusion that is not entailed by your premise.

Whether you choose to use induction, deduction, or another form of logic (35g), your decision is rhetorical. In other words, unless your instructor asks you to demonstrate a particular type of organization, no one type is unquestionably right for every written argument. The decisions you make about organization should be based on what would be most effective when writing about your subject on this occasion for the audience you have in mind.

There are, however, a few basic principles that are useful to remember.

(1) Introductions can vary.

You can begin by providing background, establishing your premise, offering a quotation, raising a question, or providing a relevant anecdote or example. (See 32f(1).)

(2) Separate reasons are best discussed in separate paragraphs.

You will usually need at least a full paragraph to develop any reason for your opinion, but some reasons could easily take several paragraphs. You might need two paragraphs to explain one reason and only one to explain another because one is more important or because you have more to say about one than the other. But if you try to discuss two separate reasons in the same paragraph, your audience may not follow you or the paragraph may lack unity and coherence (chapter 31).

(3) You can begin a paragraph with a view different from yours.

If you follow this strategy, the rest of the paragraph is available for your response and readers make only one shift between differing views. If you begin a paragraph with your view, then introduce an opponent's view, and then move back to yours, readers must shift direction twice and may miss the point. If you wait until the very end of a paragraph to respond to a different view, you could deny yourself the space you need to respond.

(4) Refutation and concessions are most effective when placed where readers will welcome them.

If you wait until the end of your argument to recognize views that differ from yours, some readers may have already decided that you are too one-sided—and may even have stopped reading. When writers are taking a highly controversial stand on a subject that has inspired strong feelings, they sometimes begin by responding to these strongly held views. Under other circumstances, however, an audience may react negatively to a writer who responds to opposing arguments before offering any reasons to support his or her own view. It is often best to offer at least one strong reason to support your case before turning to opposing views. If you keep at least one other reason in reserve, you can discuss it after your refutation and before your conclusion.

(5) Your conclusion can reinforce your purpose.

If you are writing to inquire, you might conclude with the truth you have reached. If you are writing to convince others, you might end by restating your position and summarizing your reasons for holding it. If you are writing to persuade readers to undertake a specific action, your conclusion should emphasize this point. (See 32f(2).)

Another way to organize your argument is to follow the plan recommended by classical rhetoric:

Introduction	Introduce your issue and capture the attention of your audience.
Statement of Background	Report information the members of your audience need to know before they can understand the position you are going to take.
Exposition	Interpret the information you have included and define any key terms.
Proposition	Introduce the position you are taking.
Proof	Discuss the reasons why you have taken your position.
Refutation	Show why you are not persuaded by the arguments of people who hold a different position.
Conclusion	Summarize your most important points and appeal to your audience's feelings.

Use this plan if it seems appropriate for your rhetorical situation (32a).

36f You can improve your ability to write persuasively by studying the arguments of other writers.

The following paper illustrates one student's response to an assignment in persuasive writing. As you read it, consider whether the author has argued her case effectively.

Janet Kowolsky
Professor Hayes
English 200, Section 1
25 April 1997

Making the Grade

Now that I am finishing my second semester in college, I can see that I do much better on some exams than on others. Last semester I had four midterm exams and three finals. This semester I have already had another three exams, and more will be coming up in a few weeks. The results have been all over the place even though I studied hard for each of these tests. Part of the problem is that I've always tended to do better in some subjects than in others. But that doesn't explain everything. Some of my worst results have been in my best subjects. Performance on an exam is determined not only by how much you study for it and what the questions are like. It is also determined by the circumstances under which the exam is given.

Of the ten exams I've had so far, eight were taken in class and two were taken outside of class. The eight in-class exams differed in terms of how they were set up. Three of these involved studying like crazy without having a clear sense of what I'd be asked to do. My teachers pretty much said, "Make sure you review everything we've covered so far, because this exam is cumulative." Most of them did specify whether they would ask objective or essay questions—although my history teacher last semester wouldn't even do that when someone asked. ("I'm still thinking about it," he said.) Also, they did let us know things like whether we could bring a dictionary or calculator to class. But that was about it.

The other exams were a lot less stressful. My history teacher this semester gave us a list of six questions a week before our midterm and told us she would choose three of them for our test. This was helpful because I could tell what the exam was going to be like. I still had to study a lot, because I wanted to be able to do a good job with any of these questions, but I had a lot less anxiety preparing for the test. When I was preparing for finals in December, my psychology professor and my biology professor distributed copies of previous exams so that my classmates and I could have a rough idea of what our exam was going to be like. That was also helpful.

Unfortunately, each of these exams had to be taken in a room crowded with other students and filled with tension. Whenever I wanted to pause to think, I'd look around and see other people scribbling away and worry that I was falling behind. When people would start to leave early, I'd stress out completely—thinking something must be wrong with me because I needed all the time that still remained. Then there were a range of irritations and distractions: Losing concentration when someone arrived late and squeezed into the seat next to me, listening to people rummage in their backpacks for supplies, being asked if I had an extra pen, catching sight of other students passing material between them, and feeling like I was some kind of laboratory rat under the eye of the teacher monitoring the room.

Two other tests that I had were entirely different because they were take-home exams. One of these was in my introduction to literature class; the other was in calculus. Although these two exams were set up somewhat differently, they were both excellent. I think more professors should assign take-home exams.

The big advantage of a take-home exam is that you can work on it in a quiet place where you feel safe and comfortable. The questions on my two take-homes were really challenging, but I did well on both of them because I was in my own space. Because the circumstances of a take-home exam are more comfortable doesn't mean that the exam itself has to be easy. If professors eliminated some of the stress of exam taking, they would be able to tell more accurately how much their students really know. Isn't that the purpose of exams?

Some professors may be concerned that students will cheat if they take their exams at home. I have to admit that cheating could be a problem. On the other hand, students who really want to cheat can usually find a way of doing so on regular exams and other assignments. So avoiding take-home exams does not mean that cheating goes away. And take-home exams can be designed to minimize cheating. My literature exam, for example, was an open-book essay exam. It was really useful to be able to look up quotes to back up what I wanted to say, but there's no way I could have passed the exam if I hadn't read the material and thought about it in advance. Theoretically somebody could probably get a friend to take an exam like this for him. But the same thing could happen when we have to write papers. When somebody cheats this way, the professor should be able to tell even if she wasn't there watching the person do it.

Another common argument against take-home exams is that they could become big productions. I've heard some students say that they'd rather get an exam over with in two hours than have a take-home that takes as much work as writing another big paper. I understand these concerns. My literature teacher told us that we could take as long as we wanted on the exam just as long as we handed it in on time, and I ended up spending a whole morning on it. But my calculus professor insisted that we limit ourselves to the two hours we would get during the standard final exam period. We got to choose which two hours we would devote to the exam—and where we would take it—but the exam itself took no longer than any other exam. In other words, take-homes can be designed in different ways to make them appropriate for different classes.

There are a number of other advantages to take-home exams. Finals aren't scheduled during the hours the class met, and this can be a problem for students who have jobs or who have children to take care of. The take-home provides flexibility for such students by being sensitive to their needs. And just as they are more student-friendly, they are also more professor-friendly. Teachers don't have to hang around monitoring a classroom when they've got lots of other things they could be doing. And more important, they get to read better exams. Wouldn't professors be happier to see their students doing well than to see them doing poorly?

Take-home exams can be well designed or badly designed—just like any other assignment. But the flexibility they offer makes them preferable to traditional exams. Professors who have never offered a take-home exam should experiment with them. They will get a chance to do so soon, and I hope they will take advantage of it.

Exercise 3

Write an evaluation of the preceding argument. What is its purpose? What strategies has the author used to satisfy this purpose? How well is it supported, and how well is it organized? Is there anything the author has failed to consider?

Chapter 37

Research: Finding and Evaluating Sources

Although writing from research usually takes more time than writing essays based on information already familiar to you, the process involves many of the same skills. The distinctive feature of a research assignment is that it requires you to develop a subject by drawing on outside resources and acknowledging them properly. Improving your ability to work with sources may subsequently help you with other writing assignments as well, since you may need to obtain information from sources even when you are not specifically required to do research.

Further, writing from research involves many of the same skills that you use to write essays based on familiar information.

37a Information from sources is basic to most writing.

Rather than considering the research paper as a special assignment unrelated to other kinds of writing, you should recognize that almost anything you write requires you to acquire and use information. On some occasions, you may discover that you have sufficient information from your own experience or observations. On other occasions, you may need to explore the resources of a library to discover the work of other writers or researchers who can help you. In either case, remember that you are a writer, not simply a compiler of data. No matter how many sources you use, you are the most important presence in a paper that has your name on it. Think of the paper as a **researched** paper—that is, written from research that you have evaluated and then used to advance a **thesis** (32d).

(1) Analyzing the rhetorical situation

A researched paper, like any other paper, requires that you consider occasion, purpose, audience, and subject.

Writing that responds to events in the world around you—a wedding, a birthday, a job application—takes account of one of the elements of **occasion**, perhaps the most obvious element. But occasion involves much more than that. Is the writing you are doing something you have been asked to do? Did someone ask you to do research? What kind of research is expected? For example, some papers require you to interview people, while others concentrate on print or electronic sources. What is the scope of the project? When is your deadline? What is your rhetorical stance?

Will the **purpose** (32a(1)) of your paper be chiefly expository (to report, analyze, or explain) or persuasive (to prove a point)? Are you writing to understand the information better? To show someone else that you understand? To solve a problem?

Your **audience** (32a(2)) may or may not be expert on your subject, but you should usually envision a reader who is intelligent, fair-minded, and interested in what you have to say. Similarly, you should present yourself as a writer who is thoughtful, fair-minded, and responsive to the views of others, because any sign of bias can undermine your credibility (35c) as a researcher. Your audience will also determine to a great extent how formal your paper will be, what level of language you will use (expert vocabulary, longer or shorter sentences), and what the format of the paper will be (MLA, APA, documentation styles adopted by a particular company, and so on).

You find a **subject** for a researched paper in much the same way as you find a topic for any piece of writing: You are assigned the topic (as you may be in the workplace as well as in a college class), you find a subject that interests you, or you are moved to answer a question. (See 32b.) An inquiring mind is the best equipment you can bring to this task: Choose a subject that interests you and is appropriate for your audience. If you are stuck for an idea, consider some of the methods mentioned in 32c(1). You might also try browsing on the **World Wide Web**, staying alert for sites and categories that interest you.

Once you have a subject in mind, the exploration methods discussed in 32c(1)—freewriting, listing, questioning, considering perspectives—will almost certainly help you find an interesting focus. Limiting the topic is especially important for a researched paper, since one of your main objectives is to show your ability to treat a subject in some depth within the time allowed and (usually) the length specified. But even if you begin research with a thesis, be prepared to revise it if your research findings do not support it. (See also 35b.)

A quick Web search using keywords from a subject you have in mind will help establish whether there is enough (or too much) material on your subject. (The amount of pertinent material in your college library is also an important test.) If you find dozens of relevant sources, you should probably narrow the subject to one with a more manageable scope. However, if you have difficulty finding sources, chances are that your subject is too narrow and needs to be broader. Because the best researched papers usually draw on different kinds of material, you should also reconsider any topic that would force you to rely exclusively on one type of source. A paper based only on newspaper articles, for example, could easily lack depth, and research drawn exclusively from books might overlook current information in the field. Similarly, relying solely on electronic sources is unwise, since the technology is so new that much excellent material is not yet in electronic form.

Exercise 1

Evaluate the following subjects for a ten-page researched paper. If any seem too broad, suggest a narrower topic. For example, "The Second World War" should be narrowed to something like "The Bombing of Pearl Harbor." If any seem too narrow, suggest a broader subject—for example, "Raising Wheat in Brazil" could be expanded to "The Variety of Crops in Brazilian Agriculture." Eliminate any subject that you would be unable to find reliable sources for.

censorship of the Internet
safe sex
legalization of marijuana
puns in Shakespeare
gays/lesbians in the military
animal experimentation
tofu-based salad dressings
feminism

(2) Developing a research problem and analyzing your own knowledge

An important step in doing research is to envision your topic as a research problem and then to establish what you already know about it. This step should help considerably in avoiding accidental plagiarism (see **37g**) since you will have a record of what you already know before you began researching. A **research problem** might be a question or an issue that can be resolved at least partly through research.

It may be argumentative, but it may not be a matter of opinion. For example, the thesis "animal experimentation is wrong" is not a research problem because research cannot prove a moral judgment. Research, however, can prove whether a policy is effective. The thesis "animal experimentation is necessary for medical research" is a hypothesis suitable for research.

Establishing what you already know about a topic takes freewriting and brainstorming several steps farther. Try to write down everything you know about your topic. Try to convince someone else of your thesis and write down all the information you bring to your argument. Think about where you have seen your thesis discussed and search your memory for all the information you can remember about the subject. Use the thinking strategies in chapters 35 and 32, then examine what you think you know to see if your points are matters of opinion or if they are independently verifiable. (See also 35b.)

(3) Establishing a research routine

A few words of advice: Scheduling your time is especially important because researched papers are usually assigned several weeks before they are due, and the temptation to procrastinate may be strong. Make sure to allow enough time for the long process of choosing a subject (32b), preparing a working bibliography (37b), reading extensively, taking notes (37f(2)), developing a thesis (32d), outlining (32e), drafting (32f), and revising (33b). Begin early and keep your schedule flexible. As you write your paper, you may need to return to a part of the research process that you thought you had completed. For example, when drafting your essay, you may discover that you need additional information—you may need to conduct a personal interview or return to the library for further research.

Another tool that can be very helpful is a research log, which can help you stay on schedule and keep you from having to do tasks over. It is somewhat like a journal in that you can record in it everything you do: ideas for subjects, ways to refine topics, what you already know. Not only will a research log provide a central location for recording your research activities, but it can also keep your schedule right in front of you and help keep track of tasks you have not yet completed. Further, it can be vital if you have to do any backtracking.

Here is a sample form that can help you make a realistic schedule. You may need more (or less) time for each of these activities. Adjust your schedule to conform to the way you work best.

Activity	Days Needed	Date Completed
1. Explore the campus library	1	________ ☐
2. Find a topic and develop a working hypothesis	1	________ ☐
3. Establish a search strategy	1	________ ☐
4. Develop a working bibliography	6	________ ☐
5. Take notes	6	________ ☐
6. Develop the thesis and outline	2	________ ☐
7. Draft the paper	4	________ ☐
8. Seek peer review	2	________ ☐
9. Revise the paper	1	________ ☐
10. Prepare the works cited	1	________ ☐
11. Prepare the final draft	1	________ ☐
12. Proofread	1	________ ☐

37b A working bibliography lists sources.

A working, or preliminary, bibliography contains information (titles, authors, dates, and so on) about the materials you think you might use. Write down the most promising sources you can find. Often the sources you consult will have helpful bibliographies. Draw on them, but do not use them exclusively, or else the research will no longer be yours and you will miss other sources. Some researchers find it convenient to put each entry on a separate index card, which makes it easy to add or drop a card and to arrange the list alphabetically without recopying it. Others prefer to use a computer, which can sort and alphabetize items automatically. It is also a good idea to follow consistently from the very beginning the bibliographical form you are instructed to use. The MLA bibliographic style can be found in 38a and APA style in 38d. Using the specified style from the start will save you valuable time later, when you must compile a formal list of works cited that will appear at the end of your paper. Be sure to note the address for Internet sites in case you need to visit the site again to link to other sites. Note the call number of books you consult in case you need to recheck a book after you have returned it or want to see if there are similar books shelved near it.

Primary and secondary sources As you look for sources, be aware of which ones are primary and which are secondary. Primary sources for topics in literature and the humanities are generally documents and literary works. In the social sciences, primary sources can be field observations, case histories, and survey data. In the sciences, primary sources are generally empirical—measurements, experiments, and the like. Secondary sources are commentaries on primary sources. So a critique of McKellen's adaptation of Shakespeare's *Richard III* would be a secondary source, as would results of a survey of a representative population of twenty- to thirty-year-olds or a report of the results of an experiment. Sources that summarize and explain secondary sources, such as most textbooks, are sometimes called **tertiary sources.** Learn to evaluate the quality of secondary and tertiary sources. Many are excellent commentaries, although all involve some degree of interpretation. However, some secondary sources, particularly field resources and electronic documents, may not be reliable. Unlike print sources, these are often not peer-reviewed before the information is published. That does not mean you should avoid these sources completely; it does mean you must use them carefully. (See also 37e.) Generally speaking, the closer you get to primary sources, the more reliable your information.

37c Library research requires a strategy.

College and university libraries are organized to make research as efficient as possible. Usually a map or diagram—either printed for handing out or posted on the wall—shows where various kinds of materials are located. Reference books, encyclopedias, and indexes—materials that cannot usually be checked out of the library—are located in the **reference collection,** which may also include indexing information for electronic databases, either on-line or on CD-ROM. Other books are located in the **stacks** or at the **reserve desk** and can be checked out for a specified length of time. If your library has a closed-stack policy, you request the books you need by call number from the **circulation desk.** You can find the call number in the **main catalog.** If the stacks are open, however, it may be useful to browse among the books shelved near those you have located through the catalog. **Periodicals** (magazines, journals, and newspapers in print or microform) are usually stored in a special section of the library. If your library does not have a book or periodical that you need, bear in mind that your college may participate in an interlibrary loan program, which is an arrangement among local or regional college libraries for the exchange of books and periodicals. You may also be entitled to use the facilities of other college libraries in your area. If you have difficulty locating or using any research materials, do not hesitate to ask a **reference librarian** for help.

Remember also that unless an instructor has asked you to confine yourself to printed information, your search does not need to be limited to a library. You might use information drawn from radio, television, and the Internet; from conducting interviews with experts on your topic; or from observations you have acquired through personal experience. Much of the research people do in their daily lives involves more than one approach to the issue in question. If you plan to buy a new car, for example, you may read reviews published in various magazines available in your library, interview people familiar with the cars that interest you, and take a test drive or two. A similar strategy may be appropriate for research assignments in school or at work: read, interview, and observe.

(1) Books and periodicals

Books

The first place to look is usually the **main catalog**, which can take the form of cards or computer files. The main catalog lists all books owned by the college or university and shows whether a book is in the general library or elsewhere in a special collection. Some libraries still maintain a **card catalog,** which consists of cards arranged alphabetically in drawers. Cards for each book are filed alphabetically by author, by title, and by subject or subjects. Most libraries, however, have **computerized catalogs,** which save space and make research more efficient. (See 37e.)

A library catalog, then, whether computerized or maintained on cards, identifies books by author, title, or subject. Some computerized catalog programs also allow researchers to locate sources by supplying the computer with other information, such as a keyword that may appear in the title or even a book's call number.

Although there may be a slight visual difference between the format of the computerized entry and its equivalent on a catalog card (see the following illustrations and 37e), both provide essentially the same information: author, title, place of publication, publisher, date of publication, the length and size of the book, and any special features such as a bibliography. You will also be given the book's call number, which tells you exactly where in the library the book is located.

If your library provides you with access to both card and computer catalogs, check with a librarian to see which is more current. Libraries that have computerized their catalogs may have stopped including new acquisitions in their card catalogs, and libraries that have only recently computerized their catalogs may not yet have their entire collection on-line. (See also pages 460–63.)

An entry from a computerized catalog In addition to providing all the data found on the printed card, a computerized catalog entry usually reveals the location and status of the book—information that can save a researcher time when looking for a book that has been moved to a special collection or checked out by someone else. Libraries use a number of different systems for computerizing catalogs, so expect to encounter variations on this example.

```
     Online Catalogue—BRIEF DISPLAY (1 of 1 titles)

                                          Number of holdings :1
AUTHOR         :Coursen, Herbert R.
TITLE          :Shakespearean performance as
                interpretation / H.R. Coursen
PUBLISHER      :Newark :
                University of Delaware Press ;
                London :
                Cranbury, NJ :
                Associated University Presses,
                c1992
LANGUAGE       :ENGLISH

   LIBRARY     LOCATION    COLLECTION/          STATUS/
                           CALL NUMBER          DUE DATE
   --------    ---------   ----------------     -----------
1. MAIN        MAIN        PR3091.C69 1992      In Library
 Last Page
Options:                              ⟨ENTER⟩ = scroll options
 FD = Full display    P = Prior screen    E = Extend search
  L = Limit list      O = Output          M = MARC
```

This is an example of an author card for the same source. Cards filed by title and by subject will have the same information under different headings.

```
PR
3091 Coursen, Herbert R.
.C69 Shakespearean performance as interpretation / H.R.
     Coursen.—Newark:
1992 University of Deleware Press, 1992.
      Bibliographical references (p. 253-262).
      Includes index.
      ISBN 0-874-13432-3 (alk. Paper)
```

```
1. Shakespeare, William, d 1564-1616--Stage history.
2. Shakespeare--Film and video adaptations. 3. Shake-
speare--Criticism and interpretation--History.
I. Title
```

Library of Congress Subject Headings If you are uncertain about how to search for information on your topic and if your library uses Library of Congress numbers for cataloging books (almost all academic libraries do), you can first look for your subject in the **Library of Congress Subject Headings** (*LCSH*). If your subject is indexed by that catalog, you will find a specific catalog number for books on your subject, as well as cross-references to related subject areas that may help you sharpen your focus. If you find a number indexed, write it down; then find that number in your library's own **shelf list**, which lists all the books in the library by call number. The first part of a call number indicates the subject (for example, the PR in PR3091 stands for British literature). Therefore, when you look up the call number of a book, you should find adjacent to it the call numbers of other books the library owns on that subject.

Periodicals

Since periodicals (magazines, journals, newspapers) are published frequently, they often contain some of the most recent information on your subject. A variety of periodical indexes (usually located in the reference section of the library) do for articles what the main catalog does for books. Since each index includes many publications not listed in the others, you may need to consult a number of indexes to find the information you need. Most of the print indexes listed in this section are also available electronically. For information on using these, see pages 452–53.

Indexes for general-interest periodicals If you think that articles on your subject have appeared in popular or general-interest magazines or in newspapers, you might want to consult the *Readers' Guide to Periodical Literature,* published from 1900 to the present, and a newspaper index, the best known of which is the *New York Times Index,* published since 1913 and listing articles indexed back to 1851.

MOTION PICTURE REVIEWS

Single works

See also

Cross-references

Videodiscs—Motion pictures—Reviews—Single works

Videotapes—Motion pictures—Reviews—Single works

Subtopics arranged in alphabetical order

Reservoir dogs

Film Comment il v32 p83–8 Ja/F '96. L Bush

Restoration

People Weekly il v45 p17–18 Ja 15 '96. T. Tliatto

Rolling Stone il p67 Ja 25 '96. P. Travers

Richard III

Articles on topic

The American Spectator v29 p58 Mr '96. J. Bowman

The New Republic v214 p30 F 12 '96. S. Kauffmann

New York il v29 p48–9 Ja 15 '96. D. Denby

Newsweek il v127 p58 Ja 29 '96. J. Kroll

People Weekly v45 p17 Ja 15 '96. R. Novak

Time il v147 p67 Ja 15 '96. R. Corliss

The *Readers' Guide* excerpt above (from the search Katie Frushour conducted for her paper on two film versions of *Richard III,* reprinted in the sample MLA research paper) shows that *Newsweek* published a review of the film, that the author's name is J. Kroll, and that the review—with a picture—can be found in volume 127, page 58, of the January 29, 1996, issue. (Much of the same material is available on-line.)

If you need help reading an entry, you can find a sample entry as well as a key to abbreviations in the front pages of each issue of the *Readers' Guide*.

Like the *Readers' Guide,* the *New York Times Index* arranges its authors and subjects in alphabetical order. Entries include a brief summary of the contents and an abbreviation that reveals the article's length.

Richard III (Movie)

Ben Brantley article on evil characters portrayed by Ian McKellen and Kenneth Branagh in new films Richard III and Othello: photos (M), Ja 21,II,I:2

Correction of Jan 21 article on the films Richard III and Othello, Ja 28,II,4:6

Article summary

Medium length article

Section, page, & column numbers

January 21 and 28 issues (in year of volume consulted)

For older articles of general interest, you can consult *Poole's Index,* 1802–1907, or *Nineteenth Century Readers' Guide,* 1890–99.

Indexes for special-interest periodicals Virtually every specialized field has its own periodicals, which usually provide much more detailed information than can be found in magazines or newspapers aimed at the general public. When conducting research in college, you should be familiar with indexes that cover periodicals within various professions. Some of the most useful ones are listed below.

Applied Science and Technology Index. 1958–.

Art Index. 1929–.

Biological and Agricultural Index. 1946–.

Business Periodicals Index. 1958–.

Cumulative Index to Nursing and Allied Health Literature (CINAHL). 1982–.

Education Index. 1929–.

Humanities Index. 1974–.

Index to Legal Periodicals. 1908–.

Medline. 1985–.

Music Index. 1949–.

Public Affairs Information Service (Bulletin). 1915–.

Social Sciences Index. 1974–.

The print versions of these indexes (becoming increasingly rare as libraries replace them with CD-ROM versions and discard the paper volumes) are organized like the *Readers' Guide*. Consult the front of any volume for a key to the abbreviations used in individual entries. A similar format is also used by the *MLA Bibliography*, which is essential for doing research in literature. (See **38a**.) The *MLA Bibliography* includes books as well as periodicals, and each volume is divided into separate sections covering research on the literature of different languages and time periods. Like most indexes to special-interest periodicals, the *MLA Bibliography* can be consulted in printed volumes, through a CD-ROM disk covering several years, or through an online database search. When they publish electronic versions of their indexes, some publishers change the title: *Current Index to Journals in Education* (CIJE) and *Resources in Education* (RIE) are the print volumes for research in education, while ERIC is the electronic version.

Electronic databases of scholarly materials are much easier to search and update than print versions, so most libraries have switched to them. All the CD-ROM databases in your library will probably look very much alike and can probably be searched using much the same set of commands. A different library, however, may subscribe to the same databases through a different service, and the commands and the screen designs may differ from what you are used to. The more familiar you are with the versions your library subscribes to, the easier it will be to learn how to use those in other libraries.

Abstracting services In addition to providing the bibliographical information necessary for locating sources, an abstracting service provides short summaries of the articles and books it indexes. Your library may have CD-ROM disks for such abstracts as *Academic Abstracts, Biology Abstracts, Chemical Abstracts,* and *Psychological Abstracts,* as well as for *PsychLit* or *PsychINFO,* which are both available in electronic form only, and CARL, which contains the tables of contents for most scholarly journals. (See 37e for more complete information on electronic sources and resources.) When using one of these services, you can quickly scan the short summaries and decide which seem likely to be the most useful. You may also be able to print out a list of citations, a list of citations with abstracts, and even the full text of some of the articles you discover. Here is a citation and abstract from *Academic Abstracts,* a service that covers many widely available periodicals.

Computerized abstract

```
Subject: RICHARD III    (Motion picture);
   RICHARD III Foundation
  Title: Historical Richards.
 Author: Geier, Thom
Summary: Points at the criticism received by
   the film 'Richard III' for its historical
   inaccuracy. New Jersey based Richard III
```

```
   Foundation's complaints; Details of the
   movie, including Richard III portrayed like
   Hitler.
 Source: (US News & World Report, 1/22/96,
   Vol. 120 Issue 3, p14, 1/5p, 1c)
   ISSN: 0041-5537
Item No: 9601167647

          (We subscribe to this magazine.)

       ** FullTEXT Available - Press F7 **
```

---

(2) Reference works

When doing research, you may need to consult a variety of reference works. A general encyclopedia, such as *Encyclopaedia Britannica* (now available electronically) can provide useful information, expecially at an early stage in your research. And you will almost certainly need to consult a dictionary. (See 19a and 37e.) For a detailed list of reference books and a short description of each, consult *Guide to Reference Books* by Eugene P. Sheehy and *American Reference Books Annual (ARBA)*. For a list of reference books useful when writing about literature, see pages 585–86. A few of the most widely used reference books are listed here with abbreviated bibliographical information. Note that these are reference sources: refer to them for help, but do not rely on any of them as a principal source for a college paper.

Special dictionaries and encyclopedias

Adams, James T. *Dictionary of American History*. Rev. ed. 8 vols. 1983.

Encyclopedia of American Foreign Policy. Ed. Alexander DeConde. 3 vols. 1978.

Encyclopedia of Philosophy. Ed. Paul Edwards. 4 vols. 1973.

Encyclopedia of Psychology. Ed. Raymond J. Corsini. 4 vols. 1984.

Encyclopedia of Religion. Ed. Mircea Eliade. 16 vols. 1986.

Encyclopedia of World Art. 15 vols. 1959–68. Supp. 1983, 1987.

International Encyclopedia of Higher Education. Ed. Asa S. Knowles. 10 vols. 1977.

International Encyclopedia of the Social Sciences. Ed. D. E. Sills. 8 vols. 1977. Supplements.

McGraw-Hill Encyclopedia of Science and Technology. 15 vols. 6th ed. 1987. Yearbooks.

The New Grove Dictionary of Music and Musicians. Ed. Stanley Sadie. 20 vols. 1980. Reprinted with corrections in 1995.

Biographies

Biography and Genealogy Master Index. CD-ROM. 1996.

Biography Index. 15 vols. 1946–88.

Contemporary Authors. 16 vols. 1996.

Current Biography Cumulated Index, 1940–1985. 1986. Annual supplements.

Dictionary of American Biography. 17 vols. and index. 1927–81. Supplements.

Dictionary of National Biography (British). 22 vols. 1882–1953. Rpt. 1981. Supplements.

Dictionary of Scientific Biography. 8 vols. 1970–80.

Notable American Women: 1607–1950. 3 vols. 1972. Supplements.

Notable Black American Women. 1990.

Webster's New Biographical Dictionary. 1983.

Who's Who in America. 1899–. (See also Marquis's *Who's Who Publications: Index to All Books*, revised annually.)

Almanacs and yearbooks

Americana Annual. 1924–.

Britannica Book of the Year. 1938–.

Broadcasting Yearbook. 1982–.

Facts on File. 1940–.

Information Please Almanac. 1985–.

New International Yearbook. 1907–.

Official Associated Press Almanac. 1969–.

Statesman's Year-Book. 1863–.

Statistical Abstract of the United States. 1878–.

World Almanac and Book of Facts. 1868–.

37d Field research requires special skills.

Research in the field involves interviewing, observing, experimenting, and conducting surveys.

Depending on your topic, you may want to include one or more of these other types of research. The most common alternative to library research is an **interview**. The faculty members at your college, business and professional people, and even relatives and friends can be appropriate subjects for an interview if they have relevant firsthand experience with the subject you are researching.

Since well-informed interviewers usually ask the best questions, you should consider an interview only after you have done some reading on your subject. Schedule interviews well ahead, and if you plan to use a tape recorder, ask permission. Take a professional approach to the interview: Have pens or pencils and paper ready for taking notes and fresh batteries and blank tapes for your tape recorder. Dress appropriately and be punctual. Record the time and date of the interview on tape or, if you do not use a tape recorder, at the beginning of your notes.

Begin with questions that are broad enough to give people room to reveal their own special interests; then follow up with more specific questions. Be prepared to depart from your list of planned questions whenever your subject says something of particular interest that would be useful to pursue. After the interview, send a letter thanking the interviewee. A courtesy of this sort is especially appropriate when someone has made time for you in a busy schedule or has been genuinely helpful during the interview itself.

Closely related to the interview is the **survey**, in which you ask a number of people the same set of questions and then analyze the results. You can administer the survey orally in interview fashion, or you can distribute a written questionnaire by mail or in person. Once you have a clear idea of what you want to find out, you may find the following checklist helpful in constructing a good survey questionnaire.

Checklist for Creating Survey Questions ✓

- Does each question relate directly to the purpose of the survey?
- Are the questions easy to understand?
- Are the questions designed to elicit short, specific responses?
- Are the questions designed to collect concrete data that you can analyze easily?
- Are written questions designed to give respondents enough space for their answers?

In addition to interviews and surveys, you may also have occasion to draw directly on your own **experience** or **observations**. In the paper reprinted on pages 521–41, for example, Katie Frushour incorporated her own experience viewing both the Olivier and McKellen film versions of *Richard III* with the information from her library search—a strategy appropriate for comparing the two films. For a different topic, observation might involve arming yourself with a still or video camera and/or tape recorder, writing out a plan for observing, rehearsing the observation, and taking written notes (in addition to tape) during the actual observation. But check with your instructor to see whether field research is appropriate for your research project and what kind of field research would be most productive.

37e Electronic resources are fast and efficient.

Electronic research tools enable researchers to find more information faster than ever, but the quality of the results can be uneven. Electronic research techniques require knowing how to evaluate sources as well as how to find them.

(1) Developing a research strategy

Publicly available information is stored electronically in **on-line information storage and retrieval systems** (for example, *Dialog*), on CD-ROM disks, and on the Internet. To locate and retrieve information in each of these you need a basic set of skills, as well as a group of skills particular to the kind of storage medium.

Like library sources, electronic research demands that you follow a basic search strategy.

BASIC SEARCH STRATEGY TIPS

1. Frame the topic as a thesis statement.
2. Identify main ideas and concepts.
3. Determine databases to be searched.
4. Identify the keywords.
5. Check the controlled vocabulary thesaurus (if there is one).
6. Apply a basic search logic.
7. Check system documentation on file structure and format information.
8. Log on and perform the search.
9. Identify citations to keep.
10. Refine the search strategy if the first search returned too many, too few, or irrelevant citations.

Focusing on a topic and **identifying concept areas,** the beginning steps in this strategy, echo the beginning steps for locating information in libraries. **Selecting a database** to use according to type and subject area is similar to deciding whether to consult the *MLA Annual Bibliography* or the *Social Sciences Index*. Will you use a database stored on a CD-ROM (which has the advantages of being inexpensive and relatively easy to use) or do you need to do an on-line search (which can be expensive and tricky to execute efficiently)? **Identifying keywords** is also not much different from deciding on a list of subject headings to look up in a library.

When you use print sources, you check your main concepts against the *LCSH*. (See 37c(1).) When you use a database (a collection of machine-readable information that you can retrieve using a computer), you must **check your keywords against the database thesaurus**—a list of the controlled vocabulary or official descriptors used for retrieving information. If a keyword is not part of the controlled vocabulary, a database search will turn up no rec-

ords (units of stored information). That means no information can be found using the terms you have tried, not that the database contains no information on that subject. Use the controlled vocabulary for your search terms.

Basic search logic enables you to guard against retrieving too many or too few records. A search result that says, "Found: 2,493,508 records containing the descriptor 'film'" is as useless as one that reports, "Sorry, no records found." You can use certain words (called **logical** or **Boolean operators**) to broaden or narrow your search:

or broadens a search—**young adults or single adults** finds all records that contain information about either category;

and narrows a search—**young adults and single adults** returns only those records that contain both categories;

not excludes specific items—**young adults and single adults not homeless** will exclude any records that mention homeless young single adults;

near prevents inclusion of widely separated terms—**young adults near single adults** instructs the database to list only those references to both young adults and single adults that occur within a preset number of words (this option is often not available).

After you have logged on and performed your search, evaluate the records you have retrieved and discard any that are irrelevant. If you need to narrow or broaden your search, revise your selection of keywords and use them with logical operators.

(2) Your college library as a gateway

Many college and university libraries offer students access to major electronic information storage and retrieval systems such as *First Search* or *Dialog*, which allow you to search in a large number of databases. Although some universities offer free access to these systems, students will often need to purchase access cards. If your school does not grant access to one of these, check to see if you have free access to *Academic Abstracts* or *InfoTrac*. Other databases that may be available for you to use are *CARL-Uncover* (which indexes a large number of periodicals) and *Books In Print* as well as some full-text search and retrieval databases such as *EBSCO MAGS* for periodicals and *LEXIS-NEXIS* for legal documents and newspapers, respectively. These systems allow users to search by keyword, author, and title. Most permit users to restrict searches to a specific time period, language, and type of record.

Sample search: *MLA* (using *First Search* system)

```
***** Topic Area Selection ***************
TOPIC AREA NUMBER (or Action):1
TOPIC AREA: Arts & Humanities
NO._DATABASE__________________DESCRIPTION__________________
|1 WorldCat          Books and other materials in libraries
|                    worldwide.
|2 Article1st        Indexes nearly 12,500 journals.
|3 Contents1st       Tables of contents of nearly 12,500
|                    journals.
|4 FastDoc           Index of articles with text online or by
|                    e-mail.
|5 ArtAbstracts      Leading publications in the world of the
|                    arts.
|6 HumanitiesAbs     Abstracts of articles in the humanities.
|7 MLA               Literature, languages, linguistics,
|____________________folklore_________________________________
DATABASE NUMBER (or Action): 7
******** MLA BIBLIOGRAPHY **************+
COVERAGE: Literature, languages, linguistics, and folklore
from over 4,000 journals and series published worldwide,
1963 to the present. Updated ten times per year.
© 1996 The Modern Language Association of America
```

```
+************* List of Records ***************+
DATABASE: MLA                LIMITED TO: /English
SEARCH: su:shakespeare film criticism FOUND 6 Records
NO.__________TITLE________________________AUTHOR_______YEAR
|1 Screening Shakespeare                  Pilkington, Ace   1990
|2 Criticism and the Films of             Felheim, Marvin   1986
|  Shakespeare's P...
|3 Shakespeare on Film: Some German       Bies, Werner      1983
|  Appro
|4 The Spiral of Influence: 'One          Kliman, Bernice   1983
|  Defect' in H...
|5 Sight and Space: The Perception        Styan, J. L.
|  of Shakesp
|6 Criticism for the Filmed               Homan, Sidney R   1977
|__Shakespeare_____________________________________________________
HINTS: View a record................type record number.
    Decrease number of records....type L (to limit) or A (to
    'and').
    Do a new search................type S or SEARCH.
RECORD NUMBER (or Action): 5
************* Full Record Display ***************
Record 5 of 6______________________________________________________
| NUMBER: Accession: 78-1-4052. Record: 78104052.
| UPDATE CODE: 7801
| AUTHOR: Styan, J. L.
| TITLE: Sight and Space: The Perception of Shakespeare on
|      Stage and Screen
| SOURCE: Bevington, David; Halio, Jay L.; Muir, Kenneth;
|      Mack, Maynard.
|      Shakespeare, Pattern of Excelling Nature:
|      Shakespeare Criticism in Honor of America's
|      Bicentennial from The International Shakespeare
|      Association Congress, Washington, D.C., April 1976.
|      Newark: U of Delaware P, London: Associated UP. 304
|      pp.
| PAGES: 198-209
| LANGUAGE: English
| PUB TYPE: book article
| DESCRIPTORS: English literature; 1500-1599; Shakespeare,
|______William themes and figures; Film______________________
```

Many of the same databases are available on CD-ROM: *ERIC, PsychLIT, MLA,* and indexes published by Wilson such as *Readers' Guide*. If your library has a database you need on CD-ROM, you can use the basic search strategy to find out what is indexed there. But CD-ROM searching has one disadvantage in common with print searching: Once published, the information cannot be updated without issuing a continuation. If you need up-to-the-minute information, you might need to search through one of the on-line information storage and retrieval systems to supplement what you find on CD-ROM. The advantage of CD-ROM searching is that it is usually free, whereas there is often a charge for using the same databases on-line.

(3) Using the Internet

The Internet, an international network of computers linked through telephone and fiber-optic lines, is one of the most exciting tools available to you. Detailed instructions for gaining access to and using the Internet are beyond the scope of this handbook, but inexpensive, convenient help is readily available.

The academic computing center at your school may offer workshops that will teach you how to log on to the Internet, send an e-mail message, sign up with a newsgroup, or access the World Wide Web. If not, check out one of the many helpful books, a few of which are listed below.

Gaffin, Adam. *Big Dummy's Guide to the Internet*. Electronic Frontier Foundation. [on-line]

Krol, Ed. *The Whole Internet User's Guide & Catalog*, 2nd ed. Sebastopol, CA: O'Reilly, 1995.

Reddick, Randy, and Elliot King. *The Online Student: Making the Grade on the Internet*. Fort Worth: Harcourt, 1996.

Nobody owns the Internet and there is no charge to use it, but it isn't really free. Companies, universities, the government, and other institutions bear most of the cost. You probably have access to the Internet through your academic computing account, especially if your school charges a computer use fee. If you have a computer with a **modem** (see Glossary of Terms) and your school has a data number you can dial, you can also probably do your Internet searching from home. If your room is not wired to the school network or your school does not support dial-up access, you may want to consider a local Internet service provider that offers unlimited access for a flat monthly fee that is only a little more than the price of a couple of movie tickets.

Think of the Internet not as a superhighway, but as a system using several modes of transportation. For instance, if you were taking a trip to Capri, you might go from your home to the airport in your private car, fly to Rome, take a train to Naples where you can catch the boat to Capri, and then take a bus to your hotel. If you plan to do research on the Internet, you might narrow your topic on the World Wide Web, find out which databases archive the information you need, use **Gopher** and a **file transfer protocol** or **FTP** to retrieve documents, and test out your ideas using discussion lists and Usenet newsgroups.

Electronic mail or e-mail allows you to send messages in seconds to anyone with an e-mail address anywhere in the world, and, unlike voice mail or answering machines, it allows you and your correspondent to exchange messages at times convenient for each of you. Your friend who works the graveyard shift, for instance, could send you a message at 4:00 A.M. that you could retrieve on your lunch break. E-mail can let you ask a question of a well-known scholar (assuming you know the right e-mail address), and it also lets the scholar answer at his or her convenience.

Discussion lists allow you to read messages posted to all members of a group interested in a specific topic and to post messages yourself that those dozens or hundreds of like-minded people will read. For instance, your instructor may belong to a specialized discussion list for composition teachers operated by the Alliance for Computers and Writing and called ACW-L. Participants on this list discuss issues related to using computers to teach writing. Your instructor can send e-mail messages to the **listserv address** that will redistribute them to a thousand other writing teachers around the world. Similarly, your instructor can receive replies from anyone who subscribes to the list, but everyone will be able to read the same replies. Anyone—teacher, student, publisher, software developer, or neighborhood curmudgeon—who wants to discuss the topic seriously can join the list.

To find out if there are any lists that might discuss the problems of young adults living with their parents, Adrienne Harton (see 38e) could have sent an e-mail message to listserv@listserv.net, leaving the subject line blank and including this phrase: list global/multiple-generation household. A return message would list all groups listserv can identify with that keyword. If Adrienne had not gotten the results she wanted, she could have sent another message requesting "list global/young adult." (Using "Generation-X" as the keyword returns a lot of lists related to the TV show.)

The **World Wide Web** is a huge, mostly unindexed collection of information much of which—once located—is useful for researched papers and some of which is not. The easiest way to find information on the Web is to use one of the available robotic or semirobotic search systems (often called search engines), such as Yahoo, Alta Vista, InfoSeek, or Lycos. After you type keywords into a text entry box, these engines will return a list of electronic documents (Websites) that meet the searching criteria. Most search engines encourage the use of the logical operators *and*, *or*, and *not* to make the search as efficient as possible.

Different search systems may return slightly different results because they index slightly different sets of documents or design their index databases differently. One system may search only for titles of documents, another may look at document links, and a few search the full text of every document they index. Further, some search only the World Wide Web whereas others search Usenet newsgroups and file archives. For these reasons, one engine may be better for academic information, another for general information, and yet another for business information. Until you are familiar with these tools, you should probably try them all, and you should always read the instructions (help screens). The introductory screen from Yahoo, one of the best-known search engines, shows that they are relatively simple to use.

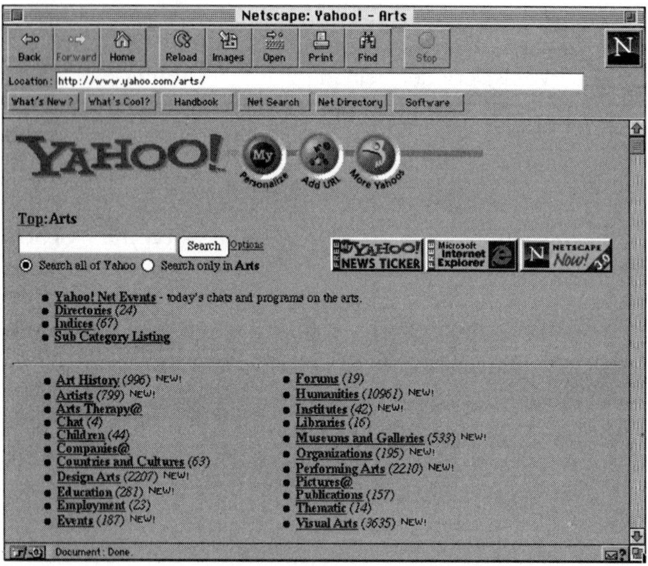

The result of the successful search will be a list of Uniform Resource Locators (URLs, pronounced as "Earls") you can use to access the page(s) you need.

As with any resource that is not moderated (compare a public free speech bulletin board in the student union), harebrained or tasteless information is readily available. However, a careful researcher will have a sense of what is appropriate and with a little checking and critical thinking can avoid what is unsuitable or unreliable.

Web pages can be accessed only with a browser. Unless you have a fast connection to the Internet, you may need to use a textual browser such as Lynx. A sample page looks much like the one Katie Frushour found on *Richard III*.

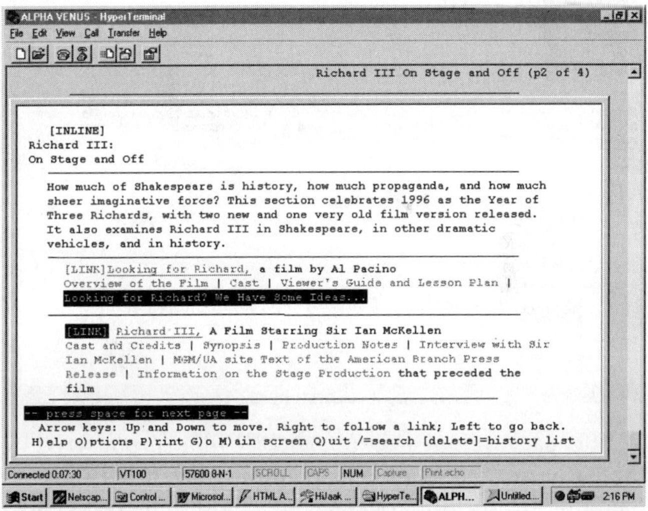

Web pages are best viewed with a graphically capable browser (the one below shows the same page retrieved with Netscape, a program free to students and faculty members) that retrieves the pictorial elements intended to make Web pages pleasant to look at and easy to read. This page begins with an image accompanied by a link to another page. **Links**, which work somewhat like a floating index, are underlined and usually change color when they have been used. To follow a link, click on the underlined text with a pointing device (mouse, touchpad, trackball) and wait until the new page appears on the screen. Scroll bars on the sides of the screen can be used to view more information.

This page on one new *Richard III* film is sponsored by the Richard III Society, an organization devoted to rehabilitating the memory of England's most maligned king—a fact that Katie had to consider when evaluating the information she found there.

FTP, Gopher, and Telnet FTP is a way of getting files from a remote computer to yours (or vice versa). It is especially valuable for getting free software, many kinds of government documents and other text files, and graphic images. You use FTP in one of two ways: You log on using "anonymous" as the user name and your e-mail address as the password, or less frequently, you log on to the remote computer with a user name and password assigned to you. The files you want are generally kept in a large directory (similar to a folder), which is usually called **pub** and which may have many subdirectories. To use FTP, you will need to learn how to navigate directories, and you will also need to have some basic understanding of what to do with a text file or a binary file once you have retrieved it (often, you cannot just start using it). FTP is powerful, but it is not friendly. For help in finding where files on a particular subject might be stored on a remote computer, you can use a keyword searching system called **Archie**. (See the academic computing service at your school for how to use it.) You fetch a text file using the command **get** plus the name of the file: get RichardIII_cast. You fetch a binary file using the command **bget** plus the filename: bget McKellen_0231.

Gopher is a system for finding and accessing files on remote computers. Gopher is a file-centered system, whereas the Web is a document-centered one, and unlike the Web, there has been no effort to standardize file types that Gopher can find. The files exist on their home computers in whatever form that computer requires. Gopher users, however, can use the files regardless of their own or the remote computer's operating system (e.g., Mac or DOS/Windows for a personal computer; UNIX, VMS, etc., for an institutional one). Gopher has two searching programs (**Veronica** and **Jughead**) for finding files in Gopherspace. Once you find the file you want, you generally have the option of printing it at your own location, retrieving it to the file space allotted to you through your college account, or cutting and pasting it into a document in your word processing program.

Telnet is a tool that allows you to use other tools at remote locations. If, for instance, your school lacks access to Gopher, you could Telnet to a school that has it. Similarly, if you are away from your school but can log on through some other school or service provider, you can Telnet to use your school's Internet facilities and your own account.

Using the Internet is an exciting, seductive way to find and use information. People are used to the idea that they have to document information they take from books and periodicals; be sure also to give proper credit for information you take from the Internet. The Internet is a new medium, and it presents new temptations and new dangers.

CAUTION Caution #1 **Guard against computer viruses.** They lurk in every part of the Internet and they can be extremely destructive to your own and your school's data. Fortunately, good, free virus checkers are available.

Caution #2 **Be conscious of security.** Do not give out your telephone number or address over the Internet. Do not tell anyone your password.

Caution #3 **Pay for what you use** unless the material is clearly freeware or public domain.

Caution #4 **Give proper credit.** *Freeware* and *public domain* mean you do not have to pay, not that you can use images or text as if they were your own.

Caution #5 The Internet offers extensive information, but **not all information.** Plenty of good sources still exist in print.

Caution #6 **Check reliability.** Evaluate the source critically. Are there errors? Is the site monitored? (Many are not.) Is the author identified and are his or her credentials given?

37f Evaluating sources requires thought; taking notes demands accuracy.

(1) Testing reliability, bias, and integrity

When you are doing research, one important consideration always is the reliability of your sources. (See 37b.) Ask the following questions about the sources you discover:

Checklist for Evaluating Sources ✓

- What are the author's credentials?
- Do others speak of the writer as an authority?
- Does the work contain evidence indicating that the author is well informed?
- Does the work contain evidence that the author is prejudiced in any way?
- Is the work recent enough to provide up-to-date information?
- Is the work published by a reputable company?
- Does the work provide documentation to support important points?
- Does the work include a bibliography that can help you to identify other sources?

Book Review Digest, which contains convenient summaries of critical opinion on a book, could help you decide which books are most dependable. *Literary Marketplace* will provide basic information about publishers. You can usually assume that university presses demand a high standard of scholarship. As for periodicals, an article published in an academic journal (as opposed to a popular magazine) has usually been reviewed by experts before publication.

Be alert for bias that may be built into a source, even if it is not obvious when you are reading. For example, an article on malpractice suits in the *Journal of the American Medical Association* is likely to be sympathetic to physicians.

Some periodicals are straightforward about identifying their affiliations. For instance, *Mother Jones* reveals its liberal credentials on its masthead, which identifies its namesake as "Mary Harris 'Mother' Jones (1830–1930), orator, union organizer, and hellraiser," and through its rhetoric:

> When the bombs explode at abortion clinics, when the tax protesters turn their guns on federal agents, the cynical politicos who mixed the cocktail of national convulsion won't be around to take the blame. In their plush backstage parlors, they will shake their heads in perfunctory pity before getting back to the business of slapping backs, trading business cards, and stirring the next round of drinks. —WILLIAM SALETAN

Subscription forms for *Conservative Chronicle, The Capitalist's Companion,* and the Conservative Book Club published in *The American Spectator* reveal its right-wing bias, but its rhetoric also makes that bias clear:

> Just when you think you've got the rules of politics figured out—that liberal Democrats won't give up the theory, rhetoric and practice of class warfare, for example, until you pry their cold, dead fingers from the wallets of the rich—along comes a one-two-three punch to send you reeling.
>
> —TOD LINDBERG

As you read your sources, learn how to find and evaluate useful passages with a minimum of time and effort. Seldom will a whole book, or even a whole article, be of use for any given researched paper. You will usually find that you must turn to many books and articles, rejecting some altogether and using others only in part. You cannot always take the time to read each book completely. Use the table of contents and the index of a book, and learn to skim the pages until you find the passages you need. When you find them, read critically. (See chapter 35.) Ask yourself if you agree with what you are reading and if the material raises any unanswered questions.

Evaluating electronic sources demands some variations on the questions in the Checklist for Evaluating Sources that follows. Since electronic sites can easily be kept up to date, look for evidence of frequent maintenance. Consider whether the electronic source has used the best available resources. For instance, if you want to look at a text of Shakespeare's play *Richard III* on-line to see material McKellen deleted from his screenplay, it would pay to determine whether the electronic version is based on the best edition. Is that edition in the public domain or does the author of the site have permission to post an electronic version? Be sure any electronic source you use is scrupulous about the copyright to the information it offers. These and other considerations are listed in the Checklist for Evaluating Electronic Sources.

Checklist for Evaluating Electronic Sources ✓

- Is there evidence of frequent maintenance?
- Have the best available resources been used?
- Is there evidence that copyright has been honored?
- Is the author acknowledged?
- Do the author and any collaborators have a reputation for being fair-minded, knowledgeable, and well informed?
- Does the presentation of the information inspire confidence in its reliability?
- Is the source located at an institution respected in the academic community?
- Does the work include citations to other sources or, in the case of hypertext, links to other reliable documents?

Exercise 2

Do preliminary reading on your research subject. Identify one source that seems reliable and another that seems biased. Write a two-paragraph evaluation in which you assess the credibility of each.

Exercise 3

Evaluate the following sources for reliability and/or bias about gun control and about abortion rights:

1. *Time*
2. *Ms.*
3. *Commonweal*
4. *National Enquirer*
5. *National Review*
6. *Consumer Reports*
7. *Newsweek*
8. *Field & Stream*
9. *Washington Post*
10. *Christian Science Monitor*

(2) Taking notes

There are probably as many ways to take notes as there are note takers; some note takers are more comfortable taking notes on 8½-by-11 paper, others on index cards, and still others using the computer. Each system has advantages and disadvantages, and you should match your choice to your project and your own work style. Whatever you use to create your notes, keep the following points in mind:

Checklist for Taking Notes ✓

- Does every note clearly identify its source?
- Is an author/title code for each source noted in the working bibliography and on every page of your notes?
- When a source has sparked your own thoughts, have you identified both the source and the fact that the note is your own idea? Mistakenly attributing your ideas to

continued

continued from previous page

✓

someone else is a kind of documentation error that gets far too little attention.

- Have you put the full bibliographic citation on the first page of every photocopy and a short form on the following pages?
- Is the bibliographic information for the source of every note accurate? Double-check to be sure. Scrupulous care now can prevent a multitude of problems later on—such as being forced to abandon important information because you lost track of exactly where it came from.
- Have you taken down verbatim—that is, copied every word, every capital letter, and every punctuation mark exactly as it was in the original—any useful passage that you think you may later quote, being especially careful to put quotation marks around any words you use directly from a source? Failure to do so as you take notes may lead to unintended plagiarism when you draft your paper.
- On photocopies, have you clearly indicated passages you intend to quote directly, passages you intend to paraphrase, and those you plan to summarize?
- Have you used different type-styles or different colors in computer files to make source identification of quoted text easy?

Using a notebook

A ring binder into which you can insert pages of notes as well as photocopies is an excellent organizational tool, particularly if you arrange it to keep your working bibliography separate from notes and photocopies and if you have a system for sorting notes into the main subject categories your work covers. Identify the source on every page of notes, and use a fresh page for each new source.

Using notecards

One of the best ways to take notes is on cards of uniform size. (Many researchers use larger cards for notes than for bibliographic references because notes often require more room. Different sizes of cards also help a writer keep the cards' functions separate.)

Show the author's name (and a short title for the work if the bibliography contains more than one work by that author) on each card, and include the exact page number(s) from which the information is drawn. If you put no more than a single note, however brief, on each card and a heading of two or three keywords at the top, you can easily arrange your cards as you prepare to write your paper.

Using photocopies

Another way to take notes is to use photocopies of short excerpts from materials you think you might quote directly. On a photocopy you can mark quotable material and jot down your own ideas as you study the source. Make sure you document the source on the photocopy.

Photocopied source with notes

paraphrase?

Olivier's use of the direct address to the camera, which defies the naturally assumed aesthetic laws of the medium, is another of those brilliant strokes whereby he brings a distinctly theatrical action to film and then gives it an impact which only cinema can. The success of its effect depends upon the fact that it amplifies elements which are implicit in the play in the character of Richard. The boldness with which he affronts the aesthetic laws of the medium is consonant with

important point

tried to mak film reflect R's ch

the assuredness with which Richard challenges the accepted procedures of royal succession and affronts the apparent spiritual order of the real.

Using computer files

If you have good keyboarding skills and are familiar with a word processing program, you may find it more efficient to use your computer for taking notes. One problem with this method, however, is that it is tempting to take down too much information verbatim. Another is that you may go too fast and make mistakes. As a result, you may not digest the information in your source well enough to use it skillfully, and you certainly run the risk of inadvertently failing to cite the source.

TIPS ON USING A COMPUTER TO TAKE NOTES

1. Create a separate master folder (or directory) for your paper.
2. Create folders within the master folder for your bibliography, notes, and portions of drafts.
3. Keep all the notes for each source in a separate file.
4. Use distinctive fonts and/or differentiators for notes on different source materials.

Using a computer to take notes makes it easy to copy and paste information into subject files and ultimately from subject files into the finished paper. But this method also makes it easy to lose track of where the note came from and increases the potential for inadvertent plagiarism.

CAUTION Systematically identify the source of each note you cut and paste. As you work the information smoothly into your text, document your sources accurately and responsibly.

Exercise 4

Select a subject that you would like to become more knowledgeable about. Consult the main catalog in your library and at least one periodical index. Propose two different ways of narrowing the subject. Write a paragraph in which you (a) report these two possibilities, (b) explain which of the two you have selected for further research, and (c) determine the number and quality of the sources that seem available. Then prepare at least four bibliography entries using cards or other means as your instructor requires.

37g Plagiarism is a serious offense.

Taking someone else's words or ideas and presenting them as your own leaves you open to criminal charges. In the film, video, music, and software business this act of theft is called **piracy**. In publishing and education it is called **plagiarism** and/or **cheating**. Whatever it is called and for whatever reason it occurs, it is wrong.

CAUTION Plagiarism is a serious offense. Carelessness is no excuse. Although the act may escape criminal prosecution, employers generally fire an employee who uses material illegally, and teachers often fail careless students.

The *MLA Handbook for Writers of Research Papers*, 4th edition (New York: MLA, 1995) advises:

> At all times during research and writing, guard against the possibility of inadvertent plagiarism by keeping careful notes that distinguish between your musings and thoughts and the

> material you gather from others. A writer who fails to give appropriate acknowledgment when repeating another's wording or particularly apt term, paraphrasing another's argument, or presenting another's line of thinking is guilty of plagiarism. You may certainly use other persons' words and thoughts in your research paper, but the borrowed material must not appear to be your creation. (26)

One purpose of this chapter is to help you to use the ideas and thoughts of others responsibly—to avoid plagiarism.

ESL Some cultures view borrowing information much differently than Americans do. For instance, in some cultures, anyone who has purchased a book and decides to quote from it can do so without citing the source or requesting (or paying for) permission. The rationale says that the person bought the words when he or she bought the book. In America, you can get in serious trouble with that kind of thinking.

You must give credit for all information you borrow except for two kinds: common knowledge and your own ideas. Common knowledge includes such information as "December has thirty-one days," and well-known proverbs ("a penny saved is a penny earned") or historical information such as the date of the Declaration of Independence.

After you have read a good deal about a given subject, you will be able to distinguish between common knowledge in that field and the distinctive ideas or interpretations of specific writers. When you use the ideas or information that these writers provide, be sure to cite your source.

As for your own ideas, if you have been scrupulous in noting your own thoughts as you took notes, you should have no difficulty distinguishing between what you knew to begin with and what you learned in your research and so must give credit for. The information in your research log that shows what you were aware of knowing before you began research can help. (See 37a(3).)

Source (from "Returning Young Adults," in *Psychology and Marketing,* 11, 1994, by J. Burnett and D. Smart, page 254)

> Both generations want their rights. The RYAs want the autonomy they have grown accustomed to and expect their parents to treat them like adults. The parents, meanwhile, have come to recognize their own rights. They may resent that the time, money, and emotional energy they planned to invest in themselves after the child's departure are instead allocated to the RYA.

Undocumented copying

They may resent that the time, money, and emotional energy they planned to invest in themselves after the child's departure are instead allocated to the RYA.

Appropriate citation

Marketing professors John Burnett and Denise Smart note that parents "may resent that the time, money, and emotional energy they planned to invest in themselves after the child's departure are instead allocated to the RYA" (254).

Quotation marks show where the copied words begin and end, and the number in parentheses at the end tells the reader the exact page on which it appears. In this case, the sentence that includes the quotation identifies the authors and establishes the context for the quotation. An alternative, more common technique for sources of lesser importance is to provide the authors' names within the parenthetical reference: (Burnett and Smart 254). If, after referring to the following checklist, you cannot decide whether you need to cite a source, the safest policy is to cite it.

Checklist for Kinds of Information to Cite ✓

- Writings, both published and unpublished
  - by direct quotation
  - by indirect quotation
  - by reference to ideas
- Opinions and judgments not your own
- Arguable points and claims
- Facts (unless widely known)
- Images and graphics such as

works of art	drawings	tables and charts
film/video	maps	advertisements
photographs	music	statistics and graphs

- Personal communication
  - private
  - public
- Electronic media
  - broadcasts
  - recordings
  - computer-generated materials

37h Integrating sources fosters mastery of information.

A research project that is a patchwork of snippets from others (even when meticulously cited) indicates that you are, at the very least, an inexperienced writer. The foundation of researched writing is always the writer's own ideas, which flow from point to point, supported and guided by research. Understanding how to evaluate sources, take notes accurately, and integrate ideas is essential.

(1) Mastering information

Digesting information has long been acknowledged as an excellent way to master what you read. However, digests are most useful when they focus on larger issues rather than details. A pattern for a research digest may help you stay on track.

Typically, depending on whether its source is an article or a book, such a digest contains from three to a dozen sentences. Each of these sentences should use a rhetorically strong verb (such as those in the checklist on page 483). The first sentence gives the author's name, the title, and the main idea of the work. The second sentence or set of sentences identifies the main points of the thesis and includes information about the methodology and kind(s) of support or argument the author used to develop these points. The third sentence or set of sentences identifies the rhetorical context—audience, occasion, facts of publication, and so on. Finally, the last sentence states the author's purpose.

(2) Integrating sources

When good research writers use borrowed material, they introduce it to readers by establishing the context from which the material came; for example, in a researched paper about the value of vitamin C, readers might find it useful to know that the author of a quotation praising the vitamin is a Nobel laureate in chemistry. Similarly, you can introduce a paraphrase by making clear why the information is important. An excellent way to introduce research is to use a phrase that indicates the author's attitude or the importance of the information. The following list of verbs that introduce quoted, paraphrased, or summarized information can be helpful in deciding how to integrate that information with your own ideas.

SIXTY-FOUR LEAD-IN VERBS

acknowledge	complain	explain	reason
add	concede	express	refute
admit	conclude	find	reject
advise	concur	grant	remark
agree	confirm	illustrate	reply
allow	consider	imply	report
analyze	contend	insist	respond
answer	criticize	interpret	reveal
argue	declare	list	see
ask	deny	maintain	show
assert	describe	note	speculate
believe	disagree	object	state
charge	discuss	observe	suggest
claim	dispute	offer	suppose
comment	emphasize	oppose	think
compare	endorse	point out	write

Writers of researched papers borrow information in three ways: quoting the exact words of a source, paraphrasing them, or summarizing them. With any of these methods, your writing will benefit if you are careful to integrate the material—properly cited, of course—into your own sentences and paragraphs. Whatever option you choose, make sure that you use sources responsibly.

CAUTION Words or ideas borrowed from other writers must not be distorted in any way, and credit must be given when borrowing occurs.

The following examples of quotation, paraphrase, and summary show MLA documentation style. For additional information on documentation, see 38a, 38c, and 38d.

(3) Using direct quotations

A quotation should contribute an idea to your paper. Select quotations only if (a) you want to retain the beauty or clarity of someone else's words or (b) you plan to discuss the implications of the words in question. Keep quotations as short as possible and make them an integral part of your text. (For examples of ways this can be done, see 38b, sample MLA research paper; 38e, sample APA research paper; and 39a, writing about literature.)

Quote **accurately**. Enclose every quoted passage in quotation marks. Any quotation of another person's words except for well-known or proverbial passages should be placed in quotation marks or, if longer than four lines, set off as an indented block. (See 16a(4).)

Cite the exact source for your quotation. If you think your audience might be unfamiliar with a source, establish its authority by identifying its author the first time you refer to it. (Note that this citation is in APA style.)

```
Family science researcher Judith S. Peck
(1991) defines the "launching" stage as "one
of the most complex stages of the family's
life cycles" (p. 150).
```

Checklist for Direct Quotations ✓

- Have I copied all the words accurately?
- Have I copied all the punctuation accurately? (See 16e.)

continued

continued from previous page

✓

- Do I need to observe a special form or special spacing? (See 16a and b.)
- Have I used ellipsis points correctly to indicate anything that is left out? (See 17i.)
- Have I avoided using ellipsis points *before* quotations that are clearly only parts of sentences?
- Have I used square brackets around everything I added to the direct quotation? (See 17g.)
- Have I used too many quotations? (Using too many quotations in a paper suggests an inability to think independently or to synthesize material.)

(4) Paraphrasing

A **paraphrase** is a restatement of a source in about the same number of words. Paraphrasing enables you to demonstrate that you have understood what you have read; it also enables you to help your audience understand. Paraphrase when you (a) use someone else's content but not his or her specific words or (b) simplify difficult material.

Your restatement of someone else's words should honor two important principles: Your version should be almost entirely in your own words, and your words should accurately convey the content of the original passage.

Using your own words

Unless you enclose an author's words in quotation marks, do not mix them with your own even if the sentence structure is different. Equally important, do not make the mistake of thinking that you can substitute synonyms for an author's words while you preserve his or her sentence structure. Both of these are plagiarism, even if you cite the source.

As you compare the source below with a paraphrase that follows, note the differences in sentence structure as well as word choice.

Source (from "Returning Young Adults," *Psychology and Marketing, 11,* 1994, by J. Burnett and D. Smart, pages 253–269)

> In general, contrary to assumptions about RYAs amassing large amounts of disposable income, the findings suggest that economic deprivation is the primary factor distinguishing the RYA from a single cohort. RYAs have an appreciably higher unemployment rate and lower income than a comparable singles group. Thus, the notion characterizing the modern RYA as a somewhat spoiled individual who wants to maintain his or her earlier lifestyle is not supported in this study.

Inadequate paraphrasing

Although many think that RYAs have large amounts of money to spend, research has shown that RYAs differ from single young adults mainly because more RYAs are unemployed or have lower incomes. Research shows that the general impression that RYAs are lazy parasites is not correct. (p. 267)

Although this passage ends with a parenthetical reference to the original sources, the reference does not reveal the size of the debt. The author could be giving credit to Burnett and Smart for the whole passage or only the last sentence—it is hard to tell. And when you compare this "paraphrase" with the original source, you will find that the author has followed the same structure. Although the wording has changed, the paraphrase in this case is so close to the original that it could be considered plagiarism.

Adequate paraphrasing

```
Burnett and Smart report research showing
that RYAs, contrary to opinion, have a more
difficult time meeting their bills than other
single young adults. Therefore, attitudes that
view them as lazy parasites are incorrect. (p.
267)
```

In this example, the page reference establishes where the paraphrase ends; the introductory "Burnett and Smart report" establishes where it begins. When you paraphrase, make sure that your audience will be able to tell whether you are paraphrasing a single sentence or more. As a general rule even in the hard sciences, which often tolerate fairly close paraphrasing in the interests of scientific accuracy, begin paraphrases with a few words indicating that you are about to restate another writer's words.

CAUTION If you simply change a few words in a passage, you have not adequately restated it. You may be charged with plagiarism if the wording of your version follows the original too closely, even if you provide a page reference to the source you used. A page reference after an inadequate paraphrase would acknowledge the source of your idea but not the extent of your debt to another writer's language.

Maintaining accuracy

Any paraphrase must accurately maintain the sense of the original. Compare the original statement below with the paraphrases.

Original Owning a boat is like standing in the shower tearing up $1,000 bills.

Inaccurate Boat owners would feel comfortable "tearing up $1,000 bills." [Changes the focus of the original.]

Accurate Owning a boat is an expensive way to get wet. [Changes the language of the original but remains faithful to the sense, even though the humor is lost.]

Of course, deliberately changing the gist of what a source says is unethical.

Unethical Boat owners are financially irresponsible masochists who enjoy being uncomfortable. [Shifts focus from the experience of boat owning to an indictment of boat owners' personalities.]

(5) Summarizing

When you summarize, you condense the main point(s) of your source as you restate them in your own words. A summary is shorter than the original source and lacks the kind of detail that fleshes out the original; it is telegraphic. Summarizing, an essential skill for writing researched papers, enables writers to report the work of others without getting bogged down in unnecessary detail. Paraphrase when you want to restate a passage so that it is easier to understand, and summarize whenever you can save space by condensing a passage (or, in some cases, an entire work).

Source (from "Boomerang Age," *American Demographics 12,* 1990, pages 25–30)

> Young adults are also taking longer to finish school. Four years after high school graduation, for example, only 7 percent of the members of the class of 1982 had a bachelor's

degree, versus 15 percent of 1972 high school graduates. Only one-fifth of the 1982 graduates had received any postsecondary degree within four years of graduation, compared with one-quarter of 1980 graduates and one-half of 1972 graduates. The gap is not as great seven years after graduation, reports the Department of Education, but is still substantial. (p. 27)

Summary

According to *American Demographics,* the number of students graduating in the traditional four years dropped significantly between 1972 and 1982. (p. 27)

CAUTION When you are summarizing, you may find it useful to retain a key phrase from your source; but if you do, put quotation marks around the words in question.

Exercise 5

Find a paragraph in two important sources that you may want to cite. After you read both paragraphs carefully, write a one-sentence summary of each. Then paraphrase the same paragraphs. Avoid using the same sentence patterns as the source. Choose your words carefully to convey the source's ideas exactly.

Exercise 6

Summarize Janet Kowolski's argument paper, page 433, and answer the following questions:

1. What is the most important sentence?
2. What are the key points of Janet's argument?
3. What was her purpose?

Chapter 38

Research: Using and Citing Sources

To write well from sources is a complex process that requires writers to perform a number of diverse tasks. These include activating the creative imagination (chapter 32), integrating it with the ability to think critically about one's own ideas and those of others (chapter 35), developing a sophisticated mastery of complex information (chapters 31, 35, and 37), and demonstrating skill at managing time and materials (chapters 8 and 37). But all that effort can be lost if a writer does not document sources accurately, a skill that demands meticulous attention to details (chapters 16, 32, and 37). Different disciplines usually employ different documentation styles, so there is no single way to document or to prepare a bibliography that can be used in every department of a college or university. Use the style your instructor specifies. The manuals listed below discuss documentation forms in detail. If you are asked to use one of these manuals, look for it in your library's reference collection, study it carefully, and make sure your notes and bibliography correspond exactly to the examples it provides.

Style books and manuals

American Chemical Society. *The ACS Style Guide: A Manual for Authors and Editors*. Washington: Amer. Chem. Soc., 1997.

American Institute of Physics. *AIP Style Manual*. 4th ed. New York: Amer. Inst. of Physics, 1990.

American Mathematical Society. *A Manual for Authors of Mathematical Papers.* Rev. ed. Providence: Amer. Mathematical Soc., 1990.

American Medical Association. *American Medical Association Manual of Style.* 8th ed. Baltimore: Williams, 1989.

American Psychological Association. *Publication Manual of the American Psychological Association.* 4th ed. Washington: Amer. Psychological Assn., 1994.

Associated Press. *The Associated Press Stylebook and Libel Manual.* Reading: Addison, 1996.

The Chicago Manual of Style. 14th ed. Chicago: U of Chicago P, 1993.

Council of Biology Editors. *Scientific Style and Format: The CBE Manual for Authors, Editors, and Publishers.* 6th ed. New York: Cambridge UP, 1994.

Gibaldi, Joseph. *MLA Handbook for Writers of Research Papers.* 4th ed. New York: Modern Language Assn., 1995.

Harvard Law Review. *A Uniform System of Citation.* 16th ed. Cambridge: Harvard Law Review, 1996.

Linguistic Society of America. *LSA Bulletin,* Dec. issue, annually.

Turabian, Kate L. *A Manual for Writers of Term Papers, Theses, and Dissertations.* 6th ed. Chicago: U of Chicago P, 1996.

United States Geological Survey. *Suggestions to Authors of the Reports of the United States Geological Survey.* 7th ed. Washington: GPO, 1991.

United States Government Printing Office. *Style Manual.* Washington: GPO, 1984.

If your instructor does not require a specific documentation style, follow the style set forth by the discipline appropriate for your paper. When you do not know what type of documentation is appropriate, go to the periodical room of your library and model your documentation on the style you find used in one of the journals in your field.

To provide you with further help, the rest of this chapter discusses the two documentation styles most widely used in college writing: MLA style, most frequently used for papers in English (38a), and APA style, most often used for papers in psychology and other courses in the social sciences (38d). Some disciplines prefer to use the footnote or endnote system of documentation, so samples of this style are provided in 38c.

38a MLA style documentation is appropriate for research papers in literary studies and foreign language courses.

As you draft a researched paper, remember that it is *your* paper. Using the headings on your cards (see page 476) and arranging your notes to follow your working plan or outline can make writing your paper easier than simply plunging in might be. Make sure to use your own words and your own style. Integrate your source material—paraphrases, summaries, quotations—with your own statements rather than making the paper a patchwork of other people's comments.

(1) Using parenthetical citations

Give proper credit by citing your sources. Traditionally, such citations took the form of notes numbered consecutively throughout the paper and placed either at the bottom of the appropriate page (footnotes) or all together at the end of the paper (endnotes). Although some disciplines still use a note system (see 38c), the MLA recommends placing citations in parentheses directly in the text. These parenthetical citations refer the reader to a list of works cited at the end of the paper. The advantage of this system is that it is easy for both writers and readers to use. The MLA suggests reserving numbered notes for supplementary or explanatory comments. The numbers are inserted in the appropriate places in the text, and the notes are gathered at the end of the paper. See page 537.

The basic elements of the parenthetical citation are the author's last name and the page number of the material used in the source. However, it is not necessary to repeat any information that is already clearly provided. In other words, omit the author's name from the parenthetical citation if you have identified it in the text of the paper, shortly before the material being cited. As you study the following examples, observe that common sense determines the information that must be included in a parenthetical citation and that this system is easy to use. (The first example is taken from the researched paper in 38b so you can see how a citation refers readers to a source listed alphabetically in the list of works cited at the end of the paper.) See also the details of punctuation and mechanics below.

A work by one author

```
Olivier creates Richard III's "central device
of coherence" by using a cyclical theme of the
crown (Brown 133).
```

In this citation, the author's name is included within the parentheses because it is not mentioned in the text. Since there is only one work by Brown in the list of works cited (on page 539), there is no need to place a title in the parentheses. However, a page number is included because the reference is to a specific passage. Note how the citation changes if the text includes more information about the source:

> Constance Brown argues that in Richard III, Laurence Olivier uses a cyclical theme of the crown to create "the central device of coherence" (133).

A work by two or three authors

> High software prices mean that "education must do without this resource, prices must come down, or new strategies for development must be devised" (Holdstein and Selfe 27).

Provide the last name of each author, punctuating as you would for items in a series. Commas are not necessary in a citation involving only two authors, for example: (Holdstein and Selfe 27).

A work by more than three authors

For a work with more than three authors, follow the bibliographic entry, giving either the first author's last name followed by *et al.* or all the last names. (Do not italicize or underline the Latin phrase.)

> In one important study, women graduates complained more frequently about "excessive control than about lack of structure" (Belenky et al. 205).

OR

> In one important study, women graduates complained more frequently about "excessive

```
control than about lack of structure"
(Belenky, Clinchy, Goldberger, and Tarule
205).
```

A multivolume work

When you cite material from a multivolume work, include the volume number (followed by a colon and a space) before the page number.

```
As Katherine Raine has argued, "true poetry
begins where human personality ends" (2: 247).
```

If your list of works cited includes only one volume of a multivolume work, then you do not need to include the volume number in the parenthetical citation.

More than one work by the same author

When your list of works cited includes more than one work by the same author, your parenthetical citations should include a shortened title that reveals which of the author's works is being cited in a particular instance. Use a comma to separate the author's name from the shortened title when both are in parentheses.

```
According to Gilbert and Gubar, Elizabeth
Barrett Browning, Emily Dickinson, and
Virginia Woolf considered poetry by women to
be forbidden and problematic (Shakespeare's
Sisters 107). That attitude was based on the
conception that male sexuality is the "essence
of literary power" (Gilbert and Gubar,
Madwoman 4).
```

This passage cites two different books by the same authors, Sandra M. Gilbert and Susan Gubar: *Shakespeare's*

Sisters: Feminist Essays on Women Poets and *The Madwoman in the Attic: The Woman and the Nineteenth-Century Literary Imagination.* The authors' names are not necessary in the first citation since they are mentioned in the text; they are included in the second citation because their names are not mentioned in connection with *Madwoman.*

You can often avoid cumbersome references by including information in the text that might otherwise have to appear parenthetically:

> **In The Madwoman in the Attic and Shakespeare's Sisters, Sandra M. Gilbert and Susan Gubar argue that the infrequent appearance of women as literary figures is a result of the repression imposed by male sexuality.**

Works by different authors with the same last name

Occasionally your list of works cited will contain sources by two authors with the same last name—for example, rhetoricians Theresa Enos and Richard Enos. In such cases, you must use the first name as well as the last.

> **Richard Enos includes a thirteen-page bibliography in Greek Rhetoric before Aristotle (141-54). In her collection of articles by prominent figures in modern rhetoric and philosophy, Professing the New Rhetorics, Theresa Enos mentions the considerable contemporary reliance on pre-Aristotelian rhetoric and includes an essay on the subject by Michael Halloran (25, 331-43).**

In these references, the citation of more than one page "(141–54)" identifies continuous pages while "(25, 331–

43)" indicates that the reference is to two separate sets of pages.

An indirect source

If you need to include material that one of your sources quoted from another work, but you cannot obtain the original source, use the following form:

The critic Susan Hardy Aikens has argued on behalf of what she calls "canonical multiplicity" (qtd. in Mayers 677).

A reader turning to the list of works cited should find a bibliographic entry for Mayers (which was the source consulted) but not for Aikens (because the quotation was obtained secondhand).

Poetry, drama, and the Bible

When you refer to poetry, drama, and the Bible, you must often give numbers of lines, acts, and scenes, or of chapters and verses, rather than page numbers. This practice enables a reader to consult an edition other than the one you are using. Nonetheless, your list of works cited should still identify your edition.

Act, scene, and line numbers (all Arabic) are separated by periods with no space before or after them. The MLA suggests that biblical chapters and verses be treated similarly, although some writers prefer to use colons instead of periods in scriptural references. In all cases, the progression is from larger to smaller units.

The following example illustrates a typical citation of lines of poetry.

Emily Dickinson concludes "I'm Nobody! Who Are You?" with a characteristically bittersweet stanza:

```
How dreary to be somebody!
How public, like a frog
To tell your name the livelong June
To an admiring bog! (5-8)
```

The following citation shows that the famous "To be, or not to be" soliloquy appears in act 3, scene 1, lines 56–89 of *Hamlet.*

```
In Hamlet, Shakespeare presents the most
famous soliloquy in the history of the theater:
"To be, or not to be . . ." (3.1.56-89).
```

Chapter 39 contains additional examples of how to quote and cite literary works.

Biblical references identify the book of the Bible, the chapter within the book, and the pertinent verses. In the following example, the writer refers to the creation story in Genesis and that the story begins in chapter 1, verse 1 and ends with chapter 2, verse 22.

```
The Old Testament creation story (Gen. 1.1-
2.22), told with remarkable economy,
culminates in the arrival of Eve.
```

Names of books of the Bible are neither italicized—underlined—(see chapter 10) nor enclosed in quotation marks (see chapter 16), and abbreviation is desirable (see chapter 11).

Punctuation and mechanics

Punctuation and numbers Commas separate the authors' names from the titles (Brown, "Olivier's *Richard III:* A Reevaluation") and indicate interruptions in a sequence of pages or lines (44, 47). Hyphens indicate continuous sequences of pages (44–47) and lines (1–4). Colons separate volume and page numbers (Raine 2: 247); one space follows the colon. Periods separate acts, scenes, and lines in drama (3.1.56–89). Periods (or colons) distinguish chapters from verses in biblical citations (Gen. 1.1 or Gen. 1:1)—see 17d.

Ellipsis points (17i) indicate omissions within a quotation: "They lived in an age of increasing complexity and great hope; we in an age of . . . growing despair" (Krutch 2). Brackets (17g) indicate interpolations within quotations: "The publication of this novel [*Beloved*] establishes Morrison as one of the most important writers of our time" (Boyle 17).

When a question mark ends a quotation (17b), place it before the closing quotation mark; then add a period after the parenthetical citation: Paulo Freire asks, "How can the oppressed, as divided, unauthentic beings, participate in developing the pedagogy of their liberation?" (33).

The MLA favors Arabic numbers throughout, except when citing pages identified by Roman numerals in the source itself (such as the front matter of a book: page vi).

Placement of citations Wherever possible, citations should appear just before a mark of punctuation in the text of the paper.

Richard Enos provides a bibliography of sources for the study of Greek rhetoric before Aristotle (141-54), and Theresa Enos's edited collection, <u>Professing the New Rhetorics</u>, includes Michael Halloran's essay "On the End of Rhetoric, Classical and Modern" (331-43).

Richard Enos's citation falls just before a comma; Theresa Enos's just before a period. However, in a sentence such as the following, the citations should follow the authors' names to keep the references separate.

```
Richard Enos (141-54) and Theresa Enos (25)
address classical rhetoric from very different
perspectives.
```

Lengthy quotations When a quotation is more than four lines long, set it off from the text by indenting ten spaces from the left margin (**16b**). The citation in this case follows the final punctuation, to avoid making it seem part of the quotation:

```
Ben Brantley further stresses the
effectiveness of Loncraine's setting as a
device to emphasize the image of tyranny. He
says:
          Setting the work in Fascist Europe,
          with Richard's Black Shirt presence
          playing on memories of Oswald Mosley
          and Edward VII's alleged Nazi
          sympathies, always made a certain
          sense. It immediately set up echoes
          of what is still perceived as the
          greatest historical example of evil
          in the 20th century: Hitler's Third
          Reich. (1)
```

When quoting more than one paragraph, indent the first line of each paragraph by three additional spaces. Do not indent if you are quoting only one paragraph (or if the first sentence quoted is not the first sentence in a paragraph).

(2) Listing the works cited—MLA style

For MLA papers, the list of sources from which you have cited information is called the **Works Cited**. (Other documentation styles differ from MLA in how they arrange and name their reference lists—see, for example, 38d.)

When you are ready to produce your final draft, eliminate from your working bibliography the cards for the items you have not cited. Arrange the remaining cards in alphabetical order by the authors' last names. If you do not use cards, number your list or have the computer sort them alphabetically. You are now ready to prepare the list of works cited that will conclude your paper. As you make your final revisions, check your citations against this list to ensure that they are complete and correct.

Arrange the list of works alphabetically by author. If a source has more than one author, alphabetize by the first author's last name. Type the first line of each entry flush with the left margin and indent subsequent lines five spaces (a hanging indentation); double-space throughout.

As you study the following MLA style entries, which cover most of the types of sources you are likely to list, observe both the arrangement of information and the punctuation. (See also pages 127–29 for a list of abbreviations that are used in works cited, notes, and tables.)

Books

Most book entries consist of three units separated by periods:

Author	Title	Publication data
Lastname, Firstname.	Title Underlined.	City: Publisher, date.

1. *Author.* Give the last name first, followed by a comma and the first name.
2. *Title.* Underline the title of the book, and capitalize all major words. (See 9c.) Always include the book's subtitle. Make the underlining continuous, not separate under each word.
3. *Publication data.* Provide the city of publication, the brief name of the publisher, and the latest copyright date shown

on the copyright page. Type a colon after the city and a comma after the publisher. To shorten the name of the publisher, use the principal name: Alfred A. Knopf becomes Knopf; Harcourt Brace becomes Harcourt; Harvard University Press becomes Harvard UP; University of Michigan Press becomes U of Michigan P.

One author

Smith, Jeanne Rosier. Writing Tricksters: Narrative Strategy and Cultural Identity in Maxine Hong Kingston, Louise Erdrich, and Toni Morrison. Berkeley: U of California P, 1997.

Use a colon to separate a main title from a subtitle.

More than one work by the same author

Angelou, Maya. A Brave and Startling Truth. New York: Random, 1995.

---. Kofi and His Magic. New York: Potter, 1996.

If you use more than one work by the same author, alphabetize the works by the first *major* word in each title. Give the author's name with the first title, but substitute three hyphens for the name in subsequent entries.

Two authors

Holdstein, Deborah H., and Cynthia L. Selfe, eds. Computers and Writing: Theories, Research, Practice. New York: MLA, 1990.

Invert the name of the first author (or editor) and place a comma after it. Do not invert the second name.

Three authors

Tate, Gary, Edward P. J. Corbett, and Nancy Myers, eds. <u>The Writing Teacher's Sourcebook</u>. 3rd ed. New York: Oxford UP, 1994.

To cite books published by universities, abbreviate "university" and "press" without periods.

More than three authors

Hawisher, Gail E., et al. <u>Computers and the Teaching of Writing in American Higher Education, 1979-1994: A History</u>. New Directions in Computers and Composition Studies. 1. Norwood: Ablex, 1996.

OR

Hawisher, Gail E., Paul LeBlanc, Charles Moran, and Cynthia L. Selfe. <u>Computers and the Teaching of Writing in American Higher Education, 1979-1994: A History</u>. New Directions in Computers and Composition Studies. 1. Norwood: Ablex, 1996.

Corporate author

Institute of Medicine. <u>Blood Banking and Regulation: Procedures, Problems, and Alternatives</u>. Washington: National Academy P, 1996.

Anonymous author

<u>You Know You're Anonymous in Washington When . . .</u>. New York: St. Martin's, 1996.

In the case of anonymous authors, begin the entry with the title. Do not use "Anonymous" or "Anon."

Editor as author

Warhol, Robyn R., and Diane Price Herndl, eds. <u>Feminisms: An Anthology of Literary Theory and Criticisms</u>. New Brunswick: Rutgers UP, 1993.

Edition after the first

Fromkin, Victoria, and Robert Rodman. <u>An Introduction to Language</u>. 5th ed. Ft. Worth: Harcourt, 1993.

Work from an anthology

Jordan, June. "Ah, Momma." <u>Double Stitch: Black Women Write about Mothers & Daughters</u>. Eds. Patricia Bell-Scott, Beverly Guy-Sheftall, Jacqueline Jones Royster, Janet Sims-Wood, Miriam DeCosta-Willis, and Lucille P. Fultz. New York: Harper, 1993. 117-18.

Use this form for an article or essay that was first published in an anthology; use it also for a story, poem, or play reprinted in an anthology. For an article or essay that was published elsewhere before being included in an anthology, use the following form:

Chaika, Elaine. "Grammars and Teaching." College English 39 (1978): 770-83. Rpt. in Linguistics for Teachers. Eds. Linda Miller Cleary and Michael D. Linn. New York: McGraw, 1993. 490-504.

Note where the essay first appeared and then show where you read it. Use the abbreviation "Rpt." for "reprinted." Both forms require you to cite the pages where the material can be found. In the second example, you must cite both the pages of the original publication and the pages of the anthologized version.

Translation

Duras, Marguerite. The North China Lover. Trans. Leigh Hafrey. New York: New Press, 1992.

Reprint

Alcott, Louisa May. Work: A Story of Experience. 1873. Harmondsworth: Penguin, 1995.

The original work was published over a century before this paperback version. Use this form for books—even relatively recent ones—that have been reissued in a new format. (For reprinted articles, see "Work from an anthology.")

A multivolume work

Odell, George C. D. Annals of the New York Stage. 15 vols. New York: Columbia UP, 1927-49.

This multivolume work was published over a period of years.

Cite the total number of volumes in a work when you have used more than one volume. If you use only one volume, include the number (preceded by the abbreviation *Vol.*) after the title and include the number of volumes in the complete work at the end of the entry:

```
Blanco, Richard L., ed. The American
     Revolution, 1775-1783: An Encyclopedia.
     Vol. 1. Hamden: Garland, 1993. 2 vols.
```

Encyclopedias and almanacs

```
Hile, Kenneth S. "Rudolfo Anaya." Contemporary
     Authors. New Revised Series, 1991.
Hopkinson, Ralph G. "Electric Lighting."
     Encyclopedia Americana. 1985 ed.
```

Full publication information is not necessary for a well-known reference work organized alphabetically. For sources that are more unusual, you should reveal more about the source:

```
Dreyer, Edward L. "Inner Mongolia."
     Encyclopedia of Asian History. Ed.
     Ainslee T. Embree. 4 vols. New York:
     Scribner's, 1988.
```

When an author's name is indicated only by initials, check the table of contents for a list of contributors. When an article is anonymous, begin your entry with the article title and alphabetize according to the first important word in the title.

A book in a series

Kelly, Richard Michael, and Barbara Kelly. The Carolina Watermen: Bug Hunters and Boat Builders. Twayne English Author Series. Winston-Salem: Blair, 1993.

When citing a book that is part of a series, provide the name of the series and the number designating the work's place in it (if any). When citing a book title containing another book title—that is, a title that would normally be underlined—do not underline the internal title. If the title within the title would normally appear in quotation marks, retain the quotation marks and underline the complete title. (See chapter 10.)

An introduction, foreword, or afterword

Morrison, Toni. Afterword. The Bluest Eye. By Toni Morrison. New York: Penguin, 1994. 209-16.

Pamphlets and bulletins

Safety Data Sheet: Kitchen Machines. Pamphlet 690. Chicago: Natl. Restaurant Assn., 1970.

Titles of pamphlets are underlined.

Government publication

McDonald, Mike. Amphibian Inventory of the Jarbidge Resource Area, Boise District. Technical Bulletin. Boise: US Bureau of Land Management, Idaho State Office, 1995.

When citing a government publication, identify the government (e.g., "United States," "Minnesota," "Great Britain," "United Nations") followed by the agency that issued the work. Underline the title of a book or pamphlet. Federal publications are usually printed by the Government Printing Office (GPO), but be alert for exceptions.

Articles

The documentation format for articles differs slightly from that for books. The three units are the same, and they are still separated by periods, but note the differences in treatment for titles and publication information.

Author	Titles	Publication data
Lastname, Firstname.	"Title of Article." Periodical	day/month/year: pages.
Lastname, Firstname.	"Title of Article." Journal	volume (year): pages.

1. *Author.* Give the last name first, followed by a comma and the first name.
2. *Article title.* Type the article title in regular (Roman) face, and put it in quotation marks with the period inside the final quotation marks. Capitalize all major words in the title. (See 9c.)
3. *Publication data.* The exact kind of information differs according to the type of periodical, but all references provide the periodical title, the date of publication, and the page numbers on which the article appeared. Continuously underline the periodical title, and capitalize all major words in the title. (See 9c.) Note that no punctuation follows the periodical title and that a colon introduces the inclusive page numbers. If the periodical provides both a volume number and a date, put the date in parentheses.

Weekly magazine or newspaper

```
Stresser, Stan. "Report from Cambodia." The
     New Yorker 18 May 1992: 43-75.

Wyatt, Edward A. "The Missing Link." Barrons
     30 Mar. 1992: 40-41.
```

MLA style abbreviates the names of months (except for May, June, and July). Volume numbers are unnecessary because specific dates are given. (To compare with APA style, see pages 551–52).

Daily newspaper

```
Ibata, David. "Information Highway to the
     Future." Chicago Tribune 17 Nov. 1992,
     final ed., sec. 1: 8.
```

When it is not part of the newspaper's name, the city's name should be given in brackets after the title: *Star Tribune* [Minneapolis]. If a specific edition is not named on the masthead, put a colon after the date and then provide the page reference. Specify the section by inserting the section number immediately before the page number. If the section is lettered, simply include the section letter next to the page number as it appears in the newspaper: A7 or 7A.

Editorial

```
Lewis, Anthony. "Black and White." Editorial.
     New York Times 18 June 1992, natl. ed.,
     A19.
```

If the editorial is not signed, begin the citation with the title.

Monthly magazine

A *journal* is a scholarly publication written for a specific profession, whereas a *magazine* is written for the general public.

Barlow, John Perry. "Is There a *There* in Cyberspace?" Utne Reader March-April 1995: 53-56.

Magazine articles are often interrupted by other articles. If the first part appears on pages 45–47 and the last on pages 213–21, give only the first page number followed by a plus sign: 45+.

Journal with continuous pagination

Diaz, Gwendolyn. "Desire and Discourse in Maria Luisa Bombal's New Islands." Hispanofila 112 (1994): 51-63.

Citing a specific issue (e.g., Sep. 1994) is not necessary when a journal's pages are numbered continuously throughout the year.

Journal with separate pagination

Leroux, Neil. "Frederick Douglass and the Attention Shift." Rhetoric Society Quarterly 21.2 (1991): 36-46.

When an issue is paged separately (each issue begins with page 1), put a period after the volume number and add the issue number.

Nonprint sources

Motion picture

Richard III. Dir. Richard Loncraine. MGM/
United Artists. 1995.

When you cite a particular performance, a screenplay, and so on, put the person's name first:

McKellen, Ian, perf. Richard III. By William
Shakespeare. Screenplay by Ian McKellen.
Dir. by Richard Loncraine. MGM/United
Artists, 1996.

Radio or television program

"'Barbarian' Forces." Ancient Warriors. Narr.
Colgate Salsbury. Dir. Phil Grabsky. The
Learning Channel. 1 Jan. 1996.

Leavitt, David. The Lost Language of Cranes.
Prod. Ruth Caleb. Dir. Nigel Finch. Great
Performances. PBS, WNET, New York. 24
June 1992.

Play

A Streetcar Named Desire. By Tennessee
Williams. Dir. Gregory Mosher. Barrymore
Theater, New York. 9 Aug. 1992.

Recording

Moby. Everything Is Wrong. Compact Disc. Mute
Records Limited, 1996.

Specify the type of recording immediately after the title. Include the manufacturer, the catalog number, and the date of issue.

Electronic media

The information required to cite sources such as software programs or databases that can be distributed on diskettes or CD-ROM disks and the information required to cite on-line sources differ in two important ways. Citations to CD-ROM disks and diskettes generally should identify the publisher, the place, and the date of publication. Citations for information obtained on-line should state the electronic address and the date of access. The date is vital because on-line information can change daily or a site can disappear between when you used it and when your reader attempts to look at it. Furthermore, because the electronic address is often the only way on-line information can be retrieved, it must be absolutely precise.

The *MLA Handbook for Writers of Research Papers,* 4th edition, offers excellent advice on how to cite many kinds of electronic sources, but it does not address sources available through FTP, the World Wide Web, Gopher, Telnet, listserv, or synchronous communication, nor does it indicate how to represent hypertext linkages such as a link from the British Library page to an outside source. Such links help establish credibility. Until the *MLA Handbook* is revised to include them, ask whether your instructor will accept the following supplementary citation formats (based on Harnack and Kleppinger's article in *Kairos*) for those kinds of sources.

E-mail

E-mail is treated much the same way personal letters and memos are treated. Give the name of the person who sent the message, a description of the message (usually the subject line), the receiver of the message, and the date.

```
Mapp, Larry G. "Rhetoric and Hypertext."
     E-mail to Suzanne Webb. 10 Mar. 1996.
```

Harnack and Kleppinger suggest adding the sender's e-mail address (enclosed in angle brackets and inserted immediately after his or her name), the kind of communication (office memo, personal e-mail), the date it was sent, and the date of access:

```
Mapp, Larry G. ⟨lgmapp@frank.mtsu.edu⟩
     "Rhetoric and Hypertext." 10 Mar. 1996.
     Personal e-mail. (11 Mar. 1996).
```

CD-ROM

For a source on CD-ROM, provide the author (if available) and the title (underlined), the publication medium, the place of publication, the publisher, and the publication date. Add the date of access last, if it is pertinent.

```
"About Richard III." Cinemania 96. CD-ROM.
     Redmond: Microsoft, 1996. 20 June 1996.
```

Publication on diskette

For publications on diskettes, provide the title, the version number, a descriptive label, the publisher or distributor, and the copyright date. Add other information at the end of the entry, including, if pertinent, the operating system and units of memory necessary for running the program. When a program is attributed to an author, insert the author's name (last name first) immediately before the title.

```
Hieatt, Constance, Brian Shaw, and Duncan
     Macrae-Gibson. Beginning Old English:
     Exercise Disk. Vers. 6.4. Diskette.
     Binghamton: OEN Subsidia. 1994. DOS.
```

More than one medium

English Poetry Plus. CD-ROM, diskette. New York: Films for the Humanities & Sciences, 1995.

Electronic texts

Many literary and historical works are available in electronic form, but not all electronically available versions are equally reliable. Be sure to use the most authoritative source and state the title, date, and editor of the source for the electronic version. Furthermore, be judicious about how much material you quote from sources. Although many electronic texts are prepared from sources now in the public domain, more are not, and you may have to get the publisher's permission to quote more than a sentence or two.

Shakespeare, William. Richard III. The Works of William Shakespeare. Ed. Arthur H. Bullen. Stratford Town Ed. Stratford-on-Avon: Shakespeare Head, 1911. Online. Dartmouth Coll. Lib. Internet. 18 June 1996.

Electronic journal

Harnack, Andrew, and Gene Kleppinger. "Beyond the MLA Handbook: Documenting Sources on the Internet." Kairos 1.2 (summer 1996): n. pag. Online. Internet. 14 Aug. 1996. Available: http://www.english.ttu/acw/kairos/index.html

Harnack and Kleppinger suggest setting off the electronic address in angle brackets to eliminate potential errors that might result from attempting to include the period that follows or the spaces resulting from line breaks in a long electronic address. Consult your instructor about which form to use.

Harnack, Andrew, and Gene Kleppinger. "Beyond the MLA Handbook: Documenting Sources on the Internet." Kairos 1.2. Summer 1996. ⟨http://www.english.ttu/acw/kairos/index.html⟩ (14 Aug. 1996).

Academic discussion list

Schipper, William. ⟨schipper@mun.edu⟩ "Re: Quirk and Wrenn Grammar." 5 Jan. 1995. ⟨ansax-l@wvnvm.wvnet.edu⟩ 12 Sep. 1996.

Archived messages from an academic discussion list

Schipper, William. ⟨schipper@morgan.ucs.mun.ca⟩ "Re: Quirk and Wrenn Grammar." 5 Jan. 1995 ⟨ansax-l@wvnvm.wvnet.edu⟩ via gopher cwis.ucs.mun.ca (12 Sep. 1996).

World Wide Web

"Richard III: On Stage and Off." Richard III Society. 22 Nov. 1995. ⟨http://www.webcom.com/~blanchrd/mckellen/index.html⟩ (7 July 1996).

Gopher

The *MLA Handbook* does not offer specific guidance about how to cite material retrieved by Gopher. Consult your instructor about whether to cite using the command-path approach or the URL enclosed in angle brackets.

Page, Melvin E. "Brief Citation Guide for Internet Sources in History and the Humanities." 20 Feb. 1996. ⟨gopher://h-net.msu.edu/00/lists/h-africa/internet-cit⟩ (7 July 1996). [OR command-path address: gopher h-net.msu.edu/00/lists/h-africa/internet-cit]

FTP

The *MLA Handbook* does not offer specific guidance about how to cite material retrieved by FTP. Consult your instructor about whether to use the command-path approach or the URL enclosed in angle brackets.

"Beowulf, fol. 192 verso." The Electronic Beowulf Project. ftp ⟨ftp://beowulf.engl.uky.edu/ftp/pub/beowulf⟩ (27 Aug. 1996). [OR command-path address: ftp beowulf.engl.uky.edu/ftp/pub/beowulf]

Both forms report that an image of manuscript page 192v is archived at beowulf.engl.uky.edu and can be downloaded from the directory ftp/pub/beowulf.

Newsgroup

May, Michaela. "Questions about RYAs." 19 June 1996. Online posting. Newsgroup alt.soc.generation-x. Usenet. 29 June 1996.

Because most newsgroups have no moderator to ensure the quality of the postings and because messages are not usually retrievable after a few weeks, use information from these sources with care. If you do use them, ask your instructor whether to include an e-mail address for the person who posted the information.

Synchronous communications

Galin, Jeff. "Teaching Writing in the Digital Age: What Makes Teaching Good These Days?" Netoric's Tuesday Cafe Discussion. MediaMOO. telnet purple-crayon.media.mit.edu/8888. (10 Sep. 1996).

Some synchronous group discussions are archived. To cite one, give the information above followed by *via* and then the address for the archive enclosed in angle brackets. A citation to the logged version of the discussion above would include the address of the Netoric Home Page and the date the log was accessed:

Galin, Jeff. "Teaching Writing in the Digital Age: What Makes Teaching Good These Days?" Netoric's Tuesday Cafe Discussion. (10 Sep. 1996). MediaMOO. telnet purple-crayon.media.mit.edu/8888 via ⟨http://www.cs.bsu.edu/homepages/siering/netoric.html⟩ (12 Sep. 1996).

Linkage data

To show a location offering a hypertext link to a source (useful for establishing the credibility of the source):

Schipper, William. ⟨schipper@morgan.ucs.mun.ca⟩ "Re: Quirk and Wrenn Grammar." 5 Jan. 1995 ⟨ansax-l@wvnvm.wvnet.edu⟩ via gopher cwis.ucs.mun.ca (12 Sep. 1996). Lkd. ⟨http://www.georgetown.edu/labyrinth⟩.

Oral sources

Lecture

```
Thompson, Lou. "Understanding The Turtle
     Diaries." Class lecture. English 3273.
     Texas Woman's University, Denton, TX. 11
     Sep. 1996.
```

Use the title if available or provide a descriptive label for an untitled lecture and give the location and date.

Interview

```
Day, Michael. Personal interview. 31 May 1996.
```

For samples of citations of other nonprint sources—such as games, filmstrips, microscope slides, and transparencies—consult Eugene B. Fleischer's *A Style Manual for Citing Microform and Nonprint Media* (Chicago: American Library Association, 1978).

(3) Final revising, editing, and proofreading

After writing and carefully documenting the first draft of your paper, make needed revisions. Check your outline to make sure the organization is logical and unified (32e). Revise each paragraph to make its purpose clear, and edit each sentence to support its paragraph. Refer to chapters 8 and 33 as needed, particularly the revising, editing, and proofreading checklists. As you revise, make sure you continue to use your sources carefully and responsibly (37g). If you have questions about final manuscript form, refer to chapter 8 and to the sample research papers in 38b and 38e.

Some instructors ask their students to submit outlines, notes, and drafts along with the final paper. Other instructors require a title page and a final outline along with the text of the paper. A title page usually gives the title of the paper, the author, the name of the course and its section number, the instructor's name, and the date—all attractively centered on the page. The MLA recommends using no title page and giving the identification on the first page before the title of the paper: see page 521. (For a sample title page that can be modified for an MLA style paper, see 38e, Sample APA research paper.)

38b Sample MLA research paper

When submitted with the text of a research paper, the final outline serves as a table of contents. In this case, a title page is advisable.

Exercise 1

Read the following paper and create an outline for it (review 32e if necessary). Your instructor will indicate whether you should create a sentence outline or a topic outline.

Exercise 2

Write a 200-word response to the following questions about the MLA paper: (a) Does the paper have a clear thesis? (b) Where is it first introduced? (c) How well is the paper organized? (d) Could it be organized in another way? (e) How well has the source material been included? (f) How well does the author include ideas of her own?

Comments

1. The identification, double-spaced, begins one inch from the top of the page and flush with the left margin. A double-spaced line precedes the centered title of the paper. A margin of one inch is provided at the left, right, and bottom.
2. Double-space between the title and the first line of the text. (A title consisting of two or more lines is double-spaced, and each line is centered.)
3. All pages (including the first one) are numbered with Arabic numerals in the upper right-hand corner, one-half inch from the top. The page number is preceded by the author's last name. Notice that no period follows the page numbers.

Frushour 1

Katie Frushour
Professor Thompson
English 200, Section 5
8 May 1997

Using Cinematic Techniques to Emphasize Theme:
Olivier's and Loncraine's Richard III

Shakespeare's plays are popular targets 1
for film adaptations, and Richard III is no exception. With his 1995 release of Richard III, Richard Loncraine is the newest addition to the field of Shakespearean directors, joining Laurence Olivier, who directed a version of the same play in 1955. While the films are true to the play's central theme of tyranny, the cinematic techniques of the two versions of Richard III are dramatically different. In order to demonstrate the tyranny of Richard, Olivier uses more traditional techniques, such as a cyclical theme, artful use of the shadow, and a careful film adaptation, while Loncraine relies on an unusual setting, clever casting, and creative film adaptation. Therefore, although different methods are employed to illuminate the common theme of tyranny, they are utilized effectively so as to emphasize the cinematic appeal of both films.

Olivier's traditional cinematic methods, 2
which were groundbreaking in his time, bring the complexity of Richard, Duke of Gloucester, to life by highlighting his malice and desire to control the crown of England. Olivier cleverly uses the cyclical theme of the crown being handed from king to king to symbolize

Comments

1. All three quotations in paragraph 2 are cited with only a page number because the authors' names are included in the text.
2. The second reference to Jorgens includes both a direct quotation and a paraphrase. Both are cited with a reference to page 137.
3. Notice how Frushour integrates the information from Jorgens into her own analysis.
4. Frushour uses her own viewing of Olivier's film for this information, and so nothing need be cited (paragraph 3).

Frushour 2

the rise and fall of Richard III, what Constance Brown justly calls "the central device of coherence" (133). Jack Jorgens concurs with Brown's assertion as he states that there "is no question that the theme of the crown is important to the film" (137). Jorgens identifies the theme of the film as the "fall and rise of state" and argues that the fall and rise are represented by the image of the crown (137). The film opens with the crowning of Edward IV, after which the audience learns of Richard's self-serving lust for the throne. The audience increasingly becomes a party to Richard's malevolent actions and his growing tyranny in his quest for power, which culminates in his possession of the crown of England. Soon after obtaining the throne, however, Richard's tyrannical methods lead to his death and the surrender of the crown to Richmond, the rightful heir. This common cycle of events creates a sense of balance in the film, which is both central to the theme and cinematically appealing.

Another cinematic technique employed by 3
Olivier is the artful use of the shadow. As Richard confides his plots to kill Clarence and to marry Lady Anne, his shadow slowly grows until it consumes the whole screen. This use of shadow symbolizes Richard's dominance and his growing tyranny. Likewise, while the audience watches Clarence describe the horrible nightmare that he sees through the window of his cell in the Tower, the camera

Comments

1. Because the quotation from Jorgens in paragraph 3 is brief, it can be run in with the text instead of being indented.
2. In paragraph 4, Frushour identifies McKellen's dual roles in the film—as main character and as the writer of the screenplay.

Frushour 3

slowly reveals the shadow of Richard on the cell door. Through this action, Anthony Davies suggests, the audience becomes an accomplice to Richard's eavesdropping and thus a confidant to his plotting (70). This action is cinematically advantageous because it involves the audience in the film, while developing Richard's tyranny. Finally, the shadow is used to emphasize the intertwining of Richard with the Duke of Buckingham, a vital alliance in Richard's quest for the crown. Jorgens describes this powerful scene: "Buckingham's shadow merges with Richard's . . . and the shadow of the murderers falls upon the crucifix in Clarence's cell as they enter to kill him" (146). The shadows of both men are shown side by side as they exit a room after plotting to meet the young Prince of Wales' escort. This visual representation of the alliance of Richard and Buckingham reinforces their ties to one another and provides a strong contrast centered on Richard's tyranny when he and Buckingham are estranged. Therefore, through the clever and inventive use of the shadow, Olivier is able to emphasize the theme of his film, while making it cinematically appealing at the same time.

Perhaps the most important of Olivier's 4
cinematic techniques is his adaptation of the play. Shakespeare plays are never performed in their entirety, as actor/screenwriter Ian McKellen states in the "Production Notes" of

Comments

1. The citation to Wilson's article, (83–84), at the end of paragraph 4 indicates that the summarized information appears on two pages.
2. Because Robert Wilson engages in a lengthy discussion about the archetypal clichés in *Richard III,* a summary of the remainder of his thesis is included in the notes and is indicated by a superscript numeral. The discussion is not included in the text because it is not directly relevant to Frushour's analysis.
3. The long quotation in paragraph 5 from *Magill's Survey of Cinema* is set off as a block, indented one inch from the left margin, because it is longer than four typed lines. Brackets indicate that the information enclosed is not part of the quotation. The ellipsis points that appear at the end of the quotation indicate that the remainder of the quoted sentence is omitted.
4. No page number is cited in the parentheses because *Magill's Survey of Cinema* is an electronic source and has no pages. Instead, the quotation can be found by searching for a distinctive phrase.
5. When using an anonymous source such as *Magill's Survey of Cinema,* use a shortened version of the title. Frushour uses the title of the article in the work: "Richard III."

Frushour 4

Loncraine's version of Richard III. Olivier generally uses traditional methods of adaptation, such as cutting characters and occasionally dialogue, which serve to clarify the plot by eliminating minor characters. He also maintains the stereotypes of the characters that were defined by Shakespeare. Robert Wilson points out that Olivier uses Shakespeare's archetypal clichés of Lady Anne and Richard III (83-84).[1]

However, Olivier also adds scenes to the film that are not in the play. One of these key additions is described in Magill's Survey of Cinema: 5

> [Olivier] interpolated the coronation of Edward IV from the end of Henry VI, Part 3 (the play that preceded Richard III in Shakespeare's history cycle) into the beginning of the film. This accomplished two things: it gave the audience a bit of welcome background to the action commencing on screen, and it also gave Olivier a framing device to use. . . . ("Richard III")

This adaptation is important to the theme of the film because it provides an insight into the events that lead to Richard's coronation, and it provides the cyclical theme of the three crownings, which is important to the film both thematically and cinematically. Olivier also adds Mistress Shore to the opening scenes. Her presence at the coronation 6

Comments

1. The reference to Brown in paragraph 6 includes Brown's name because the name is not mentioned in the text immediately preceding the reference.
2. The reference to Stark in paragraph 7 acknowledges that Frushour got the idea that there is renewed interest in Shakespeare because of Branagh's productions from Stark's article. No page is cited because Frushour used the online version of the source.
3. Kauffmann's complaints about the film are given in a footnote because they are not directly relevant to Frushour's analysis.
4. In paragraph 7, ellipsis points in the quotation from Kersey and from Kroll (see original text below) show that nonessential information is omitted.

   Source: Kroll, Jack. "Richard III—My Kingdom for a Movie." Newsweek 29 Jan. 1996: 58.

   Loncraine gives you true movie visuals and rhythms as Richard rises to power, polishing off all the men, women, and children in his way, in an England of art deco and prewar tensions.
5. The citation to Kersey in paragraph 7 refers to a Newsgroup posting for which no page number is available. The Works Cited list, however, gives the full electronic address for the source.

and brief interaction with Edward IV emphasize Edward's lasciviousness (Brown 14), which parallels Richard's lust for power. These brief scenes work to enforce the image of Richard as tyrant and are an important part of the cinematic beauty of Laurence Olivier's Richard III.

Loncraine's release of Richard III in 7
1995 takes a more contemporary approach to Shakespeare. Fueled by a renewed interest in Shakespeare resulting from Kenneth Branagh's success in bringing the playwright to the big screen (Stark), the film sparked a controversy concerning Loncraine's choice of setting. Loncraine uses a fictional, fascist, art deco London circa 1930 for the setting of his film, which adds to its cinematic capabilities. Although critics such as Stanley Kauffmann complain that Loncraine's setting is unbelievable,[2] Jack Kroll states in his article concerning the recent release, "Loncraine gives you true movie visuals and rhythms as Richard rises to power . . . in an England of art deco and prewar tensions" (58). The setting parallels the tyranny of Richard. It becomes more militaristic as his obsession for the crown drives him to greater tyranny. Richard's tyranny fuels his rise to power, which "parallels Nazi Germany . . . with his introduction at a Nuremberg-style rally just prior to his coronation" (Kersey). Ben Brantley further stresses the effectiveness of

Comments

1. Notice that the page number for the blocked quotation from Brantley in paragraph 7 comes after the final period, whereas for quotations that are run into the text, such as Kroll's, the page number comes before the period.
2. Newspapers are cited by giving both the page number and the section in which the article appears. (Sime 1C) in paragraph 8 is an example.

Frushour 6

Loncraine's setting as a device to emphasize the image of tyranny. He says:

> Setting the work in Fascist Europe, with Richard's Black Shirt presence playing on memories of Oswald Mosley and Edward VII's alleged Nazi sympathies, always made a certain sense. It immediately set up echoes of what is still perceived as the greatest historical example of evil in the 20th century: Hitler's Third Reich. (1)

This setting, complete with "a wild boar on the flags instead of a swastika" (Kersey) and modeled from the modern image of tyranny and fascism--Hitler's Germany, intensifies the audience's perception of Richard III's rule. The altered setting makes the film more appealing to audiences with a strong mental picture of Hitler's rule. McKellen states, "We weren't trying to bring the play Richard III to as many people as possible, but trying to make a film . . . that would appeal to as many people as possible" (Sime 1C). The audience relates Richard to Hitler through the cinematic images Loncraine creates, enforcing both the theme and the cinematic appeal of the film. 8

From a cinematic standpoint, Loncraine also makes a few casting decisions that relate the plot (and in turn the theme) of the film to the audience. The "Production Notes" from Richard III explain: 9

Comments

1. Brackets in the blocked quotation in paragraph 9 indicate that the production notes include only the actor's surname.
2. No page number is necessary for the blocked quotation in paragraph 9 because it is a citation to a Web page. In this instance, a paragraph number is given instead, according to advice (rather than a requirement) in the *MLA Handbook*. However, the full electronic address appears in the Works Cited.

Frushour 7

> [Robert] Downey [Jr.] and Annette Bening play Americans. Their casting . . . grew out of the fact that in the play Queen Elizabeth and her brother, Earl Rivers, are outsiders. They are not members of the aristocracy and Loncraine and McKellen wanted to find a twentieth-century equivalent. (Paragraph 15)

Loncraine's choice to cast two Americans in the small but important roles of Queen Elizabeth and her brother emphasizes the role of both characters as outsiders by equating their exclusion from the aristocracy to an average American's exclusion from royalty in Britain today. Thus, a seemingly minor part of the cinematic production, casting, enables Loncraine to demonstrate a crucial element of the plot, further enhancing the film's theme and cinematic appeal.

Finally, like Olivier's film, the most 10
important technique emphasizing the theme of Loncraine's film while making it cinematically favorable is adaptation. Ian McKellen, who wrote the screenplay in addition to playing Richard, makes numerous character cuts, rearranges or drops lines, and combines scenes to adapt Shakespeare's play. Characters like Lords Dorset, Grey, and Northumberland and Queen Margaret are eliminated, and their lines are given to other characters in the play. To increase the pace of the film, McKellen combines two scenes between Richard and Lady

Comments

1. The citations in paragraph 10 refer to the two identically authored and titled films. The director's name is included to distinguish one version from the other.
2. The citation in paragraph 10 to the interview with McKellen includes the title to avoid confusion with other electronic sources that quote McKellen. Since the reference is to a Web page, there is no page number.

Frushour 8

Anne (Loncraine, Richard III), so that she is successfully wooed in one scene rather than two (Olivier, Richard III). This reduction in scenes emphasizes the power that Richard has over Anne and allows the audience to compare it to the power he acquires as the movie gains momentum. This scene is so powerful that even in his negative review of Loncraine's film, Kauffmann describes the scene between Anne and Richard as intrinsically interesting (30). Yet, despite the major alterations that McKellen makes to reduce the four-hour play to just under one hundred minutes, he insists on preserving the spirit of Shakespeare. He says, in an on-line interview, "I will not betray his words." McKellen emphasizes the fact that although the characters are changed, lines rearranged, and scenes added or dropped, the words remain true and convey the proper image to the audience ("Richard III: Interview with Sir Ian McKellen"). This dedication to the spirit of Shakespeare's Richard III, while making cinematically advantageous alterations to the text, enables Loncraine to focus on the tyranny of Richard.

Forty years allows for numerous cinematic 11
improvements, yet in Olivier's version of the play, Richard's tyranny is stressed using traditional methods that are just as cinematically appealing today as they were in 1955. Likewise, Loncraine's Richard III introduces a dramatic twist to the film, opening it for cinematic reinterpretation

Comments

1. Notes are usually put at the end of the text and titled *Notes*. They are coordinated with their location in the text by a superscript number that comes before the indented first line of the note and also at the appropriate location in the text.
2. Footnotes fell out of general use because of the difficulty of arranging text around them. Rather, the information was placed on a separate page at the end of the text, which has the additional advantage of making it easy for a reader to set the notes side-by-side with the page being read. In-text citation is even easier to manage, and in an electronic source, a hypertext link (which generally offers fuller information) often accomplishes the same purpose as a note.

Frushour 9

while preserving the tyrannical theme. Therefore, it is this artful and careful presentation of the films that allows both directors to successfully emphasize the tyranny of Richard III while employing vastly different, yet equally effective, cinematic techniques.

Frushour 10

Notes

[1]Wilson states that Lady Anne continues to represent the angel image that is set in opposition to the devil image represented by the character of Richard III (83-84). He further explains that as the angel, Lady Anne's assigned duty is to reform the fallen man, Richard III. Richard III, the devil, is defined by his symbolic rape of the weakened victim, Lady Anne.

[2]Kauffmann argues that by changing the setting to Fascist times, Loncraine succeeds only in creating an unbelievable story line and distorts Shakespeare's original intentions. Kauffmann says, "Are we to believe that this power-greedy homicidal malcontent was a fascist? Nonsense. He had nothing in his head except schemes for personal advancement" (30).

Comments

1. All works cited as sources in the paper and only those should be included in the list of works cited.
2. Alphabetize entries according to the author's last name. Works with more than one author are alphabetized under the name of whichever writer is listed first in the source itself.
3. Observe the use and placement of periods and commas, especially in relation to parentheses and quotation marks. A colon separates a title from a subtitle and the place of publication from the publisher's name. A colon also precedes page numbers of articles from periodicals. Some authorities recommend using angle brackets to set off an electronic address in citations to electronic sources as shown in the alternate citations below.
4. Alternate citation for Kersey:

Kersey, Alan. ⟨kersey@aol.com⟩ "Review: Richard III (1995)" ⟨rec.arts.movies.reviews⟩ (9 July 1996).

5. Alternate citation for "Richard III: Interview with Sir Ian McKellen":

"Richard III: Interview with Sir Ian McKellen." Richard III Onstage and Off. 22 Nov. 1995. ⟨http://www.webcom.com/~blanchrd/mckellen/film/mckell.html⟩ (3 July 1996).

Frushour 11

Works Cited

Brantley, Ben. "Mesmerizing Men of Ill Will." New York Times 21 Jan. 1996, late ed.: 1+.

Brown, Constance. "Olivier's Richard III: A Reevaluation." Focus on Shakespeare Films. Ed. Charles W. Eckert. Englewood Cliffs: Prentice, 1972. 131-45.

Davies, Anthony. Filming Shakespeare's Plays: The Adaptations of Laurence Olivier, Orson Welles, Peter Brook, and Akira Kurosawa. Cambridge: Cambridge UP, 1988.

Jorgens, Jack J. Shakespeare on Film. Bloomington: Indiana UP, 1977.

Kauffmann, Stanley. "Stanley Kauffmann on Films: Shrinking Shakespeare." The New Republic 12 Feb. 1996: 30-31.

Kersey, Alan. "Review: Richard III (1995)." 6 May 1996. Online posting. Newsgroup rec.arts.movies.reviews. Usenet. 9 July 1996.

Kroll, Jack. "Richard III--My Kingdom for a Movie." Newsweek 29 Jan. 1996: 58.

Richard III. By William Shakespeare. Screenplay by Ian McKellen. Dir. Richard Loncraine. MGM/United Artists, 1995.

Richard III. Dir. Laurence Olivier. British Broadcasting Company, 1955.

"Richard III: Interview with Sir Ian McKellen." 20 Dec. 1995. Online. Internet. 3 July 1996. Available http://www.webcom.com/~blanchrd/mckellen/film/mckell.html

Comments

1. An anonymous source (such as Magill's Survey of Cinema or "Richard III: Production Notes") is alphabetized under the first important word in the title.
2. Alternate citation for "Richard III: Production Notes":

```
"Richard III: Production Notes." Richard III
    Onstage and Off. 20 Dec. 1995. ⟨http://
    www.webcom.com/~blanchrd/mckellen/film/
    notes.html⟩ (3 July 1996).
```

3. Inclusion of the issue number and date indicates that each issue of this journal is paged separately.

Frushour 12

"Richard III." Magill's Survey of Cinema. CD-ROM. Salem: Salem Press, Inc., 1996.

"Richard III: Production Notes." 20 Dec. 1995. Online. Internet. 3 July 1996. Available http://www.webcom.com/~blanchrd/mckellen/film/notes.html

Sime, Tom. "Now Is McKellen's Winter of Content: Acclaimed Shakespearean Finally Wins Film Stardom in Richard III." Dallas Morning News 4 Feb. 1996: 1C.

Stark, Susan. "His Naked Villainy: Sir Ian McKellen Is No Garden-Variety Richard III." The Detroit News 20 Jan. 1996: n. pag. Online. Internet. 3 July 1996. Available http://www.detnews.com/menu/stories/32720.htm

Wilson, Robert F., Jr. "Shakespeare and Hollywood: Two Film Clichés." Journal of Popular Film and Television 15.2 (1987): 83-84.

38c Some disciplines use the note style of documentation.

Although the MLA has recommended parenthetical documentation since 1984 (and the influential *Chicago Manual of Style* since 1982), some disciplines in the humanities still use either footnotes or endnotes for documentation. The information is provided here in case you are instructed to follow a note style of documentation.

Both footnotes and endnotes require that a superscript number be placed wherever documentation is necessary. The number should be as near as possible to whatever it refers to, following the punctuation (such as quotation marks, a comma, or a period) that appears at the end of the direct or indirect quotation.

Footnotes should be single-spaced four lines below the last line of text on the same page where the documentation is necessary. Double-space between footnotes if more than one appears on any one page. **Endnotes** should be double-spaced on a separate page headed *Notes*.

The following notes use the same sources as those used for "Listing the works cited—MLA style" on pages 500–18. By comparing the model footnote with its corresponding works cited entry, you will see differences between the two forms. (These numbered notes are arranged in a pattern for your convenience. They are numbered sequentially, as your notes would be for documentation. But your notes would not necessarily begin with "a book by one author" followed by "a book by more than one author," etc.)

A book by one author

[1]Jeanne Rosier Smith, Writing Tricksters: Narrative Strategy and Cultural Identity in

Maxine Hong Kingston, Louise Erdrich, and Toni Morrison (Berkeley: U of California P, 1997) 143.

Indent five spaces, then give the note number (without punctuation) followed by a space. Additional lines in a note should be flush with the left margin. Note that an abbreviation for "page" is not used before the page number at the end of the note.

A book by more than one author

[2]Deborah H. Holdstein and Cynthia L. Selfe, eds., Computers and Writing: Theories, Research, Practice (New York: MLA, 1990) 124.

If the book has more than two authors, use commas to separate the authors' names.

[3]Gail E. Hawisher, Paul LeBlanc, Charles Moran, and Cynthia L. Selfe, Computers and the Teaching of Writing in American Higher Education, 1979-1994: A History. New Directions in Computers and Composition Studies. 1 (Norwood: Ablex, 1996) 201.

A multivolume work

[4]George C. D. Odell, Annals of the New York Stage, vol. 15 (New York: Columbia UP, 1949) 243.

[5]Richard L. Blanco, ed., The American Revolution, 1775-1783: An Encyclopedia, vol. 1 (Hamden: Garland, 1993) 2 vols. 377.

An edited book

[6]Robyn R. Warhol and Diane Price Herndl, eds., Feminisms: An Anthology of Literary Theory and Criticisms (New Brunswick: Rutgers UP, 1993) 165.

A work in an anthology

[7]June Jordan, "Ah, Momma," Double Stitch: Black Women Write about Mothers & Daughters, eds. Patricia Bell-Scott, Beverly Guy-Sheftall, Jacqueline Jones Royster, Janet Sims-Wood, Miriam DeCosta-Willis, and Lucille P. Fultz. 1991 (New York: Harper, 1993) 117-18.

An introduction, preface, foreword, or afterword

[8]Toni Morrison, afterword, The Bluest Eye, by Toni Morrison (New York: Penguin, 1994) 209-16.

An article from a newspaper

[9]David Ibata, "Information Highway to the Future," Chicago Tribune 17 Nov. 1992, final ed., sec. 1: 8.

An article from a magazine

[10]Stan Stresser, "Report from Cambodia," The New Yorker 18 May 1992: 63.

An article from a journal with continuous pagination

[11]Gwendolyn Diaz, "Desire and Discourse in Maria Luisa Bombal's New Islands" Hispanofila 112 (1994): 51-63.

38d APA style documentation is appropriate for research papers in psychology and most social sciences.

(1) Using parenthetical citations

In APA style, the basic elements of a parenthetical citation in the text are the author's last name, the year of publication, and the page number if the reference is to a specific passage in the source. If the author's name is mentioned in the text of the paper, give the date alone or the date and the page number in parentheses. In the following examples, note the details of punctuation and the treatment of the page number.

A work by one author

One writer has stated, "Prisons can be divided into specific social groups organized by type of crime" (Liptz, 1979, p. 235).

OR

Liptz has stated, "Prisons can be divided into specific social groups organized by type of crime" (1979, p. 235).

OR

```
Liptz (1979) has stated, "Prisons can be
divided into specific social groups organized
by type of crime" (p. 235).
```

Unlike MLA style, APA style requires the abbreviation *p.* (or *pp.* for "pages") before the page reference. Use commas to separate the author's name from the date and the date from the page reference.

A work by two authors

```
There is evidence that students in second and
third grade respond favorably to guidance from
elementary school students in higher grades
(Bowman & Myrick, 1987).
```

Use the ampersand (&) to separate the authors' names.

A work by more than two authors

```
One recent study has shown that people who
fear failure are not susceptible to hypnosis
(Manganello, Carlson, Zarillo, & Teeven,
1985).
```

For works with *three to five authors*, cite all the authors in the first reference, but in subsequent references give only the last name of the first author followed by *et al.* ("Manganello et al." in this case). For works with *more than six authors*, provide only the last name of the first author followed by *et al.*, even in the first citation.

Anonymous works

Use a shortened version of the title to identify an anonymous work:

```
Chronic insomnia usually requires medical
intervention ("Sleep," 1993).
```

In this case, the author has cited a short article identified in the bibliography as "Sleep disorders: What can be done about them."

Two or more works within the same parentheses

```
Much animal experimentation may be both
unnecessary and cruel (Mayo, 1983; Singer,
1975).
```

Use a semicolon to separate different studies, and arrange them in alphabetical order.

(2) Listing the references—APA style

Format the "References" (alphabetical list of works cited) in the APA style your instructor specifies. (See the commentary on final manuscript style, page 555.) As the fourth edition of the *Publication Manual* asserts, **final manuscript style** allows considerable freedom to format documents to enhance readability. Some instructors prefer that the first line of each entry in the references list be typed flush left and that the second and subsequent lines of each entry be indented three spaces—called a hanging indent. Other instructors prefer that you indent the first line of each entry five spaces and type subsequent lines flush with the left margin. The *Publication Manual* urges instructors to specify the style they prefer for the final manuscript.

The reference entries below have a hanging indent, but as the *Publication Manual* asserts, they could have been formatted just as correctly with an indented first line—the recommended approach for **copy manuscript** (see page 555). Whichever format you use, be consistent and observe all details of indention, spacing, and mechanics.

Books

Most book entries consist of four units separated by periods:

1. *Author.* Give the author's last name and use initials for the first and middle names. For entries that contain more than one author, invert all names and put an ampersand (&) before the last one. (If two authors have the same last name and initials, spell out their first names and list the references in the alphabetical order of their first names.)

2. *Date.* Put the date in parentheses after the author's name. By including the date near the beginning of the entry, APA style draws attention to its importance.

3. *Title.* Capitalize only the first word in titles and subtitles. Do not capitalize other words (except for proper names that would be capitalized in other contexts). Separate titles and subtitles with a colon, and underline the title and any period immediately following it.

4. *Publication data.* Give only enough of the publisher's name so that it can be identified clearly.

Book by one author

Riordan, C. H. (1997). Equality and achievement: An introduction to the sociology of education. New York: Longman.

More than one work by the same author

If you use more than one work by the same author, list the works in order of the publication date, with the earliest first. Repeat the author's name for each work.

Gates, H. L. (1995). Colored people: A memoir. New York: Vintage.
Gates, H. L. (1997). 13 ways to look at a black man. New York: Random House.

Book by two or more authors

Fish, B. C., & Fish, G. W. (1996). The Kalenjiin heritage: Traditional religious and sociological practices. Pasadena, CA: William Carney Library.

Contrast APA style with MLA style, which inverts only the name of the first author in a multiauthor work. (See page 502.)

An edition after the first

Kelly, D. H. (1989). Deviant behavior: A text-reader in the sociology of deviance (3rd ed.). New York: St. Martin's.

Translation

Freud, S. (1960). <u>Jokes and their relationship to the unconscious</u> (J. Strachey, Trans.). New York: Norton. (Original work published 1905)

Cite the date of the translation and include the date of the original publication at the end of the entry. In text, use the following form: (Freud, 1905/1960).

A government document

Department of Transportation. (1996). <u>Liability cost and risk analysis studies: Bus liability review for six transit systems</u> (DOT-T-96-13). Washington, DC: Technological Sharing Program.

Treat the issuing agency as the author when no author is specified. Include a document or contract number (but not a library call number) if either number is printed on or in the document.

Works with no author

Use the first significant words of the title to cite anonymous materials in the text, underlining the title of a book. Unless Anonymous is specifically designated as the author of a work, do not use it for in-text citations or the list of references.

Directory of Mental Health Providers in Texas. (1996). Austin: State Employees' Insurance Agency.

Articles

Capitalize only the first word and any proper nouns in article titles, and do not put quotation marks around titles. (If the article has a subtitle, use a colon to separate the title and the subtitle and capitalize the first word of each.) For an article in an edited book, provide both the title of the article and the title of the book in which it appears. Give the name of the editor and the complete page numbers of the article. For an anonymous article, place the article title where the author's name would normally appear, and alphabetize by the first important word in the title.

Boomerang age. (1990). American Demographics, 12, 25-30.

The title of a journal is capitalized differently from article or book titles. Underline the volume number and the commas preceding and following it (but not the issue number) so it will be distinct from the page reference (which is not preceded by *p.* or *pp.*).

Journal: Continuous pagination

Lenfant, C. (1996). High blood pressure: Some answers, new questions, continuing challenges. JAMA, 275, 1605-1606.

Journal: Separate pagination

```
Kolakowski, L. (1992). Amidst moving ruins.
   Daedalus, 121(2), 43-56.
```

Place the issue number in parentheses immediately after the volume number but do not underline it.

Monthly or weekly magazine

```
Levy, D. H. (1992, June). A sky watcher
   discovers comets and immortality.
   Smithsonian, 23, 75-82.
```

For a monthly magazine, give the year first, followed by a comma and the full spelling of the month. For a weekly magazine, provide the exact date: (1997, February 18).

Newspaper

```
Baker, R. (1996, July 23). Down with all of
   that! New York Times, p. A119.
```

Work in an anthology

```
Chlad, F. L. (1991). Chemical storage for
   industrial laboratories. In D. A. Pipitone
   (Ed.), Safe storage of laboratory chemicals
   (pp. 175-191). New York: Wiley.
```

Book review

Becker, J. G. (1992). The dilemma of choice [Review of the book Psychiatric aspects of abortion]. Contemporary Psychology, 37, 457-458.

When a review is titled, place the subject of the review in brackets after the review title. When a review is untitled, use the material in brackets as the title, but retain the brackets to show that this "title" is a description.

Pyles, A. R. (1997) [Review of Pre-Adolescent Female Friendships]. School Psychologist, 2, 57-59.

Nonprint sources

Film

Doran, Lindsay (Producer), & Lee, Ang (Director). (1995). Sense and sensibility [Film]. London: Mirage.

Recording

Fellows, W. (Speaker). (1993). Nutritional needs for women with AIDS (Cassette Recording No. 8294). Madison, WI: Nutritionworks.

Electronic media

The APA *Publication Manual* suggests the following formats for references to electronic media. Note that the final period is omitted for all because trailing periods can cause difficulty in retrieving files:

Lastname, I. (date). Title of article. *Name of Periodical* [On-line], *xx*. Available: Specify path

Lastname, I. (date). Title of article or chapter. In *Title of full work* [On-line]. Available: Specify path

Lastname, I., Lastname, I., & Lastname, I. (date). *Title of full work* [On-line]. Available: Specify path

Computer program

O'Reilley, R. (1993). Prostyle [Computer software]. Bloomington, MN: Wordcorp. (OTR-71148).

On-line journal

Crump, E. (1995, February). RhetNet, a cyberjournal for rhetoric and writing [30 lines]. ACW Connections [On-line serial]. Available E-mail: acw-mem@unicorn.acs.ttu.edu or World Wide Web: http://prairie_island.ttu.edu/acw/acw.html

World Wide Web page

Salvo, M. (1996, August). Kairos. Available: http://acw.english.ttu.edu/acw/kairos/index.html

Cite e-mail, newsgroup, or bulletin board messages in the text but do not list them in the references. Not usually archived in any systematic way, these kinds of sources cannot be systematically retrieved and are regarded as ephemeral—short-lived and transitory.

38e Sample APA research paper

The APA *Publication Manual* specifies two different styles of manuscripts, the **copy manuscript** and the **final manuscript**. The *Manual* explains,

> The author of a thesis, dissertation, or student paper produces a "final" manuscript; the author of a journal article produces a "copy" manuscript (which will become a typeset article). The differences between these two kinds of manuscripts help explain why the requirements for theses, dissertations, and student papers are not necessarily identical to the manuscripts submitted for publication in a journal. (p. 331)

The copy manuscript style is used for a document that will be sent to a publisher and set in type. The final manuscript style should be used for such documents as student papers, lab reports, master's theses, and doctoral dissertations.

Copy manuscripts, the APA *Publication Manual* explains, "must conform to the format and other policies of the journal to which they are submitted" (p. 332). Final manuscript style, however, permits a "number of variations from the requirements described in the *Publication Manual*" (p. 332) and should conform to the requirements of an individual university, department, or instructor. The *Manual* further advises that it is

> not intended to cover scientific writing at an undergraduate level, because preferences for style at that level are diverse. Instructions to students to "use the *Publication Manual*" should be accompanied by specific guidelines for its use. (p. 332)

Generally speaking, a **title page** includes three elements, all of which are double-spaced. The **running head** is a shortened version of the **title** and appears in the upper left-hand corner of the title page. It will also appear in the upper right-hand corner of every page, including the title page, which is counted as page 1. (If you use this title page as a model for a paper in MLA style, do not include the running head or the page number.) The title appears next in upper- and lowercase letters and is centered. The **author's name** or **byline** appears below the title and is followed by the author's affiliation. If an instructor asks that the course number be included, it will generally appear as the affiliation. Unless the instructor specifically requires it, the instructor's name and the date the paper is due are not included. (A final manuscript may also include an **abstract,** a 100- to 200-word summary of the paper. This is the length of most abstracts in APA journals.)

The body of the paper, the **discussion,** should normally be double-spaced and include in-text citations as specified in the *Publication Manual.* Variations in spacing to promote readability, however, are not only permitted, but encouraged.

A fourth essential component of the final manuscript, the **references,** is a list of all the references cited in the text. It does not usually include any references not cited. However, any material that is especially pertinent or that informs the whole paper may be included if it is considered essential. When that is the case, the reference list becomes a bibliography. For additional examples of APA style documentation, see the following student essay and the commentary on it printed on the left-hand pages.

Comments

1. Student papers should be prepared in **final manuscript style** (see page 555), double-spaced with in-text citations as specified in the APA *Publication Manual.* Depending on the particular requirements of your department or instructor, requirements for final copy may differ from those for copy manuscript style described in the body of the *Manual.*
2. A **title page** includes three double-spaced elements: running head, title, and author's full name and affiliation. Center the title and author horizontally (but not necessarily vertically).
3. The **running head** is a shortened version of the title. It appears in the upper right-hand corner of every page and the upper left of the title page, which is counted as page 1.
4. If an instructor asks that the course number be included, it generally appears instead of the affiliation. Unless specifically required, the instructor's name and the date the paper is due are not included.

Running head: GENERATION X

Generation X: Moving Back Home

Adrienne Harton

Texas Woman's University

Comments

1. An abstract is a short summary of a paper. The APA *Publication Manual* requires that an abstract be supplied on the second page of any essay that is to be submitted for publication (copy manuscript style). Check with your instructor to see if an abstract is required for your paper.
2. Harton's abstract is slightly over 60 words, a reasonable length for a short paper. The usual length is 100 to 120 words.

Generation X 2

Abstract

Young adults are returning to their parents' homes in record numbers. Research indicates that education, occupation, and personal lifestyles all contribute to the economic hardships of young adults. The generation born between 1964 and 1980 faces financial difficulties just like previous generations, but parents of this generation seem more willing, almost obligated, to support their adult children.

Comments

1. In her opening paragraph, Adrienne Harton draws on personal experience to catch her audience's interest.
2. At the beginning of paragraph 2, Harton explains what RYA means. Thereafter, she uses the abbreviation without explanation.

Generation X 3

Generation X: Moving Back Home

Jim and Carole Wilson appear to be a comfortable couple in their 50s, married for 30 years. The Wilsons own a home, drive nice cars, and were able to pay for a college education for all three of their children. The Wilsons deviate from the stereotypical couple, though, because one of their college-educated children has moved back home. Scott, the oldest child, quit his temporary job (waiting tables "while I look for something better") and resumed residence in his old bedroom. Unfortunately for parents like the Wilsons, this syndrome has become increasingly common in the past 10 years. Grown children are returning to the nest or sometimes never leaving at all. The primary impetus for this phenomenon is economic: Young adults are moving back home because of educational opportunities or the lack of them, occupational difficulties, and personal lifestyle choices. 1

The RYA (Returning Young Adult) phenomenon is a family development syndrome looked at as circular in the family's attempt to "launch" the young adult members into independence. The young adult leaves home to experience adult independent living, returns home, hopefully to leave again, this time successfully. The act of emerging from the core family home and assuming responsibilities 2

Comments

1. Paragraph 3 describes RYA by using demographic evidence.
2. Note that the long quotation—a quotation of more than 40 words—in paragraphs 2, 7, 9, and 11 is indented five spaces only, per APA style. (See **16b**.)

and, in essence, finding a place in the world can often be unsuccessful financially for many young adults. Peck (1991) defines the "launching" stage as "one of the most complex stages of the family's life cycles" (p. 150). According to Natalie Swartzberg (1991)

> American family young adulthood can be defined as usually beginning in the early twenties . . . when the young person is launched from the family of origin, and ending sometime in the early thirties, when the young adult is firmly esconced in a job and is capable of intimacy. (p. 77)

For the most part, the reason for the RYA syndrome is economics.

Before analyzing the financial reasons why people in their 20s are returning to their parents' homes, researchers first determine the characteristics of this group. Burnett and Smart (1994) define RYAs: "To be a true RYA, both the individual and parents expected the child to leave home, the child actually did leave home but, because of the need for economic support, returned" (p. 255). The RYA phenomenon is also called the crowded nest or "boomerang effect." The number of children in the RYA generation who return to live with their parents seems surprisingly high. "About 3

Comments

1. Paragraph 5 on page 568 includes statistical evidence that will support Harton's analysis. Note that she relies heavily on one source, *American Demographics* (which, however, is a long statistical study). When introducing the Holtz study, Harton works the author's name into the text. Notice also that the page numbers follow the quote.
2. Paragraph 6 on page 569 includes a citation to a source with two authors and to a source that is a government document.

Generation X 5

40 percent of young adults return to their parents' home at least once. Men and women are equally likely to return home until age 25, but men are more likely to return after that age" ("Boomerang age," 1990, p. 26). With almost half of the 20-something generation moving home, a family with two or more children can almost surely anticipate an RYA. Another intriguing statistic is that males are more likely to live with their parents than females: "Men are more than twice as likely as females to live with their parents" (Burnett & Smart, 1994, pp. 257–258). Over 70% of those male RYAs have a yearly income of less than $10,000, also. From the data, researchers can typify the RYA as a male in his early 20s with a low-paying job or no job.

Determining the characteristics of the RYA's family is another important control. The RYA family often has an above-average income (Burnett & Smart, 1994, p. 254), which actually helps influence adult children to move home since most of them likely have not accumulated all the material comforts their parents have attained. Parents of young adults actually wield great influence in determining whether or not the child becomes an RYA. However, the economic circumstances of RYAs are almost always the deciding factor in moving back home. Knowing these characteristics of RYAs and their families leads to a more in-depth analysis of financial considerations and the RYA syndrome. 4

Generation X 6

5 Education affects young adults in two ways with regard to moving home. Either the RYA is attending college and cannot afford to live on his or her own, or the RYA chose not to further his or her education and cannot be self-sustaining on the paycheck alone. In the first case, research shows that more young adults are going to college, and almost half of first-year college students have a job ("Boomerang age," 1990, p. 30). Furthermore, many students start at 2-year colleges and so take longer to finish, and students also now take longer to choose a major. Such statistics show that young adults are spending more time in college than ever before. Living with one's parents effectively decreases a student's financial burden. Holtz (1995) claims, "The average college undergraduate was taking more than six years to earn a degree; fewer than half graduated after the traditional four years of study" (p. 124). An economic chain reaction exists for college students living at home. "Because people are delaying marriage, they are living with their parents longer. They are delaying marriage because they're going to school. They're going to school because most well-paying jobs now require a college degree" ("Boomerang age," 1990, p. 26). Of course, these RYAs have sound and smart reasons for living with their parents, but what about the RYAs who are not continuing their education?

Generation X 7

Some RYAs simply cannot afford to live away from home on a small salary. The typical 25-year-old working man has a median income less than the poverty level for a single person (Holtz, 1995, p. 158). Obviously, returning to one's childhood home makes sense whether the young adult is trying to save money or to maintain a particular lifestyle. While long-term prospects for the educated RYA are more promising, the average income for males without a college degree has fallen (Levy & Michel, 1991, p. 45). Many RYAs do not even have jobs. According to the U.S. Census (1993), the unemployment rate for young adults living at home is 30 to 35%. Whether RYAs' unemployment is a result of attending college or of a lack of proper education, the best financial decision to make is to move home with Mom and Dad. As one young Gen X'er put it: "Those theories I got in college were great, but now that reality is here, I need to figure out if they really work." 6

Jobs obviously affect economic situations of young adults. Some RYAs hold jobs and some do not, but for both groups, the dilemma is not having enough money to maintain a desired lifestyle and pay the bills too. One study notes, "As the U.S. economy shifts from manufacturing to services, it sharply reduces the number of entry-level jobs available to people who don't have much schooling" ("Boomerang age," 1991, p. 30). Another 7 problem relates directly to postsecondary education and choosing a major in college. As the business and technology sectors grow faster than areas grounded in liberal arts, college students should plan for long-term job security by selecting a marketable major. Although unemployment seems to be an undesirable predicament, RYAs have a parental safety net, as illustrated by E. L. Klingelhofer (1989):

> The inability to find appropriate work has not been as catastrophic a burden as it once might have been because the parents were able to support the child, to help out, to tide him or her over. And, as the individual quest for work wore on and eventually, wore out, what had been thought of as a temporary arrangement imperceptibly became a permanent one. (p. 86)

Whereas unemployment once meant failure, embarrassment, and perhaps even homelessness, now it seems to be an opportunity to return home.

8 Even for young adults with jobs, moving home can be a solution to financial problems. RYAs change careers with great frequency. As research reveals, "Young adults have the highest rate of occupational mobility. Thirty percent of employed men aged 16 to 19, and 22 percent of those aged 20 to 24, changed occupations" compared with 10 percent for all

Generation X 9

workers ("Boomerang age," 1990, p. 52). Apparently, grown children choose to live with their parents to find some stability during professional uncertainty. Furthermore, the jobs that young adults, even when college educated, obtain may not yield enough money to survive away from home. A college education can be very expensive, especially over 6 years. Some young adults who shoulder their entire college debts cannot afford to live away from home while paying student loans (Kuttner, 1995, p. M5). Regardless of whether an RYA has a job or not, the economic sense of moving back home exceeds the need for independence.

The final financial reason why grown 9
children are returning to the nest encompasses personal lifestyle decisions: delayed marriage and middle-class comfort. The average age of marriage has steadily increased since the 1970s. Littwin (1986) concludes:

> Commitment to a relationship is just as difficult for them as commitment to a career or point of view. It is one act that might define them and therefore limit their potential. Besides, it is difficult to be in a relationship when you still don't know who you are. (p. 219)

With the option of moving home, young 10
adults do not feel the pressure or the necessity to marry early. Even when people do

Comment

1. Harton cites the personal communication from Karl James in paragraph 11 in the text but, as with other nonrecoverable sources such as personal letters, e-mail, and bulletin board postings, does not list it in the references.

marry early and divorce, research shows that many young adults return to their parents' homes to recover and stabilize (Klingelhofer, 1989, p. 86). RYAs can opt to live with their families as an alternative to marriage or to reestablish themselves after a divorce. In either scenario, the RYA is more financially stable than if he or she lived alone.

Some RYAs return to the nest to attain the material comforts of a middle- to upper-class home that they enjoyed and expected as dependents. Adult children now receive allowances, their own rooms, telephones, cars, personal freedom. Why should they leave the nest? For wealthier families, adult children moving home is a particular problem. Littwin (1986) says: 11

> The affluent, perfect parent is the ideal target for rebellion-and-rescue. . . . The young adult resents that he has been given so much that he cannot give himself. He has been cared for too well and too conscientiously. (p. 140)

A potential RYA, still a student at a private university and for whom his parents pay all expenses, recently complained about the constraints his full-time summer job placed on his lifestyle, "I don't see how you and Dad get anything done when you have to work 40 hours a week" (K. James, personal communication, August 15, 1996). In an instant-gratification-seeking

Comments

1. Harton's concluding paragraph 32f(2) follows the traditional model of summarizing the preceding points and suggesting a direction for future study.
2. A strong final statement, the quotation Harton uses to conclude her essay contains an implicit challenge to Generation X. Note also that it is introduced by a colon (17d(1)).

generation, returning to the nest is just easier than earning comfort.

In conclusion, young adults are moving back home for a variety of reasons. Of course, people of the 20-something generation would not be able to return home without parental acquiescence. Future research will reveal if RYAs develop a pattern of adult dependence on their parents, but for now, research proves that grown children are moving back home for a myriad of financial considerations. And, perhaps, as one Gen X'er bemoans: "We as a generation have yet to produce any defining traits, except perhaps to show a defeatist belief that we will do worse than our parents" (Janoff, 1995, p. 10). 12

Comments

1. The reference list is organized alphabetically and begins on a new page. The last name is always given first, and initials are provided for first and middle names. The date of publication is always given parenthetically, immediately after the author's name. (See 38d(2).)
2. Observe the use of periods and commas, the style of capitalization for book and article titles, and the different capitalization style for journal titles. Underline book and journal titles, and carry continuous underlining of periodical titles through the volume number.
3. If Harton's instructor had specified a final manuscript format that called for the first line of each entry to be indented five spaces, the first two entries would look like this:

```
     Boomerang age. (1990). American
Demographics, 12, 25-30.
     Burnett, J., & Smart, D. (1994).
Returning young adults. Psychology and
Marketing, 11, 253-269.
```

4. Notice that the entry for Colligan's electronic article specifies its length as seven paragraphs. Citations for electronic sources sometimes refer to a specific paragraph where citations to print sources would refer to page numbers.

Generation X 12

Bibliography

Boomerang age. (1990). American Demographics, 12, 25-30.

Burnett, J., & Smart, D. (1994). Returning young adults. Psychology and Marketing, 11, 253-269.

Cipriano, E. (1996). Who is this generation formerly known as x? Seriously [On-line serial], 6(1). Available FTP: spc.5yr.edu/seriously/generation

Colligan, P. (1996, March 19) Go Pat go? No Pat no? [7 paragraphs]. CGX [On-line serial], 3(4). Available E-mail: conservgenx@teleport.com

Holtz, G. T. (1995). Welcome to the jungle: The why behind "Generation X." New York: St. Martin's Griffin.

Janoff, J. B. (1995, April 24). A gen-x Rip Van Winkle. Newsweek, 127, 10.

Klingelhofer, E. L. (1989). Coping with your grown children. Clifton, NJ: Humana Press.

Kuttner, R. (1995, June 25). The new elite: Living with mom and dad. Los Angeles Times, p. M5.

Levy, F., & Michel, R. C. (1991). The economic future of American families: Income and wealth trends. Washington, DC: Urban Institute.

Littwin, S. (1986). The postponed generation: Why American youth are growing up later. New York: William Morrow.

Peck, J. S. (1991). Families launching young adults. In F. H. Brown (Ed.), Reweaving the family tapestry: A multigenerational approach to families. (pp. 149-168). New York: Norton.

Schwartzberg, N. (1991). Single young adults. In F. H. Brown (Ed.), Reweaving the family tapestry: A multigenerational approach. (pp. 77-93). New York: Norton.

U.S. Department of Commerce, Bureau of the Census. (1993). 1990 Census of Population. Washington, DC: U.S. Government Printing Office.

Chapter 39

Writing for Special Purposes

The information conveyed throughout this handbook will benefit you in different writing situations. The essentials of English grammar (1–4, 6–7, 25) and the principles of effective sentence structure (23, 24, 26, 29, 30)—as well as conventions for using appropriate diction (19–22), punctuation (12–17), and mechanics (8–11, 18)—are always relevant. Advice about planning and drafting (32), developing (31d, 32c), and revising and editing (33) applies to most writing that you will need to do in college and in your profession. Other advice, such as how to write arguments (36) and work with sources (38), applies to specific purposes. This chapter will introduce you to principles that govern two additional situations: writing about literature (39a) and effective business communication (39b).

39a Writing about literature increases understanding of it.

Like all writing in specialized fields, literature has its own vocabulary. When you learn it, you are not just learning a list of terms and definitions. You are grasping concepts that will help you understand literature and write about it effectively. This section introduces these concepts and provides basic guidelines for writing about literature. Your instructor can give you further help.

Writing about literature involves using the principles of good writing. Consider the rhetorical situation, especially your audience and your purpose (32a), and explore, limit, and focus your subject (32c) as you read and write. Work toward formulating a thesis statement (32d) that can be supported from the work itself, and plan how to organize your thoughts so that your essay will have a sound structure.

(1) Prepare for writing by reading, reflecting, and planning.

You cannot write effectively about a literary work that you have not read. Begin the process of writing about literature by reading carefully and noting your personal response. Think critically about these impressions and be open to new ideas as you plan your essay.

(a) Explore your personal response to literature.

As you read, take notes and jot down ideas. Trust your own reactions. What characters do you admire? Did the work remind you of any experience of your own? Did it introduce you to a world different from your own? Were you amused, moved, or confused? These first impressions can provide the seeds from which strong essays will grow. You may find that you need to modify your initial impressions as you study the work more closely or as writing takes you in a direction that you did not originally anticipate. But writing about literature begins with active, personal engagement with what you read.

You can facilitate this engagement by freewriting (see 32c) or by keeping a journal in which you record your reactions and questions. These methods of exploring a subject can help you discover what you think or what you want to understand. In addition to generating topics for writing, they provide a useful method for identifying questions you could raise in class. Here is a piece of freewriting on "Lullaby," a short story discussed in the paper that begins on page 592. The author quickly wrote whatever came to mind, confident that doing so would help him discover a topic for an essay.

I felt really sad when I finished this story. Looks like the characters are about to die. A form of suicide? What would Chato have said if he was alert? Ayah must be very unhappy. Doesn't seem to have anything left to live for. One thing I didn't understand though is why she laughs when she sees the shoes her husband is wearing. Does she think it's funny? She seems peaceful watching the sky though I think nature calms her down. At other times she seems angry.

After briefly noting how the story made him feel, the author of this excerpt then moves on to ask three questions, each of which could lead to an essay through the exploration of possible answers. Another essay could explore Ayah's relationship with nature: Is it true that "nature calms her down" and, if so, why? Note also that this excerpt does not consist entirely of grammatically correct sentences. When you freewrite about literature, write whatever comes to mind without worrying about whether or not you are correct. You are thinking on paper, not editing an essay.

(b) Analyze, interpret, explicate, and evaluate.

Although you may have occasion to write papers in which you simply explore your personal response to a work of literature and relate it to your own life, writing papers about a literary work usually requires you to focus on the work itself. Your personal response may help you discover a direction you want to explore, but as you explore you will often need to look at a work by analyzing it, interpreting it, or evaluating it. A short paper may do only one of these; a long paper may do all three.

Analyze (see 31d(6)) a work of literature by breaking it into elements and examining how such elements as setting, characters, and plot combine to form a whole. How do the elements interact? How does one element contribute to the overall meaning of the work? For example, in her paper on *King Lear* (beginning on page 599), Susan Ferk demonstrates how the characters in the subplot comment on and intensify the main plot and theme.

Interpret a work by asking what it means, bearing in mind of course that a work may have more than one meaning. Support your interpretation by referring to elements in the work itself. For example, in his paper on "Lullaby" (beginning on page 592), Tom Villalta cites evidence to support his belief that the story shows how Native American culture has been violated. Interpretation is closely related to analysis and allows writers to draw freely on any part of a work that can be used to explain its meaning.

An interpretation that attempts to explain every element in a work is called an **explication** and is usually limited to poetry. When explicating William Wordsworth's "A Slumber Did My Spirit Seal," a writer might note that the "s" sound reinforces the hushed feeling of sleep and death in the poem. But it would also be necessary to consider the meaning of "slumber," "spirit," and "seal," as well as why the words in this line are arranged as they are (as opposed to "A Slumber Sealed My Spirit" or "My Spirit Was Sealed by My Slumber").

Evaluate a work by asking how successful the author is in communicating its meaning to readers. Like interpretation, evaluation is a type of argument in which a writer cites evidence to persuade readers to accept a clearly formulated thesis. (See chapter 36.) In her paper on Galway Kinnell (beginning on page 610), Susan Schubring argues that "The Milk Bottle" successfully conveys "the division between mind and body in humans." An evaluation of a literary work should consider both strengths and weaknesses if there is evidence of both.

CAUTION Although **summarizing** a literary work can be a useful way to make sure you understand it, do not confuse summary with analysis, interpretation, or evaluation. Those who have read the literary work are unlikely to benefit from reading a summary of it. Do not submit a summary unless your instructor has asked for one.

(c) Choose a subject and decide how you want to develop it.

If your instructor asks you to choose your own subject, your first step should be to reflect on your personal response (39a(1)). Reviewing your response may enable you not only to choose a subject but also to formulate a tentative thesis. The purpose of your paper in this case would be to persuade readers to agree with your view. Also try some of the methods suggested in 32c to explore the work in question. If you generate more than one possible topic, decide which one seems most original.

Choose a topic that would be interesting both to write and read about. Readers are usually interested in learning what *you* think. If you choose an easy topic, you may find yourself repeating what many others have already said. As a rule, try to avoid writing the obvious. However, do not let the quest for originality lead you to choose a topic that would be too hard to develop adequately.

Apply strategies of development (31d). You might **define** why you consider a character heroic, **classify** a play as a comedy of manners, or **describe** a setting that contributes to a work's meaning. Perhaps you could **compare and contrast** two poems on a similar subject or explore **cause-and-effect** relationships in a novel. Why, for example, does an apparently intelligent character make a bad decision?

(d) Reread carefully.

Experienced readers understand that a literary work can provoke different responses from different readers. You can also have a significantly different response when rereading a work—even a work you think you understand already. Whenever possible, reread any work that you are planning to write about. If its length makes doing so not feasible, at least reread the chapters or scenes that impressed you as especially important or problematic.

If you have a tentative thesis, rereading a work will help you find the evidence you need to support it. You are likely to find evidence that you did not notice on your first reading or that will require you to modify your thesis. To establish yourself as a credible source (**35d**), use evidence appropriate for your purpose (**35c**) and present it fairly.

A good way to note evidence, ideas, and concerns is to annotate as you read. Because experienced readers are actively engaged with their reading, they often keep a pen or pencil at hand so they can mark passages they may wish to study, ask about, or draw on when writing.

(e) Do research when appropriate.

Both writers and readers often favor papers that are focused on a person's individual response, analysis, interpretation, or evaluation. But by reading criticism that reveals what other readers think of a given literary work, you can engage in a dialogue. When you draw on the ideas of other people, however, remember that you must use those sources responsibly (**37g**), and that even when you incorporate them you must still advance a position that is clearly your own. Few readers enjoy papers that offer little more than a collection of quotations.

When you read criticism, remember that a work of literature rarely has a single meaning. Three different critics may offer three radically different interpretations. Your responsibility is not to determine who is right but to determine the extent to which you agree or disagree with the differing views you encounter. Read critically (chapter **35**) and formulate your own thesis (**32d**).

Chapter **37** explains how to do research. To locate material on a specific writer or work, consult your library's catalog (**37c**) and the *MLA Bibliography,* an index of books and articles about literature. Like most indexes to special interest periodicals (p. 451), the *MLA Bibliography* can be consulted in printed volumes, through an on-line database search, or through access to a CD-ROM disk covering several years.

You may also locate useful information in the following reference books:

Cambridge History of English Literature. 15 vols. Cambridge: Cambridge UP, 1907–33.

Davidson, Cathy N., et al., eds. *The Oxford Companion to Women's Writing in the United States.* New York: Oxford UP, 1995.

Drabble, Margaret, ed. *The Oxford Companion to English Literature.* 6th ed. New York: Oxford UP, 1996.

Elder, John, ed. *American Nature Writers.* 2 vols. New York: Scribner's, 1996.

Elliott, Emory, et al., eds. *Columbia Literary History of the United States.* New York: Columbia UP, 1988.

Evory, Ann, et al., eds. *Contemporary Authors.* New Revision Series. Detroit: Gale, 1981–.

Hart, James D., ed. *The Oxford Companion to American Literature.* 6th ed. New York: Oxford UP, 1995.

Hazen, Edith P., ed. *The Columbia Granger's Index to Poetry*. 10th ed. New York: Columbia UP, 1993.

Holman, C. Hugh, and William Harmon, eds. *Handbook to Literature*. 7th ed. New York: Macmillan, 1995.

Howatson, M.C., ed. *The Oxford Companion to Classical Literature*. 2nd ed. New York: Oxford UP, 1989.

Klein, Leonard. *Encyclopedia of World Literature in the 20th Century*. 2nd ed. 5 vols. New York: Ungar, 1981–84.

Levernier, James A., and Douglas R. Wilms, eds. *American Writers Before 1800*. 3 vols. Westport: Greenwood, 1983.

New Cambridge Bibliography of English Literature. 5 vols. Cambridge: Cambridge UP, 1969–77.

Preminger, Alex, et al., eds. *The Princeton Handbook of Poetic Terms*. Princeton: Princeton UP, 1986.

For an example of a paper that incorporates research about literature, see the essay by Susan Schubring (beginning on page 610).

CAUTION Research is not appropriate for all assignments. Your instructor may want only your own response or interpretation. If your instructor has not assigned a researched paper, ask if one would be acceptable.

(2) Write essays about fiction.

Although the events have not happened and the characters may never have existed, serious fiction expresses truth about the human condition through such components as **setting, character,** and **plot.** In "Lullaby" (1979), Leslie Silko tells the story of a Navajo family headed by an old woman named Ayah and her crippled husband, Chato. Moving between the present and the past, Silko reveals that they have lost their three children. The oldest, Jimmie, died in a helicopter crash while serving in the army; the younger two, Danny and Ella, have been taken away by the state. At the end of the story, Ayah decides to freeze to death with her husband after they have been walking home from town, where Chato has been drinking. Here is an excerpt from the conclusion:

> He was walking along the pavement when she found him. He did not stop or turn around when he heard her behind him. She walked beside him and she noticed how slowly he moved now. He smelled strong of woodsmoke and urine. Lately he had been forgetting. Sometimes he called her by his sister's name and she had been gone for a long time. Once she had found him wandering on the road to the white man's ranch, and she asked him why he was going that way; he laughed at her and said, "You know they can't run that ranch without me," and he walked on determined, limping on the leg that had been crushed many years before. Now he looked at her curiously, as if for the first time, but he kept shuffling along, moving slowly along the side of the highway. His gray hair had grown long and spread out on the shoulders of the long overcoat. He wore the old felt hat pulled down over his ears. His boots were worn out at the toes and he had stuffed pieces of an old red shirt in the holes. The rags made his feet look like little animals up to their ears in snow. She laughed at his feet; the snow muffled the sound of her laugh. He stopped and looked at her again. The wind had quit blowing and the snow was falling straight down; the southeast sky was beginning to clear and Ayah could see a star.
>
> "Let's rest awhile," she said to him. They walked away from the road and up the slope to the giant boulders that had tumbled down from the red sandrock mesa throughout the centuries of rainstorms and earth tremors. In a place where the boulders shut out the wind, they sat down with their backs against the rock. She offered half of the blanket to him and they sat wrapped together.
>
> The storm passed swiftly. The clouds moved east. They were massive and full, crowding together across the sky. She watched them with the feeling of horses—steely blue-gray

horses startled across the sky. The powerful haunches pushed into the distances and the tail hairs streamed white mist behind them. The sky cleared. Ayah saw that there was nothing between her and the stars. The light was crystalline. There was no shimmer, no distortion through earth haze. She breathed the clarity of the night sky; she smelled the purity of the half moon and the stars. He was lying on his side with his knees pulled up near his belly for warmth. His eyes were closed now, and in the light from the stars and the moon, he looked young again.

She could see it descend out of the night sky: an icy stillness from the edge of the thin moon. She recognized the freezing. It came gradually, sinking snowflake by snowflake until the crust was heavy and deep. It had the strength of the stars in Orion, and its journey was endless. Ayah knew that with the wine he would sleep. He would not feel it. She tucked the blanket around him, remembering how it was when Ella had been with her; and she felt the rush so big inside her heart for the babies. And she sang the only song she knew to sing for babies. She could not remember if she had ever sung it to her children, but she knew that her grandmother had sung it and her mother had sung it.

Setting **Setting** involves time—not only historical time, but also the length of time covered by the action. It also involves place—not only the physical setting, but also the atmosphere created by the author. The time sequence in "Lullaby" is in one sense brief: The story begins and ends on the same day. But within this day, Ayah remembers experiences that she had throughout her life, ultimately making the time sequence several decades. The physical setting is the countryside near Cebolleta, a small town in the American Southwest. The contrast between the town and the open countryside complements the conflict of cultures within the story.

Plot The sequence of events that make up the story is the **plot**. Unlike a narrative, which simply reports events, a plot establishes how events relate to one another. Narrative asks "What comes next?"; plot asks "Why?" For example:

Narrative	The king died, and the queen died.
Plot	The queen died because the king died.

Depending on the author's purpose, a work of fiction may have a complicated plot or almost no plot at all. The plot of "Lullaby" is fairly simple. After years of loss, drought, and racism, a Navajo woman and her husband freeze to death. This plot reveals the conflict between cultures that the story is designed to convey.

Characters The **characters** carry the plot forward and usually include a main character, called a **protagonist**, who is in conflict with another character, with an institution, or with himself or herself. In "Lullaby," Ayah is the protagonist. She is in conflict to a degree with her husband, but more important, she is in conflict with the Anglo culture into which her husband has unsuccessfully tried to integrate. By examining a character's conflict, you can often discover a story's **theme**.

Point of view The position from which the action is observed—the person through whose eyes the events are seen—is the **point of view**. It may be that of a single character within the story or of a narrator who tells the story. Many works of fiction are told from a single point of view, but some shift the point of view from one character to another. "Lullaby" is told from Ayah's point of view. We know her thoughts throughout the story but not those of other characters. In this case, the narrator is **partially omniscient**—that is, partially all-knowing. A narrator who knows the thoughts of all characters is **omniscient**. A story told by a character who refers to herself or himself as "I" employs the **first-person** point of view. (Do not confuse this character with the author.) When the narrator does not reveal the thoughts of any character, the story is being told from the **dramatic** or **objective** point of view.

Tone Conveyed by point of view—as well as by diction and sentence structure—**tone** is the author's attitude toward the events and characters in the story or even, in some circumstances, toward the readers. The tone of the narrator in "Lullaby" is somber and respectful, helping to establish sympathy for Ayah and her husband. Another story could have an ironic, humorous, wry, or bitter tone. By determining a work's tone and the impact it has on you as a reader, you can gain insight into the author's purpose. (See 33a.)

Symbolism A common characteristic of fiction, **symbolism** is also used in drama and poetry. A **symbol** is an object, usually concrete, that stands for something else, usually abstract. On one level, it is what it is; on another level, it is more than what it is. In writing about a particular symbol, first note the context in which it appears. Then think about what it could mean. When you have an idea, trace the incidents in the story that reinforce that idea. According to the paper by Tom Villalta, Jimmie's blanket in "Lullaby" symbolizes "how little government aid benefits Native Americans." It could also be said to symbolize the love Ayah had for the son who had used the blanket.

Theme The main idea of a literary work is its **theme.** Depending on how they interpret a work, different readers may identify different themes. To test whether the idea you have identified is central to the work in question, check to see if it is supported by the **setting, plot, characterization,**

tone, and **symbols**. If you can relate these components to the idea you are exploring, then that idea can be considered the work's theme. In his paper on "Lullaby," Tom Villalta argues that the story's theme is that Native American culture has been damaged by the American government.

As you read and write, ask yourself the following questions:

Checklist for Analyzing Fiction ✓

- From whose point of view is the story told?
- What is the narrator's tone?
- Who is the protagonist? How is his or her character developed?
- With whom or what is the protagonist in conflict?
- How does one character compare with another?
- What symbols does the author use?
- What is the theme?
- How does the author use setting, plot, characters, and symbolism to support the theme?

Sample student paper about fiction

In the following paper, a student interprets "Lullaby," identifying what he believes the theme to be and arguing on behalf of his interpretation. His assignment was as follows:

> Reread "Lullaby" and look for conflicts within the story. Decide which of these conflicts is, in your opinion, the most important. Write an essay of approximately four pages in which you (a) describe that conflict, (b) determine whether the story leads you to sympathize with either side of that conflict, and (c) explore why this conflict is worth reading about. Be sure to support your interpretation with evidence from the story.

Villalta 1

Tom Villalta
Professor Miller
English 195, Section 1
12 March 1997

Killing with Kindness

1 Leslie Marmon Silko's short story "Lullaby" explores the loss of Native American culture as a majority culture halfheartedly tries to compensate Native Americans for the injustice they have suffered in the past. If we examine the losses Native Americans experience and compare them with the "benefits" Ayah and her family receive, be they medical, financial, or educational, we find that Native Americans are still being exploited.

2 We are introduced to Ayah's losses in the very beginning of the story when we first glimpse the deep scar that her son's death has left on her. We learn that "she did not want to think about Jimmie. So she thought about the weaving and the way her mother had done it" (43). This passage suggests that thinking of her son still hurts her. It also suggests that the culture she turns to for comfort has already been supplanted: traditional weaving is something to be remembered from the past rather than practiced in the present. Ayah is left with Jimmie's old army blanket to keep her warm; she no longer has a family to comfort her or the skill to weave new blankets.

3 Like the loss of Jimmie in a foreign war, Ayah's other losses are either directly or

Villalta 2

indirectly associated with the American government. For many years, government policies were shaped by the belief that the melting of minority cultures into the majority culture benefited minority cultures. Access to the majority culture's medicine, money, and language was expected to benefit minorities. But Ayah is a victim of such aid.

We get a clear indication of this 4
victimization when Ayah's children are taken away from her. While it would seem that the doctors came with good intentions, their methods of treatment conflict with Native American customs. Ayah states, "I want a medicine man first" (46). But she does not get a medicine man; she gets white doctors who come with their own kind of aid, using their own kind of means. It is also significant that the children's symptoms indicate that they have tuberculosis, an ailment Europeans brought to America. When the children are allowed home for a brief visit, Danny has lost the ability to speak Navajo easily, and Ella no longer remembers her mother.

Ayah is thinking about her lost children 5
at the end of the story, as she is preparing for her own death, the ultimate loss she will experience. Silko writes that Ayah "felt the rush so big inside her heart for the babies" (51). This memory signifies the importance they had in her life and reinforces the dramatic effect the white man's actions had on her. Trying to help according to their own

values, the white doctors had, in effect, stolen Ayah's children.

6 Welfare subsidies also illustrate how attempts at compensation have contributed to the Native Americans' plight. Ayah's apparent desire to distance herself from government aid is an indication that she prefers to live within her own culture, untouched by the potentially addictive compensation society gives to Native Americans. The story made me feel that contact with money, the most basic and versatile of American gifts, hurts Native Americans rather than helps them. Welfare money buys material goods, and it is these goods that are destroying Ayah's husband and the culture to which he belongs. Conveying Ayah's point of view, the narrator notes, "if the money and the wine were gone, she would be relieved because then they could go home again" (49). Ayah is not angry with her husband for spending the money; she just wants to be through with it. It means nothing to her. Ayah's attitude when accepting the money reinforces her apparent disdain for financial compensation. She does not tell us that the family needs the money every month, but that they went to get the money "because it was time to do this" (50). In this statement, she cites habit as the compelling force in getting the money rather than need or desire for it.

7 Chato, Ayah's husband, exemplifies what trusting the dominant society can do to Native Americans. Chato has tried to integrate

Villalta 4

himself into American society by becoming educated in both English and Spanish. But the story shows that learning the language of a majority culture can be dangerous. Chato teaches his wife how to sign her name, and Ayah's signature leads directly to the loss of her children. Ayah reflects that "it was like the old ones always told her about learning their language or any of their ways: it endangered you" (47). She notes that Chato is "a stranger"; he has tried too hard to melt into a society that is unwilling to accept him. His reward is the loss of a leg, the loss of his job, the loss of his dignity, and eventually the loss of his life.

In the end, when Ayah "tucked the blanket around him" (50), it was clear to me that both Ayah and her husband would die: "Ayah knew that with the wine he would sleep. He would not feel it" (51). The blanket, a symbol of how little government aid benefits Native Americans, will not save them from freezing to death. The medical, financial, and educational benefits all seem, in Ayah's case, to be equally useless. They are misdirected and incorrectly prescribed solutions to problems created over many centuries. Just like Jimmie's blanket, they cover serious problems with unwanted material goods. The result in "Lullaby" is death--the death of three Native Americans, and, perhaps, the culture they represent. 8

Villalta 5

Work Cited

Silko, Leslie. "Lullaby." Storyteller. New York: Seaver, 1981. 43-51.

In this paper, Tom Villalta argues that the theme of "Lullaby" is that Native Americans have been exploited and their culture threatened. This thesis is first introduced at the end of paragraph 1 and is restated in the second half of paragraph 8. The second sentence of the opening paragraph establishes the basic structure of the essay: A discussion of losses leads to a discussion of benefits. The reference in paragraph 1 to medical, financial, and educational benefits prepares readers for a discussion of each, and this expectation is fulfilled in paragraphs 4 through 7. And at the end of paragraph 7, Villalta returns to the idea of loss, as he prepares for a conclusion that links loss to benefits on the grounds that the benefits have contributed to the loss.

Exercise 1

Write an outline for this paper. Compare your outline with the assignment given on page 591. Write a comment of approximately one hundred words in which you evaluate how successfully the paper fulfills the assignment. Imagine that the author of this paper will read your comment. Try to be specific and helpful.

Exercise 2

In consultation with your instructor, choose a short story other than "Lullaby" and complete the assignment on page 591.

(3) Write essays about drama.

Although it is written to be filmed or performed on a stage, drama can also be read, which is probably the way you will encounter it in your course work. In a performance, the director and the actors imprint the play with their own interpretations; in a book or script, you have only the printed word and the imagination you bring to it. Drama has many of the same elements as fiction, but they are presented differently.

Dialogue **Dialogue** is the principal medium through which we see action and characterization when reading a play. Examine dialogue to discover motives, internal conflicts, and relationships among characters.

Characters Often identified briefly in a list at the beginning of the play, the **characters** are developed largely through what they say and what is said about them and to them. In Ibsen's *A Doll's House,* for example, Nora's development can be traced through her gestures and her speech. The play opens with her reciting lines like "Me? Oh, pooh, I don't want anything." It concludes with her deciding to leave her husband and declaring, "I must educate myself." In writing about drama, you might compare characters or analyze their development and its significance through their dialogue and their actions.

Plot **Plot** in drama is similar to plot in fiction and is usually advanced by conflict between characters. Although there may be time lapses between scenes, the story line must be developed within the place constraints of the play. **Subplots** similar to the one outlined in the sample student paper that follows may reinforce the theme of the main plot.

You might examine in a paper how dialogue, characterizations, setting, and stage directions for gestures and movement further the action.

As you read and write, ask yourself the following questions:

Checklist for Analyzing Drama

- How are the characters depicted through dialogue?
- What is the primary conflict within the play?
- What motivates the characters to act as they do?
- Are there any parallels between different characters?
- How does setting contribute to the play's action?
- What is the theme of the play?
- If there is more than one story in the play, how do they relate to one another?

Sample student paper about drama

The following student paper discusses the significance of the subplot in *King Lear*. The writer chose to respond to the following question:

> Does the conflict between Edmund and Gloucester contribute to the meaning you find in *King Lear*, or is this conflict an unnecessary distraction from the main action of the play?

Ferk 1

Susan K. Ferk
Professor Dorgan
English 211
10 April 1997

The Subplot as Commentary in King Lear

To a careless eye, the subplot involving Gloucester, Edgar, and Edmund in Shakespeare's King Lear may appear to be trivial, unnecessary, and a simple restatement of the theme of the main story. On close examination, however, it is clear that Shakespeare has skillfully introduced a second set of characters whose actions comment on and intensify the main plot and theme. 1

The first scene of King Lear sets up comparison and contrast between Lear and Gloucester. Gloucester jokes about his bastard son while Lear angrily banishes his favorite daughter. By the end of the second scene, we realize how important their children are to both men and yet how little they really know them. Both are easily deceived: Lear by Goneril and Regan, who convince him of their love with flowery words, and Gloucester, who is convinced by very little evidence of Edgar's plot against his life. The audience is set up to accept Lear and Gloucester as old fools. Neither takes responsibility for what has happened. Gloucester says "these late eclipses" (1.2.96) have brought about these changes, and Lear blames Cordelia for her losses. Neither realizes or acknowledges that his own foolishness has brought about these events. 2

Ferk 2

3 Gloucester, however, does comment on Lear's actions in scene 2. He is amazed that the king has limited his power so suddenly. When Edmund suggests that "sons at perfect age, and fathers declined, the father / should be as ward to the son, and the son manage his / revenue" (1.2.68–70), Gloucester is enraged by what he thinks are Edgar's words. He calls Edgar unnatural, and since this is exactly the action taken by Lear with his daughters, we can assume that he thinks Lear's act was unnatural also.

4 At Goneril's palace Lear foreshadows Gloucester's fate when he says "Old fond eyes, / beweep this cause again, I'll pluck ye out" (1.4.278–79). In the same way that Lear fears for his eyes because of Goneril, so does Gloucester lose his eyes because of Edmund. At the end of act 1, Lear foreshadows his own destiny, "Oh, let me not be mad, not mad, sweet heaven!" (1.5.38).

5 Shakespeare brings together the two plots in act 2 scene 2 when Regan, Cornwall, Gloucester, and Edmund meet at Gloucester's castle. Cornwall's offer of employment to Edmund, made on the pretense of his royal service, seems logical to the members of the audience, who know the similarity of their true natures. It is interesting to note that Gloucester calls Edmund his "loyal and natural boy" (2.1.85), while Lear names Goneril a "degenerate bastard" (1.4.230).

6 Lear arrives at the castle and is outraged when Cornwall and Regan do not meet

him. However, Lear decides that perhaps
Cornwall is ill and unable to come. Likewise,
throughout the remainder of act 2 Lear tries
to imagine that Regan and Cornwall love and
respect him, and he makes excuses for them
when their actions do not conform to his
expectations. Lear has more at stake here than
Regan's love. If she proves as evil as Goneril
(and she proves even more so), then Lear
cannot deny that he was wrong in supposing
these two daughters more loving than his
banished Cordelia. Lear soon acknowledges that
the disease of his daughters is in his own
blood. The realization of his errors and his
loss of power and Cordelia drive him to the
madness seen in act 3.

Gloucester and Lear meet in scene 4 of 7
act 3 in the midst of a raging storm, Lear's
madness, and Gloucester's despair. Gloucester
has not suffered the worst, but his words
begin to echo those of Lear in earlier scenes.
He says, "Thou sayest the King grows mad: I'll
tell thee, friend, / I am almost mad myself"
(152-53). Gloucester helps the king into the
hovel and cares for him like a child, similar
to the way Edgar later helps Gloucester after
his eyes are plucked out.

Death begins in act 3 scene 7. A servant 8
dies defending Gloucester, and Cornwall is
fatally wounded. In the confusion, Gloucester
realizes his mistakes and his former
blindness. After losing his sight, he can now
see. When he is turned out, his wanderings in
the country remind us of Lear in the storm.

Ferk 4

Likewise, in his despair, Lear has learned to see.

9 Gloucester and Lear share many similarities at this point. Both men at the height of their afflictions desire the company of Tom o'Bedlam, who represents wisdom. They also acquire a sense of justice and care for less fortunate men. Lear looks after his fool in the storm, and Gloucester calls for clothes for Tom. Their similarities intensify the pain and change in each man. Also, Shakespeare's use of a king and a nobleman both suffering from their foolishness emphasizes the universality of man's suffering. On the other hand, they do not suffer in the same way. Gloucester does not lose his mind, and Lear does not try suicide.

10 In the end, the story comes full circle. Edgar tells Gloucester his identity and asks his father's forgiveness, thus causing Gloucester's heart to break "Twixt two extremes of passion, joy and grief" (5.3.202). Lear also dies, with Cordelia in his arms, trying so hard to believe her alive that it strains his heart as well. These men have learned much, but as in real life, wisdom in old age and recognizing one's children for what they are do not always bring peace and happiness. The dismal final scenes of this play, in which almost everyone dies, serve to emphasize Shakespeare's intent to show two unfortunate characters who suffer from foolishness and Fortune's wheel.

Ferk 5

Work Cited

Shakespeare, William. The Tragedy of King Lear. The HBJ Anthology of Drama. Ed. W. B. Worthen. Ft. Worth: Harcourt, 1993. 174-214.

Susan Ferk supports her thesis by comparing and contrasting the characters of Lear and Gloucester as they move through the play. In act 1, the plots are separate, but she points out how they move together in act 2 and proceed along parallel lines, crossing only occasionally. She traces this progression throughout the play, following the characters' actions and dialogue while emphasizing the significance of each plot in reinforcing and intensifying the other.

Exercise 3

Select a recent film or television drama. Write a short essay in which you identify the theme and show how the actions of the characters reveal that theme.

(4) Write essays about poetry.

Poetry shares many of the components of fiction and drama. It too may contain a narrator with a point of view, and dramatic monologues and narrative poems may have plot, setting, and characters. But poetry is primarily characterized by its concentrated use of connotative **diction, imagery, allusions, figures of speech, symbols, sound**, and **rhythm**. Before starting to write a paper about a poem, try to capture the literal meaning of the poem in a sentence or two; then analyze how the poet transfers that meaning to you through the use of the following devices.

Speaker The first-person *I* in a poem is not necessarily the poet. It may be a character, or **persona**, that the poet has created to speak the words. In some poems, such as Robert Frost's "Home Burial," there may be more than one speaker. Although there are times when the poet may be the speaker, you often need to distinguish between the two when writing about poetry.

Diction The term **diction** means "choice of words," and the words in poetry convey meanings beyond the obvious denotative ones. (See 20a(2).) As you read, check definitions and derivations of key words in your dictionary to find meanings beyond the obvious ones. How do such definitions and derivations reinforce the meaning of the poem? How do the connotations of these words contribute to the poem's meaning?

Imagery The **imagery** in a poem is a word or phrase describing a sensory experience. Notice the images in the following lines from the poem "Meeting at Night," by Robert Browning, about a lover journeying to meet his sweetheart.

> Then a mile of warm sea-scented beach;
> Three fields to cross till a farm appears;
> A tap at the pane, the quick sharp scratch
> And a blue spurt of a lighted match,
> And a voice less loud, through its joys and fears,
> Than the two hearts beating each to each!

The feeling, the smell, and the sound of the beach; the sounds of the tap at the window, the scratch of a match being lighted, the whispers, and the hearts beating; and the sight of the two lovers in the match light, embracing—all are images conveying the excitement and anticipation of lovers meeting in secret.

Allusion An **allusion** is a brief, unexplained reference to a work or a person, place, event, or thing (real or imaginary) that serves to convey meaning compactly. Writing about the way she came to see her father, Sylvia Plath describes him in "Daddy" as "A man in black with a Meinkampf look. . . ." *Mein Kampf,* German for "my struggle" is the title of Hitler's political manifesto. Although Plath does not directly compare her father to Hitler, she links the two by making an allusion.

Paradox A **paradox** is a seemingly contradictory statement that makes sense when thoughtfully considered. In a poem about searching for religious salvation, John Donne writes, "That I may rise and stand, o'erthrow me. . . ." At first glance, the wish to be overthrown seems to contradict the desire to "rise and stand." On reflection, however, the line makes sense: The speaker believes that he will rise spiritually only after he has been overwhelmed by the God he is addressing.

Personification The attribution to objects, animals, and ideas of characteristics possessed only by humans is called **personification**. In the following lines, Emily Dickinson personifies death, portraying it as a man driving a carriage.

> Because I could not stop for Death—
> He kindly stopped for me—
> The Carriage held but just Ourselves—
> And Immortality.

Simile A **simile** is a comparison using *like* or *as* to link dissimilar things. (See 20a(4).)

> You fit into me
> like a hook into an eye
> a fish hook
> an open eye

In these lines, Margaret Atwood uses sewing and fishing items to describe a disturbing personal relationship.

Metaphor A comparison that does not use *like* or *as,* **metaphor** is one of the figures of speech most frequently used by poets. (See 20a(4).) In the following example from "Walking Our Boundaries," Audre Lorde uses a metaphor to describe how it feels to wait for a lover's touch.

> my shoulders are
> dead leaves
> waiting to be burned to life.

Overstatement Also called **hyperbole, overstatement** is a deliberate exaggeration used for ironic or humorous effect. In "To His Coy Mistress" by Andrew Marvell, the speaker describes how much time he would invest in courting the woman he admires if life were not so short.

> An hundred years should go to praise
> Thine eyes, and on thy forehead gaze;
> Two hundred to adore each breast,
> But thirty thousand to the rest.

Understatement Like **overstatement, understatement** is used for ironic or humorous effect. In this case, however, a serious matter is treated as if it were a small concern. Writing in "Musée des Beaux Arts" about indifference to human suffering, W. H. Auden describes a painting in which a boy with wings is falling from the sky.

> In Breughel's *Icarus*, for instance: how everything turns away
> Quite leisurely from the disaster; the ploughman may
> Have heard the splash, the forsaken cry,
> But for him it was not an important failure; the sun shone
> As it had to on the white legs disappearing into the green
> Water; and the expensive delicate ship that must have seen
> Something amazing, a boy falling out of the sky,
> Had somewhere to get to and sailed calmly on.

Sound **Sound** is an important element of poetry. **Alliteration** is the repetition of initial consonants, **assonance** is the repetition of vowel sounds in a succession of words, and **rhyme** is the repetition of similar sounds either at the end of lines (end rhyme) or within a line (internal rhyme). When you encounter such repetitions, examine and analyze their connection to each other and to the meaning of a line or a stanza or a poem. For instance, notice how the repetition of the *w* and the *s* sounds in the following lines from Elinor Wylie's "Velvet Shoes" sound like the soft whisper of walking in a snowstorm.

> Let us walk in the white snow
> In a soundless space;

Whenever possible, read poetry aloud so you can hear the sound of it.

Rhythm The regular occurrence of accent or stress that we hear in poetry is known as **rhythm**, and the rhythm is commonly arranged in patterns called **meters**. Such meters depend on the recurrence of stressed and unstressed syllables in units commonly called **feet**. The most common metrical foot in English is the **iambic**, which consists of an unstressed syllable followed by a stressed one (pr̆océed). A second common foot is the **trochaic**, a stressed syllable followed by an unstressed one (fíftў). Less common are the three-syllable **anapestic** (ŏvĕr-cóme) and the **dactylic** (párăgrăph). A series of feet make up a line to form a regular rhythm, as exemplified in the following lines from Coleridge's "Frost at Midnight."

> T̆he Fróst pĕrfórms ĭts sécr̆et mínĭstrý,
> Ŭnhélped bў ány wínd. T̆he ówlĕt's crý
> C̆ame lóud—ănd hárk, ăgáin! lóud ăs bĕfóre.

Note the changes in rhythm and their significance—the ways in which rhythm conveys meaning. The second line contains a **pause** (**caesura**), which is marked by the end of the sentence and which adds special emphasis to the intrusion of the owlet's cry.

When you study a poem, ask yourself the following questions:

Checklist for Analyzing Poetry ✓

- What words have strong connotations?
- What words have multiple meanings?
- What images convey sensation?
- What figures of speech does the poet use?
- How does the poet use sound, rhythm, and rhyme?
- What does the poem mean?
- How do the various elements of the poem combine to convey meaning?

An essay about poetry need not necessarily explore all of these questions, but considering them helps you understand what the poet has accomplished—important preparation for whatever the focus of your essay will be.

Sample student paper about poetry

The following student essay, which begins on page 610, is about "The Milk Bottle," a poem by Galway Kinnell. The assignment was as follows:

> Choose one of the poets we have discussed this semester; then go to the library and locate at least three articles about this poet. Write an essay of six to eight pages in which you analyze one of this poet's works and determine how your response fits within critical views of the poet's work. Use MLA style documentation.

Schubring 1

Susan Schubring
Professor Miller
English 103, Section 3
5 May 1997

The Thrill of Change

1 Galway Kinnell's poem "The Milk Bottle" is about the division between mind and body in humans, a division that pulls us in two directions at once. The body desires change and is happiest when it is flowing, unconsciously, with the universe. But the conscious mind fights change, knowing that change ultimately brings us closer to death, "Kinnell's principal theme for more than two decades" (Dickstein 12). Tragically, in this tug-of-war between desire and fear, the tug of fear is often stronger, producing a life-long resistance to change that can bring only unhappiness.

2 The entire poem takes place near a tide pool, where the speaker is closely observing the many creatures of the sea. One, a snail holding up its spiral shell, is moving slowly. Another, possibly a clam, is not moving at all, but "clamps / itself down to the stone" (4-5). A third creature, a sea anemone, is sucking at the speaker's finger, doing what it likes to do best: "eat / and flow" (8-9). As the speaker watches these sea creatures, he starts to see connections between them and humans.

3 According to Richard Calhoun, Kinnell often uses animals in his poetry to reveal "an unsuspected kinship" and suggest "a mythology

of the common fate of living things" (18). Kinnell himself has argued that

> The best poems are those in which you are not this or that person, but anyone, just a person. If you could go farther, you would no longer be a person but an animal. If you went farther still you would be the grass, eventually a stone. (*Walking* 23)

Stones seem so far removed from humans, 4
and yet in this poem the sea creatures "half made of stone" (10) tell our story. The speaker notes that we are like the creatures in that we both "thrill / to altered existences" (10-11)--we thrive on change. The similarity between us and them is further emphasized in a metaphor in which the human moving forward through life is like the snail moving through the tide pool. Caesura helps re-create the hesitant movement of the snail: "we ourselves, / who advance so far, then stop, then creep / a little, stop again . . ." (11-13).

The connection between the snail and the 5
human actually began back in the first lines of the poem when the speaker described the snail's shell as a "fortress foretelling / our tragedies" (3-4). Then in lines 13 through 17 the reader begins to understand what our tragedy is. Every breath we take is "the bright shell / of our life-wish encasing us" (14-15). What is our life-wish?--to be a part of the changing universe, to move forward, experiencing all that the world has to offer.

This is the body's unconscious desire, just as breathing is an unconscious act. But--and here is the tragedy--like the snail that hides under its shell when it sees danger, our conscious minds suddenly take over; we see how scary change can be, and we "gasp / it all back in" (15-16). Unlike the body, the mind is aware of time--the past and the future--and can see that "any time / would be OK / to go" (16-18). This phrase can be taken two ways. First, we are aware that each breath brings us closer to death and that we can die at any time. Second, it means that we have a concept of "future": there is plenty of time ahead, so why bother changing now? The result of this awareness of time is tragic: we stop moving, we resist change, we stop flowing with the universe--and in the process we stop being happy. Ironically, efforts to avoid death produce a stagnancy and a vague dissociation from nature that is a kind of living death.

6 The solution the speaker sees to this dilemma is to somehow "separate out / time from happiness" (23-24). Lovers seem to be able to do it. Most of the time lovers are unconsciously flowing with the wonderful feeling of being in love, but then they "wake up at night and see / they both are crying" (19-20). These words recall what critic Gary Blank has described as a "fitful wakening to mortality's finite character" (583): the lovers are suddenly aware that time changes everything--someday their love will end, through death or change of heart. But quickly

Schubring 4

they realize that it does not matter because "already / we will have lived forever" (21-22). They have separated out time from happiness. Their happiness now is so overwhelming that time means nothing.

In lines 25-28, the speaker wonders whether it is possible to do what the lovers have done, to somehow get rid of 7

> the molecules scattered throughout
> our flesh that remember, skim them
> off, throw them at non-conscious
> things, who may even crave them. . . .
> (25-28)

In this metaphor, memory is simply molecules on the surface of our bodies, easily scraped off and thrown away. Sounds simple enough--but is it possible?

In the very next line, we see that the answer is probably no. Ironically, even as the speaker is wishing we could get rid of our memory and our consciousness of time, he finds himself caught up in his own memory--a memory of "one certain / quart of milk" (29-30). He remembers back to his childhood in 1932, when the milkman set a bottle of milk on the doorstep, and he, just a child, brought it in the house. On one level, this is only a simple, sweet memory about the olden days, back when the milkman made daily deliveries and milk came in bottles. But there are clues that something more is going on here. Why, for instance, was the milk bottle brought in and "not ever set down" (37)? Certainly, if the milk bottle were simply a milk bottle, it 8

Schubring 5

would have been set down by now, after 30, 40, maybe 50 years have passed! Perhaps the "certain quart of milk" is a metaphor for a particular memory, clinking against other milk bottle memories in his mind. He has carried this memory in his mind for years like a milk bottle that was never set down.

9 But the milk bottle takes on another meaning as the poem continues. In lines 38-50, as the speaker stands by the tide pool, a sea eagle flying overhead "rings its glass voice" (39) and the reader is reminded again of the glass milk bottle. And then when the speaker talks of first dreams rising and flowing in waves, it is as if the dreams are milk flowing from that bottle after all these years. Milk, so pure and white, is a wonderful metaphor for dreams. It brings to mind mother's milk, a source of nourishment. But where are the dreams flowing?--"out there where there is nothing" (44). "Out there" is the future, and the future does not exist except in the mind. The speaker concludes that what is real is "the meantime" (50)--not the past or the future, but now. The meantime overflows with the abundance that life has to offer; it "streams and sparkles over everything" (52).

10 In the last lines the emphasis is again on change and on the continuous flow of the universe. It is interesting to note that the entire poem replicates the idea of the continuity of life. There are no stanza breaks; the poem just runs on and on without any stops--just as there is no stopping the flow of time and the changes it brings: the

Schubring 6

sea eagle will eventually "cry itself back down into the sea" (47) and die, as will the sea creatures, and we ourselves. The powerful love the young lovers feel will fade with time, or die. The milk of dreams stored in a bottle will spoil over time, and the old glass bottle will eventually "shatter . . . / in the decay of its music" (45-46). The cry of the eagle and the decaying music of the bottle create a mournful tone, a note of sadness, that one critic suggests comes from "our inability to do much but hold on for an instant and experience the passing" (Marusiak 357).

If humans are to escape the tragedy of letting the fears of our conscious minds take over and "gasp" at change, then we must become more like the "non-conscious" creatures of the sea. In many ways, when we were babies, before time wove all of its tangles in our minds, we were like the sea anemone in the beginning of the poem. As infants, Kinnell has said, we were "not yet divided into mind and body" and so we "felt joyous connection with the things around us" ("Poetry" 230). Unaware of the concept of past and future, babies are able to experience the fullness of "the meantime." They find complete happiness in sucking on a finger or drinking milk from their mother's breast. Like the sea anemone, a baby's primary concern is "to eat / and flow." 11

Kinnell challenges us, in "The Milk Bottle," to come to grips with the inevitability of change, the certainty of death--and then allow ourselves to flow, 12

Schubring 7

becoming part of the continuous life/death cycle of the planet. The division between mind and body, the pull between desire and fear, still exists. But we must make a choice: we can fight change every step of the way; we can be afraid of it and hide under our shells. Or we can "thrill" to change, swim in the overflowing sparkle of the meantime.

Schubring 8

Works Cited

Blank, Gary. Rev. of Mortal Acts, Mortal Words, by Galway Kinnell. Magill's Literary Annual: Books of 1980. Ed. Frank N. Magill. Englewood Cliffs: Salem P, 1981. 582-86.

Calhoun, Richard K. Galway Kinnell. New York: Twayne, 1992.

Dickstein, Morris. "Intact and Triumphant." Rev. of Selected Poems, by Galway Kinnell. The New York Times Book Review 19 Sep. 1982. 12+.

Kinnell, Galway. "The Milk Bottle." Mortal Acts, Mortal Words. Boston: Houghton, 1980. 67-68.

---. "Poetry, Personality, and Death." Field 4 (1971): 56-75. Rpt. in Claims for Poetry. Ed. Donald Hall. Ann Arbor: U of Michigan P, 1982. 219-37.

---. Walking down the Stairs: Selections from Interviews. Ann Arbor: U of Michigan P, 1978.

Marusiak, Joe. "Where We Might Meet Each Other: An Appreciation of Galway Kinnell and William Everson." The Literary Review 24 (1981): 355-70.

Exercise 4

Write a short explication of the following poem. Then locate two different discussions of it in the library or on the World Wide Web. Summarize these discussions and show how they relate to your own interpretation of the poem.

Sonnet 73

That time of year thou mayst in me behold
When yellow leaves, or none, or few, do hang
Upon those boughs which shake against the cold,
Bare ruined choirs, where late the sweet birds sang.
In me thou see'st the twilight of such day
As after sunset fadeth in the west;
Which by and by black night doth take away,
Death's second self, that seals up all in rest.
In me thou see'st the glowing of such fire,
That on the ashes of his youth doth lie,
As the deathbed whereon it must expire,
Consumed with that which it was nourished by.
This thou perceiv'st which makes thy love more strong,
To love that well which thou must leave ere long.

—WILLIAM SHAKESPEARE

(5) Use proper form in writing about literature.

Writing about literature follows certain special conventions.

Tense Use the present tense when discussing literature, since the author is communicating to a present reader at the present time. (See 7b.)

Sherwood Anderson lets the boy speak for himself.

Documentation When writing about a work from a book used in the course, you usually do not need to give the source and publication information for the book. However, you should indicate if you are using another edition or anthology. One way of doing so is to use the MLA form for works cited, as explained in section 38a, although in this case your bibliography might consist of only a single work. (See the examples on pages 596 and 603.)

An alternative way of providing this information is by acknowledging the first quotation in an explanatory note and then giving all subsequent references to the work in the body of the paper.

> [1]Tillie Olsen, "I Stand Here Ironing," Literature: Reading, Reacting, Writing, ed. Laurie Kirszner and Stephen Mandell, 3rd ed. (Fort Worth: Harcourt, 1997) 154. All subsequent references to this work will be by page number within the text.

If you use this note form, you may not need a works cited list to repeat the bibliographical information. Check with your instructor about the reference format he or she prefers.

Whichever format you use for providing the publication data for your source, you must indicate specific references whenever you quote a line or passage. References to short stories and novels are by page number; references to poetry are by line number; and references to plays are usually by act, scene, and line number. This information should be placed in the text in parentheses directly after the quotation, and the period or comma should follow the parentheses. (See 16e and 38a.)

Poetry For **poems** and **verse plays,** type quotations of three lines or less within your text and insert a slash (17h) with a space on each side to separate the lines.

> "Does the road wind uphill all the way?" / "Yes, to the very end"—Christina Rosetti opens her poem "Uphill" with this two-line question and answer.

Quotations of more than three lines should be indented one inch (or ten spaces) from the left margin, with double-spacing between lines. (See pages 167–68.)

Author references Use the full name in your first reference to the author of a work and only the last name in all subsequent references. Treat male and female authors alike: Dickens and Cather, not Dickens and Miss Cather.

39b Effective business communication is necessary in most professions.

Effective business communication requires a strong sense of audience (32a), an ability to write clearly and efficiently (chapter 21), and an understanding of business conventions. These conventions are changing as technology redefines the workplace. Thanks to fax machines and e-mail, for example, many business people find themselves writing more than ever. They also have to take responsibility for their own writing. Although there are still some executives who dictate a letter for someone else to edit and type, many more business people are expected to write for themselves. The computers on their desks provide instant access to a wide range of written communication.

(1) Use e-mail effectively in the workplace.

When first introduced, e-mail was perceived as a vehicle for fast communication that did not need to be as carefully written as a memo or a letter, and it is still perceived that way in academic and research environments where the use of the powerful but user-unfriendly UNIX and VAX systems can make editing difficult. The speed with which you can send an e-mail message continues to be one of its advantages, but businesses now generally use sophisticated messaging programs such as cc:Mail or Lotus Notes that make correcting typographical errors in messages easier and, therefore, as important as it would be in any business communication.

E-mail is, however, a less formal medium than the traditional business letter or memo, so you will need to balance its implicit informality with a businesslike attention to detail. Since most businesses are hierarchical, the tone (**33a**) of your e-mail should be suited to your own place in this hierarchy and the recipient's, that is, neither coldly formal nor overly familiar. Furthermore, in business, e-mail tends to be used for brief comments or requests and for social occasions (such as announcing a retirement party), whereas longer documents such as responses to reorganization plans and employee evaluations are generally still handled by letter or memo.

Be aware, also, that e-mail is not really private. Not only may your recipient keep your message in a file, print it out, or forward it to someone else, but it may remain on the company's main computer. Most businesses operate e-mail on their own networks, so the system administrator also has access to what you have written. Under these circumstances, you could be embarrassed or lose influence within your organization if your communication is poorly written. Present yourself well by reviewing every message to eliminate errors and inappropriate remarks.

Take care to spell your recipient's name correctly at the To: prompt, and be sure to enter an accurate and descriptive subject line. Busy people use the subject line to identify messages they need to respond to immediately, those they can safely postpone for a few hours, and those they can postpone indefinitely. Furthermore, many people find unnecessary e-mail inefficient and time-wasting. Send copies to anyone who is mentioned in your message or who has some other legitimate reason for being included, but do not send out copies of your messages indiscriminately. (See also 8.)

Checklist for Business E-mail ✓

- Is my tone appropriate for my audience and occasion? Have I refrained from using sarcasm or irony? If I have used humor, can I be sure that it will be understood?
- Do I sound like the kind of person I want or need to be while at work? Am I signaling that I am competent and resourceful, helpful and accommodating?
- Is my content clear, concise, focused, and accurate? Have I made any statements or errors that would embarrass me if copies of this message were distributed elsewhere?
- Does my subject line describe the content of my message?
- If I need a response, have I established the kind of response I need and when I need it?
- Have I sent copies to everyone who should receive one? To anyone who need not?
- Am I respecting the privacy of others or am I forwarding a personal message without permission?
- Have I respected copyright law by crediting any quotations, references, and sources?

(2) Write effective memos.

Like e-mail, memos are used to communicate a variety of information within an organization. Although e-mail is ideal for sending brief announcements and requests for information, many business writers prefer the more formal memo when communicating detailed information such as policy directives, activity reports, and monthly action reports. While the length of the memo varies according to its purpose, the basic format is relatively standardized. A memo begins with essentially the same information provided by the message header of an e-mail. The person or persons to whom the memo is addressed appear in the first line, the person who wrote it in the second, the date in the third, and the subject in the fourth.

If the memo is long, it sometimes begins with a statement of purpose and then gives a summary of the discussion. This summary helps a manager or executive decide which memos to read carefully and which to skim. The discussion is the main part of the memo and may benefit from the use of headings to highlight key parts. If appropriate, the memo closes with recommendations for action to be taken. You should clearly state in this part of the memo who is to do what and when. In the following example, excerpted from a longer memo, you can see how the writer opens with a statement of purpose.

An example of memo format

To: Regional Sales Managers
From: Alicia Carroll, National Sales Director
Date: January 26, 1997
Re: Performance review

Now that we have final sales figures for 1996, it is clear that sales are growing in the South and West, but declining in the Northeast and Midwest. These results can be traced to numerous factors and should not be seen as a reflection of individual performance. Each of you will soon receive a confidential evaluation of your work. The purpose of this memo is to share information and to outline goals for the coming year.

(3) Write effective business letters.

Standard business stationery is 8½ × 11 inches for paper and 4 × 10 inches for envelopes. In the workplace, you usually use company letterhead that can be fed right into the office printer. If you are writing a business letter from home and do not have letterhead, use only one side of white, unlined paper. On occasion, a business writer may handwrite a short note—either to provide a quick cover letter for forwarded material or to signal a personal relationship. In most cases, however, business letters should be word processed or typed.

Check to see if your company or organization has a policy about letter format. Most companies use a block format for regular correspondence (see page 626), though an indented format is sometimes used for personal business correspondence such as thank-you notes, congratulations, and the like.

A business letter has six parts: (a) heading; (b) inside address; (c) salutation; (d) body; (e) closing, which consists of the complimentary close and signature; and (f) added notations.

The **heading** gives the writer's full address and the date. Depending on your format, place the date flush left, flush right, or centered just below the letterhead. On plain stationery, place the date below your address. Arrange the letter so that it will be attractively centered on the page—flush with the left-hand margin, as in the letter on page 626. Notice that the heading has no ending punctuation.

The **inside address**, placed two to six lines below the heading, gives the name and full address of the recipient. Use the postal abbreviation for the state name. (For a list of these, see **11b**.)

Place the **salutation** (or greeting) flush with the left margin, two spaces below the inside address, and follow it with a colon. When you know the surname of the addressee, use it in the salutation unless you are writing to someone who prefers to be addressed by first name. When writing to a woman, use Ms. unless this person has expressed a preference for Miss or Mrs. or can be addressed by her professional title.

Dear Ms. Samuelson: Dear Mayor Rodriquez:

Dear Dr. Gillespie: Dear Mr. Trudeau:

In letters to organizations or to persons whose name and gender you do not know, current styles recommend omitting the salutation or using the office or company name:

Dear Mobil Oil:

Dear Registrar:

For the appropriate forms of salutations and addresses in letters to government officials, military personnel, and so on check an etiquette book or the front or back of your dictionary.

In the **body** of the letter, single-space inside paragraphs and double-space between them. If you use a block format, do not indent the first line of each paragraph. If you use an indented format, indent first lines five to ten spaces.

Follow the principles of good writing. Organize information so the reader can grasp immediately what you want. Be clear and direct; do not use stilted or abbreviated phrasing:

Your letter
~~The aforementioned letter~~

as soon as possible
Please send this to me ~~ASAP.~~

The **closing** is double-spaced below the body. If your letter is in block style, type it flush with the left margin; if it is in indented style, align it with the heading. Use one of the complimentary closes common to business letters, such as the following:

Formal	**Less Formal**
Very truly yours,	Sincerely,
Sincerely yours,	Cordially,

Place your full name four lines below the closing and, if you are writing on company or organization business, your title on the next line.

Notations, placed flush with the left margin two lines below your title, indicate any materials you have enclosed with or attached to the letter (*enclosure* or *enc., attachment* or *att.*), who will receive copies of the letter (*cc: AAW, PTN* or *c: AAW, PTN*), and the initials of the sender and the typist (*DM/cll*).

Model business letter (block format)

LETTERHEAD CONTAINING RETURN ADDRESS

Willcox, Davern, and Smith

529 Lake Side Boulevard **Chicago, IL 60605** **312-863-8916**

September 1, 1997

Dr. Elizabeth Boroughs
Fairchild Clinic
1710 Sheridan Ave.
Lakewood, IL 60045

} INSIDE ADDRESS

Dear Dr. Boroughs: } SALUTATION

I have just given final approval to several organizational changes designed to ensure closer attention to the individual needs of our clients. Everyone here is excited about these changes, and I am writing to advise you of the one that will affect you most directly.

Effective the first of November, our certified public accountants will specialize in the areas in which they have the greatest expertise. Although we have always tried to direct clients to the accountant best suited to their needs, most staff members have had a diverse workload. This diversity worked well when the company was smaller, but it has become problematic during the past few years as we doubled the size of our staff in response to our growing list of clients.

- BODY

As you probably know, tax laws have changed considerably in recent years. The new codes are complex, and interpretation continues to evolve. Given the complexity of the codes, the importance of guiding clients through effective tax planning, and the availability of highly trained personnel, accountants in our company will henceforth work within one of three divisions: corporate, small business, and individual.

Richard Henderson, who has prepared your taxes for the past three years, will now be working exclusively with individual clients. I have reviewed your tax records with him, and we agree that Grace Yee, one of our new associates, will give the Fairchild Clinic the best help we can offer. Although she is new to our staff, she comes to us with twelve years of experience working mostly with medical groups.

You can expect to hear separately from both Rick and Grace, but I wanted to let you know myself that Willcox,

Davern, and Smith remains committed to serving you and your business.

Sincerely,	Complimentary Close	CLOSING
Ted Willcox	Signature	
Edward Willcox	Typed Name	
President	Title	

EW/nfd } NOTATION

(4) Write effective application letters.

Writing a letter of application is an essential step in applying for a job. This letter usually accompanies a résumé (39b(5)), and it should do more than simply repeat information that can be found there. Your letter provides you with the chance to sound articulate, interesting, and professional. Make the most of the opportunity.

Address your letter to a specific person. If you are responding to an advertisement that mentions a department without giving a name, call the company and find out who will be doing the screening. A misspelled name creates a bad impression, so make sure you spell that person's name correctly when you write.

In your opening paragraph, you should state the position you are applying for, how you learned about it, and—in a single sentence—why you believe you are qualified to fill it. Devote the paragraphs that follow to describing the experience that qualifies you for the job. If your experience is extensive, you can establish that fact and then focus on how you excelled in one or two specific situations. Mention that you are enclosing a résumé, but do not summarize it. Your goal is to get a busy person to read the résumé. Few people enjoy reading the same information twice.

In addition to stating your qualifications, you might also indicate why you are interested in this particular company. Demonstrating that you already know something about it will help you appear to be a serious candidate. Extensive information on most companies is available directly from them in their annual reports. You can also find information by searching a good newspaper index or the World Wide Web. (See page 465.)

In your closing paragraph, offer additional information and make a specific request. Instead of settling for "I hope to hear from you soon," tell your reader how and where you can be reached and also mention any relevant information about your schedule during the next few weeks. Then try to arrange for an interview. At the very least, indicate that you are available for an interview and would enjoy the opportunity to exchange information. Some writers also indicate that they will telephone on a particular date to see how their application is doing.

Assume that your audience is busy and that there are many applications. These assumptions make it important for you to be concise (chapter **21**). A good letter of application should run between one and two pages, depending on your experience. As you revise (**33b**), delete anything that is nonessential. To keep your letter to a single page, you may need to choose a smaller than usual font before you print it out—but make sure that the text is still easily readable.

Model application letter

431 Felton Ave.
St. Paul, MN 55102
April 5, 1997

Mr. Thomas Flanagan
Tristate Airlines
2546 Ashton Ave.
Bloomington, MN 55121

Dear Mr. Flanagan:

I am writing to apply for the position of Assistant Director of Employee Benefits in the Human Resources Department of Tristate, as advertised in this morning's Star Tribune. My education and experience are well suited to this position, and I'd welcome the chance to be part of a company that has shown so much growth during a period when other airlines have been operating at a loss.

As you can see from my résumé, I majored in Business Administration with an emphasis in human resources. Whenever possible, I have found campus activities and jobs that would give me experience in working with people. As an assistant in the Admissions Office at the University of Southern Minnesota, I worked successfully with students, parents, alumni, and faculty. The position required both a knowledge of university regulations and an understanding of people with different needs.

I also benefited from working as an administrative intern last summer in the personnel division of Central Bank & Trust, a department that handles the benefits for almost three thousand employees. Although banking may seem far removed from the airline industry, I learned procedures for monitoring benefits that are easily transferable. When I was working there, new computers were installed for the division, enabling us to use more powerful and comprehensive programs. Because I have extensive experience with computers, I was able to help other employees make the transition.

I am very much interested in putting my training to use at Tristate and hope that we can schedule an interview sometime during the next few weeks. I will be here in St. Paul until May 7, when I leave to spend a week visiting my family in Iowa (515-283-1652). If I haven't heard from you by then, I will telephone to see if the position is still available.

Sincerely,

Marcia Baumeister

Marcia Baumeister

enc.

(5) Write effective résumés.

A résumé is a list of a person's qualifications for a job and is enclosed with a letter of application. It is made up of four categories of information:

1. Personal data: name, mailing address, telephone number
2. Educational background
3. Work experience
4. References

Most businesses appreciate résumés that highlight your experience and abilities.

Make your résumé look professional. Like the letter of application, the résumé is a form of persuasion designed to emphasize your qualifications for a job and get you an interview. Since there is usually more than one applicant for every job, your résumé should make the most of your qualifications. If you keep your résumé in a computer file, you can easily tailor it to each job you apply for so you can present your qualifications in the best light. After reading all the letters and résumés received, a potential employer usually decides to interview only the most qualified candidates.

Writing a résumé requires the same planning and attention to detail as writing a paper. First, make a list of the jobs you have had, the activities and clubs you have been part of, and the offices you have held. Amplify these items by adding dates, job titles and responsibilities, and a brief statement about what you learned from each of them. Delete any items that seem too weak or tangential to be persuasive.

Résumés can be organized in a number of ways. One is to list experience and activities in reverse chronological order, so that your most recent experience comes first. This is a good plan if you have a steady job history, without gaps that are hard to explain, and if your most recent experience is worth emphasizing. If older experience is more directly relevant to the job for which you are applying, you can emphasize it by giving your work history chronologically. An alternative way to organize a résumé is to list experience in terms of job skills rather than jobs held. This plan is especially useful when your work history is modest but you know you have the skills for the job in question.

However you choose to organize your résumé, remember that presentation is important (chapter 8b). Your résumé is, in effect, going to someone's office for a kind of job interview, so make sure it is well dressed for the occasion. Use good-quality paper (preferably white or off-white) and a laser printer. Use boldface to mark divisions and experiment with different fonts. Although the design of your document should look professional, resist the impulse to create fancy letterhead or other design features that can make the overall effect too busy to be effective. When in doubt, choose simplicity. For sample résumés, see pages 635–37.

Checklist for Résumé Writing ✓

- Make sure to include your name, address, and telephone number; unless relevant to the job, leave out personal data such as age and marital status.
- Identify your career objective simply, without elaborating on future goals. Reserve a detailed discussion of your plans until asked about them during an interview (and even then make sure they enhance your appeal as a candidate). Your interest should be to match your qualifications to the employer's needs.
- Mention your degree, college or university, and pertinent areas of special training.

continued

continued from previous page

✓

- Even if an advertisement asks you to state a salary requirement, any mention of salary should usually be deferred until the interview.
- Whenever possible, make the relationship between jobs you have had and the job you are seeking clear.
- To show that you are an efficient, well-organized, thoughtful person, use a clean, clear format and make sure the résumé is neat, orderly, and correct.

For further information on application letters, résumés, and interviews, you may find it helpful to consult one of the following books.

Angel, Juvenal L. *The Complete Résumé Book and Job Getter's Guide.* 3rd ed. New York: Pocket, 1990.

Besson, Taunee. *Résumés.* 2nd ed. New York: Wiley, 1996.

Bolles, Richard N. *What Color Is Your Parachute? A Practical Manual for Job-Hunters and Career-Changers.* Berkeley: Ten Speed, annual.

Eyler, David R. *Job Interviews that Mean Business.* 2nd ed. New York: Random, 1996.

Ferris, Donna MacDougall. *The Practical Job-Search Guide.* Berkeley: Ten Speed, 1996.

Moreau, David. *Take Charge of Your Career.* Washington: Kiplinger, 1996.

Petras, Kathryn, and Ross Petras. *The Only Job Hunting Guide You'll Ever Need.* Rev. ed. New York: Simon, 1995.

Reed, Jean. *Résumés that Get Jobs.* 8th ed. New York: Simon, 1996.

Smith, Michael H. *The Résumé Writer's Handbook.* 3rd ed. New York: Harper, 1994.

Chronological résumé

Marcia Baumeister
431 Felton Ave.
St. Paul, MN 55102
(612) 228-1927

Career Objective: A management position specializing in the administration of employee benefits.

Work Experience:

Intern, Central Bank & Trust, June–August 1996.
Provided information to new employees, helped the personnel department get on-line with new information technology, and entered data for changes in medical benefits.

Student Assistant, Admissions Office, University of Southern Minnesota, January 1995–May 1997.
Responded to queries from parents and prospective students, conducted campus tours, planned orientation meetings, and wrote reports on recruitment efforts.

Tutor, University Writing Center, September 1994–May 1997.
Tutored students in business writing for six hours a week and worked as needed with other clients. Provided computer assistance, including ways to access information on the World Wide Web.

Education:

University of Southern Minnesota, B.S. with honors, 1997. Majored in Business Administration with an emphasis in human resources. Minors in Economics and

Communications. Recipient of the 1997 Grable Award for university service.

Active in Management Club, Yearbook, Alpha Phi Sorority

References available on request.

Emphatic résumé

MARCIA BAUMEISTER
431 Felton Ave.
St, Paul, MN 55102
(612) 228-1927

CAREER OBJECTIVE

A management position specializing in the administration of employee benefits

MANAGEMENT SKILLS

Familiarity with all contemporary models of effective management; good writing and communication skills; experience with planning and evaluating meetings; experience with programming and tracking information electronically; ability to teach computer skills.

PERSONNEL EXPERIENCE

Assisted in the transfer of data on medical benefits for approximately three thousand employees at Central Bank & Trust in St. Paul; provided benefit information to employees; worked with students, parents, and faculty at the University of Southern Minnesota as an information specialist with an emphasis on student benefits.

ADDITIONAL EXPERIENCE

Tutored students in writing, helped edit the yearbook, gave campus tours, and served as a liaison between my sorority and the university.

EDUCATION

University of Southern Minnesota, B.S. with honors, 1997. Majored in Business Administration with an emphasis in human resources. Minors in Economics and Communication. Recipient of the 1997 Grable Award for university service.

EXTRACURRICULAR

Active in Management Club, Yearbook, Alpha Phi Sorority

References available on request.

Exercise 5

Choose one of the following:

1. Write a letter to a former teacher to express appreciation for recommending you for a summer job.
2. In a letter, call the attention of your representative in city government to repairs needed on neighborhood streets.
3. Write a letter to an automobile company complaining about the performance of a car it manufactured.
4. Write a memo to the members of an organization you belong to recommending a change in procedures.
5. Prepare a résumé, and then write a letter of application for a position you are qualified to fill.

Glossary of Usage

The following short glossary covers the most common usage problems. It also distinguishes between written and spoken English and formal and informal styles. An expression that may be acceptable in spoken English or in a letter to a friend is labeled **informal** and is usually not acceptable in academic or business writing. Formal written style is sometimes referred to as "edited American English." The following are labels used in this glossary.

Formal	Words or phrases listed in dictionaries without special usage labels; appropriate in college writing.
Informal	Words or phrases that dictionaries label *informal, slang,* or *colloquial;* although often acceptable in spoken language, not generally appropriate in college writing.
Unacceptable	Words or phrases labeled in dictionaries as *archaic, illiterate, nonstandard, obsolete, substandard;* generally not accepted in formal or informal writing.

You may also wish to consult 18b for a list of words that sound alike but have different meanings.

a, an Use *a* before the sound of a consonant: **a** yard, **a** U-turn, **a** one-term president. Use *an* before a vowel sound: **an** empty can, **an** M.D., **an** ax, **an** X-ray.

accept, except *Accept* means "to receive"; *except* means "to exclude": I **accept** your apology. All **except** Joe will go.

accidently A misspelling of *accidentally.*

adapt, adopt *Adapt* means "to change for a purpose"; *adopt* means "to take possession": You must **adapt** to extreme cold. The company will **adopt** a new policy.

adverse, averse *Adverse* means "antagonistic" or "unfavorable"; *averse* means "opposed to": We would have gone had it not been for **adverse** weather conditions. After seeing the weather report, I was **averse** to going on the trip.

advice, advise *Advice* is a noun, and *advise* is a verb: I accept your **advice.** Please **advise** me of the situation.

affect, effect The verb *affect* means "to influence" or "to touch the emotions." The noun *effect* means "result of an action or antecedent": Smoking **affects** the heart. His tears **affected** her deeply. Drugs have side **effects.** The **effect** on sales was good. When used as a verb, *effect* means "to produce an effect": The medicine **effected** a complete cure.

aggravate Widely used for *annoy* or *irritate.* Many writers, however, restrict the meaning of *aggravate* to "intensify, make worse": Noises **aggravate** a headache.

ain't Unacceptable in writing unless used in dialogue or for humorous effect.

allusion, illusion An *allusion* is a casual or indirect reference. An *illusion* is a false idea or an unreal image: The **allusion** was to Shakespeare. His idea of college is an **illusion.**

alot A misspelling of the overused and nonspecific phrase *a lot.*

already, all ready *Already* means "before or by the time specified." *All ready* means "completely prepared."

alright Not yet a generally accepted spelling of *all right,* although it is becoming more common in journalistic and business writing.

altogether, all together *Altogether* means "wholly, thoroughly." *All together* means "in a group": That book is **altogether** too difficult, unless the class reads it **all together.**

a.m., p.m. (OR **A.M., P.M.**) Use only with figures: The show will begin at 7:00 **p.m.** OR at seven in the evening [NOT at seven in the *p.m.*]

among, between Prepositions with plural objects (including collective nouns). As a rule, use *among* with objects denoting three or more (a group), and use *between* with those denoting only two (or twos): danced **among** the flowers, whispering **among** themselves; reading **between** the lines, just **between** you and me.

amount of, number of Use *amount of* with a singular non-count noun: The **amount of** rain varies. Use *number of* with a plural count noun: The **number of** errors was excessive. See **number** and **1c(2)**.

and etc. *Etc.* is an abbreviation of the Latin *et* ("and") *cetera* ("other things"). Omit the redundant *and.* See also **etc.**

another, other *Another* is followed by a singular noun: **another** book. *Other* has no plural and is followed by a plural noun: **other** books.

ante, anti *Ante* is a prefix meaning "before," "in front of": **anteroom.** *Anti* is a prefix meaning "opposed to," "hostile": **antiwar.**

anxious Not to be used as a synonym for "eager."

anyone, any one; everyone, every one Distinguish between each one-word and two-word compound. *Anyone* means "any person at all"; *any one* refers to one of a group. Similarly, *everyone* means "all," and *every one* refers to each one in a group.

Was **anyone** hurt?	Was **any one** of you hurt?
Everyone should attend.	**Every one** of them should attend.

anyways, anywheres Unacceptable for *anyway, anywhere.*

apt, liable, likely *Apt* is generally accepted and now used interchangeably with *liable* and *likely* before an infinitive. *Liable* is generally limited to situations that have an undesirable outcome: He is not **likely** to get sick. He is **liable** to get sick. (See **liable, likely.**)

as 1. As a conjunction, use *as* to express sameness of degree, quantity, or manner: Do **as** I do. As a preposition, use *as* to express equivalence: I think of Tom **as** my brother [Tom = brother]. Use *like* to express similarity: Tom is **like** a brother.

2. Use *if, that,* or *whether* instead of *as* after such verbs as *feel, know, say,* or *see:* I do not know **if** [NOT as] my adviser is right.
3. In subordinate clauses, prefer *because* to introduce a causal relationship or *while* to introduce a time relationship: **Because** [NOT as] it was raining, we watched TV. **While** [NOT as] it was raining, we watched TV.

assure, ensure, insure *Assure* means "to state with confidence." *Ensure* and *insure* are sometimes used interchangeably to mean "make certain." *Insure* has the further meaning of "to protect against loss": Marlon **assured** me that he would vote for my ticket. I **ensured** (or **insured**) that Vincent had his tickets before I left home. Bing **insured** her car against theft.

as to Imprecise; use the clearer *about:* He wasn't certain **about** [NOT as to] the time.

awful Unacceptable for the often overused adverb *awfully:* She is **awfully** [NOT awful] intelligent.

awhile, a while *Awhile,* an adverb, is not used as the object of a preposition: We rested **awhile.** [COMPARE We rested for **a while.**]

bad Unacceptable as an adverb: Bill danced **badly** [NOT bad]. Acceptable as a subject complement after sense verbs such as *feel, look, smell.* See 4b.

because Unacceptable in the expression *is because,* since the *to be* form signifies equality between the subject and what follows. See 27.

being as, being that Wordy and imprecise; use *since, because.*

beside, besides Always a preposition, *beside* usually means "next to," sometimes "apart from": The chair was **beside** the table. As a preposition, *besides* means "in addition to" or "other than": She has many books **besides** those on the table. As an adverb, *besides* means "also" or "moreover": The library has a fine collection of books; **besides,** it has a number of valuable manuscripts.

better Unacceptable for *had better:* We **had better** [NOT better] run the spell check. See **had better.**

between See **among, between.**

biannual, biennial *Biannual* means twice in one year, while *biennial* means every two years.

bring, take Both words describe the same action but from different standpoints. Someone *brings* something *to* the speaker's location, while someone else *takes* something *away* from the speaker's location: **Bring** your book when you come here. I **take** my notes home with my book.

busted Unacceptable as the past tense of *burst.*

but what, but that Informal after expressions of doubt such as "no doubt" or "did not know." Use *that:* I do not doubt **that** [NOT but what] they are correct.

can, may *Can* refers to ability and *may* refers to permission: I **can** [am able to] drive fifty miles an hour, but I **may** not [am not permitted to] exceed the speed limit. Contemporary usage allows *can* and *may* denoting possibility or permission to be used interchangeably.

can't hardly, can't scarcely Unacceptable for *can hardly, can scarcely.*

capital, capitol A *capital* is a governing city; it also means "funds." As a modifier, *capital* means "chief" or "principal." A *capitol* is a statehouse; the *Capitol* is the U.S. congressional building in Washington, D.C.

censor, censure *Censor* (verb) means "to remove or suppress because of moral or otherwise objectionable ideas"; a *censor* (noun) is a person who suppresses those ideas. *Censure* (verb) means "to blame or criticize"; a *censure* (noun) is an expression of disapproval or blame.

center around Informal for *to be focused on* or for *to center on.*

chairman, chairperson, chair *Chairman* is misused as a generic term. *Chairperson* or *chair* is generally preferred as the generic term.

cite, site, sight *Cite* means "to mention." *Site* is a locale. *Sight* is a view or the ability to see: Be sure to **cite** your sources in your paper. The president visited the disaster **site.** What a tragic **sight!**

compare to, compare with *Compare to* means "regard as similar" and *compare with* means "examine to discover similarities or differences": The instructor **compared** the diagram **to** [NOT with] the finished product. The student **compared** the first draft **with** [NOT to] the second.

complement, compliment *Complement* means "to complete" or "to supply needs." *Compliment* means "to express praise." *Complimentary* means "given free," as in "**complimentary** tickets": Their personalities **complement** each other. Betsy **complimented** Jim on his performance.

continual, continuous *Continual* means recurring at regular intervals: He coughed **continually.** *Continuous* means recurring without interruption: He talked **continuously.**

different than, different from Both are widely used, although *different from* is generally preferred in formal writing.

disinterested, uninterested *Disinterested* means "impartial" or "lacking prejudice": a **disinterested** referee. *Uninterested* means "indifferent, lacking interest."

don't Unacceptable when used for "doesn't": My father **doesn't** [NOT don't] dance.

drug Unacceptable as the past tense of *dragged.*

due to Usually avoided in formal writing when used as a preposition in place of *because* or *on account of:* **Because of** [NOT due to] holiday traffic, we arrived an hour late.

effect See **affect, effect.**

e.g. Abbreviation from Latin *exempli gratia* meaning "for example." Replace with the English equivalent *for example* or *for instance.* Do not confuse with **i.e.**

elicit, illicit *Elicit* means "to draw forth." *Illicit* means "unlawful": It is **illicit** to **elicit** public funds for your private use.

emigrate from, immigrate to The prefix *e-* (a variant of *ex-*) means "out of." To *emigrate* is to go out of one's own country to settle in another. The prefix *im-* (a variant of *in-*) means "*into.*" To *immigrate* is to come into a different country to settle. The corresponding adjective or noun forms are *emigrant* and *immigrant:* The Ulster Scots **emigrated from** Scotland to Ireland and then **immigrated to** the southern United States. (COMPARE **export, import.**)

eminent, imminent *Eminent* means "distinguished"; *imminent* means "about to happen": Linda Hughes is an **eminent** scholar. The storm is **imminent.**

ensure See **assure, ensure, insure.**

enthused Informal usage, not accepted in formal writing. Use *enthusiastic.*

especially, specially *Especially* means "outstandingly"; *specially* means "for a particular purpose, specifically": This is an **especially** nice party. I bought this tape **specially** for the occasion.

-ess A female suffix now considered sexist, therefore unacceptable. Use *poet, author, actor,* and *waiter* or *server* instead of *poetess, authoress, actress,* and *waitress.*

etc. From the Latin *et cetera* meaning "and other things." In formal writing substitute *and so on* or *and so forth.* Since *etc.* means "and other things," *and etc.* is redundant.

everyone, every one See **anyone, any one.**

except See **accept, except.**

explicit, implicit *Explicit* means "expressed directly or precisely." *Implicit* means "implied or expressed indirectly": The instructions were **explicit.** There was an **implicit** suggestion in her lecture.

farther, further Generally, *farther* refers to geographic distance: six miles **farther.** *Further* is used as a synonym for *additional* in more abstract references: **further** delay, **further** proof.

fewer, less *Fewer* refers to people or objects that can be counted; *less* refers to amounts that can be observed or to abstract nouns: **fewer** pencils, **less** milk, **less** support.

figure Informal for *believe, think, conclude,* or *predict,* all of which are more precise.

folks Informal for *parents.*

former, latter *Former* refers to the first of two; *latter* to the second of two. If three or more items are mentioned, use *first* and *last:* Sean and Ian are both British; the **former** is from Northern Ireland, and the **latter** is from Scotland.

genus Singular form for *genera.* Takes a singular verb: The genus **is** . . . .

go, goes Inappropriate in written language for *say, says:* **I say** [NOT go], "Hello there!" Then he **says** [NOT goes], "Glad to see you!"

good, well *Good* is an adjective frequently misused as an adverb; *well* is an adverb: He dances **well** [NOT good]. He had a **good** time. *Well* in the sense of "in good health" may be used as a subject complement interchangeably with *good* in such expressions as "Pedro doesn't feel **well** (or **good**)."

great Overworked for more precise words such as *skillful, good, clever, enthusiastic,* or *very well.*

had better (meaning *ought to*) Do not omit the verb *had:* We **had better** go home.

had ought (meaning *ought to*) Omit the verb *had:* We **ought to** go home.

half a, a half, a half a Use *half of a, half a,* or *a half.*

hanged, hung *Hanged* refers specifically to "put to death by hanging": She was **hanged** at dawn. *Hung* is the usual past participle: He had **hung** the picture.

he Used inappropriately as a generic term that possibly could refer to a woman. See 6b, 19j.

heighth Unacceptable for *height.*

hisself Use *himself.*

hopefully Means "with hope." Used inappropriately for *I hope* or *it is hoped.*

i.e. Abbreviation for the Latin *id est,* meaning "that is." Use *that is* instead. Do not confuse *i.e.* with **e.g.**

if, whether Use *if* to mean *in the event that; whether* suggests alternatives. I can't go **if** you drive; **whether** I go depends on who is driving.

illusion See **allusion, illusion.**

imminent See **eminent, imminent.**

implicit See **explicit, implicit.**

imply, infer *Imply* means "suggest without actually stating," and *infer* means "draw a conclusion based on evidence": He **implied** that he was angry, but I **inferred** that he was satisfied.

incidently A misspelling of *incidentally.*

ingenious, ingenuous *Ingenious* means "creative or shrewd." *Ingenuous* means "innocent or unworldly": Terry's **ingenious** plan worked without complication. The criminal's **ingenuous** smile was misleading.

in regards to Unacceptable for *in regard to.*

irregardless Use *regardless.*

its, it's *Its* is a possessive pronoun, as in "The dog buried **its** bone." *It's* is a contraction of *it is,* as in "**It's** a beautiful day."

kind, sort Used interchangeably. Singular forms are modified by *this* or *that,* plural forms by *these* or *those:* **This kind (sort)** of argument is unacceptable. **These kinds (sorts)** of arguments are unacceptable.

kind of a, sort of a Use *kind of* and *sort of:* This **kind of** [NOT kind of a] book. . . .

lay, lie Use *lay (laid, laying)* in the sense of "put" or "place." Use *lie (lay, lain, lying)* in the sense of "rest" or "recline." *Lay* takes an object (to **lay** something), while *lie* does not. See also 7a(2).

Lie	He had **laid** [NOT lain] the book on the table. The man was **laying** [NOT lying] the carpet.
Lay	He had **lain** [NOT laid] down to take a nap. The woman was **lying** [NOT laying] on the bed.

learn Unacceptable for *teach, instruct, inform:* He **taught** me [NOT learned me] bowling.

leave Unacceptable for *let* in the sense of allowing: **Let** [NOT leave] him have the hammer.

less See **fewer, less.**

liable, likely *Liable* usually means "exposed" or "responsible" in an undesirable sense. *Likely* means "probably," "destined," or "susceptible": If you wreck the car, you are **liable** for damages. With her brains, she is **likely** to succeed.

like Although widely used as a conjunction in spoken English, *as, as if,* and *as though* are preferred for written English.

lose, loose *Lose* is a verb: did **lose,** will **lose.** *Loose* is chiefly an adjective: a **loose** belt.

lots Informal for *many, much.*

mankind Considered offensive because it excludes women. Use *humanity, human race.*

many, much *Many,* used with plural nouns, refers to numbers: **many** stores, too **many** cats; *much,* used with singular nouns, refers to amount: **much** courage.

may be, maybe *May be* is a verb phrase; *maybe* is an adverb: The rumor **may be** true. **Maybe** the rumor is true.

may, can See **can, may.**

media, medium *Media* is plural; *medium* is singular.

morale, moral *Morale* (a noun) refers to a mood or spirit: **Morale** was high. *Moral* (an adjective) refers to correct conduct or ethical character: a **moral** decision. *Moral* (as a noun) refers to the lesson of a story: the **moral** of the story.

most Use *almost* in expressions such as "almost everyone," "almost all." Use *most* only as a superlative: **most** writers.

much See **many, much.**

myself Use only when preceded by an antecedent in the same sentence: Chin and **I** [NOT myself] went swimming. BUT **I** made **myself** go swimming.

nauseous, nauseated Frequently confused. *Nauseous* means "producing nausea"; *nauseated* means "enduring nausea": I felt **nauseated** when I smelled the **nauseous** spoiled meat.

nowhere near Informal. Use *not nearly:* I had **not nearly** [NOT nowhere near] enough money.

nowheres Unacceptable for *nowhere.*

number As subjects, *a number* is generally plural and *the number* is singular. Make sure that the verb agrees with the subject: **A number** of possibilities **are** open. **The number** of possibilities **is** limited. See also **amount of, number of.**

of Often mistaken for the sound of the unstressed *have:* "They must **have** [OR would **have**, could **have**, might **have**, ought to **have**, may **have**—NOT must of] gone home.

off of Use *off* in phrases such as "walked **off** [NOT off of] the field."

OK, O.K., okay Informal usage. All three are acceptable spellings. It is often better to replace *OK* with a more specific word.

on account of Use the less wordy *because:* I went home **because** [NOT on account of] I was tired.

ought See **had ought.**

plus Acceptable as a preposition. Weak when used instead of the coordinating conjunction *and.* I telephoned and [NOT plus] I sent flowers.

p.m. See **a.m., p.m.**

precede, proceed To *precede* is to "go ahead of"; to *proceed* is to "go forward": His song will **precede** the fight scene. He will **proceed** with the song.

principal, principle The adjective or noun *principal* means "chief" or "chief official." The noun may also mean "capital." The noun *principle* means "fundamental truth": The **principal** factor in the salary decision was his belief in the **principle** of sexual equality.

raise, rise *Raise (raised, raising)* means "to lift or cause to move upward, to bring up or increase." *Rise (rose, risen, rising)* means "to get up, to move or extend upward, ascend." *Raise* (a transitive verb) takes an object; *rise* (an intransitive verb) does not: Retailers **raised** prices. Retail prices **rose** sharply. See **7a(2)**.

rarely ever Use either *rarely* alone or *hardly ever:* He **rarely** (or **hardly ever**) [NOT rarely ever] goes to the library.

real, really Use *real* as an adjective, *really* as an adverb. *Real* is often misused in the following expression where it is an adverb modifying the adjective *beautiful:* It is a **really** [NOT real] beautiful day.

reason why Redundant. Use *reason:* The **reason** I went home was that I was ill.

regard, regarding, regards Use *in regard to, with regard to,* or *regarding.*

sensuous, sensual *Sensuous* refers to gratification of the senses in response to art, music, nature, and so on; *sensual* refers to gratification of the physical senses.

shall, will Used interchangeably in contemporary American English.

sit, set Use *sit* in the sense of "be seated" and *set* in the sense of "to place something": Jonathon **sat** under the tree. Maria **set** the cookies on the table. See 7a(2).

so Overused as an intensifier; use a more precise modifier: She was **intensely** [NOT so] focused.

some Informal and vague when used as a substitute for such words as *remarkable, memorable:* She was a **remarkable** [NOT some] athlete.

someone, some one Distinguish between each one-word and two-word compound. See **anyone, any one; everyone, every one.**

sometime, sometimes, some time *Sometime* is an adverb meaning "at an unspecified time"; *sometimes* is an adverb meaning "at times"; *some time* is an adjective-noun pair meaning "a span of time": Let's go to the movie **sometime. Sometimes** we go to the movies. They agreed to allow **some time** to pass before going to the movies together again.

somewheres Unacceptable for *somewhere.*

sort, sort of See **kind, sort** and **kind of a, sort of a.**

specially See **especially, specially.**

stationary, stationery *Stationary* means "in a fixed position"; *stationery* means "writing paper and envelopes."

sure Informal when used as an adverb, as in "I **sure** like your new hat." Use *certainly* or *undoubtedly*.

take See **bring, take.**

thataway, thisaway Unacceptable for *that way* and *this way.*

that, which Use *that* with a restrictive clause: The cup **that** is on the table is full (distinguishes a specific cup that is full). Use *which* with a nonrestrictive clause: The cup, **which** is on the table, is full. ("which is on the table" gives nonessential information). Read the two example sentences aloud to notice the different intonation patterns. Some writers, however, prefer to use *which* for restrictive clauses if it does not cause confusion. See 12d.

their, there, they're, there're *Their* is the possessive form of *they; there* is ordinarily an adverb or an expletive; *they're* is a contraction of *they are; there're* is a contraction of *there are:* **There** is no explanation for **their** behavior. **They're** making trouble **there** on the ball field. **There're** no tickets left.

theirself, theirselves Use *themselves.*

them Unacceptable when used as an adjective: **those** apples OR **these** apples [NOT them apples].

then Sometimes incorrectly used for *than.* Unlike *then, than* does not relate to time. He's better than [NOT then] he knows.

this here, that there, these here, them there Redundant; use *this, that, these, those.*

thusly Use *thus.*

to, too Distinguish the preposition *to* from the adverb *too:* When the weather is **too** hot to play ball, they go **to** the movies.

toward, towards Both acceptable. *Toward* is preferred in American usage.

try and Informal for *try to:* I will **try to** [NOT try and] see him today.

type See **kind.**

unique Because it means "one of a kind," it is illogical to use *unique* with a comparative, as in *very unique*. Do not confuse with *unusual*.

utilize Often pretentious; *use* is preferred.

wait on Unacceptable as a substitute for *wait for*.

ways Unacceptable for *way* when referring to distance: It's a long **way** [NOT ways] from home.

where Informal as a substitute for *that:* I saw on TV **that** [NOT where] she had been elected.

where . . . at, where . . . to Omit the superfluous *at, to:* **Where** is the library [OMIT at]? **Where** are you moving [OMIT to]?

which When referring to persons, use *who* or *that*. See **that, which.**

whose, who's *Whose* indicates possession: **Whose** book is this? *Who's* is the contraction of *who is:* **Who's** going to the movie?

with regards to See **regard, regarding, regards.**

you all A regionalism for the plural of *you*. Not acceptable for formal writing.

your, you're *Your* is the possessive of *you:* in **your** house. *You're* is a contraction of *you are:* **You're** gaining strength. See also **its, it's.**

Glossary of Terms

This glossary presents brief explanations of frequently used terms. Consult the index for references to further discussion of most of the terms and for a number of terms not listed.

absolute phrase A grammatically unconnected part of a sentence—generally a noun or pronoun followed by a participle (and sometimes modifiers): We will have a cookout, **weather permitting** [noun + present participle]; **The national anthem sung for the last time,** the old stadium was closed [noun + past participle with modifier]. Some absolute phrases have the meaning (but not the structure) of an adverb clause. See **1d(3)**, **24a**, and 30b(4). See also **phrase** and **sentence modifier.**

abstract A summary of the main points of a piece of writing, usually placed at the very beginning of the work.

abstract noun A noun that expresses qualities, concepts, and emotions that cannot be perceived through the senses: truth, justice, fear, future. See 20a(3).

accusative case See **case.**

acronym A word formed by combining the initial letters of a series of words: laser—light amplification by stimulated emission of radiation.

active voice The form of a transitive verb indicating that its subject performs the action the verb denotes: Emily *sliced* the ham. See 7 and 29d(1). See also **passive voice, verb,** and **voice.**

adjective The part of speech modifying a noun or a pronoun. *Limiting adjectives* restrict the meaning of the words they modify: *that* pie, *its* leaves. *Descriptive adjectives* name a quality of a noun, including degrees of comparison: *red* shirt, *bigger* planes. *Proper adjectives* are derived from proper nouns: *Spanish* rice. See 9c. Two or more adjectives separated by a comma, instead of by coordinating conjunctions, are referred to as *coordinate* *adjectives:* A *brisk, cold* walk. See 12c(2). *Interrogative adjectives* are used to ask questions: *Whose* book is it? See also **degree** and **predicate adjective.**

adjective clause A subordinate clause used as an adjective: people *who bite their fingernails.* An adjective clause may be restrictive. See 1e(2), 12d, and 25a(3). See also **clause.**

adjective phrase A phrase used as an adjective: The woman *carrying the large notebook* is my sister. See 1d(3). See also **phrase.**

adverb The part of speech modifying a verb, an adjective, or another adverb: *rapidly* approached, *too* bitter, *very graciously* accepted. An adverb may also modify a verbal, a phrase or clause, or the rest of the sentence: *Usually,* an artist does her best work when she is focusing *entirely* on the task at hand.

adverb clause A subordinate clause used as an adverb. An adverb clause may indicate time, place, cause, condition, concession, comparison, purpose, or result: *Although he is usually quiet* [concession], everyone listens to him *when he speaks* [time], *because he makes good suggestions* [cause]. See 1e(2), 12b(1), and 30b(1). See also **clause** and **conditional clause.**

adverbial conjunction See **conjunctive adverb.**

adverb phrase A phrase used as an adverb. An adverb phrase may indicate time, place, cause, condition, concession, comparison, purpose, or result. See 1d(3) and 24a(2). See also **adverb clause.**

agreement The correspondence in number and person of a subject and verb (*the dog barks, dogs bark*) or in number and gender of a pronoun and its antecedent (the *team* boarded *its* bus, the *members* carrying *their* bags). See chapter 6.

allusion A brief, unexplained reference to a work or to a person, place, event, or thing that the writer expects the reader to be familiar with. See also 39a(8).

ambiguity The capability of being understood in two or more different ways: "Reading alone comforts me" could mean "*Reading by myself* comforts me" or "*Only reading* comforts me."

analogy A rhetorical device using the features of something familiar (and often concrete) to explain something unfamiliar (and often abstract), or similarities between things that are not usually associated.

analysis A separation of a whole into its constituent parts.

analytical reading A reader's active engagement by the writer's ideas and how the ideas are expressed; paying attention to content and form.

antecedent A word or group of words that a pronoun refers to. The antecedent may follow (but usually precedes) the pronoun: *Pets* can be polite or rude, like *their* trainers. See chapter 28.

antonym A word that means the opposite of another: *follow* is the antonym for *lead*.

APA American Psychological Association. See 38d–e.

appeal The means of persuasion in argumentative writing; relies on reason, authority, and/or emotion.

appositive A noun or noun phrase placed next to or very near another noun or noun phrase to identify, explain, or supplement its meaning. Appositives may be restrictive. See 12d(2), 24a(3), 30b(4), and 30c(3).

appropriate Writing suitable for the audience, purpose, and occasion.

argument A kind of writing that uses various rhetorical strategies and appeals to convince the reader of the truth or falsity of a given proposition or thesis. See **appeal** and **thesis**.

article *The, a,* or *an* used as adjectives before nouns: *the* cups, *a* cup, *an* extra cup. *The* is a definite article. *A* (used before consonant sounds) and *an* (used before vowel sounds) are indefinite articles. See 22a.

audience The person or persons for whom the writing is intended. See 32a. A specific audience has considerable knowledge of the subject. A general audience does not have expertise on the subject but is willing to read about it.

auxiliary A form of *be, have,* or *will* that combines with a verb to indicate voice, tense, or mood: *was* going, *had* gone, *will* go. Modals such as *will, would,* and *may* are also considered auxiliaries. See 7 and 22b.

balanced sentence A sentence with grammatically equal structures. See 29g.

bibliography A list of books, articles, essays, or other material, usually on a particular subject.

binary See **file.**

Boolean operator(s) Words used to broaden or narrow computer database searches. These include *or, and, not,* and *near.* See page 460.

brainstorming A method of generating ideas about a subject; involves listing ideas as they occur in a session of intensive thinking about the subject. See 32c.

browser Software that finds and displays Web pages. Most browsers can display images as well as text.

cardinal number See **number.**

case The form or position of a noun or pronoun that shows its use or relationship to other words in a sentence. The three cases in English are the *subjective* (or nominative), which is usually the subject of a finite verb; the *possessive* (or genitive), which indicates ownership; and the *objective* (or accusative), which functions as the object of a verb or preposition. See 5 and 15a.

cause and effect A rhetorical strategy by which a writer seeks to explain why something happened or what the results of a particular event or condition were or will be. See 31d(4).

CD-ROM Acronym for Compact Disk—Read Only Memory. CD-ROM disks store large amounts of information—as much as 300,000 pages.

citation Notation (usually parenthetical) in a paper that refers to a source. See 38a(1) and 38d(1).

chronological order The arrangement of events in a time sequence (usually the order in which they occurred).

claim A conclusion that a writer expects readers to accept. Should be supported by accurate and representative source material. See chapter **35**.

classification and division A rhetorical strategy in which a writer sorts elements into categories (*classification*) or breaks a topic down into its constituent parts to show how they are related (*division*). See **31d(6)**

clause A sequence of related words within a sentence. A clause has both a subject and a predicate and functions either as an independent unit (*independent clause*) or as a dependent unit (*subordinate clause,* used as an adverb, an adjective, or a noun). See **1e** and **24**. See also **sentence.**

I saw the moon. It was glowing brightly [sentences].

I saw the moon, for **it was glowing brightly** [independent clauses connected by a coordinating conjunction]

I saw the moon, **which was glowing brightly** [adjective clause].

I saw the moon **because it was glowing brightly** [adverb clause].

I saw **that the moon was glowing brightly** [noun clause—direct object].

cliché An expression that may once have been fresh and effective but that has become trite and worn out with overuse. See **20c**.

coherence The principle that all the parts of a piece of writing should stick together, one sentence leading to the next, each idea evolving from the previous one. See **25** and **31b**.

collaborative writing A method of writing involving a cooperative effort between two or more persons.

collective noun A noun singular in form that denotes a group: *flock, jury, band, public, committee.* See **6a(8)**.

colloquialism A word or phrase characteristic of informal speech. "He's *grumpy*" is a colloquial expression describing an irritable person. See chapter **19**.

comma splice, comma fault A punctuation error in which two independent clauses are joined by a comma with no coordinating conjunction. See chapter 3.

Comma Splice	Patricia went to the game, her brother stayed home.
Revised	Patricia went to the game, **and** her brother stayed home.

common gender A term applied to words that can refer to either sex (*parent, instructor, salesperson, people, anyone*). See 19i.

common noun A noun referring to any or all members of a class or group (*woman, city, apple, holiday*) rather than to a specific member (*Susan B. Anthony, Las Vegas, Winesap, New Year's Day*). See **noun.**

comparative degree. See **degree.**

comparison and contrast A rhetorical strategy in which the writer examines similarities and/or differences between two ideas or objects. See 31d(5).

complement A word or words used to complete the sense of a verb. Although the term may refer to a direct or indirect object, it usually refers to a subject complement, an object complement, or the complement of a verb like *be*. See 1b.

complete predicate A simple predicate (a verb or verb phrase) with any objects, complements, or modifiers: We *ate the fresh homemade pie before the salad.* See **predicate.**

complete subject A simple subject (a noun or noun clause) with any modifiers: *Everyone at the picnic* liked the pie. See 1b. See also **subject.**

complex sentence A sentence containing one independent clause and at least one subordinate clause: *My neighbor noticed a stranger* [independent clause] *who looked suspicious* [subordinate clause]. See 1f, 24, and 30c(1). See also **clause.**

compound-complex sentence A sentence containing at least two main clauses and one or more subordinate clauses: *When the lights went out* [subordinate clause], *there was no flashlight* *at hand* [independent clause] *so we sat outside and gazed at the stars* [independent clause]. See **1f**. See also **clause.**

compound predicate Two or more predicates having the same subject: Clara Barton *nursed the injured during the Civil War* and *later founded the American Red Cross.* See **2a** and **30c(2)**. See also **predicate.**

compound sentence A sentence containing at least two independent clauses and no subordinate clause: *The water supply was dwindling* [independent clause], so *rationing became mandatory* [independent clause]. See **1f**, **12a**, and **14a**. See also **clause.**

compound subject Two or more subjects of the same verb: *Women, men,* and *children* call the crisis center.

concession Agreeing with a point made by your opponent in response to your own argument. Doing so increases a writer's credibility, making the opposition more likely to agree with his or her argument.

conclusion A sentence, paragraph, or group of paragraphs that brings a piece of writing to a satisfying close, usually by summarizing, restating, evaluating, asking a question, or encouraging the reader to continue thinking about the topic. See **32f(2)**.

concrete, concrete noun Concrete nouns refer to things that can be experienced through the senses: *cologne, sunset, onions, thorns.* Concrete nouns make writing clear, vivid, and lively. COMPARE **abstract noun.**

conditional clause An adverb clause (beginning with such conjunctions as *if, unless, whether, provided*) expressing a real, imagined, or nonfactual condition: *If she does a good job,* I will pay her. See **7d**. See **clause.**

conjugation A set or table of the inflected forms of a verb that indicates tense, person, number, voice, and mood. See chapter 7.

conjunction A part of speech (such as *and* or *although*) used to connect words, phrases, clauses, or sentences. *Coordinating conjunctions (and, but, or, nor, for, so, yet)* connect and relate words and word groups of equal grammatical rank: Color-blind people can usually see blue, *but* they may confuse red with green *or* with yellow. See 1c(7) and 26. See also **correlatives.**

Subordinating conjunctions (such as *although, if, when*—see list on page 25) mark a dependent clause and connect it with a main clause: *When* Frank sulks, he acts *as if* he were deaf. See chapter 24.

conjunctive adverb A word (*however, therefore, nevertheless*) that serves not only as an adverb but also as a connective. See 3b, 14a, and 31b(3).

connective A word or phrase that links and relates words, phrases, clauses, or sentences (*and, although, otherwise, finally, on the contrary, which, not only . . . but also*). Conjunctions, conjunctive adverbs, transitional expressions, relative pronouns, and correlatives function as connectives. See 31b(3).

connotation The suggested or implied meaning of a word through the associations it evokes in the reader's mind. See 20a(2). See also **denotation.**

consonant A class of speech sounds represented in English by any letter other than *a, e, i, o,* or *u.*

context The surrounding information that helps give a particular word, sentence, or paragraph its meaning: *cabinet* means "a group of leaders" in a political context and "a place for storage" in a building context. Context also refers to circumstances surrounding the composition of a piece of writing—the occasion, the purpose, the audience, and what the writer and reader already understand about the topic. See 32a.

contraction Condensing two words into one by adding an apostrophe to replace the omitted letter or letters: *aren't, don't.* Contractions are used primarily in spoken or informal written language.

contrast See **comparison and contrast.**

controlling idea The central idea of a paragraph or essay, often expressed in the paragraph's **topic sentence** or the essay's **thesis** statement. See 31a and 32d.

conventional Language that complies with the accepted rules of formal written English, generally termed *correct.*

coordinating adjective See **adjective.**

coordinating conjunction One of seven connectives: *and, but, for, or, nor, so, yet.* See **1c(7)**, **12a**, **24**, and **26**. See also **conjunction.**

coordination The use of grammatically equivalent constructions to link ideas, usually (but not always) those of equal weight. See **12c(2)**, **24b**, and **26**.

correlatives One of five pairs of linked connectives: *both . . . and; either . . . or; neither . . . nor; not only . . . but also; whether . . . or.* Correlatives link equivalent constructions: *both* Jane *and* Fred; *not only* in Peru *but also* in Mexico. See **26c**.

count, noncount nouns Count nouns are individual, countable entities and cannot be viewed as a mass (*word, finger, remark*). Noncount nouns are a mass or a continuum (*humor*). See chapter **1**.

credibility The reliability of a person or evidence. See **35d**.

critical thinking/reading/writing The ability to analyze and synthesize ideas: to distinguish between fact and opinion, to recognize the importance of evidence and logic, to evaluate for credibility, and to avoid common fallacies. See chapter **35**.

cumulative sentence A sentence in which the subject and predicate come first, followed by modifiers. (Also called a loose sentence.) See **29b**.

dangling modifier A word or phrase that does not clearly refer to another word or word group in the sentence. See **25b**.

data Accepted fact or evidence. In computer language, information stored in computer-readable form.

database A kind of electronic filing system. Computer databases are usually organized hierarchically so that computers can find information more quickly. An *electronic database system* is a group of databases such as Dialog or CARL Uncover. Most such systems are *retrieval* databases—users can get information from them but cannot add to them.

declension A set or table of inflected forms of nouns or pronouns. See the examples on page 55.

deduction A form of logical reasoning that begins with a generalization (*premise*), relates a specific fact to that generalization, and forms a *conclusion* that fits both. See **35f**. COMPARE **induction.**

definition A brief explanation of the meaning of a word, as in a dictionary. Also, an extended piece of writing, employing a variety of rhetorical strategies, to explain what something is or means. See **31d(7)**.

degree The form of an adverb or adjective that indicates relative quality, quantity, or manner. The three degrees are as follows: *positive,* a quality of a single element; *comparative,* between two elements; and *superlative,* among three or more elements. Examples of sets of degree include *good, better, best* and *fast, faster, fastest.* See **4c**.

demonstratives Four words that point out (*this, that, these, those*): **Those** are as good as **these** [pronouns]. **Those** curtains have never been cleaned [adjective].

denotation The literal meaning of a word as commonly defined. See **20a(1)**. See also **connotation.**

dependent clause A subordinate clause. See **clause.**

description A rhetorical strategy using details perceivable by the senses to portray a scene, object, performance, and so on. See **31d(2)**.

details Specific information, such as facts, sensory data, or examples, that clarifies and explains.

determiner A word (such as *a, an, the, my, their*) that signals the approach of a noun: **the** newly mown *hay.*

development The elaboration of an idea through organized discussion filled with examples, details, and other information. See **31c**.

dialect A variety of language characteristic of a region or culture. Dialects are distinguished by vocabulary, pronunciation, and/or syntax: British English, Low German, and Cantonese. See chapter **19d**.

dialogue A reproduction in writing of conversation by two or more people, real or fictional. See **9e**, **16a**, and **19b**.

dial-up access Refers to using a modem and a telephone line to connect a computer to a network.

diction The writer's choice of exact, idiomatic, and fresh words, as well as appropriate levels of usage. See chapters **19** and **20**.

direct address A name or descriptive term (set off by commas) designating the one or ones spoken to: Play it again, *Sam.*

direct object A noun (or noun clause) naming *whom* or *what* after a transitive active verb: Emily sliced the *ham.* See **1b(2)**. See also **object.**

direct quotation A repetition of the exact spoken or written words of others: "Where an opinion is general," writes Jane Austen, "it is usually correct." See **16a** and **37g**.

discussion list See **listserv.**

documentation The citing of sources in a researched paper to conform to a given style, such as MLA or APA. See chapter **38**.

double negative The nonstandard combination of two negatives, which has a negative meaning: We ca*n't* do *nothing* about the weather. See **4e**.

draft, drafting A working version of a piece of writing. The process of putting ideas in writing so they can be revised and edited. See **32f–g**.

edited American English (EAE) The term adopted by the National Council of Teachers of English for the formal style expected in most college writing. EAE observes conventional rules of spelling, punctuation, mechanics, grammar, and sentence structure.

editing Reworking sentences for clarity, sense, and conformity to conventional rules of spelling, punctuation, mechanics, grammar, and sentence structure.

electronic mail See **e-mail.**

electronic resources On-line research tools that enable the computer user to access publicly available information. These may include CD-ROM, databases, and Internet access. See **electronic mail, database, CD-ROM,** and **World Wide Web.**

electronic sites Publicly available files on a computer that can be accessed through the Internet.

ellipsis Three or four spaced periods that indicate material omitted from a quotation. See **17i**.

elliptical construction The omission of words while retaining the meaning: Cats are cleaner than pigs [are].

e-mail Electronic mail; transfers messages over a communications network. E-mail may be limited to a single network, but most often refers to messages sent via the Internet.

emoticon A small icon made up of punctuation characters. It shows how a sender wants a message to be interpreted; e.g., a smiling emoticon (for example, :-), often called a smiley) indicates a joke.

emphasis Special weight or importance given to a word, sentence, or paragraph by any of a variety of techniques. It may also mean stress applied to one or more syllables in a word. See chapter 29.

essay A brief piece of nonfiction writing on a single topic in which a writer typically states the thesis in the introduction, develops several points in support of that thesis, and concludes.

ethos Can be translated as "arguing honorably" and is employed when you tell others the truth and treat them with respect. Many writing theories have suggested that effective arguments use not only ethos, but also **logos** (the logical use of language) and **pathos** (the use of language to stir the feelings of an audience). See page 428.

etymology The origin and historical development of a word, its derivation.

euphemism An indirect or "nice" expression used instead of a more direct one: *Correctional facility* instead of *jail*. See chapter 20.

evaluation The process of finding and judging useful passages from source material. See **37f**.

evidence Facts, statistics, examples, testimony, sensory details, and so on that support generalizations.

example Any fact, anecdote, reference, or the like used to illustrate an idea. See **31c**.

expletive A signal of a transformation in the structure of a sentence that occurs without changing the meaning. The expletive *there* shifts the order of subject and verb in a sentence: *There* were over four thousand runners in the marathon. [COMPARE Over four thousand runners were in the marathon.] The expletive *it* transforms the main clause into a subordinate clause: It is apparent that the plane is late. [COMPARE Apparently, the plane is late.] See **6a(5)**.

expository writing See **referential writing.**

expressive writing Writing that emphasizes the writer's own feelings and reactions to a topic. See **32a**.

fact A reliable piece of information that can be verified through independent sources or procedures. A **fact** differs from an **opinion.** See **opinion.**

fallacy A false argument or incorrect reasoning. See **35h**.

faulty predication The use of a predicate that does not logically belong with a given subject: One superstition is a black cat. [The verb should be *involves.*]

figurative language The use of words in an imaginative rather than a literal sense. See **20a(4)**.

file A collection of computer-readable information. *Binary* files contain information readable only by computers unless the file is decoded. People can read *text* files (often called ASCII files) without having to decode them.

finite verb A verb form that can function as the only verb in the predicate of a sentence: They *ate* a can of pork and beans. Verb forms classified as gerunds, infinitives, or participles cannot. See **predicate;** contrast **verbal.**

first person See **person.**

flaming Heated, confrontational exchanges on e-mail.

focus The narrowing of a subject to a manageable size; also the sharpening of the writer's view of the subject. See 32c and 32d.

formal/informal writing style Considering the rhetorical situation (your audience, purpose, and occasion) to determine if you need to use a formal or informal style. You should master a formal style employing edited American English for most college and business writing, but you should also master an informal style for personal letters and other kinds of self-expression. See 19 and 32a and the Glossary of Usage.

fragment A group of words that begins with a capital letter and ends with a period but forms only part of a sentence. See chapter 2.

freewriting A method of finding a writing topic by composing for a specified length of time without stopping to reflect, reread, or correct errors.

freeware Software available free of charge. Freeware programs are often available for downloading from the Internet; however, the computer user should be aware of the potential transmission of a computer virus. See **virus.**

FTP Abbreviation for File Transfer Protocol. People use FTP for transferring files on the Internet. See page 468.

function words Words (such as prepositions, conjunctions, auxiliaries, and articles) that indicate the functions of other words in a sentence and the grammatical relationships between them.

fused sentence Two or more sentences run together, with no punctuation or conjunctions to separate them. Also called a run-on sentence. Unacceptable in formal writing. See chapter 3.

gender The grammatical distinction that labels nouns or pronouns as masculine, feminine, or neuter. In English, grammatical gender usually corresponds with natural gender.

general/specific, generalization *General* words are all-embracing, indefinite, sweeping in scope: *food. Specific* words are precise, explicit, limited in scope: *spaghetti carbonara*. The same is true of *general* and *specific* ideas. A *generalization* is vague and may be untrue.

genitive case See **case.**

gerund A verbal (nonfinite verb) that ends in *-ing* and functions as a noun. Gerunds may take objects, complements, or modifiers: *Riding* a bike is good exercise. [The gerund phrase—*riding* and its object, *bikes*—serves as the subject of the sentence.] A noun or pronoun serving as the subject of the gerund takes the possessive case: *His* [or *Jim's*] *bicycle riding* is good exercise.

Gopher A menu-based program for finding files on the Internet. See page 469.

grammar The system of rules by which words are arranged into the structures meaningful in a language.

graphics Images or pictures that can be displayed on a computer screen.

hardware In computer terminology, the tangible components of the computer system such as the keyboard, the monitor, and the components inside the system box.

helping verb A verb that combines with another verb to indicate voice, tense, or mood. See **auxiliary** and **modal.**

historical present A tense used to describe events in literature or history that are permanently preserved in the present: The tragedy *is* that Iago *deceives* Othello. See **7b** and **39a**.

homophones Words that have the same sound and sometimes the same spelling but differ in meaning (*their, there,* and *they're* or *capital* meaning funds and *capital* meaning government city). See **18b**.

hyperbole An intentional overstatement made for rhetorical effect. See **39a(8)**. COMPARE **understatement.**

idiom A fixed expression (within a language) whose meaning cannot be deduced from its elements: *put up a fight; to mean well.* See **20b**.

illustration In writing, the use of specific details to give substance and interest to a subject. See **31c**.

imperative mood See **mood.**

indefinites The article *a* or *an* (*a* banana, *an* insect), as well as pronouns (*anyone, everybody*) and adjectives (*any* car, *few* problems, *several* questions) that do not specify distinct limits.

independent clause See **clause.**

indicative mood See **mood.**

indirect object A word (or words) naming the one (or ones) indirectly affected by the action of the verb: Emily sliced *me* some ham. See **object.**

indirect question A question phrased as a statement, usually a subordinate clause: We can ask *whether Milton's blindness was the result of glaucoma,* but we cannot be sure. See 27c.

indirect quotation A report of the written or spoken words of another without using the exact words of the speaker or writer: The registrar said *that the bank returned my tuition check*. COMPARE **direct quotation.**

induction A form of logical reasoning that begins with evidence and interprets it to form a conclusion. See 35e. COMPARE **deduction.**

infinitive A verbal (nonfinite verb) used chiefly as a noun, less frequently as an adjective or adverb. The infinitive is usually made up of the word *to* plus the present form of a verb (called the *stem* of the infinitive). Infinitives may have subjects, objects, complements, or modifiers: Lashanda wanted *to continue* the debate. [*Debate* is the object of the infinitive *to continue; to continue the debate* is the object of the verb *wanted*.]

infinitive phrase A phrase that employs the infinitive form of the verb: *to go to the store, to run the race*. See **phrase.**

inflection A change in the form of a word to show a specific meaning or grammatical function:

Verb	*talk, talks, talked*
Noun	*dog, dogs, dog's, dogs'*
Pronoun	*he, him, his; they, them, their, theirs*
Adjective	*thin, thinner, thinnest*
Adverb	*rapidly, more rapidly, most rapidly*

informal Although often acceptable in spoken language, words or phrases that dictionaries label **informal, colloquial,** or **slang** are not generally appropriate in college writing. See chapter 19 and **formal/informal writing style.**

informative writing See **referential writing.**

intensifier A modifier used for emphasis: *very* excited, *certainly* pleased. See **qualifier.**

intensive/reflexive pronoun The *-self* pronouns (such as *myself, himself, themselves*). The *intensive* is used for emphasis: The teenagers *themselves* had the best idea. The *reflexive* is used as an object of a verb, verbal, or preposition: He blames *himself;* she bought a present for *herself.* An intensive or reflexive pronoun always refers to another noun or pronoun in the same sentence that denotes the same individual or individuals.

interjection A word (one of the eight parts of speech) expressing a simple exclamation: *Hey! Oops!* When used in sentences, mild interjections are set off by commas. See 17c.

Internet An international network of computers linked through telephone and fiber-optic lines.

interpretation Use of inductive reasoning to help understand facts in order to reach probable and believable conclusions and avoid sweeping conclusions that can be easily challenged. See 35e.

interrogative A word like *which, whose,* or *why* used to ask a question: *Which* is the more expensive? [pronoun] *Whose* lights are on? [adjective] *Why* are treasury bills a good investment? [adverb]

interrogative adjective See **adjective.**

intransitive verb A verb (such as *appear* or *belong*) that does not take an object. See chapter 7. See also **verb** and **transitive verb.**

introduction The beginning of an essay, often a single paragraph, that engages the reader's interest and indicates, usually by stating the thesis, what the essay is about. See 32f(1).

invention The process of using strategies to generate ideas for writing. See **31d** and **32b–c**.

inversion A change in the usual word order of a sentence: Into the valley of death rode the five hundred. See **29f**.

irony A deliberate inconsistency between what is stated and what is meant. Irony may be verbal or situational. See **20a(4)**.

irregular verb A verb that is not inflected in the usual way—that is, by the addition of *-d* or *-ed* to the present form to form the past tense and past participle. Examples include *begin, began, begun* and *lend, lent, lent.*

jargon Technical slang, appropriate as a shortcut to communication when the audience is knowledgeable about the topic and the terms; it should be avoided in writing intended for a more general audience. See **19g**.

journal A special-interest periodical (*Rhetoric Review, Environmental Legislation*). Also a notebook in which a writer records personal thoughts and experiences.

journaling Keeping a **journal.**

justification Inserts spaces between words so that every line is the same length and makes the right or left margin, or both margins, straight.

linking verb A verb that relates the subject complement to the subject. Words commonly used as linking verbs are *become, seen, appear, feel, look, taste, smell, sound,* and forms of the verb *be:* She *is* a writer. The bread *looks* burned. See **1a**, **4b**, and **5f**.

listing An informal way of gathering ideas about a writing topic in which a writer lists any ideas that he or she has about the subject. See p. 345.

listserv A list of e-mail addresses to which messages can be automatically broadcast as if they were sent to a single user: a *discussion list* or a *mailing list.*

logic The presentation of ideas that shows a clear, predictable, and structured relationship among those ideas. See chapters **23** and **35**.

logical operator(s) See **Boolean operator(s).**

log on The process by which a user provides a username and a password in order to be recognized by a computer system and allowed to use its programs.

logos See **ethos.**

loose sentence See **cumulative sentence.**

main clause See **clause.**

main idea The part of the paragraph or paper to which all the other ideas relate. See **topic sentence** and **thesis.**

mechanics The form of words and letters, such as capitals, italics, abbreviations, acronyms, and numbers.

memory The way a computer stores information. Simply put, the main memory of the computer resides on chips and refers to the amount of information the computer can process at one time. Computers also store information by writing it to a storage device such as a fixed hard disk or a removable floppy disk. *RAM,* an acronym for Random Access Memory, is used to mean the main memory of a computer. *ROM,* for Read Only Memory, generally refers to the basic memory the computer needs to use its operating system.

metaphor An imaginative comparison between dissimilar things without using *like* or *as.* See 20a(4) and 39a(8).

misplaced modifier A modifier placed in an awkward position, usually far away from what it modifies: I read that there was a big fire *in yesterday's newspaper.* I read in yesterday's newspaper that there was a big fire. [Place the modifier after the verb *read.*] Sometimes a misplaced modifier confuses the reader because it could qualify either of two words: To do one's best *sometimes* is not enough. *Sometimes* to do one's best is not enough. To do one's best is *sometimes* not enough. [Place the adverb closer to the verb.] See 25a.

mixed construction A garbled sentence that is the result of an unintentional shift from one grammatical pattern to another. See 23c(2).

mixed metaphor A metaphor that confuses two or more metaphors: Playing with fire will drown you. See 23c(1).

MLA Modern Language Association. See 38a–b.

modal A helping verb (not conjugated) that shows ability (*can, could*); permission or possibility (*may, might*); determination, promise, or intention (*shall, should; will, would*); obligation (*ought*); or necessity (*must*).

modem Acronym for *mo*dulator-*dem*odulator. A modem is a device that allows a computer to transmit data over telephone lines.

modifier A word or word group that describes, limits, or qualifies another: a *true* statement, walked *slowly,* yards *filled with rocks,* the horse *that jumped the fence.* See chapters 4 and 25.

mood The way a speaker or writer regards an assertion—that is, as a declarative statement or a question (*indicative* mood); as a command or request (*imperative*); or as a supposition, hypothesis, recommendation, or condition contrary to fact (*subjunctive*). Verb forms indicate mood. See 1f and 7e.

mouse See **pointing device.**

narration A rhetorical strategy that recounts a sequence of events, usually in chronological order. See 31d(1).

netiquette Internet etiquette.

network A group of two or more linked computer systems.

nominalization The practice of using nouns instead of active verbs: She *made a list* of the schedule changes. [COMPARE She *listed* the schedule changes.] Excessive nominalization produces a wordy style.

nominative case See **case.**

nonfinite verb A verb form (verbal) used as a noun, adjective, or adverb. A nonfinite verb cannot stand as the only verb in a sentence. See 1c and 2a. See also **verbal.**

nonrestrictive Nonessential to the identification of the word or words referred to. Set off by commas. A word or word group is nonrestrictive (parenthetical) when it is not necessary to the meaning of the sentence and can be omitted: My best friend, *Pauline,* understands me. See 12d.

nonstandard Speech forms that are common in informal writing but that should be avoided in formal writing. See chapter **19**.

noun A part of speech that names a person, place, thing, idea, animal, quality, or action: *Mary, America, apples, justice, goose, strength, departure.* A noun usually changes form to indicate the plural and the possessive case, as in *man, men; man's, men's.* See **1c(2)**.

TYPES OF NOUNS

Common	a **woman**, the **street**, some **dogs** [general classes]
Proper	**Ms. Wentworth**, in **Dallas**, the **White House** [capitalized, specific names—**9a**]
Collective	a **team**, the **committee**, my **class** [groups]
Concrete	A **truck**, the **cup**, my **foot**, two **fish** [tangibles]
Abstract	**love**, **justice**, **fear** [ideas, qualities]
Count	two **cents**, sixteen **bytes**, an **assignment**, many **revisions** [singular or plural—often preceded by adjectivals telling how many]
Noncount	much **concern**, more **consideration**, less **revenue** [singular in meaning—often preceded by adjectivals telling how much]

noun clause A subordinate clause used as a noun. See **1e**. See also **clause.**

number The inflectional form of a word that identifies it as singular (one) or plural (more than one): *river–rivers, this–those, he sees–they see.* See **6a** and **18d(5)**. *Cardinal numbers* express quantity: *two (2), thirty-five (35). Ordinal numbers* indicate order or rank: *second (2nd), thirty-fifth (35th).*

object A noun or noun substitute governed by a transitive active verb, by a nonfinite verb, or by a preposition. See **1b(2–3)** and **1c(6)**.

A *direct object,* or the *object of a finite verb,* is any noun or noun substitute that answers the question *what?* or *whom?* after a transitive active verb. A direct object frequently receives, or is in some way affected by, the action of the verb: Bill hit the *ball.*

What did he hit? A direct object may be converted into a subject with a passive verb. See **voice.**

An *object of a nonfinite verb* is any noun or its equivalent that follows and completes the meaning of a participle, a gerund, or an infinitive: Building a *house* takes time. She likes to grow *flowers.*

An *indirect object* is any noun or noun substitute that states *to whom* or *for whom* (or *to what* or *for what*) something is done. An indirect object ordinarily precedes a direct object: She gave *him* the keys. I gave the *floor* a good mopping. It is usually possible to substitute a prepositional phrase beginning with *to* or *for* for the indirect object: She gave the keys *to* him.

An object of a preposition is any noun or noun substitute that a preposition relates to another word or word group: They play ball in the *park.* [*Park* is the object of the preposition *in.*]

object complement A word that helps complete the meaning of such verbs as *make, paint, elect, name.* An object complement refers to or modifies the direct object: They painted the cellar door *blue.* See **1b(3)** and **4b**. See also **complement.**

objective case See **case.**

on-line server A server available for remote access. A server is a machine that houses software for delivering information on a *network.* See **network.**

opinion Ideas that may or may not be based on fact. See **35b**.

ordinal number See **number.**

overgeneralization Lacking specificity. See **general/specific, generalization.**

paradox A seemingly contradictory statement that actually may be true. See **39a(8)**.

paragraph Usually a group of related sentences unified by a single idea or purpose but occasionally as brief as a single sentence (or even a single word or phrase). The central, or controlling, idea of a paragraph is often explicitly stated in a *topic sentence.* A paragraph is marked by the indention of its first line or some other defining device.

parallelism The use of corresponding grammatically equal elements in sentences and paragraphs. It aids the flow of a sentence, making it read smoothly, and also emphasizes the relationship of the ideas in the parallel elements. See chapter **26**.

paraphrase A sentence-by-sentence restatement of the ideas in a passage, using different words. See **37h(4)**.

parenthetical documentation See **documentation.**

parenthetical element Nonessential words, phrases, clauses, or sentences (such as an aside or interpolation) usually set off by commas but often by dashes or parentheses to mark pauses and intonation: *In fact,* the class, *a hardworking group of students,* finished the test quickly. See **12d**, **17e(2)**, and **17f**.

participle A verb form that may function as part of a verb phrase (was *thinking,* had *determined*) or as a modifier (a *determined* effort; the couple, *thinking* about their past).

The *present participle* ends in *-ing* (the form also used for verbal nouns: see **gerund**). The past participle of regular verbs ends in *-d* or *-ed;* for past participles of irregular verbs, see **7a**. See also **irregular verb.**

Functioning as modifiers in *participial phrases,* participles may take objects, complements, and modifiers: The bellhop *carrying the largest suitcase* fell over the threshold. [The participle *carrying* takes the object *suitcase;* the whole participial phrase modifies *bellhop*.] See **25b(1)**.

particle A word like *across, away, down, for, in, off, out, up, with* combined with a verb to form idiomatic usages in which the combination has the force of a single-word verb: The authorities refused to *put up* with him.

parts of speech The classes into which words may be grouped according to their form changes and their grammatical relationships. The traditional parts of speech are *verbs, nouns, pronouns, adjectives, adverbs, prepositions, conjunctions,* and *interjections.* Each of these is discussed separately in this glossary. See also **1c**.

passive voice The form of the verb showing that its subject is not the agent performing the action of the verb but rather receives that action: The ham *was sliced* by Emily. See 7 and 29d(1). See also **active voice.**

pathos See **ethos.**

pentad A method of exploring a subject. The pentad considers the five dramatic aspects: the act, the actor, the scene, the agency, and the purpose.

perfect tenses The tenses formed by the addition of a form of *have* and showing complex time relationships in completing the action of the verb (the present perfect—*have/has eaten;* the past perfect—*had eaten;* and the future perfect—*will/shall have eaten.*

periodic sentence A sentence in which the main idea comes last. See 29b. COMPARE **cumulative sentence.**

person The form of pronouns and verbs denoting or indicating whether one is speaking (*I am*—first person), is spoken to (*you are*—second person), or spoken about (*he is*—third person). In the present tense, a verb changes its form to agree grammatically with a third-person singular subject (*I watch, she watches*). See 6a and 27b.

personal pronoun Any one of a group of pronouns—*I, you, he, she, it,* and their inflected forms—referring to the one (or ones) speaking, spoken to, or spoken about. See chapter 5.

personification The attributing of human characteristics to nonhuman things (animals, objects, ideas): "That night wind was breathing across me through the spokes of the wheel." —WALLACE STEGNER. See 39a(8).

perspective A manner of considering a subject. A perspective can be static, dynamic, or relative. See p. 347.

persuasive writing A form of writing intended chiefly to change the reader's opinions or attitudes or to arouse the reader to action. See 32a.

phrasal verb A unit consisting of a verb plus one or two uninflected words like *after, in, up, off,* or *out* (see **particle**) and having the force of a single-word verb: We *ran out* on them.

phrase A sequence of grammatically related words without a subject and/or a predicate. See 1d and 2a. See **verbal.**

plagiarism The use of another writer's words or ideas without acknowledging the source. Akin to theft, plagiarism has serious consequences and should always be avoided. See **37g**.

plural More than one. COMPARE **singular.**

pointing device A device used to control the cursor (or pointer) on the display screen. To control the cursor with a *mouse,* the user rolls a small box-like device across a hard surface. The user turns a ball resting in a stationary holder to operate a *trackball* and moves a finger across a sensitive pad to use a *touchpad.*

point of view The vantage point from which the subject is viewed. See **27e**. It also refers to the stance a writer takes—objective or impartial (third person), directive (second person), or personal (first person).

positive See **degree.**

possessive case See **case.**

predicate A basic grammatical division of a sentence. A predicate is the part of the sentence comprising what is said about the subject. The *complete predicate* consists of the main verb and its auxiliaries (the *simple predicate*) and any complements and modifiers: We ***chased the dog all around our grandmother's farm.*** [*Chased* is the simple predicate; *chased* and all the words that follow make up the complete predicate.]

predicate adjective The adjective used as a subject complement: The bread tastes *sweet.* See **1c(4)** and **4b**. See also **linking verb.**

predicate noun A noun used as a subject complement: Bromides are *sedatives.* See **1c(2)** and **5f**. See also **linking verb.**

predication The act of stating or expressing something about the subject. See **faulty predication.**

prefix An added syllable or group of syllables (such as *in-, dis-, un-, pro-*) placed before a word to form a new word: *adequate–inadequate.* A prefix ordinarily changes the meaning.

premise An assumption or a proposition on which an argument or explanation is based. In logic, premises are either major (general) or minor (specific); when combined correctly, they lead to a conclusion. See 35f. See also **syllogism.**

preposition A part of speech that links and relates a noun or noun substitute to another word in the sentence: The dancers leapt *across* the stage. [The preposition *across* connects and relates *stage* (its object) to the verb *leapt.*] See page 17 for a list of phrasal prepositions.

prepositional phrase A preposition with its object and any modifiers: *in the hall, between you and me, for the new van.*

present and past participle See **participle.**

prewriting The initial stage of the writing process, concerned primarily with planning.

primary source In research or bibliographies, the source that provides unedited, firsthand facts.

principal parts The forms of a verb that indicate the various tenses: the present (*give, jump*); the past (*gave, jumped*); and the past participle (*given, jumped*). See 7a.

process, process writing See **writing process.**

process analysis A rhetorical strategy either to instruct the reader how to perform a procedure or to explain how something occurs. See 31d(3).

progressive verb A verb phrase consisting of a present participle (ending in *-ing*) used with a form of *be* and denoting continuous action: *is attacking, will be eating.*

pronoun A part of speech that takes the position of nouns and functions as nouns do. See 1c(3), 5, 6a, 6b, and 28. See also **noun** and the separate entries for the types of pronouns listed below.

Personal Pronoun **She** and **I** will drive to Conway.

Relative Pronoun Jack is a person **who** enjoys life.

Indefinite Pronoun **Each** of us played against **somebody.**

Intensive Pronoun **I myself** am an agronomist.

Reflexive Pronoun Jane enjoyed **herself** at the fair.

Demonstrative Pronoun **This** is closer than **that.**

Interrogative Pronoun **What** is it? **Who** said that?

proofreading Checking the final draft of a paper to eliminate typographical, spelling, punctuation, and documentation errors. See 8c and 33d.

proper adjective See **adjective.**

proper noun See **noun.**

purpose A writer's reason for writing. The purpose for nonfiction writing may be predominantly expressive, expository, or persuasive, though all three aims are likely to be present in some measure. See 32a. See also **expressive writing, persuasive writing,** and **referential writing.**

qualifier Any modifier that describes or limits: *Sometimes* movies are *too* gory to watch. Frequently, however, the term refers only to those modifiers that restrict or intensify the meaning of other words. See **intensifier.**

quotation Repeated or copied words of another, real or fictional. See 16a and 37g.

RAM See **memory.**

reading preview To scan a piece of writing for the main ideas. Critical readers use this method to scan a reading assignment quickly to determine an assignment's main purpose, thereby allowing them to think about it critically.

reciprocal pronoun One of two compound pronouns expressing an interchangeable or mutual action or relationship: *each other* or *one another.*

record A set of related information usable by a computer.

redundant Needlessly repetitious, unnecessary.

referential writing Writing whose chief aim is to clarify, explain, or evaluate a subject in order to inform or instruct the reader. Also called expository or informative writing. See 32a.

reflexive pronoun See **pronoun.**

refutation A writer's introduction of reasons why others may believe differently followed by an explanation showing why these reasons are not convincing. See p. 426.

regular verb A verb that forms its past tense and past participle by adding *-d* or *-ed* to the present form (or the stem of the infinitive): *love, loved; laugh, laughed.* See chapter 7.

relative clause An adjective clause introduced by a relative pronoun: the programs *that provide services.*

relative pronoun A noun substitute (*who, whom, whose, that, which, what, whoever, whomever, whichever, whatever*) used to introduce subordinate clauses: He has an aunt **who** *is a principal* [adjective clause introduced by the relative pronoun *who*]. OR **Whoever** *becomes treasurer* must be honest [noun clause introduced by the relative pronoun *whoever*]. See chapter 5.

restrictive A word, phrase, or clause that limits the word referred to by imposing conditions or by confining the word to a particular group or to a specific item or individual: Every student *who cheats* will be removed from the class. [The restrictive clause *who cheats* imposes conditions on—restricts—the meaning of *every student.* Only those students *who cheat* will be removed.] See 12d. See also **nonrestrictive.**

retrieval database A database system that allows users to search by keyword, author, or title and that may often provide the full text of a document.

revision Part of the writing process. Writers revise by rereading and rethinking a piece of writing to see where they need to add, delete, move, replace, reshape, and even completely recast ideas.

rhetoric The art of using language effectively. Rhetoric involves the writer's **purpose** (32a), the **audience** (32a), the discovery and exploration of a subject (32b and 32c), its arrangement and organization (32e), the style and tone in which it is expressed (32a), and the form in which it is delivered (8 and 32a).

rhetorical question A question posed for effect without expectation of a reply: Who can tell what will happen?

rhetorical situation The relationship between the writer, the audience, and the context that determines the appropriate approach for a particular situation.

run-on sentence See **fused sentence.**

scroll bar A bar on the side or bottom of a computer window that allows the user to control what part of the displayed file is visible.

search engine A program that searches documents for a specific word (keyword) and returns a list of all documents containing that word.

secondary source A source that analyzes or interprets **primary source** material.

sentence A grammatically independent unit of expression. A simple sentence contains a subject and a predicate. Sentences are classified according to structure (simple, complex, compound, and compound-complex) and purpose (declaratory, interrogatory, imperative, exclamatory). See chapter 1.

sentence modifier An adverb or adverb substitute that modifies the rest of the sentence, not a specific word or word group in it: *All things considered,* Middle America is a good place to live. OR *Yes,* the plane arrived on time.

server A computer that manages network resources; for example, a Web server, a network server, or a mail server.

sexist language Language that arbitrarily excludes one sex or the other or that arbitrarily assigns stereotypical roles to one or the other sex: A secretary should keep *her* desk tidy. [COMPARE Secretar*ies* should keep *their* desks tidy.] See 6b and 19i.

simile The comparison of two dissimilar things using *like* or *as.* See 20a(4) and 39a(8).

simple tenses The tenses that refer to present, past, and future time.

singular One. See **number.** COMPARE **plural.**

slang The casual vocabulary of specific groups or cultures, usually considered inappropriate for formal writing. Occasionally, slang can be effective if the writer carefully considers purpose and audience. See chapter **19**.

software Computer programs that enable the user to perform specific tasks.

space order A concept often used to organize descriptive passages. Details are arranged according to how they are encountered as the observer's eye moves vertically, horizontally, from far to near, and so forth. See **31b(2)**.

split infinitive The often awkward separation of an infinitive by at least one adverb: *to* quietly *go*. See **infinitive.**

squinting modifier An ambiguous modifier that can refer to either a preceding or a following word: Eating *often* makes her sick. See **25a(4)**.

standard American English See **edited American English.**

stipulative definition A definition that specifies how a certain term will be used within a certain context. See **23e(2)**.

style An author's choice and arrangement of words, sentence structures, and ideas as well as less definable characteristics such as rhythm and euphony. See **27d**.

subject A basic grammatical division of a sentence. The subject is a noun or noun substitute about which something is asserted or asked in the predicate. It usually precedes the predicate. (In imperative sentences subjects are implied, not stated.) The *complete subject* consists of the *simple subject* and the words associated with it: *The **woman** in the gray trench coat* asked for information [simple subject—*woman;* complete subject—*the woman in the gray trench coat*]. COMPARE **predicate.** May also refer to the main idea of a piece of writing.

subject complement A word or words that complete the meaning of a linking verb and that modify or refer to the subject: The old car looked *shabby* [predicate adjective]. *The old car was an eyesore* [predicate noun]. See **1b**, **4b**, and **5f**. See also **linking verb.**

subjective case See **case.**

subjunctive mood See **mood.**

subordinate clause See **clause.**

subordinating conjunction See **conjunction.**

subordination The use of dependent structures (phrases, subordinate clauses) that are lower in grammatical rank than independent ones (simple sentences, main clauses). See chapter 24.

suffix An added sound, syllable, or group of syllables placed after a word to form a new word, to change the meaning of a word, or to indicate grammatical function: *light, lighted, lighter, lightest, lightness, lightly.*

summary A concise restatement briefer than the original. See 37h(5).

superlative degree See **degree.**

syllogism A three-part form of deductive reasoning. See 35f.

synonym A word that has a meaning similar to that of another word.

syntax Sentence structure; the grammatical arrangement of words, phrases, and clauses.

synthesis **Inductive reasoning** whereby a writer begins with a number of instances (facts or observations) and uses them to draw a general conclusion. See 35e.

tag question A question attached to the end of a related statement set off by a comma: She's coming, *isn't she?* See 3a.

Telnet A program that connects a computer to a network server. The user then has access to programs and functions as if he or she were in the same physical location as the server. See page 470.

template A pattern that serves as a model. Some writers create computer templates (like a fill-in form) if they often use the same standard layout.

tense The form of the verb that denotes time. Inflection of single-word verbs (*pay, paid*) and the use of auxiliaries (*am paid, was paid, will pay*) indicate tense. See chapter 7.

thesis The central point or main idea of an essay. It is one of the main ways an essay is unified (see **unity**). A specific, clearly focused thesis statement helps the writer make all the other elements of the essay work together to accomplish his or her purpose. See also 32d.

tone The writer's attitude toward the subject and the audience, usually conveyed through diction and sentence structure. Tone affects the reader's response.

topic The specific, narrowed idea of a paper. See **subject.**

topic sentence A statement of the central thought of a paragraph, which, though often at the beginning, may appear anywhere in it. Some paragraphs may not have a topic sentence, although the main idea is clearly suggested.

touchpad See **pointing device.**

trackball See **pointing device.**

transitions Words, phrases, sentences, or paragraphs that relate ideas and provide coherence by linking sentences, paragraphs, and larger units of writing. Transitions may be expressions (words or phrases such as *moreover, first, nevertheless, for example,* and so on) or structural features a writer uses, such as parallelism or repetition of key words and phrases. When they link larger units of writing, transitions may take the form of sentences or even brief paragraphs. See 36b.

transitive verb A type of verb that takes an object. Some verbs may be either transitive or intransitive depending on the context: They *danced* [transitive] the polka. They *danced* [intransitive] all night. See **verb** and **intransitive verb.**

truth In deductive reasoning, the veracity of the premises. If the premises are true, the conclusion is true. An argument may be true but invalid if the relation between the premises is invalid. See 35f. See also **validity.**

unacceptable Words or phrases labeled in dictionaries as *archaic, illiterate,* or *substandard;* generally not accepted in formal or informal writing.

understatement Intentional underemphasis for effect, usually ironic. See 39a(8). See also **hyperbole.**

Uniform Resource Locator See **URL.**

unity All the elements in an essay contributing to developing a single idea or thesis. A paragraph is unified when each sentence contributes to developing a central thought. See **31a** and **32d**.

URL Acronym for Uniform Resource Locator, which allows the computer user to locate resources on the Internet. A URL consists of several parts: the protocol to be used (e.g. (http://; ftp://; gopher://), the Internet address and domain name, and the path to the file. Here is the URL for the Library of Congress: http://lcweb.loc.gov/homepage/lchp.html. In this example *http://* indicates that the World Wide Web protocol is to be used, *lcweb.loc.gov* indicates the domain name for the Library of Congress, and */homepage/lchp.html* indicates the particular file—the main page.

Usenet A worldwide bulletin board system that is available on the Internet. It contains over 2,000 ***newsgroups*** on a wide variety of topics. People interested in a topic can subscribe to a newsgroup, where they can discuss the topic with like-minded people.

validity The structural coherence of a deductive argument. An argument is valid when the premises of a syllogism are correctly related to form a conclusion. Validity does not, however, actually refer to the truthfulness of an argument's premises. See **35f**. COMPARE **truth.**

verb A part of speech denoting action, occurrence, or existence (state of being). Inflections indicate tense (and sometimes person and number) and mood of a verb. Verbs may be either transitive or intransitive. See **1a** and **7**. See also **inflection, mood, voice, transitive verb,** and **intransitive verb.**

verbal A nonfinite verb used as a noun, an adjective, or an adverb. Infinitives, participles, and gerunds are verbals. Verbals (like finite verbs) may take objects, complements, modifiers, and sometimes subjects: Sarah went *to see a movie.* [*To see,* an infinitive, functions as an adverb modifying the verb *went.* The object of the infinitive is *movie.*] See **gerund, infinitive, nonfinite verb,** and **participle.** See also **1d**.

verb phrase See **phrase.** See also **1d**.

virus A tiny, often destructive program that can replicate itself. Usually an executable program, a virus is generally transferred by infected disks and bulletin board files. Some viruses can be transferred across networks.

voice The form of a transitive verb that indicates whether or not the subject performs the action denoted by the verb. A verb with a direct object is in the *active voice*. When the direct object is converted into a subject, the verb is in the *passive voice*. A passive verb is always a verb phrase consisting of a form of the verb *be* (or sometimes *get*) followed by a past participle. See 7 and 29d(1).

Active Voice	The batter **hit** the ball. [The subject (*batter*) acts.]
Passive Voice	The ball **was hit** by the batter. [The subject (*ball*) does not act.]

Speakers and writers often omit the *by* phrase after a passive verb, especially when the performer of the action is not known or is not the focus of attention: Those flowers *were picked* yesterday. We just heard that a new secretary *was hired*.

vowel A speech sound represented in written English by *a, e, i, o, u,* and sometimes *y*.

Website See **World Wide Web.**

word order The arrangement of words in sentences. Because of lost inflections, modern English depends heavily on word order to convey meaning.

Nancy gave Henry $14,000.	Henry gave Nancy $14,000.
Tony had built a garage.	Tony had a garage built.

word processing An electronic method of producing text. The writer performs a number of computer operations, such as inputting, inserting, deleting, moving, blocking, and so forth, to facilitate writing.

World Wide Web (WWW) A system of Internet servers that store documents formatted in a special computer language (HTML). These documents are called *Web pages* and a location containing several such pages is called a *Website*. Web pages can provide links to other sites as well as to graphics, audio, and video files. Users can jump to the linked sites by clicking on designated spots in the document. See page 465.

writing process The various activities of planning (gathering, shaping, and organizing information), drafting (setting down ideas in sentences and paragraphs to form a composition), revising (rethinking, reshaping, and reordering ideas), editing (checking for clear, effective, grammatically correct sentences), and proofreading (checking for correct spelling, mechanics, and manuscript form). The writing process sets no particular sequence for these activities but allows writers to return to any activity as necessary.

WWW See **World Wide Web.**

Copyright and Acknowledgments

Excerpt from *Reader's Guide to Periodical Literature*, 1990, p. 440. Copyright © 1990 by The H.W. Wilson Company. Material reproduced with permission of the publisher.

Excerpts from poems "I'm Nobody! Who Are You?" and "Because I Could Not Stop for Death" by Emily Dickinson. Reprinted by permission of the publishers and the Trustees of Amherst College from *The Poems of Emily Dickinson*, Thomas H. Johnson, ed., Cambridge, Mass.: The Belknap Press of Harvard University Press, Copyright © 1951, 1955, 1979, 1983 by the President and Fellows of Harvard College.

Excerpt from poem "You fit into me . . ." from *Power Politics* by Margaret Atwood, copyright © 1971, 1996. Reprinted with the permission of the House of Anansi Press, North York, Ontario.

Excerpt reprinted by permission from *Merriam-Webster's Collegiate ® Dictionary*, Tenth Edition © 1996. Merriam-Webster, Incorporated.

Excerpt from *The New York Times Index*. Copyright © by The New York Times Company. Reprinted by permission.

Specified three line excerpt from "To be of use" from *Circles on the Water* by Marge Piercy. Copyright © 1982 by Marge Piercy. Reprinted by permission of Alfred A. Knopf, Inc.

Specified eight line excerpt from "Musée des Beaux Arts" from *W. H. Auden.: Collected Poems* by W. H. Auden, edited by Edward Mendelson. Copyright © 1940 and renewed 1968 by W. H. Auden. Reprinted by permission of Random House, Inc.

Excerpt from "Lullaby" by Leslie Marmon Silko. Copyright © 1981 by Leslie Marmon Silko. Reprinted by permission from

Storyteller by Leslie Marmon Silko, published by Seaver Books, New York.

Excerpt from "Walking Our Boundaries" from *The Black Unicorn* by Audre Lorde. Copyright © 1978 by Audre Lorde. Reprinted by permission of W.W. Norton & Company, Inc.

Excerpt sample page reprinted by permission from Yahoo!. Text and artwork copyright © 1996 by Yahoo!, Inc. All rights reserved. Yahoo! and the Yahoo logo are trademarks for Yahoo!, Inc.

Sample web pages from Netscape and Lynx, "Richard III: On Stage and Off," © 1996, 1997, The Richard III Society, Inc. Used with permission.

Index

Numbers and letters in color refer to rules; other numbers refer to pages.

ESL Index

Entries in this index identify topics basic to ESL usage. Numbers and letters in color refer to rules; other numbers refer to pages.

MLA Documentation Style

This index refers to items in the parenthetical citations, the works cited list, and the student papers in chapters 38 and 39. The italics indicate the page on which a given form is illustrated in a paper.

APA Documentation Style

This index refers to items in the parenthetical citations, the reference list, and the student paper in chapter 38. The italics indicate the page on which a given form is illustrated in a paper.

Checklists